i

THE AESTHETICS
OF THE
ROUGON-MACQUART

José Porrúa Turanzas, S.A.
EDICIONES

Director General:
José Porrúa Venero

Director:
Constantino García Garvía

Sub-Director General:
Enrique Porrúa Venero

Executive Director: American Division: Bruno M. Damiani

stuðia humanitatis

DIRECTED BY
Bruno M. Damiani
The Catholic University of America

ADVISORY BOARD

THE AESTHETICS
OF THE
Rougon-Macquart

BY
JOHN A. FREY

studia humanitatis

PUBLISHER, PRINTER AND DISTRIBUTOR
José Porrúa Turanzas, S. A.
Cea Bermúdez, 10 - Madrid-3
España

Dep. legal M. 34.917.-1978

I. S. B. N. 84-7317-076-8

IMPRESO EN ESPAÑA
PRINTED IN SPAIN

Ediciones José Porrúa Turanzas, S. A.
Cea Bermúdez, 10 - Madrid-3

TALLERES GRÁFICOS PORRÚA, S. A.
JOSÉ, 10 - MADRID-29

M. Emile Zola, par Gill, cover of *L'Eclipse*, April 16, 1876.

For Helmut and Herta Hatzfeld

TABLE OF CONTENTS

Pages

ABBREVIATIONS

All citations from *Les Rougon-Macquart* will be indicated by short title in the text, and refer to the edition of the *Bibliothèque de la Pléiade, édition intégrale publiée sous la direction d'Armand Lanoux, Etudes, Notes et Variantes par Henri Mitterand (Paris,* 1960). Unless otherwise indicated the italics are mine.

VOLUME I:

La Fortune des Rougon: *Fortune*
La Curée: *Curée*
Le Ventre de Paris: *Ventre*
La Conquête de Plassans: *Conquête*
La Faute de l'abbé Mouret: *Faute*

VOLUME II:

Son Excellence Eugène Rougon: *Son Excellence*
L'Assommoir: *Assommoir*
Une Page d'amour: *Page*
Nana: *Nana*

VOLUME III:

Pot-Bouille: *P.B.*
Au Bonheur des dames: *Bonheur*
La Joie de vivre: *Joie*
Germinal: *Germinal*

VOLUME IV:

L'Oeuvre: *Oeuvre*
La Terre: *Terre*
Le Rêve: *Rêve*
La Bête humaine: *Bête*

VOLUME V:

L'Argent: *Argent*
La Débâcle: *Débâcle*
Le Docteur Pascal: *Pascal*

FOREWORD AND ACKNOWLEDGMENTS

The idea of this book began in my Zola seminars about eight years ago. At that time, it seemed appropriate, on the basis of stylistic evidence, to try to establish some links between naturalism, impressionism and even symbolism. A reading of the Zola bibliography, especially the new Zola criticism, confirmed that many critics were doing similar things. A historical reading of the bibliography in Paris showed that, at least for impressionism, the very first Zola critics had also been aware of these parallels. Studying the Zola manuscripts and *dossiers*, it became apparent that Zola himself was never the pure naturalist that a positivistic literary history had made of him.

The procedure then was to scrutinize very closely *Les Rougon-Macquart*, basing myself in classical stylistic methodology. The final result is quite different from my original speculations. Thus, while this study will try to demonstrate aesthetic affinities between naturalism, impressionism and symbolism, it will at the same time insist upon the necessary limitations, imposed not just by the facts, but also by genre.

Reevaluating Zola's place in late nineteenth-century French literature led to speculations on the evolution of modern French literary history. For this reason, I have tried to read both Zola and the impressionists in terms of the radical break with classical tradition brought about by Jean-Jacques Rousseau. In this sense we can see Zola as a romantic, as we can, along with many art historians, see impressionism as the last and most resplendent manifestation of the romantic spirit, before art, and at least poetry, turn to abstractionism.

I am deeply indebted to those critics who are rewriting, with insights and intuitions which this study can only feebly imitate, the history of modern art forms, especially Wylie Sypher, Robert Rosenblum and above all, Helmut Hatzfeld. To Professor Hatzfeld I am grateful for years of conversation with him on this and related topics.

The American painter, Stephen Pace, and his wife, Pamela, were invaluable to me with their comments on the creative process, and with their appraisals of nineteenth and twentieth century paintings. The counsel of my colleagues here in Washington, Professor Peter L. Morris of The Catholic University of America, Professor Jean-Max Guieu of Georgetown University, and Professors James F. Burks, J. Michael Tubbs and Jean-François Thibault of The George Washington University was heeded and followed.

The entire manuscript was patiently prepared by Esther Naylor, administrative assistant of the Department of Romance Languages and Literatures of my university.

Finally, I would thank my students who usually were able to modify my viewpoint by conclusion of a seminar, the very solicitous staff of the *Bibliothèque nationale,* and the graduate committee on research at The George Washington University for its financial support.

JOHN A. FREY
The George Washington University
December, 1976

Chapter I

THE HISTORICAL JUNCTURE OF REALISM, IMPRESSIONISM AND SYMBOLISM

Criticism of the last thirty years has made it clear that the standard and simplistic definition of Zola's naturalism is erroneous. Yet it would be naive and dangerous to impose any label of impressionism or symbolism on Zola simply because we now recognize their importance in the total structure of his work.

Zola's own contradictory statements on the nature of art have been of little help to literary history, and he is partly responsible for sending criticism down a narrow positivistic road which led not to but away from the center of his work. The appearance in 1880 of the *Roman experimental,* when he had already written nine of the twenty volumes of the *Rougon-Macquart,* helped to fix the idea of a doctrinaire naturalism which became standard text and classroom teaching until very recent times. Yet the nine volumes written before 1880 present contradictions to the statement found in the *Experimental Novel* and subsequent theoretical writings.

We know that the pure naturalistic Zola of literary history does not exist. It would even be difficult to support the idea, in the face of recent critical investigations, that creativity is primarily with Zola a rational operation (1).

This means that the external history of naturalism should

---

(1) Martin Kanes, «Zola, Balzac and 'La Fortune des Rougon',» *French Studies,* 18 (1964), 212.

be rewritten as the evidence from interior criticism shifts radically away from the events of naturalistic history as it is presently understood. The misunderstanding of the meaning of the debate of naturalism is due to our inability to read properly the naturalistic archives, and is parallel to the misreading which still goes on for romanticism. We do not as yet, for example, understand the relationship between the conservative and liberal *salons* of the 1820's, so labelled mainly because of political leanings, and the ultimate triumph of Hugo over Stendhal in theoretical romantic aesthetics. A proper beginning would be to use the standard Beuchat history (2) as a preliminary checklist of documents, and then to make a fresh evaluation of them in the light of the new textual criticism of Zola's writings. This might be initiated along the lines suggested by Professor Hemming's inquiry (3) into the possible Russian origins of Zola's idea of naturalism, with all that it implies for humanistic or spiritual insights of Russian realism as opposed to the theoretically cold and detached spirit of realism in France.

The fact that Zola's work was not just controversial, but misunderstood or misevaluated from the very beginning should have made it clear that the deterministic thesis is not at the heart of his aesthetic doctrine. The lowest level of misunderstanding was the charge of pornography. His work seems innocent enough today in the face of our own erotic literature, but more importantly the generation of critics who used the yardstick of morality is gone. We now see that adverse criticism not as a real indictment of immorality, but more as a disguise for what was rightfully felt to be an assault on a standard of value or taste which seemed to be disappearing as modernism, with confidence, asserted itself in all the arts in the concluding days of the nineteenth century. This relativity of evaluation is chosen to do justice to Zola, and not to upset higher aesthetic principles.

The real problem, of course, for literary history was not the question of morality or immorality, but rather, how to

---

(2) Charles Beuchat, *Histoire du naturalisme français*, I, II (Paris, 1949).

(3) F. W. J. Hemmings, «The Origin of the terms 'Naturalisme', 'Naturaliste',» *French Studies,* 8 (1954), 109-121.

classify Zola. It is then that the real failure of the positivisitic critical apparatus becomes apparent. Positive and negative criticism immediately noted in the scientific Zola what they would call his «romanticism», his «lyricism», even poetic aspects (4), and since then critics have pointed out that indeed Zola pays little practical attention to his formal theories. It has been shown, through a careful study of the *dossiers* that documentation plays a minor role in the novelistic craft of Zola (5), that in some of the most important novels there is a total absence of any biological determinism (6). Guy Robert observes that Louis Desprez' objection to Zola's determinism would have been pertinent if «... Zola romancier ne faisait souvent bon marché des principes hautement affirmés par Zola critique» (7). The very early work of Sherard (8) in a primitive manner is stating the same thing when he speaks

---

(4) Maurice Le Blond, *Emile Zola, son évolution, son influence* (Paris, 1903), 6, saw the question clearly as early as November, 1902: romantic critics accuse Zola of immorality, whereas, realists object to his lyricism. The young and astute naturalistic critic, Louis Desprez, after having criticized *La Faute de l'abbé Mouret* for its lyricism, discovered with hindsight that this had all along been a hallmark of Zola's art: «En vous le lyrique et l'observateur se mêlent...,» *Lettre* XXI, 8 mars, 1885, in *Lettres inédites de Louis Desprez à Emile Zola, Introduction et notes de Guy Robert* (Paris, 1952), 111. Another sympathetic reader cited by Robert (25) was Maupassant who, in *Le Gaulois*, 14 janvier, 1882, spoke of Zola's novels as poems. In his book, *Emile Zola* (Paris, 1883), Maupassant speaks of Zola as a «... romantique ... dans tous ses procédés ...,» 292. Brunetière's attack on Zola focuses on his romanticism. He calls him a «... romantique attardé...» whose novels are marked by the spirit of 1830, Ferdinand Brunetière, *Le Roman naturaliste* (Paris, 1892), 346 and 155. John Rewald, *Cézanne et Zola* (Paris, 1936), 125, expresses the idea that Cézanne outgrew his romanticism, substituting for romantic dreams the direct representation of his sensations in front of nature, while Zola, in spite of naturalism, remained a sentimental romantic.

(5) Guy Robert, *Emile Zola, Principes et caractères généraux de son oeuvre* (Paris, 1952), 55.

(6) Jean Fréville, *Zola semeur d'orages* (Paris, 1952), 64. Fréville's belief is supported by André Wurmser, «Ancienne maison Balzac, Zola successeur,» *Europe*, (nov.-déc., 1952), 51.

(7) *Lettres de Desprez à Zola*, 51.

(8) Robert Sherard, *Emile Zola: a Bibliographical and Critical Study* (London, 1893), 132-33.

of the absence of thesis and the difficulties Zola had in finding a plot line for *L'Assommoir*. Angus Wilson makes the strongest affirmation against the naturalistic thesis which he sees as never being permitted to inhibit the creative spirit of the writer. Wilson feels that the whole controversy would have been avoided if Céard had not introduced Zola to the work of Claude Bernard which leads directly to the writing of *Le Roman expérimental* (9). That is, the naturalistic theory looks like a post-dated elaboration which cannot be confirmed by the textual practice: «... il y a chez Zola désaccord entre son enseignement et son oeuvre» (10). The bulk of the accumulated evidence reveals a Zola who never abandoned an aesthetic ideal which refuses the limitations of the naturalistic thesis (11). Angus Wilson would go as far as to place Zola almost in the camp of art for the sake of art (12).

---

(9) *Emile Zola, an Introductory Study of his Novels* (London, 1952), 30.

(10) Alexandre Zévaès, *Zola* (Paris, 1946), 271.

(11) Aesthetic transcendentalism might be an appropriate term for Zola, if we accept the evaluation of an entire line of critics who have tried to modify the pure naturalistic interpretation. In the face of this evidence, it is to be wondered how the rigorous naturalistic thesis ever caught on. See F. Doucet, *L'Esthétique de Zola et son application à la critique* (Paris, 1923), 100; Alexandre Baillot, *Emile Zola, le penseur, le critique* (Poitiers, 1924), 77, for very pertinent remarks on the letters of the young Zola. Idealism and aesthetic concerns which we might want to limit to the young Zola can be seen as perpetuating themselves across his entire career. In 1869, Zola defends Flaubert's *Education sentimentale* against the attacks of Duranty: «Lorsque j'entends la critique reprocher à Gustave Flaubert de ne rien apporter ... je suis tenté de crier à mes confrères: Tant pis pour vous, si les sens vous manquent. Ce que l'auteur apporte, ce sont les profondeurs inconnues de l'être, les sourds désirs, les violences, les lâchetés, toutes les impuissances et toutes les énergies traduites par les niaiseries de la vie journalière. Et ce n'est pas un simple greffier. C'est un musicien doué dont les poèmes sont faits pour des oreilles sympathiques. Si vous n'entendez pas, c'est que le sang ou la bile vous étouffent ... Pour moi, l'*Education sentimentale* comme *Mme Bovary* est une pure symphonie.», quoted by Maurice Parturier, *Zola et Duranty, notes et documents* (Paris, 1948), 17. Thirteen years later, Louis Desprez restates to Zola the latter's remarks on the preface to *Les Frères Zemganno*, making it clear that naturalism is not to be limited to the positive: «Le naturalisme ne restreint pas l'horizon

Wilson's reading of the *Rougon-Macquart* attaches Zola to the high and almost metaphysical realism of the nineteenth century Russian novelists. *La Bête humaine* seems to have for him something to do with *Crime and Punishment*; the great human dignity of Gervaise is underlined; the concept of nobility and redemption in *La Terre* is parallel to Dostoevsky's *The House of the Dead* or *The Idiot* (13).

Neither the labels romantic or naturalist can situate Zola's place in literary history. Wilson seems to be on the right track. Zola is not a romantic. One of Zola's great discoveries, revealed in novels like *Pot-Bouille,* is that the high romanticism of the poets of the 1820's had lost its idealistic surge at the end of the century, and, debased, became a sentimental masking of bourgeois immorality, which infects even the lower classes (Nana) as they engage in upward social mobility. Berthe of *Pot-Bouille* is more soulless than Emma Bovary. Duveyrier of the same novel, with his cheap histrionics, what Zola calls his «... besoin de cultiver la petite fleur bleue des romances, dans ses gros appétits de mâle» (*P. B.,* 131), represents the perversion of romanticism, and Zola is the first writer to unmask it. *Une Page d'amour* is no more a romantic novel than *Madame Bovary*. The plight of Hélène is not that of the cardboard heros and heroines of romantic prose, sexless, soulless, without problems. Hélène is psychologically studied, the novel is made out of the tension between recognizable obligations toward her own innate decency, maternal obligation to her child, a fundamental belief in middle class stability, and her passion for the married Dr. Deberle.

Likewise, the naturalistic reading of *L'Assommoir* as a

... Il est la nature et l'homme dans leur universalité, avec leur connu et leur inconnu ... Lorsque M. de Goncourt, lorsque d'autres romanciers naturalistes surajoutent leur fantaisie au vrai, ils gardent leur méthode d'analyse, ils prolongent leur observation au-delà de ce qui est. Cela devient un poème, mais cela reste une oeuvre logique.», *Lettres de Desprez à Zola*, 57. This constant adjustment by Zola of the naturalistic thesis to the greater exigencies of art may be seen across his entire life, especially by a careful reading of the letters.

(12) *Zola*, 52.
(13) *Ibid.*, 103, 112, 118.

sociology of the poor must be the lowest possible aesthetic reading of this great novel. If this novel is successful, it is not because it engenders in the reader a courageous stance for social reform, but rather because the aesthetic construct leads, as all great art should, to moral pondering. Gervaise's plight touches us because she has the great dignity of a classical heroine in spite of her low origins. Simply put, she is not vulgar. Criticism should lead us to a true aesthetic reading of Zola, and such a reading and analysis finally will put into oblivion the over-stated naturalistic theory.

To label Zola an impressionist is tempting from both a historical and a textual point of view; it is a temptation which should be refused. Zola's involvement personally with the painters, especially his friend Cézanne, his defense of the new painters, his art criticism, and the application to literature of painterly techniques make the label of impressionism attractive. Considered, historically, however, it seems to be less a question of a specific painterly mode, and more one of naturalism and impressionism both being seen as a renewal of art under the general impulse of what is referred to as modernism. In reading the documents, it becomes apparent that the battle between the new and the traditional art, highlighted at the official salons, particularly in 1863, is truly a struggle for something felt as «realistic» or «modern» over the academic forms. Realism, when it becomes a descriptive label, looks somewhat like what we today call impressionism. This seems to be part of the meaning of the discussion of Manet in Zola's *Mes Haines* (1866). The issues are clearly seen in a book by Fernand Desnoyers, *Salon des Refusés — La Peinture en 1863* (Paris, 1863), a pro-modern document. Desnoyer's work is filled with attacks on the jury of 1863 which, in an arbitrary manner, refused the new painters because of their realism. His discussions of landscape paintings insist on the necessity of having «air» in these paintings, and calls for an exact rendering of color as opposed to strict academic coloring. His argument for realism is truly describing new painterly techniques which will evolve into impressionism.

Zola is interested in these questions, the new frontiers of art, not just as it becomes a question in the salons, but also for his own literary development. In an article on Cervantes and Gustave Doré of 1863, he ponders the relationship between the stylistic procedures of the painter and the poet:

> ... savoir quels sont les véritables domaines du peintre et du poète, et où s'arrête pour chacun d'eux la puissance de rendre des idées et des spectacles? Je sais que cette puissance a des bornes, que jamais le poète n'immobilisera parfaitement son sujet, que jamais le peintre ne fera penser et agir ses personnages (14).

From the beginning of his career Zola seems exclusively surrounded by painters, and a whole series of articles dating from the 1860's come to the defense of the new painters, and seem to imply that impressionism and what is to be naturalism are part of the same movement (15). A letter of Stassov to Tourgueniev in 1875 expresses the desire to correspond with Zola who is seen as «... le meilleur critique de l'époque» (16). That Zola senses a common purpose in the avantgarde of painting and literature is seen in his review of Halévy's play, *La Cigale,* in which there apparently is much poking of fun at the new painters:

> Je veux croire qu'an fond Mss Meilhac et Halévy sont pleins d'affection pour ces artistes novateurs qui cherchent à peu près en peinture ce qu'eux-mêmes cherchent au théâtre, la vie moderne, le côté intense et incisif des choses, les aspects multiples du grand Paris (17).

By the late 1870's it is apparent that there is some confusion in the public's mind as to differences between impressionism and naturalism (18). It is the original study of Louis Desprez

---

(14) Emile Zola, «Cervantès et Gustave Doré,» *Le Journal populaire de Lille,* 23 décembre, 1863, 4.

(15) See, for example, Zola, *Mon Salon V* in *L'Evénement illustré,* 1er juin, cited by Rewald, 62-63, and *Le Voltaire,* 19 juin, 1880, cited also by Rewald, 108.

(16) Cited by P. Duncan and V. Erdely, *Zola, Lettres de Paris* (Geneva, 1963), 15-16.

(17) Emile Zola, «Revue dramatique et littéraire,» *Le Bien public,* 15 octobre, 1877, 1.

(18) John A. Frey, «Louis Desprez and his *Evolution naturaliste,*» *Romance Notes,* XII, no. 2 (1971), 1-5.

in 1884, however, which dares to call the art of Balzac, Flaubert, Daudet, the Goncourt brothers and Zola impressionist (19), meaning to him the introduction of materialism into literature. Zola does not seem to have been too happy with such an appellation, which proves that no decisive point can be made (20). Impressionism as a label only describes tendencies; it is not a system.

The situation of impressionism in literature becomes more complicated during this period because of the attacks on impressionism as a destructive force for literature. These attacks come likewise from the conservatives and from the positivists (21).

Slowly, the term impressionism slips into the descriptive vocabulary of the Zola critics, first as they try to evaluate the historical situation (22), then to use the term to describe

---

(19)   Louis Desprez, *L'Evolution naturaliste* (Paris, 1884), 90.

(20)   Robert cites a letter of Zola to Desprez in 1884: «Je n'aime pas beaucoup votre 'impressionnisme' qui rapetisse l'horizon et met l'art dans la sensation seule.» *Lettres de Desprez à Zola,* 79.

(21)   Robert cites Brunetière's article in the *Revue des deux mondes* of November 1, 1883 on «... l'excès de décomposition analytique de l'impressionnisme et sur son impuissance à composer.» *Lettres de Desprez à Zola,* 27.   In a curious work, *Degeneration,* Max Nordau (trans. anon. from the 2nd German ed., New York, 1895), devotes an entire chapter in Book IV (473-505) to a study of realism.   Most of the discussion treats Zola and his school and makes absolutely no distinction between realism and impressionism, both of which are considered degenerate: «A very much worse error than desultory, cold-blooded description in imaginative writing is impressionism.» (485); «M. Zola's disciples boast of his art of description and his 'impressionism'.» (484); «Poetical impressionism ... is a complete misconception of the essence of imaginative work; it is the negation and suppression of it.» (485); «Such is the procedure of impressionism.   The writer gives himself the air of a painter; he professes to seize the phenomenon, not as a concept, but to feel it as simple sensation.» (486); «He (Zola) shows at times an unhealthy predominance of the sensations of smell in his consciousness, and a perversion of the olfactory sense which make the worst odours, especially those of all human excretions, appear to him particularly agreeable and sensually stimulating» (502).

(22)   Maurice Le Blond, *Emile Zola, son évolution,* 23, cites, without any textual reference, a document from Zola of 1896 in which he states that naturalism and impressionism were fused. Thirty-five years later the following was written: «Dès la fin du Second Empire, le naturalisme littéraire et l'impressionnisme pic-

particular descriptive techniques in specific novels (23), and finally as a useful term for describing ever-accelerating tendencies in the nineteenth century novel and in the art of Zola in particular (24). In the strict sense of the word, impressionism belongs to the field of painting and means the elimination of everything which is non-optical (25). In this case Zola could not be an impressionist. As a writer he will rely upon, want to rely upon, the abstract as fundamental to

---

tural se confondirent en un seul courant. Les mêmes principes: l'amour de la nature, du plein air, de la lumière, de la réalité, de la vie frémissante, s'appliquèrent à l'un et à l'autre. L'Impressionnisme devint en quelque sorte l'expression esthétique du naturalisme. Ils eurent les mêmes détracteurs et les mêmes apôtres. Les mêmes formules leur convinrent.», Marcel Batilliat, *Emile Zola* (Paris, 1931), 31.

(23) «It (*Le Ventre de Paris*) may be called Zola's first successful attempt at impressionism: and it is, at this date of 1873, the book in which Zola most closely approximated the 'artistic style' the 'écriture artiste' practiced by the Goncourts.», Elliott M. Grant, *Emile Zola* (New York, 1966), 70. Joan-Yvonne Dangelser as early as 1938 had spoken of the impressionism of *La Faute de l'abbé Mouret* in *La Description du milieu dans le roman français, de Balzac à Zola* (Paris, 1938), 208-209.

(24) Again Wilson is the most daring when he writes that «It is not 'Naturalism' but impressionistic technique which explains Zola's greatness.», *Emile Zola*, 55. The remarks of Fréville are more restrained, but do insist upon the interplay of impressionism and naturalism, *Zola, semeur d'orages*, 18, 19, 23. Robert stresses an inclination toward impressionistic description: «... une tendance, qui alla en s'accentuant, à en juxtaposer les éléments plus qu'à les organiser.», *Emile Zola, principes et caractères*, 22-23. In all instances each critic is speaking of the technical utilization of impressionism. Once it is fully understood that impressionism and realism share the same ideology it may be possible to speak of impressionism as the basic stylistic expression of realism.

No work in this area would be possible without: Arnold Hauser, *The Social History of Art*, II (New York, 1952); Helmut Anthony Hatzfeld, *Literature Through Art* (New York, 1952; reprinted University of North Carolina Press, 1969), the remarks (Chapter VI) on impressionism are especially helpful, as well as his counsel on the danger of comparing the arts (211-223); the seminal study of Ruth Moser, *L'Impressionnisme français* (Geneva, 1952); the trailblazing work of Wylie Sypher, *Rococo to Cubism in Art and Literature* (New York, 1960). The work of Professor Joy Newton in this area may prove to be decisive.

(25) Hauser, *Social History of Art*, II, 874.

his craft. Therefore, we should properly speak of Zola's literary modifications of impressionistic technique.

The question of symbolism does not present the same historical difficulties as impressionism. For all of Zola's pretense to objectivity, it was Taine himself who found his work too subjective, too poetic (26). And contrary to the general symbolist reaction, Mallarmé was, it would seem, a great admirer of Zola (27). Zola's own position on these symbolist questions cannot be perceived easily. His attitudes on Wagner are qualified. He seems to express enthusiasm from the viewpoint of musical and dramatic revival, and yet grave reservations from the viewpoint of the resuscitating of national myth (28).

As with impressionism, Zola criticism across the ages has marked his inclination toward symbolic structure. This is so widespread, so universal, that there is no need to cite any

---

(26) Zévaès points out that Zola had sent Taine the first five volumes of the series, and then quotes Taine's letter to Zola, April, 1875, in which a gentle but negative criticism is offered of Zola's subjectivity and «symphonic» effects in *La Faute de l'abbé Mouret*. Taine writes: «L'effet total est celui d'une symphonie; on perd pied; on est à cent pieds de la terre et de la prose.», *Zola*, 50. Zévaès goes on (51) to record what must have been Taine's disgust with *L'Assommoir* and *Germinal* for which he must have felt «... une sorte d'horreur sacrée.»

(27) See *Dix-neuf lettres de Stéphane Mallarmé à Emile Zola, avec une introduction de Léon Deffoux, un commentaire de Jean Royère* (Paris, 1929). Royère, the symbolist poet, makes a pertinent commentary on these letters from Mallarmé which would make of Zola a type of symbolist poet in the novel form. He speaks at some length of the affinities of the two writers, referring to them both as mystical atheists: «Zola et Mallarmé sont deux mystiques athées. Le naturalisme épique de Zola correspond dans une certaine mesure au *Cérémonial* de Mallarmé ... Baudelaire, dont la mystique est transcendentale, aurait eu horreur de Zola, mais n'eut pas aimé de coeur Mallarmé en tant que grand poète de la foule ... ce panthéisme ou plutôt cette panthéification systématique de son cerveau (Zola's) est très mallarméen.», 73-74.

(28) A basis for an understanding of this problem can be found in Alfred Bruneau, *A l'Ombre d'un grand coeur* (Paris, 1931). Bruneau was Zola's collaborator on a series of lyrical and musical dramas of a symbolic nature. The discussion of Wagner can be found from pages 65-101 and thereabouts. See also Jean-Max Guieu, «Le Théâtre lyrique d'Emile Zola,» (doctoral dissertation, The University of Maryland, 1975).

particular critic since practically all speak of it. It is a question of «poem» novels, of motifs, of symbols, and of myths. This is practically the center of recent Zola criticism. There is no doubt that Zola was seeking some sort of transcendence in his novels. He is trying to ponder the mysteries of human existence. Here he is absolutely contrary to Flaubert whose nihilism is apparent from the time of *Madame Bovary* and which can be described as desperate in the unfinished *Bouvard et Pécuchet.*

This study, while aiming to make a stylistic appraisal of the art of the *Rougon-Macquart,* must take into consideration the elements of impressionism and symbolism which may be components of the work of Zola. In the particular sense of a movement in France called symbolism, it would be naive to suggest that Zola is in any sense a symbolist, for of course he is not. The novel form, however, by borrowing as it must from other genres, does lend itself to symbolic representation, if only in its reliance on figurative language, which is always at the basis of symbolism. With the exception of Stendhal and the Flaubert of the *Education sentimentale,* metaphorical structure is basic to the modern novel from Balzac to Proust.

The affinities of three movements almost contemporaneous with each other, Zola's naturalism, Mallarmé's symbolism, and the impressionism of the painter seem valid, but the approximations must always be qualified. Impressionism and symbolism seem intertwined. It is no accident that Débussy put Mallarmé's *L'Après-midi d'un Faune* to music when Mallarmé thought that he had already done so. A study of Mallarmé's vocabulary would reveal it to be impressionistic, and like the impressionists, his aesthetic doctrine stresses suggestion over precision, to evoke not the thing but the effect produced by it (29).

---

(29) Unlike the impressionists, Mallarmé was not interested in the ephemeral for its own sake, but as the very way of capturing an essence. Perhaps both the painters and the poet had the same thing in mind. Mallarmé writes toward the conclusion of *Crise de vers*: «Je dis: une fleur! et, hors de l'oubli où ma voix relègue aucun contour, en tant que quelque chose d'autre que les calices sus, musicalement, se lève, idée même et suave, *l'absente de tous bouquets.*» Stéphane Mallarmé, *Oeuvres complètes* (Paris, 1945), 368.

We try to see then the relationships between three movements or tendencies which even within themselves enjoyed
no basic unity, for there are impressionisms, symbolisms and
naturalisms. What, beyond tendency and bent, could possibly
unite Manet, Monet and Renoir, Baudelaire, Rimbaud, Verlaine,
Mallarmé and Valéry, Zola, the Goncourt brothers, Huysmans,
Daudet and Maupassant? Of the three tendencies only naturalism could show an almost solid commitment to a materialistic
ideology.

But this confusion of aim is normal enough to any time
period committed to renewal, to the seeking of new roads,
which is exactly the cultural climate at the end of the
nineteenth century, when art is just waiting to move into
total abstraction. If we take just the small area of theatrical
renewal, the work of Lugné-Poe at the *théâtre de l'Oeuvre,*
or Antoine and the free theatre, a study of both repertories
proves that Lugné-Poe was not exclusively reserved to
symbolism, and Antoine was not just a super-realist.

None the less, Mallarmé's symbolism, impressionism in
painting, and Zola's naturalism, all three, do share a common
commitment to science, and in that manner all three perhaps
do reveal the last outbursts of nineteenth century positivistic
thinking. The impressionists thought of themselves as truly
scientific in their approach, relying heavily upon the optical
sciences. Mallarmé's new poetic seems to reside heavily in
the new science of philology. Zola's «scientism» hardly needs
any comment.

Yet Zola has a mind which prefers analogy to analysis, a
nonscientific and subjective vocabulary which moves through
metaphor into allegory and on to symbolic procedure, even
when we know it to be constructed. After the *Rougon-
Macquart,* the symbolic mode of Zola is properly called
visionary.

Wylie Sypher has said that romanticism should have led
directly to expressionism (30). This would seem to mean that
the new, deeply subjective romantic feeling only finds its form
in the early twentieth century, modern sentiment in quest of

(30) *Rococo to Cubism,* 65.

a mold in which to find expression. It would seem that the first outpouring of romantic sentiment, while strong, overflowing perhaps, found no single expressive form. Thus romanticism seems to be composed of multiple stylizations, not just in literature, but also in painting. While conceding that impressionism and symbolism are not the forms or final resting places for modern sentiment, it can be argued that as techniques, they did succeed in grouping together in a new, super, positive sensitivity the scattered emotionalisms of the early romantics. Whether or not cubism or expressionism succeed in giving formal, object substance to modern subjectivity is still an open and debatable question.

This study proposes to make of Zola neither an impressionits nor a symbolist. Zola's impressionistic technique, for example, could properly be studied without any reference at all to the painters, for in literature it could be proven to be simply a derivative of Flaubert, an over all literary tendency which gains momentum with him and then develops radically and laterally with Zola and the Goncourt brothers.

Rather it is proposed first of all to show how impressionistic techniques, grammatically based, proliferate into multiple stylistic devices, especially in the great descriptive passages on light and color, and that this formal descriptive pattern is derived from the subjective sentiment introduced into the modern world by Rousseau, to explode into impressionistic sensitivity in the two media, literature and art.

Then it can be shown that impressionism, in Zola at least, implies not just light and color, but their movement, and impressions of all the senses mobilized. Movement seems to be the dynamic principle of Zola's work, a movement which at first is perceived as impressionistic, but then invades the entire structure, moving beyond impressionistic design of capturing the ephemeral, arriving at a statement indicating that life is nothing more than constant change, sometimes creative and uplifting, often indicative of decay and destruction. While Zola may rely greatly on techniques which seem for literature proximate to what we see in impressionistic painting, at the same time his world in movement is meant to be symbolic even if not achieved. The parallels to the painters will be obvious, as will the evident restrictions. The same may be said of symbolic procedure. There are parallels to the high symbolic poem, but then there are the limitations of the novelistic genre.

This study will leave the existing schools intact, but will offer a stylistic and structural scrutiny of the twenty volumes of the *Rougon-Macquart* that will show that ideologies and their expressions were closer in the last part of nineteenth century than had previously been believed.

The history of modern French literature will be written when we have thoroughly explored the external history, movements, contacts, and debates, and measure what the artists say about what they are doing together with the textual evidence we have of what they actually have done or not done. At the basis of any such work is a careful analysis of the creative language of the writer, verified sometimes through concomitant structural layers. It may well be that a new generation of critics, armed with the tools of a new and more scientific methodology, may find the way to organize our fragmented knowledge of modern literature (31).

---

(31) Such a work may be the study of Alain de Lattre, *Le Réalisme selon Zola, Archéologie d'une intelligence* (Paris, 1975), which attempts a new and acceptable definition of realism in Zola, and which could potentially be applied to other writers of the nineteenth century.

CHAPTER II

FROM SENTIMENT TO IMPRESSION

Deep, subjective response to nature, joining man's psychological interior to the world about him, might be seen as the organizing force behind aesthetic theory as it is elaborated across the nineteenth century in both literature and painting. Impressionism may be the last and richest expression of romanticism, a positive subjectivity affirming life through light and color, and achieved with a technical formality unknown to the generation of the French Revolution and Napoleon. That is, the highly refined romantic feeling of nature engenders, at the end of the century, precise literary and artistic techniques by which this sentiment can receive formal expression. Nature will no longer simply be felt, but sensed, that is, truly seen and heard.

If Zola, in some manner, magnifies life, translating nature into verifiable perceptions, the basis for this is found in his deep love for and awareness of the exterior world. Subjectivity and sensitivity are the interior feelings from which he develops a mastery of light and color in a manner to make of literature a rival or companion to the work of the painters.

Exaltation in nature is manifest across the twenty volumes of the *Rougon-Macquart* in the rich descriptions of the gardens and parks of Plassans and Paris: the moonlight atmospheres of the Aire Saint-Mittre (*La Fortune des Rougon*), the elegant Bois de Boulogne and parc Monceau (*La Curée*), sunny gardens (*La Coquête de Plassans*), the primeval *Paradou* (*La Faute de l'abbé Mouret*), Dr. Deberle's bourgeois garden (*Une Page d'amour*), the bishop's *clos* (*Le Rêve*), and Dr. Pascal's small estate (*Le Docteur Pascal*). There is also the city man's enjoyment of country life as experienced in the long idyll of Claude and Christine (*L'Oeuvre*), or simply a day in the country as enjoyed by Florent and Claude (*Le Ventre de Paris*) or by the employees of the Au Bonheur des Dames. Vast panoramas are described, the wheat fields of La Beauce in *La Terre,* the mournful plain of *Germinal,* the nightmarish northern landscapes invaded by the Prussians in *La Débâcle,* the kaleidoscopic visions of town and nature between Paris and Le Havre in *La Bête humaine.* And since impressionism is basically an urban art, Zola's natures include cityscapes, the grimy proletarian atmospheres of *L'Assommoir* (with the correlative of the *corons* of *Germinal*), the vast skyscapes of Paris found in *L'Oeuvre, Une Page d'amour,* and in the great scene of baptism of the Imperial Prince in *Son Excellence Eugène Rougon.* There are impressionistic still lifes (*Ventre de Paris*) and Second Empire scenes, too multiple to list, from the racetrack natures of *Nana* to the gray tones of Paris courtyards in *Pot-Bouille.* Seascapes form the backdrop for *La Joie de vivre,* and visionary landscapes of the mid-east as dreamed by the romantics act as a thematic recall for the quixotic Christian Capitalists of *L'Argent.* A hypersensitivity to rural and urban environments is characteristic of all the novels of the series; it is often felt by the characters, and is totally enjoyed by Emile Zola.

For the historical critics, Zola's Provençal origins explain his intoxication with nature, particularly, the central role of sun and light in his work (1), resulting in a type of lyricism or romanticism (2). It is Angus Wilson, however, who successfully joins the biography to structure, explaining that the vivid nature of Provence had heightened Zola's senses, endowing him with an «... almost pathologically nervous sensitivity...» which will produce a realistic art which can be called «impressionistic» (3).

Zola's descriptive art should be understood within the general concept of nature first propagated by Rousseau and

---

(1) Doucet, 24.
(2) *Ibid.,* 24-25.
(3) Wilson, 8.

the romantics. His felt rather than seen landscapes are exteriorizations of the innermost sentiments of the soul or psyche. Looking across the pages of *Rêveries d'un promeneur solitaire*, it is not difficult to create a minimal but representative list of general and abstract adjectives and nouns: *heureux, délicieux, agréable, charmant, triste, beau, limpide, riant, content, vif, tendre, doux; charmes, bonheur, douceur, plaisir, délices, joie, rêveries, fraîcheur, contentement, paix.* Rousseau imparts to us his subjective reaction to nature, but we cannot say that it has been visually described:

> En sortant d'une longue et douce rêverie, en me voyant entouré de verdure, de fleurs, d'oiseaux et laissant errer mes yeux au loin sur les romanesques rivages qui bordoient une vaste étendue d'eau claire et cristalline, j'assimilois à mes fictions tous ces aimables objects et me trouvant enfin ramené par degrés à moi-même et à ce qui m'entouroit, je ne pouvois marquer le point de séparation des fictions aux réalités; tant tout concouroit également à me rendre chère la vie recueillie et solitaire que je menois dans ce beau séjour (4).

The text hovers between slight concrete detail rendered through general plural nouns and descriptive listings and abstractions. Similar processes are noted as the romantic movement develops, in Senancour and Chateaubriand, in Lamartine, especially in his neo-classical light and shadow romanticism. With Victor Hugo, however, the concrete and visual detail gains ground as it will continue to do in the second half of the century (starting with Baudelaire).

Although it will be demonstrated that Zola's descriptive style goes beyond the models of Rousseau, the latter's patterns persist in the *Rougon-Macquart*. Impressionistic natures evolve from their romantic sensibility. If not identified, the following citations from Zola could easily be attributed to Rousseau:

---

(4) Jean-Jacques Rousseau, *Oeuvres complètes*, I, *Les Confessions, Autres textes autobiographiques* (Paris: Bibliothèque de la Pléiade, 1959), *Cinquième promenade*, 1048. Hereafter all citations from Rousseau will refer to the Pléiade edition, and page number will be indicated following the text.

2

«... une mélancolie douce...» (*Fortune*, 9); «... le grand ciel tiède...» (*Fortune*, 26); «... les clartés discrètes de la lune» (*Fortune*, 27); «... la voûte religieuse des feuillages...» (*Faute*, 1382); «cet astre discret...» (*Faute*, 1383).

Landscapes in French romantic poetry are predominantly of the sad variety with little positive Wordswordian outlook recorded. Such landscapes do occur in Zola, and at first glance, seen out of context, they do resemble the descriptions offered by the melancholy romantic poets: «Mais cette aube grise éclairait d'une *infinie tristesse* Bazeilles et Balan...» (*Débâcle*, 543); «Le gros bruit de la Meuse continuait, une plainte d'*infinie tristesse* semblait avoir passé dans l'ombre croissante» (*Débâcle*, 563).

Zola's natures are often sad and melancholic, even frightening. They are also joyful, however. This is what can be called Zola's lyrical weather reports. That is, in almost any novel, even the bleakest, there is a persistent and positive outlook on nature and atmospheric conditions which we conclude is derived from the sentiments of Zola himself. The lyric joy which emanates across the pages of the *Rougon-Macquart* is perhaps unequalled in the second half of the nineteenth century. These joyful atmospheres are very dense in Dr. Deberle's August garden of *Une Page d'amour,* but this lyric joy is felt, again and again, in the badminton game sequence in *La Conquête de Plassans,* in the horse race scene in *Nana,* with Claude and Christine in the country in *L'Oeuvre.* If not in form, then at least in spirit these descriptions are impressionistic, recording in a very modern way the joy of life found in nature. If put in contrast with romantic prose descriptions, the America of Chateaubriand, for example, it would be clear how far literature has moved from romantic picturesque to the impressionistic idea of unrestrained pleasure in nature (5). Romantic nature produces sensations of awe and fear, emanating from *genre pittoresque* fascination with Niagara Falls, Mt. Etna, storm scenes and shipwrecks. Zola is not limited to this single perspective. Indeed, emotions of fear, awe, and fright are frequently provoked, especially by scenes

---

(5) Sypher's *From Rococo to Cubism* discusses the development of romantic picturesque in detail.

of dirt, decay and destruction, but in spite of this, Zola's own positive outlook toward natural phenomena dominates even the blackest of novels, as the following selected weather reports would indicate: «... sous le soleil blond de cette matinée d'octobre, c'étaient des mares d'or, des mares de pourpre, une richesse de manteau...» (*Son Excellence*, 177); «... dans la douce et pâle journée d'octobre» (*Bonheur*, 389); «... un blond soleil d'été...» (*Bonheur*, 676); «C'était par une journée exquise, au grand ciel limpide...» (*Oeuvre*, 117); «La nuit d'août était superbe, chaude, criblée d'étoiles» (*Oeuvre*, 321); «... devant la fenêtre ouverte, par laquelle entrait la radieuse matinée de mai» (*Rêve*, 846); «... la radieuse matinée d'avril triomphait au-dessus du champ de massacre...» (*Bête*, 1269); «... un ardent et pur dimanche d'août resplendit sur Mulhouse...» (*Débâcle*, 419); «... par une éclatante journée de la fin du mois d'août...» (*Pascal*, 1204). It is apparent that Zola continues the tradition of Rousseau, but with intensified lyric feeling and the specifically added detail of light.

Flaubert's descriptive realism is selective; Balzac's is cumulative. Zola's dense descriptive style would seem to attach him to Balzac. Technically, however, Zola looks more like Flaubert than Balzac, both concerned with scientific accuracy, especially in light and color descriptions, a precision which is rare in the first half of the nineteenth century. The description of the sunrise over Carthage in *Salammbô* illustrates Flaubert's ability to manipulate light and is the literary basis for the art of Zola:

> Mais une barre lumineuse s'éleva du côté de l'Orient. A gauche, tout en bas, les canaux de Mégara commençaient à rayer de leurs sinuosités blanches les verdures des jardins... et tout autour de la péninsule carthaginoise une ceinture d'écume blanche oscillait tandis que la mer couleur d'émeraude semblait comme figée dans la fraîcheur du matin. Puis à mesure que le ciel rose allait s'élargissant... (6).

---

(6) Gustave Flaubert, *Salammbô* (Paris: Classiques Garnier, 1959), 18.

Light and color are accidental properties, and normally would first be expressed through the adjective, then the noun, and finally the verb and adverb. Nineteenth century French, however, with its nominal tendencies, will increasingly employ the noun and the verb in lieu of the adjective, in accord with the impressionistic inclination of modern French. If the adjective is substantivized (*le vert*), or if the adjective is replaced by a true noun (*la verdure*), that which grammatically had been considered accidental is indeed substantive. The adjective remains dominant but is seen within a new stylistic constellation in which is noted an increased use of noun and verb.

Furthermore, the adjective in the nineteenth century will be placed with noticeable frequency in the affective position, preceding the noun it is modifying. The primary placing of the adjective reveals a lyrical or symbolical intent, and probably begins with Rousseau, as his emphatic and expansive subjectivism replaces the majestic baroque *cursus* of classicism and the brittle *esprit* of the rococo *philosophes* (Voltaire). Affective adjectival word order underlines Rousseau's distrust of men and his attraction to a consoling nature (7):

> Ayant donc formé le projet de décrire l'état habituel de mon âme dans *la plus étrange position* où se puisse jamais trouver un mortel... (*Deuxième promenade*, 1002).
> ... ne pouvant dans les antres même des alpes échapper aux *cruelles mains* des hommes, acharnés à me tourmenter (*Septième promenade*, 1071).
> ... mais loin d'y trouver le *calme heureux* que j'y goûte aujourd'hui j'y portois l'agitation des *vaines idées* qui m'avoient occupé dans le salon (*Huitième promenade*, 1083).
> ... je me plaisois à côtoyer les *verdoyantes rives* de l'Isle dont les *limpides eaux* et les ombrages frais... (*Cinquième promenade*, 1044).
> ... pour parcourir des yeux le *superbe* et *ravissant coup d'oeil* du lac... (*Cinquième promenade*, 1045).

---

(7) It is interesting that Rousseau's contemplation of nature leads to a conclusion, which while forming the basis of the entire *mal du siècle* of romanticism, at the same time identifies him

This procedure of Rousseau continues across the nineteenth century, not confining itself to the lyrical, but embracing a whole spectrum of adjectives used affectively for novelistic end. The tendency toward abstract or emotional quality will remain. Throughout the *Rougon-Macquart* Zola uses the abstract affective adjective: «... la *douce fraternité* qui règne entre ivrognes...» (*Fortune*, I, 117); «... un air d'*adorable fausseté*» (*Curée*, 322); «Toute sa *monstrueuse personne*...» (*Argent*, 37). Affective adjectives underscore the horror of war in *La Débâcle*: «... la Champagne... acheva de dérouler ses champs pauvres, d'une *désespérante* monotonie» (468); «... le *terrible* convoi était parti...» (515); «Dans Remilly, une *effrayante* confusion d'hommes...» (524); «Devant la *furieuse* résistance du village...» (633; «... ils assistèrent à une *effrayante* scène...» (769); «... l'*inévitable* dénouement» (877). *Le Docteur Pascal* records Clotilde's love for Pascal through an insistence upon her qualities put in the affective position: «... une *adorable jeunesse*...» (918); «... son *exquise* jeunesse blonde...» (934); «... cette *fine* créature de charmes et d'amour» (937); «... sa *triomphante* jeunesse» (985); «... dans le *divin* élancement de sa taille mince» (1025).

Flaubert is the first writer to use the techniques of literary impressionism in a consistent manner. But Flaubert's impressionism is primarily syntactical, with other impressionistic modes used sparingly. Zola, the Goncourt brothers and Pierre Loti come closest to a literary exploitation of light and color in the painterly sense, but even with these novelists there is always a substratum of simple non-impressionistic coloration:

---

psychologically as the first impressionist, in the sense of capturing the very modern idea of the impermanence of life: «Tout est dans un flux continuel sur la terre: rien n'y garde une forme constante et arrêtée, et nos affections qui s'attachent aux choses extérieures passent et changent nécessairement comme elles.», *Cinquième promenade*, 1046; «Tout est sur la terre dans un flux continuel qui ne permet à rien d'y prendre une forme constante. Tout change autour de nous. Nous changeons nous-mêmes et nul ne peut s'assurer qu'il aimera demain ce qu'il aime aujourd'hui.», *Neuvième promenade*, 1085. To Rousseau and the romantics, flux produces insecurity and ennui. The impressionists, and then much of the twentienth century accept as normal the idea of life as movement and change. With the impressionists there is an absolute delight in fixing in the work of art ephemeral phenomena.

«... en face de l'étroite maison *jaune* où il était né...» (*Débâcle,* 492); «... la semence *blonde*...» (*Terre,* 367); «Deux lampes, voilées de papier *rose,* éclairaient le salon...» (*P. B.,* 46); «Un instant, sur le chemin qui devenait *rose*...» (*Germinal,* 1581); «... la grande chambre *bleue*» (*Nana,* 1238). Simple color markings are frequently reinforced by the most neutral, linguistically normal modifications possible: *cru, pâle, blond, tendre, foncé, clair, fade, vif, sombre, livide, louche, opaque, mou, gros:* «... une étoffe *havane clair*» (*Nana,* 1207); «... grosses lèvres d'un *rose pâle*...» (*Germinal,* 1172); «... les volants de sa longue jupe de soie *cerise pâle*» (*Son Excellence,* 274); «Deux petits arbres se détachaient nettement, d'un *vert cru*...» (*Nana,* 1099); «... des gerbes d'un *pourpre vif*...» (*Débâcle,* 886); «... le dôme du Panthéon est d'un *bleu tendre* extraordinaire» (*Son Excellence,* 295); «... des becs de gaz... la chauffaient d'un coup de *lumière crue*» (*Nana,* 1195); «Une *lueur louche*... entrait par les fenêtres» (*Nana,* 1193).

The *-âtre* suffix, the effacing of color contour, suggesting imprecision of color, the destruction of spectral boundaries, forms the most minimal impressionistic color unit. It is a dominant pattern in Zola, the most used of all his simple color devices: «... entre les bourrelets rosâtres, l'enfant apparaissait» (*Joie,* 1096); «... oliviers grisâtres...» (*Oeuvre,* 41); «... toute la voûte d'un reflet rougeâtre» (*Bête,* 1037); «... les grands arbres nus de l'hôtel Beauvilliers, violâtres sur le ciel pâle» (*Argent,* 205); «... le ventre ballonné, dejà verdâtres,...» (*Débâcle,* 765); «... des chrysanthèmes... dardant de courts rayons éteints, blanchâtres, violâtres, rosâtres» (*Faute,* 1348); «... l'effacement jaunâtre d'un lot de concombres» (*Ventre,* 627); «Son cou rougeâtre avait un gloussement continu...» (*Conquête,* 1006); «La piéce s'échauffait, s'emplissait d'une fumée bleuâtre» (*Curée,* 455). Zola uses the *-âtre* suffix to create happy atmospheres, above all, skyscapes. It is rarely utilized for naturalistic physiognomies.

The procedures become more complicated as light and color are manipulated through noun, verbal and complex adjectival constructions. The adjective of color itself will be surrounded by simile and metaphor, a process unique to literature, in order to give a more accurate idea of the particular nuance.

The nineteenth century turns color adjectives into color nouns. While grammatically there is no neuter in French, the modern writers create a stylistically neuter color noun out of the syntactically expressed masculine (*ce qui est vert*) which becomes noun with masculine definite article (*le vert*). This is a daring achievement, and Zola is one of the more ostentatious practitioners of this style: «... le rouge saignant des dahlias» (*Ventre*, 622); «... les blés... d'un vert bleu... tranchait sur le vert noir des betteraves» (*Germinal*, 1251); «L'air, d'un gris argenté...» (*Nana*, 1253). The neuter has also a plural: «... des verts noyés dans des jaunes» (*Ventre*, 627). *Le noir* is so frequently combined with *encre* that it must be considered a frozen expression: «... ses cheveux... d'un noir d'encre...» (*Page*, 808).

The feminine is more normal to the language: «... la blancheur éclatante de la nappe...» (*Curée*, 338); «... une muraille de verdure...» (*Faute*, 1361); «... la route... d'une blancheur de craie...» (*Terre*, 368).

Nouns which by extension may imply color assume the function of adjectival modifiers either through direct attachment to the noun or through prepositional joinings with *de* and *en*. A similar process is observed in contemporary American English with the descriptive labels on cans of paint: «pea green», «cranberry red», «desert brown», «pumkin yellow». Zola uses nouns which by analogy to fruit, dead leaves, pottery, straw, flowers, bottles, give an idea of color. These constructions are sometimes very common in the language, often they are very original: «... une salle... peinte en *vert pomme*...» (*Germinal*, 1149); «... dans une robe *feuille-morte*» (*P. B.*, 139); «... des rechampis *jaune paille* de la calèche» (*Curée*, 319); «... deux gros yeux *bleu faïence*...» (*Terre*, 379). Color in a specific object (*azur*, for example, the blue of the atmosphere and the sea) can have such a long psychological and literary tradition that it is easily converted into adjective: «... une cravate bleu de ciel...» (*Terre*, 751); «... un soubassement en marbre vert de mer...» (*Bonheur*, 761). Often the color noun is attached directly: «... avec ses cheveux carotte...» (*Bonheur*, 526); «... avec de longs rubans cerise» (*Oeuvre*, 73). Au Bonheur des Dames, a modern department store, knows the value of nominal style for advertisement: «... les soies légères aux transparences de cristal, *vert Nil, ciel indien, rose de mai, bleu Danube*» (*Bonheur*, 487).

In such constructions, Zola is attempting to get as close as possible to an exact translation in literature of the nuance of color, much as the painters were breaking down the fundamental colors of the spectrum—red, orange, yellow, green, blue, indigo and violet. The abstract, *couleur de* followed by a noun «... sous la tente *couleur de chair*...» (*Curée*, 484) suggesting color is a common formula in the *Rougon-Macquart*, equalled only by the *-âtre* suffix: «... le soleil couchant, couleur de rouille...» (*Son Excellence*, 87); «Son tas de cheveux blonds, couleur d'avoine fraîche...» (*Assommoir*, 709); «... son visage couleur de vieux mur...» (*Assommoir*, 735); «... le soleil, couleur de blé mûr...» (*Oeuvre*, 117); «Le ciel était couleur de cendre...» (*Conquête*, 1190).

Closer to painting is the literary creation of light and color spaces —blocks, patches— similar to distinct placings or densities on a canvas. These become delineated spots in Zola's descriptions, and are formulated from *tache, masse, nappe,* and *teinte,* which are related to *couleur de,* but are less abstract, more visual. The new terms suggest volume, somewhat amorphous, in that the contours may be missing, but nevertheless are well-defined in their topography.

At the most literal visual level, a mass may be indeed just that, the bulk of a mountain range scarcely discernible in the pale moonlight: «... *la masse des Garrigues* dormait, à peine blanchie d'une teinte laiteuse» (*Fortune*, 162). An identifiable object may disappear into a mass for psychological reasons as in this impression of the abbé Faujas:

> Une jeune femme, ayant levé brusquement la tête, eut même un geste contenu de terreur, en apercevant cette masse noire devant elle. L'impression fut défavorable... (*Conquête*, 949).

Such techniques, while basically literary are at the same time impressionistic, for they efface contour. The geometric structure of Saint-Eustache is replaced by a dark color patch: «... la masse grise de l'église» (*Ventre*, 609). Grays and blacks, frequently contrasted with light and white, seem to dominate, and may be used to efface an individual: «... elle faisait une *masse noire* contre la *blancheur* d'un pilier...» (*Conquête*, 1063), or unite individuals into a group: «... sur le trottoir, une masse noire de consommateurs occupaient les tables du café de Madrid» (*Nana*, 1111). This last example, in addition to recalling *boulevard* paintings, is typical, in the smallest syntactical unit, of impressionistic syntax with subject identified last.

Tache may be employed to put a single color in relief: «... deux taches rouges sur la peau blanche...» (*Germinal*, 1299). As with *masse* the use may be literary, with figurative meaning dominating, but being pushed all the same in a painterly direction. The abbé Faujas is presented as casting a spot of «grief» (figurative), a literary blackness, onto the white walls of the Mouret household, combining real color with figurative color: «... la haute figure noire du prêtre faisait une tache de deuil sur la gaieté du mur blanchi à la chaux» (*Conquête*, 906). Through impressionistic syntax, *tache* gives primacy to color, the accidental quality, over the object itself. Object is not effaced but minimized: «... la grande tache rouge du rideau...» (*Nana*, 1095); «... la tache verte des arbres...» (*Son Excellence*, 85); «... un petit vieux... dans la tache verte d'une lampe, lisant un journal vert avec des mains vertes» (*Nana*, 1261).

Nappe, hovering between its literal and figurative meanings, is often used to measure light filling a space: «Dans les coulisses, éclairées de violentes nappes de lumière...» (*Nana*, 1217); and *teinte*, suggesting color complexity, seems liquid and flowing: «... Le ciel... d'une teinte laiteuse...» (*Page*, 1084).

Another grouping of nouns, *éblouissement, clarté, buée, lueur, luisant, lumière, miroitement, rayon, rayonnement*, indicates weakness and intensity of light, dullness and brilliance, reflection, and is often combined with analogies to metals and materials: «... l'eau... avait dans le noir un luisant de miroir d'étain...» (*Bonheur*, 529); «Le ciel, chargé de pluie, avait une lueur rousse qui éclairait faiblement le chemin» (*Conquête*, 1188).

A mixture of light and matter is found in the reiterated use of *pluie, poudroiement* and *poussière* which are reserved almost exclusively for the description of sunrays or hair: «... sous ce poudroiement de rayons, les maisons... se brouillaient, s'effaçaient...» (*Bête*, 997); «... sous la pluie de petites frisures blondes, qui noyaient le bleu cerné de ses yeux...» (*Nana*, 1346); «Dans la poussière jaune du soleil qui entrait par la porte du jardin, sa soutane râpée semblait toute rouge...»

(*Conquête*, 907). This last example seems a literary imitation of the impressionistic «blue trees, green skies», the dull brown-black cassock glowing red in the sunlight. Color is impermanent and subject to change.

Flamme, flamboiement and *incendie* all relate to the idea of fire, the simultaneous display of heat, light and flame; the mind can, at least connotatively, turn them to the colors red and yellow with their variations. Traditionally, a figurative meaning is meant as when Octave Mouret supervises the arrival of merchandise: «... dans ses yeux clairs, cette débâcle de marchandises qui tombait chez lui... mettait une courte flamme» (*Bonheur*, 422). As with the romantics nothing more than intensity of gaze is intended: «... ses yeux de flamme...» (*Joie*, 827). True light effects, however, are produced in a variety of literary manners. There is attention to small detail: «On voyait la flamme blanche de la baïonnette...» (*Germinal*, 1491); sunsets and intensity of the sun's rays: «... dans un dernier flamboiement du soleil» (*Germinal*, 1437); a type of impressionistic exaggeration which would be missed by the average viewer: «... le visage enflammé, sous le flamboiement de ses cheveux rouges» (*Pascal*, 959).

Color, becoming, manifesting itself on another color or on an object, is transmitted through the very effective *bleuissement*: «... le bleuissement nocturne de la neige» (*Terre*, 438); «le bleuissement des violettes...» (*Ventre*, 622); «... le bleuissement des maisons d'une rue...» (*Bonheur*, 532).

Verbal light and coloration parallel and dominate of course over the noun, the most frequently used being: *tacher, luire, miroiter, se moirer, rayonner, refléter, allumer, éclairer, ensanglanter, incendier, flamber, pâlir,* plus of course all the color verbs. More so than with the nouns we have nuances of reflected light: simple light on an overcast day; sun effects; natural light on embroideries, coppers and lamps; the light of the city. Special light and color effects are noticed with small details: the light of a cigarette; shining hat; the reflected light of stars, hair, craniums and noses.

Grammatically speaking the past participle tends to record static and fixed states, and consequently, when recording light and color, resembles most the stable light and color adjective with which this chapter started. Zola's propensity for the concrete expression, however, leads to achievements as painterly as possible, even with the past participle, in which the mobility of the verb is still felt and creates the nuance: «Pas une voix ne montait de Paris *ouaté* de neige» (*Bête,* 1205); «... au milieu de la nappe élargie de la rivière, très bleue, *moirée* de vert...» (*Son Excellence,* 87); «... son vieux paletot marron, *verdi* par les pluies» (*Oeuvre,* 15); «... les portières de Karamanie et de Syrie, *zébrées* de vert, de jaune et de vermillon» (*Bonheur,* 471); «... la nappe toute *noircie* de la cendre des cigares» (*P. B.,* 191).

The present participle either as verbal medium or as adjective is the most dynamic form possible when it has the vitality of the present tense. The situation stems from a very early confusion of the Latin participle and the Latin gerund. Historically, in the nineteenth century at least, the present participle has enjoyed an intimacy and interplay with the imperfect.

The present participle as adjective transmits the light mutations of a skyscape which acts as a scenic drop for the conversations of the strolling, idealistic, avant-garde painters Claude and Bongrand: «Et l'un et l'autre continuaient à vaguer, chacun parlant pour lui, très haut, sous les étoiles pâlissantes» (*Oeuvre,* 89). It can indicate the subtle but on-going processes of aging: «... la tête nue, embroussaillée d'épais cheveux roux grisonnants» (*Terre,* 406). The humid, milky white, camelia-like skin of an artist's *odalisque* seems to be vanishing in greater and greater degrees of paleness: «... la peau moite et *pâlissante,* de la pâleur laiteuse des camélias» (*Oeuvre,* 24). In these examples the subject is undergoing change.

The participle may be used transitively with gerund character. The redness found in bricks is intensified to the observing Etienne: «... il avait l'éblouissement du soleil devenu brûlant, incendiant l'horizon, rougissant les briques sous la crasse du charbon» (*Germinal,* 1251). The usual Zola doubling, then tripling process is operative, always getting closer to the exact nuance, *brûler,* synonymous of *flamber* and *incendier, brûlant > incendiant > rougissant.* The sensation of heat is turned into the visual perception of redness. The transitive participle may be used to impose color on a dark backdrop, green on black turning scarlet (bright red) to a violet shading:

Ces hautes flammes vertes dansaient en l'air, comme

flottantes et suspendues, tachant la nuit sans l'éclairer, ne tirant du noir que la double rangée des gilets écarlates qu'elles rendaient violâtres (*Son Excellence*, 183).

The imposition of color on object is deftly accomplished through the use of transitive verbs, usually in the imperfect, where they may connote *durée*. Various transmissions of white, especially in the achromatic atmospheres of *La Fortune des Rougon* and *Le Rêve*, spread across the series: «La lune blanchissait toute la clairière, ...» (*Germinal*, 1380); «Au ciel, la lune... les blanchissait d'une transparence laiteuse» (*Reve*, 927); «Le soleil y blanchissait les vieilles dalles...» (*Pascal*, 1050). There is also: «... le gai soleil printanier *jaunissait* tout un angle de la place Gaillon» (*P. B.*, 173); «C'était Bordenave, en effet, se promenant... avec un chapeau que le soleil rougissait» (*Nana*, 1389); «... avec ses volets gris que *verdissent* les coups de pluie de l'ouest» (*Bête*, 1025); «... les graisses qui *jaunissaient* déjà ses mains de mécanicien, ...» (*Bête*, 1026).

Intransitive descriptions are very impressionistic, pushing literature almost to a direct rivalry with painting. Intransitive constructions are quasi-nominal, presenting an on-going visualization to the reader. The intransitive participle presents an impressionistic subject undergoing processes of light and color modification: «... tout un infini de terres *grises, poudroyant* sous le ciel *bleu*...» (*Débâcle*, 584); «... le *reflet* des candélabres *brûlant* dans un verre de champagne» (*Nana*, 1181); «... une eau de *satin bleu, blanchissant* dans un *reflet* de *miroir*...» (*Oeuvre*, 102).

Parallel to the dense use of intransitive participle is the use of intransitive verbs in the imperfect. The on-going and becoming process is, of course, brought about with light and color verbs revealing the seemingly autonomous modifications taking place on a subject. For light, the principle verb is *pâlir* either stated simply, combined with color, or fused in a Baudelairian type *correspondance* as these examples would indicate: «La petite lampe *pâlissait*...» (*P. B.*, 31); «Parfois quand la flamme des lampes *pâlissait* et *bleuissait* davantage...» (*Germinal*, 1294); «... les épaules nues *pâlissaient*, sous les *notes vives de l'orchestre*» (*Nana*, 1422). The transition to color is made with *blanchir*, the most used color in the *Rougon-*

Macquart: «... lorsque le ciel blanchissait...» (*Bête*, 1145); «... la maison du passeur blanchissait...» (*Débâcle*, 525). Full color works in the same manner: «... Dans la *lueur* du foyer, les poils noirs du signe qu'elle avait au coin des lèvres *blondissaient*» (*Nana*, 1163); «... un portrait de l'acteur Vernet *jaunissait* à la chaleur du gaz» (*Nana*, 1196); «... en regardant au loin les toits des Tuileries, qui *bleuissaient* dans une *poussière de soleil*» (*Son Excellence, 51*); «... des dômes de monuments *bleuissaient*» (*Oeuvre*, 101); «... des cheveux *grisonnaient*, ...» (*Argent*, 310). Intransitive color may fuse with pure literary mode as in this example where the facade of an apartment house undergoes a progression of whiteness, working out of the idea of *nudité*, which implies the moral hypocrisy of the bourgeoisie: «... sous la pâle clarté, sa nudité blanchissait» (*P. B.* 292).

This process is intensfied with the reflexives which play the role of an obsolete passive voice: «... les murailles *jaunes se marbraient* de taches verdâtres...» (*Bonheur*, 544); «... le ciel *de suie se cuivrait*...» (*Germinal*, 1235).

In literature, it is hard to make the simile work for impressionistic effect, but Zola does try. In literature, as in painting, metamorphosis (change) of the raw material (object) is implied, as it is in high symbolist poetry, in the sense of Mallarmé. Simile is less poetic than metaphor because of the joining term which divides abstractly and intellectually the two orders of experience. In poetry, simile often twists the poem into allegory (one to one abstract relationships) while metaphor urges on to symbol. Simile not only means intellectualization instead of direct sense seizing of the material, but also theme, problem or thesis. The light and color similes are stylistically the equivalent of the expressions *couleur de* and of *le blanc* over *la blancheur*.

But how can simile be avoided by the novelist, especially a prolific one like Zola who, competing with the painters must seek out every linguistic, grammatical, rhetorical and stylistic means to present light and color to the inner eye of his reader.

Starting with the similes and metaphors of color, a few examples will illustrate how Zola vacillates between what could be called purely literary color, and more painterly attempts at nuance and exactness. «... des figuiers gigantesques... étirant leurs branches comme des bras grisâtres las de sommeil...»

(*Faute,* 1363), for example, is so pale in its color that hardly any visualization is posssible, especially when reinforced by the abstract concept of «arms fatigued with sleep». Better yet is the attempt to render yellow flowers with the parallel of a bed of liquid gold: «Le long des marches coulait un ruissellement de giroflées pareil à une nappe d'or liquide» (*Faute,* 1350). The depiction of a field of algae: «... le Baudrier de Neptune, cette ceinture de cuir verdâtre, aux bords frisés, qui semble taillée pour la poitrine d'un géant» (*Joie,* 862), is striking in that the metaphor of a greenish leather belt with curly edges seems almost like a scientific description of the plant, while the more literary concluding simile seems to be a fancy way of indicating its size. Yet the figure shows what will be made clear shortly, namely, that the usual procedure with Zola will be to combine color and light with both metaphor and simile. Parallel procedures are noticed with the light fields. Naturally enough fire-light can be seen as starlight; but while perhaps very apt to give the idea of the vast expanse of an army encampment, the following simile remains literary, for «stars» is too abstract for high visualization: «... les feux des cent mille hommes endormis éclairaient les cinq lieues de plaine, *comme une traînée d'étoiles*» (*Débâcle,* 467). More interesting is the light description of a bed of flowers, likened to sparks from a fireplace, and then refined and intensified in the conclusion of the figure: «.. des champs de géraniums et de pélargoniums, sur lesquels semblaient courir des flammèches ardentes, le rouge, le rose, le blanc incandescent d'un brasier» (*Faute,* 1352).

The most successful rendering of color and light is to be found when Zola utilizes analogies to precious metals and stones, rich metallic artifacts, expensive cloth, draperies, curtains, seashells, rich iron works, fine crystal. In their density they seem innovative in the art of nineteenth century fiction, and the only parallel is Flaubert (*Salammbó*), while the obvious origin is the poetry of Baudelaire. Here is a sampling: «... le soleil oblique faisait de la rondeur de l'eau un grand miroir d'argent poli, reflétant la face éclatante de l'astre» (*Curée,* 592); «... les pelouses s'étendaient, *noyées de clarté, pareilles à des champs d'émeraudes,* jusqu'à *la dentelle lointaine de la porte* de la Muette» (*Ibid.*); «Des chardons... plantaient des *candélabres de bronze vert...*» (*Faute,* 1350-1351). A rich cluster of metalliferous images describes vegetation in the *Paradou*: «... des houx... faisaient des haies, qui ressemblaient à des ouvrages délicats de serrurerie, à des grilles de bronze noir, de fer forgé, de cuivre poli...» (*Faute*, 1385). The obvious procedure here is to offer a field of closely related images, hoping by the multiplicity and progressive classification, as in other cases of impressionistic testing, to convey meaning to the reader. The very opposite of *mot juste,* it is a kind of literary impressionistic excess.

A very literary mode, of dubious painterly value, but stemming from a rather old tradition, is the comparison of nature's light and color to young girls, parts of their bodies, their articles of clothing. This is first seen in the Silvère-Miette idyll of *La Fortune des Rougon* where it is a question of moonlight and shadow serving as backdrop to the young lovers during their cemetery rendezvous. In *La Curée,* it is the lyrical rendering of the Seine River as a beautiful girl, viewed from the belvedere of the *hôtel* Béraud; it is also the call of sex in the Bois de Boulogne and in the parc Monceau. Its most important use is found in *La Faute de l'abbé Mouret* where all of nature joins Albine in an affirmation of life (and sexuality) seen principally in terms of light (as life) and color. The *chef-d'oeuvre* of Claude Lantier in *L'Oeuvre,* a gigantic landscape of Paris with the ideal woman superimposed upon it provides a very complicated fusion of ideal feminine beauty and landscape. Finally the fusion of woman and nature runs as a general motif all across *La Terre.*

Zola sharply separates passages of exaltation in nature from erotic nature. Lyric nature and erotic nature are not usually mixed. In *La Curée* the lyrical passages are confined to the viewings of the Seine by Renée, and they usually occur at her father's house, during those moments when she is evaluating her complex and guilty sexual life, with regrets for lost innocence and youth. In *La Faute de l'abbé Mouret,* the new Eden alternates lyrical and erotic imagery as the mood varies from the innocent games of childhood to serious sexual exchanges as Serge and Albine each day come closer and closer to the tree of forbidden knowledge.

Intoxication with nature in these descriptions seems to emanate directly from Zola as he continues the tradition of Rousseau. Basically the form is literary, with color being mere adornment: «... les Alsophila... comme des dames vertes, avec leurs larges jupes garnies de volants réguliers...» (*Curée*, 486). More drastic is the following simile in which light is transformed into a purely literary image, concentrating on the lyrical meaning of light for the author. The rays of the setting sun produce joy in Zola. He transforms light into a striking image of young girls, dressed in white, entering a church for betrothal ceremonies:

> Au loin, le long des colonnades, il y avait des coups de soleil couchant, pareils à un défilé de filles en robes blanches, entrant dans l'église, pour des fiançailles, au sourd ronflement des orgues (*Faute*, 1381).

The expanded simile actually destroys any light concept and we delight in a literary conceit. A metamorphosis of cornflowers into peasant bonnets is enriched by changing «bleuets» into «ruchés de bleu,» a clothing term (by analogy to beehives). The flowers, like bonnets, seem ready to fly off like a swarm of bees:

> ... de grands *bleuets* balançaient leurs légers *bonnets de paysanne ruchés de bleu*, menaçant de *s'envoler* par-dessus les moulins à chaque souffle (*Faute*, 1369).

High poetic pleasure is derived from Zola's botanical classifications turning about the accoutrements of women, as in this powder-puff dative: «... des agératums à houppettes bleu céleste...» (*Faute*, 1348).

The most striking, however, are the sustained light and color figurations of the Seine as found in *La Curée*. The Seine becomes brightly dressed young girls, the boats hugging its shores are transformed into a black velvet ribbon:

> Par les beaux jours, par les matinées de ciel bleu, elles se trouvaient ravies des belles robes de la Seine; c'étaient des robes changeantes qui passaient du bleu au vert, avec mille teintes d'une délicatesse infinie; on aurait dit de la soie mouchetée de flammes blanches, avec des ruches de satin; et les bateaux qui s'abritaient aux deux rives la bordaient d'un ruban de velours noir. Au loin, surtout, l'étoffe

devenait admirable et précieuse, comme la gaze enchantée d'une tunique de fée; après la bande de satin gros vert, dont l'ombre des ponts serrait la Seine, il y avait des plastrons d'or, des pans d'une étoffe plissée couleur de soleil. Le ciel immense, sur cette eau, ces files basses de maisons, ces verdures des deux parcs, se creusait (La *Curée*, 403).

While the painter can of course attempt «velvet» tones, only the literary artist can evoke «admirable and precious material», or the «enchanted gauze of a fairy tunic». A comparison of this text with the river and plain description beginning the second part of *Madame Bovary* shows not only how subjective the Zola passage is, but also how it is inundated with light and color by comparison with the more selective and judicious Flaubert:

La prairie s'allonge sous un bourrelet de collines basses pour se rattacher par derrière aux pâturages du pays de Bray, tandis que, du côté de l'est, la plaine, montant doucement, va s'élargissant et étale à perte de vue ses blondes pièces de blé. L'eau qui court au bord de l'herbe sépare d'une raie blanche la couleur des prés et celles des sillons, et la campagne ainsi ressemble à un grand manteau déplié qui a un collet de velours bordé d'un galon d'argent (8).

The Flaubert text remains more abstract and literary than that of Zola.

From lyric descriptive mode to quasi-symbolic eroticism in the manner of Baudelaire is just a step. Zola boldly establishes direct parallels between plant life and human sexuality. The Chinese hibiscus plant of Renée's hothouse has «... des bouches sensuelles de femmes...» (*Curée*, 356). Hovering between abstraction and materialization is the description of the spring waters in *La Faute de l'abbé Mouret*:

Et, du premier bassin, elles s'en allaient, elles allongeaient des bras d'une blancheur pure; elles

---

(8) Gustave Flaubert, *Madame Bovary* (Paris: Classiques Garnier, 1961), 65. Hereafter all citations from this novel will refer to this edition and page will be indicated following the text.

3

rebondissaient, pareilles à des nudités joueuses d'enfant; elles tombaient brusquement en une chute, dont la courbe molle semblait renverser un torse de femme, d'une chair blonde (*Faute*, 1385).

Plant life in these two novels takes on forms of the female body, qualified with light, color and various textures, quite frequently metallic ones. Analogous processes are noted with merchandise in *Au Bonheur des dames* and with the food products in *Le Ventre de Paris*.

Zola's light and color imagery applied to women and their adornments is simply a more painterly illustration of a tendency which goes back to the early years of romanticism, the depicting of idealized feminine beauty in terms of whiteness and blondness, the confusion of nudity and nakedness, part of which stems from the romantic neo-classical misunderstanding of the then recently discovered Greek statuary. The examples in romanticism are numerous, the alabaster arms of the dying Atala, the many representations of the sylph-like drowning Ophelia, the contrasting shadow and light atmospheres of Lamartine's *Elvire* poems. Zola in a sense answers the riddle of Gautier's «Symphonie en blanc majeur», a parnassian *tour de force,* which concludes with the question as to how to put a little «rose» in all of that whiteness, meaning how to turn a white statue of a nude (idealized beauty) into a flesh and blood woman. Albine, a sentimental woodland nymph, is first perceived as pure light:

> Puis, il y eut une course légère, un murmure de robe coulant sur l'herbe, pareil à un frôlement de couleuvre. L'abbé Mouret, debout devant la fenêtre, suivait au loin une tache blonde glissant entre les bois de pins, ainsi qu'un reflet de lune (*Faute*, 1275).

Count Muffat perceives the moving Nana: «Muffat suivait ce profil si tendre, ces fuites de chair blonde se noyant dans des lueurs dorées, ces rondeurs où la flamme des bougies mettait des reflets de soie... Nana était toute velue, un duvet de rousse faisait de son corps un velours» (*Nana*, 1271). Idealized or sensual beauty reduced to pure form, a blond spot, a moonbeam? In the same sense as the first perception of the muse by the poet in the first night poem, written exactly forty years before *La Faute de l'abbé Mouret*?

> Comme il fait noir dans la vallée!
> J'ai cru qu'une forme voilée
> Flottait là-bas sur la forêt.
> Elle sortait de la prairie;
> Son pied rasait l'herbe fleurie;
> C'est une étrange rêverie;
> Elle s'efface et disparaît (9).

Similar in intent, Zola's text relies more heavily on light. The problem is basically the same however. Musset's poet cannot distinguish ideal love from sexual love, as is proven in «La Nuit d'août». And Father Mouret suffers from the same dichotomy, pursuing the ideal of the Blessed Virgin and Albine, as the romantics had confused Mary and Eve, with full-blown flesh and blood woman winning out in the second part of the novel. It is there that the elusive light of Albine is transformed into Gautier's desired «rose» when Zola describes Albine as being «... une grande *rose*, une des *roses pâles*, ouvertes du matin» (*Faute*, 1341). And Renée is compared to a flower: «... elle ressemblait à une grande fleur, rose et verte...» (*Curée*, 357).

A summary of most of the processes discussed in this section —adjective, noun, verb, simile, metaphor— is found in the very rich light field of *Au Bonheur des dames*, the department store at four in the afternoon during a parasol sale:

> Il était quatre heures, les rayons du soleil à son coucher entraient obliquement par les larges baies de la façade, éclairaient de biais les vitrages des halls; et, dans cette clarté d'un rouge d'incendie, montaient, pareilles à une vapeur d'or, les poussières épaisses, soulevées depuis le matin par le piétinement de la foule. Une nappe enfilait la grande galerie centrale, découpait sur un fond de flammes les escaliers, les ponts volants, toute cette guipure de fer suspendue. Les mosaïques et les faïences des

---

(9) Alfred de Musset, «La Nuit de mai,» *Poésies nouvelles* (Paris: Classiques Garnier, 1958), 35.

frises miroitaient, les verts et les rouges des peintu-
res s'allumaient aux feux des ors prodigués. C'était
comme une braise vive, où brûlaient maintenant les
étalages, les palais de gants et de cravates, les girandoles de rubans et de dentelles, les hautes piles de
lainage et de calicot, les parterres diaprés que
fleurissaient les soies légères et les foulards. Des
glaces resplendissaient. L'exposition des ombrelles,
aux rondeurs de bouclier, jetait des reflets de métal.
Dans les lointains, au-delà de coulées d'ombre, il
y avait des comptoirs perdus, éclatants, grouillant
d'une cohue blonde de soleil (*Bonheur*, 642).

This passage unites the key elements of which we have been
speaking. The main components are dense noun fields of light
and somewhat of color, verbal light and color, verbal movement
of light and color —backed up by adverbial precision as to
angles of entry. And not too surprisingly, very little emphasis
on adjective. While a substratum of object is still discernible
in the display of objects for sale —gloves, ties, ribbons, laces,
parasols— these objects tend to be submerged, effaced, if not
destroyed by the invasion of light in movement and the metaphorical transformations of the objects. Movement is not just
stylistically presented, but is also found in the very structure
of the store with its wrought iron flying bridges. Movement
culminates in a riot of light, the formlessness of which is
stressed with *grouillant* and *cohue,* seen as stylistic superlative
equivalents of *nappe* and *fond,* the light patches which begin
the passage. Combined with the metaphorical constructs of
palais and *girandoles,* the department store is turned into
something magical. The concluding *cohue blonde de soleil* is
something like a first step which may turn romantic feeling
into the abstract art of the twentieth century.

This passage also illustrates for us another aspect of literary
impressionism as it relates to the noun and the verb. If nominal
style is a necessary component of literary impressionism, at the
same time the evidence of the bulk of this chapter cannot
substantiate any decreased role for the verb. The noun has
increased in value; but the verb has remained vital, particularly
in conveying states of movement and states of becoming, for
which nouns would not be pertinent. Literary impressionism
means an increased use of nominal style for the purpose of

putting into affective and primary position that which in logical constructs would be accidental and secondary. Once color and light fields have been substantivized, however, literature will still choose the verbal path to set these fields in motion through manipulation of the past and present participles, and verbs in the imperfect, used transitively and intransitively, with both reflexive and pronominal forms. If we have tended to believe that impressionism implies nominal style, we are correct, with the qualification that this indicates a new role not just for the noun, but relatively speaking, for the verb as well.

Characteristic of the art of Zola is the clustering of light terms, but mainly color terms. This occurs frequently enough in the *Rougon-Macquart* to merit analysis so that literary versus painterly intent may be verified. The following description of stained glass, while dazzling in its small orchestration, is basically serving narrative purpose, when we recall that Félicien's occupation is repairer of stained-glass windows:

> ... il y avait ... des verres de toutes les couleurs ... les bleus, les jaunes, les verts, les rouges, pâles, jaspés, fumeux, sombres, nacrés, intenses (*Rêve*, 930).

Equally literary, serving the plot, are these repetitions of white: Madame Baudu's (*Au Bonheur des dames*) whiteness betrays her anemia, but also types her as representative of a dying class, the small merchants, by contrast with the dazzling light of the new style of mercantilism; the white hair of Caroline Hamelin in *L'Argent* means a strange and haunting beauty; the «whiteness» of Dr. Pascal fuses with the Biblical motif which we shall explore later:

> La première était une petite femme mangée d'anémie, toute *blanche,* les cheveux *blancs,* les yeux *blancs,* les lèvres *blanches* (*Bonheur*, 396).
> ... c'était ses cheveux *blancs* superbes, une royale couronne de cheveux *blancs...* Dès vingt-cinq ans, elle était devenue toute *blanche.* Ses sourcils, restés noirs et très fournis, gardaient une jeunesse, une étrangeté vive à son visage encadré d'*hermine...* Mais certainement, cette tosin *blanche,* cette *blancheur* envolée de fins cheveux de *soie, adoucissait* sa physionomie un peu dure... (*Argent*, 57-58).

... tandis que ses cheveux *blancs,* sa barbe *blanche,*
poussaient plus drus, d'une abondance léonine, dont
le flot de *neige* le rajeunissait (*Pascal,* 1068).

That this is a type of literary repetition in no way related to
light and color for its own sake can be proven if we present
similar patterns of repetition without color or light. Mouret
visits the apartment of abbé Faujas, feigning to inspect a water
leak, but actually hoping to learn something: «Pas un papier
sur la table, pas un objet sur la commode, pas un vêtement aux
murs: le bois nu, le marbre nu, le mur nu» (*Conquête,* 926).
Renée, at the costume ball, dresses in a Tahitian costume which
reveals most of her body to the guests. It is also a moment
of self-examination in which she tries to figure out where she
went wrong in life. Zola conveys this idea to us through the
reiterated use of *nu* which builds as motif across the chapter:

> Elle était en Otaïtenne... Et rien autre. Elle était
> nue (*Curée,* 555).
> Et le collier et le bracelet de corail lui semblaient
> plus jolis sur la peau de son cou et de son bras.
> Etait-ce ce jour-là qu'elle avait commencé à se
> mettre nue? (*Curée,* 573).
> Qui donc l'avait mise nue? (*Curée,* 574).
> Ils l'avaient mise nue (*Curée,* 575).
> Sa nudité l'irritait (*Ibid.*).
> Alors, elle jeta sur ses épaules une pelisse de
> fourrure, pour ne pas traverser le bal toute nue
> (*Curée,* 577).
> Par moments, il lui semblait qu'un souffle de
> vent allait enlever les robes. Ces épaules nues, ces
> bras nus, ces chevelures nues qui volaient... comme
> l'image tumultueuse de sa vie à elle, de ses nudités,
> de ses abandons (*Curée,* 580).

The repetitions herein are essentially the same as the repetitions
of colors with which this section began, proving, I think, that
in most instances the repetitions of color serve basically novelistic purpose (10).

_____

(10) Repetition as a literary device has been studied by Calvin
S. Brown in *Repetition in Zola's Novels* (Athens, Georgia, 1952).

Yet another purpose is served by these color and light clusters— the expression of lyric joy experienced by the narrator. Berthe's wedding outfit, for example, hammers away at the idea of whiteness, expressing perhaps the only joyful moment in a rather drab and pessimistic novel:

> ... et Berthe parut, en robe de soie *blanche*, toute fleurie de fleurs *blanches*, la couronne *blanche*, le bouquet *blanc*, la jupe traversée d'une guirlande *blanche*, qui s'en allait mourir sur la traîne, en une pluie de petits boutons *blancs*. Dans cette *blancheur* elle était charmante... (*P. B.*, 140-141).

In *Une Page d'amour* the motif of white underlines the sentimentality of the Paris bourgeoisie, unable to distinguish a funeral from a spring garden party. Madame Deberle, the *animatrice*, has the idea of making «... des funérailles touchantes...» (1072): «Son rêve était d'avoir un défilé de petites filles en robe *blanche*» (*Ibid.*). And Jeanne, in her casket, seems to be queen of this assembly of little fairies.

> Jeanne était encore couchée, les mains jointes; et comme Marguerite, comme les demoiselles Levasseur, elle avait une *robe blanche, un bonnet blanc, des souliers blancs*. Une couronne de *roses blanches*, posée sur le bonnet, faisait d'elle la reine de ses petites amies, fêtée par tout ce monde qui attendait en bas (1074).

As in this case of a leitmotif in white, the dresses of Jeanne and her little friends recall to Hélène happier days when the little group was assembled for a costume party. White clustering thus serves the psychological temporal narrative, the bright colors of the past being contrasted with the white of the present:

> Alors, quand le jardin fut tout blanc, en face de cette bande lâchée de petites filles, Hélène eut un souvenir. Elle se rappela le bal de l'autre belle saison, avec la joie dansante des petits pieds. Et elle revoyait Marguerite en laitière, sa boîte au lait à la ceinture, Sophie en soubrette, tournant au bras de sa soeur Blanche, dont le costume de Folie sonnait

un carillon. Puis, c'étaient les cinq demoiselles Levasseur, des Chaperons Rouges qui multipliaient les toquets de satin ponceau à bandes de velours noir; tandis que la petite Guiraud, avec son papillon d'Alsacienne dans les cheveux, sautait comme une perdue, en face d'un Arlequin deux fois plus grand qu'elle. Aujourd'hui, toutes étaient blanches. Jeanne aussi était blanche, sur l'oreiller de satin blanc, dans les fleurs. La fine Japonaise (Jeanne at the costume party), au chignon traversé de longues épingles, à la tunique de pourpre brodée d'oiseaux, s'en allait en robe blanche (1078).

In the passage just cited it is apparent that the color clusters are being accompanied by complementary lyrical elements, *la joie dansante des petits pieds, boîte au lait, sonnait un carillon, papillon d'Alsacienne,* the naming of the various costumes, the hustle and bustle of activity of little children. The idea of funeral and death is having superimposed on it the lyrical celebration of spring, the dresses metaphorically turned into the freshness of the first season: «... les robes étaient la candeur même du printemps» (1078). The little girls kneeling in the cemetery are compared to white sparrows: «Les petites filles agenouillées se levaient comme un vol de moineaux blancs (1081). And the last sentence of the chapter shifts from white to gold as the Paris spring is celebrated by Zola: «A l'horizon, Paris blondissait sous la radieuse matinée de printemps» (1083). His exaltation in a springtime nature is contrasted with the evasive white of the sentimental funeral. His lyric white unites with the narrative white of Hélène's recall of the past. Finally white adds the painterly dimension in this chapter along the lines we have been discussing: the blond hair of one little girl contrasts with the whiteness of the veil, reinforced with simile to give the impression of gold on white:

Marguerite Tissot, dans son *nuage de mousseline,* avec ses grands yeux, semblait une vierge enfant; ses cheveux blonds s'échappaient du petit bonnet, mettaient comme une pèlerine brochée d'or sous la blancheur du voile (1073).

Little boys in their black suits put black spots on the whiteness:

Le salon, peu à peu, s'emplissait d'une tombée de
neige. Quelques garçons en redingote, tachaient de
noir cette pureté (1074).

In the sun the whiteness of the dresses intensifies, producing
a moire effect: «Les robes blanches se gonflaient dans le soleil,
se moiraient de transparences...» (1077).

La Terre provides a very fine example of color impressions
of La Beauce:

> ... il distingua de loin le *vert jaune* du blé, le *vert
> bleu* de l'avoine, le *vert gris* du seigle, des pièces à
> l'infini, étalées dans tous les sens, parmi les plaques
> rouges des trèfles incarnat (531).

Buteau, like an impressionistic painter, observes the very finely
nuanced colorations. This example is a case in point of how
Zola will sacrifice at times his novelistic art to his own delight
in rendering a colorful natural landscape, for Buteau the
peasant, in the context of the novel, would not be capable of
such observations.

Certainly the best example of color clustering is the *tour
de force* of the white sale, *la grande exposition de blanc* found
in *Au Bonheur des dames*. The passage is quoted in its entirety
in order to give a total feeling of this aspect of Zola's art:

> Ensuite, les galeries s'enfonçaient, dans une blan-
> cheur éclatante, une échappée boréale, toute une
> contrée de neige, déroulant l'infini des steppes ten-
> dues d'hermine, l'entassement des glaciers allumés
> sous le soleil. On retrouvait le blanc des vitrines du
> dehors, mais avivé, colossal, brûlant d'un bout à
> l'autre de l'énorme vaisseau, avec la flambée blanche
> d'un incendie en plein feu. Rien que du blanc, tous
> les articles blancs de chaque rayon, une débauche
> de blanc, un astre blanc dont le rayonnement fixe
> aveuglait d'abord, sans qu'on pût distinguer les dé-
> tails, au milieu de cette blancheur unique. Bientôt
> les yeux s'accoutumaient: à gauche, la galerie Mon-
> signy allongeait les promontoires blancs des toiles
> et des calicots, les roches blanches des draps de lit,
> des serviettes, des mouchoirs; tandis que la galerie
> Michodière, à droite, occupée par la mercerie, la
> bonneterie et les lainages, exposait des constructions

— 41 —

blanches en boutons de nacre, un grand décor bâti avec des chaussettes blanches, toute une salle recouverte de molleton blanc, éclairée au loin d'un coup de lumière. Mais le foyer de clarté rayonnait surtout de la galerie centrale, aux rubans et aux fichus, à la ganterie et à la soie. Les comptoirs disparaissaient sous le blanc des soies et des rubans, des gants et des fichus. Autour des colonnettes de fer, s'élevaient des bouillonnés de mousseline blanche, noués de place en place par des foulards blancs. Les escaliers étaient garnis de draperies blanches, des draperies de piqué et de basin alternées, qui filaient le long des rampes, entouraient les halls, jusqu'au second étage; et cette montée du blanc prenait des ailes, se pressait et se perdait, comme une envolée de cygnes. Puis, le blanc retombait des voûtes, une tombée de duvet, une nappe neigeuse en larges flocons: des couvertures blanches, des couvre-pieds blancs, battaient l'air, accrochés, pareils à des bannières d'église; de longs jets de guipure traversaient, semblaient suspendre des essaims de papillons blancs, au bourdonnement immobile; des dentelles frissonnaient de toutes parts, flottaient comme des fils de la Vierge par un ciel d'été, emplissaient l'air de leur haleine blanche. Et la merveille, l'autel de cette religion du blanc, était, au-dessus du comptoir des soieries, dans le grand hall, une tente faite de rideaux blancs, qui descendaient du vitrage. Les mousselines, les gazes, les guipures d'art, coulaient à flots légers, pendant que des tulles brodés, très riches, et des pièces de soie orientale, lamées d'argent, servaient de fond à cette décoration géante, qui tenait du tabernacle et de l'alcôve. On aurait dit un grand lit blanc, dont l'énormité virginale attendait, comme dans les légendes, la princesse blanche, celle qui devait venir un jour, toute-puissante, avec le voile blanc des épousées (768-769).

If those elements which do not make some reference to whiteness or lightness were italicized it would be seen that very little of the paragraph escapes this literary assault of white. Using the basic categories of this chapter we see a statistically impressive array of noun, verb and adjective fields of white, light, and movement. This long description contains only twelve sentences, and within them there are twenty-four metaphorical transformations balanced and fused with thirty identifiable white objects displayed, and five specialty sections listed. The text fuses the figurative and the real, emphasizing effacement of the real in order to idealize it. Subject is effaced, much in the manner of a too close viewing of an impressionistic painting, but the nuanced fields of white more approximate a later art, that of abstract expressionism, of which, as has been suggested earlier, Zola may have been a literary ancestor. The disappearance of subject is first of all a fact: the bright light blinds the viewer, details cannot be distinguished, but finally the eyes get use to the effect. Then object is subordinated to metaphors and similes of whiteness, nordic topographies. Zola the narrator must identify the galleries to the left and the right, so dazzled are reader and customer by all of this whiteness. In a series of coordinate clauses, the galleries are assumed into a bursting whiteness. This is followed or backed up by five clausal steps, each clause taking us deeper into whiteness through a series of northern glacial images. This process of constantly adding a term is characteristic of the Zola sentence and is further illustrated with the following sentence: «Puis (1) le blanc retombait des voûtes, (2) une tombée de duvet, (3) une nappe neigeuse, (4) en larges flocons: des couvertures blanches, (5) des couvre-pieds blancs, (6) battaient l'air, (7) accrochés, (8) pareils à des bannières d'église». Thus the clause moves from the general abstraction of white to three figurations which then move into two identifiable objects in white, finally to their movement and placement, concluding with a simile. Careful attention is given to the idea of form in this passage. At first, form and space seem vague, then more precise, on the one hand *échappée, construction, décor,* on the other, figurative, northern geographies, ice and snow regions. We go through a whole gamut of analogies of white, much like Gautier's «Symphonie en blanc majeur» or the condensed white fields of Mallarmé's swan sonnet, but with the added dimensions imposed by the art of the novel. The final metamorphosis of white into virginal whiteness, the white princess awaiting the bridegroom at the conjugal bed, fuses with the role of Denise in the novel. The motif of white is found throughout Chapter XIV, in descriptions of many of the specialized counters, and acts as a kind of structural motif. The reader, at page 794, with only nine pages left, wonders how Zola will get back to his narration, so intoxicated is he with his white descriptions. Will Denise leave, or will she marry Octave? Finally it should be noted that this passage is highly nominal with noun fields standing out in rich relief. If in the preceding display of greens from *La Terre* we noted nominal impressionistic word order, «le vert-jaune du blé», we go forward another step here with a uniquely literary color joining metaphor in a primary position: «les promontoires blancs/des toiles...»; «les roches blanches/des draps...». And while the style is highly nominal we note again that it is richly verbal, reiterating the idea that increased nominal structure does not preclude strong verbal patterns of movement. To the contrary it seems a basic component of the art of Zola.

The discussion of the *exposition de blanc* leads naturally into the final consideration of this chapter, the great tableaux of the *Rougon-Macquart,* on the basis of which Zola has been termed a literary impressionist. Following the novels sequentially, the great light and color tableaux are the following: the rain of gold scene in *La Curée* wherein Saccard and Angèle have an evening dinner on Montmartre overlooking Paris, and the evening Boulevard scene of Renée at the café Riche in the same novel; the great and almost gratuitous scenes of the *Le Ventre de Paris*; the most celebrated of all the tableaux, the formal five tableaux of Paris which conclude the five sections of *Une Page d'amour*: (1) Paris at ten in the morning of a beautiful February day, (2) an impressionistic sunset, (3) a September evening, capturing as many nuances of light as possible in a starscape, (4) a destructive rainstorm over Paris in which the city appears «englouti», with the Biblical furor of the Great Flood, and (5) Paris seen under snow, a scene greatly used to explain the final psychological stance of Hélène; the great descriptive tableaux of Paris found in *L'Oeuvre,* particularly in Chapters IV and VIII, plus the very paintings of Claude; the fusion of sunset with the actual burning of Paris during the *Commune* at the end of *La Débâcle.* These tableaux utilize the techniques that have been discussed, in a prolonged and sustained manner, and are not always gratuitous but frequently integrated into the narration. The great tableaux present the final evidence for the basic point of this chapter, namely that there is a relationship between light and color impressionism, and the lyrical feeling of the romantics which seems to engender these impressions. That is, we move from romantic sensation to descriptive impressions. The lyric feeling noticed in many of the examples analyzed so far is demonstrable in almost all of the great paintings of the *Rougon-Macquart*. The third description of Paris in *Une Page d'amour* is of a romantic, impressionistic starlit night. In this scene, Hélène is trying to struggle through a sentimental problem, to give into her sentiments for Henri, or to marry a good honest bourgeois. The descriptions herein are the weakest possible from the viewpoint of impressionism, the correspondance between Hélène and the city is diminished by the interpolation of her conversation with the priest (the impressionistic tableaux are most effective when the observer is alone), and there is a technical reliance on disparate simile and metaphor. Hélène is pleased with some of the lights, and frightened by others. Nevertheless, with Zola trying to capture as many nuances of light as he can, the passage is a good demonstration of a light and color description hovering between impressionism and traditional romantic subjectivity.

> Que d'étoiles! murmura l'abbé Jouve. Elles brillent par milliers... Alors, elle leva les yeux, regardant le ciel d'été. Les constellations plantaient leurs *clous d'or.* Une planète, presque au ras de l'horizon, luisait *comme une escarboucle,* tandis qu'une *poussière d'étoiles* presque invisibles *sablait* la *voûte* d'un *sable pailleté d'étincelles...* (966).

The above is almost a perfect balancing of literary (figurative) light with painterly tendencies. Hélène, looking at the sky, experiences a feeling of peace, followed by a description which does frighten her:

> ... les yeux toujours levés, éblouis et pris d'un léger frisson en face de ce *fourmillement d'astres qui grandissait.* Derrière les milliers d'étoiles, d'autres milliers d'étoiles apparaissaient, et cela sans cesse, dans la profondeur infinie du ciel. C'était un continuel épanouissement, une braise attisée de mondes brûlant du feu calme des pierreries. La voie lactée blanchissait déjà, développait ses atomes de soleil, si innombrables et si lointains qu'ils ne sont plus,

à la rondeur du firmament, qu'une écharpe de lumière (*Ibid.*).

The impressionistic detail has now been all but obliterated, to be replaced by what? A fearful sentiment of the vast and ever continuing, endless spaces of the firmament. This is not the old Pascalian fear of the infinite spaces. It is exactly, in the second half of the nineteenth century, the romantic inquietude provoked by the contemplation of the constellations, and so well evoked in the poetry of Victor Hugo. The romantic *frisson* has been inherited by the bourgeoisie of the Second Empire. Hélène, in working out a personal problem, whether or not to enter into an adulterous relationship with Dr. Deberle, is imposing on the sky her psychological problem. This problem, as Zola reveals it, has dimensions of spirituality to it, for Hélène seeks a decent and pure love (11). New stars, however, conclude the scene, the stars which are the lights of Paris, the temptations of an adulterous affair. These lights gain as the chapter concludes and have the intensity of fire and sunset. What is observed here in the third tableau is a mixture of lyric awe and pondering of destiny through a skyscape tinged with impressionistic light and color. It is a blend which joins the new light of impressionism with romantic subjectivism.

Lyrical impressionism means also metaphorical transformations of the raw material. In one of the great tableaux of *L'Oeuvre* we can observe this process in operation. If the impressionism is enfeebled by a simple literary listing of the sights of Paris observed by Claude and Christine —Isle de la Cité, Pont-Neuf, la Préfecture, pont des Saints-Pères, Hôtel de ville, Saint Gervais, etc., true impressionistic metamorphoses

---

(11) See the discussion by Professor Robert Rosenblum of the importance of the night sky in nineteenth century painting. Rosenblum explains that «... For Van Gogh, as for so many Romantics, the night sky could provide one of the most passionate metaphors of the mysteries of the universe.» *Modern Painting and the Northern Romantic Tradition* (New York, 1975), 93. Hélène's contemplation of the night sky seems to have some parallels with this motif in nineteenth century painting as discussed by Rosenblum. It should also be said that Professor Rosenblum's book is truly a pioneering work in exploring the evolution towards the abstract art of the twentieth century out of its romantic roots.

do accompany them. Poplar trees are changed into powerful green masses: «... les peupliers du terre-plein *verdissaient en une masse puissante*...» (*Oeuvre*, 213); the movement of the yellow public transports and the multicolored moving vans is changed into the impressionistic movement of children's toys:

> Le long du Pont-Neuf, *de grands omnibus jaunes,* des *tapissières bariolées,* défilaient avec une *régularité mécanique de jouets d'enfant* (*Ibid.*).

Across the pont des Arts, seen as the second plane of a painting, a crowd of pedestrians in movement appears to be a cavalcade of ants on horseback:

> Puis, au milieu, la Seine vide montait, verdâtre avec des petits flots dansants, fouettée de blanc, de bleu et de rose. Et le pont des Arts établissait un second plan, très haut sur ses charpentes de fer, d'une légèreté de dentelle noire, animé du perpétuel va-et-vient des piétons, une chevauchée de fourmis, sur la mince ligne de son tablier (*Oeuvre*, 212-13).

This citation very well joins color impressionism, movement, and metaphor, the transformation of the pedestrians into ants anticipating the famous transformation of the Eiffel tower by Apollinaire in «Zone,» without of course the very buoyancy of the shepherd image of Apollinaire. But this is among the first examples of metaphorical modernism.

The great tableaux illustrate that ultimately Zola turns his light and color impressionism into highly visual metaphors usually denoting destruction and collapse, through intensive movement within them. One of the most sustained fields in this regard is the last tableau of *Une Page d'amour.* As in the preceding ones of the same novel, the process is to move from a series of impressionistic elements, single elements in the syntax, to the culminating image. This scene is dominated by the idea of snow. Zola transforms Paris into a series of mountain ranges in which the original elements almost completely disappear. It is a metaphorical process which seems to be even beyond impressionism, bordering on total abstraction. In common with impressionism, however, it is analogous to the procedure of approaching the painting until all the original elements of design, however weak, are no longer recognizable. Here the procedure is somewhat different because of the nature of the literary work. Instead of losing identity into impressionistic dots and spots, the literary impressionist adds the dimension of figuration, simile and metaphor, to replace one reality, Paris under the December morning snow, by a series of nature snow paintings, attached mainly to the ambiance of mountains. This is just a stylistic step removed from Mallarmé's fusion of two distinct realities. In Zola the fusion is still apparent since one part of the phrase announces the concrete reality (towers of Notre-Dame) even though the second half is simile or metaphor: «La Seine roulait des eaux terreuses, entre ses berges qui la bordaient *d'hermine*» (1091); «... les tours de Notre-Dame surmontaient de leurs *pics neigeux*» (*Ibid.*); «Saint-Augustin, l'Opéra, la tour Saint-Jacques étaient *comme des monts où règnent les neiges éternelles*» (*Ibid.*). Better yet because of the word order is: «... *les cimes blanchies* des Invalides, de Saint-Sulpice, du Panthéon...» (*Ibid.*). Zola comments upon the disappearance of the original forms:

> Des rues se devinaient à des fentes grises, des carre-fours semblaient s'ètre creusés dans un craquement. Par files entières, les maisons avaient disparu (*Ibid.*).

Ultimately even the metaphorical structure disappears. Rather an expressionistic and abstract field of white is created. Like the abstract metaphors of Mallarmé, objects are announced only to be destroyed. Here, in Zola, the original material such as Notre-Dame or the Pantheon disappears into simile and metaphor of ice peaks. Paris finally is seen as a semi-abstract glacial lake, approximating as much as this is possible in the novel, the lake inhabited by Mallarmé's swan:

> Les nappes de neige, ensuite, se confondaient, se perdaient en un lointain éblouissant, en un lac dont les ombres bleues prolongeaient le bleu du ciel (*Ibid.*).

It should be pointed out that Zola does not always and everywhere create tableau in this metaphorical-impressionistic fashion. The great fire scene at the conclusion of *La Conquête de Plassans* is narrated almost totally with an eye for accurate and simple realistic detail. To see in this, however, any indication that Zola had not as yet developed impressionistic techniques is refuted by the generous samplings utilized in this chapter from preceding novels, especially *Le Ventre de Paris,* which is considered one of his most impressionistic. The minimization of impressionistic light in *La Conquête de Plassans* probably has more to do with the heavy and sensational narration—neighbors sitting in chairs watching the fire as they would a fireworks display; Madame Faujas carrying her giant of a son down the stairway of the burning house; the scene shift to the dying Marthe Mouret. Zola's description of the fire seems almost like a newspaper account. It is rendered simply and directly: «La maison flambait alors, du rez-de-chaussée au second étage, comme une immense torche» (*Conquête,* 1206).

The assumptions of this chapter have been the following: Romantic lyricism of the variety found starting in Rousseau's natures is transformed in Zola, a Zola who shares and surpasses Rousseau's sensitivity to nature, certainly under the influence of the artistic theories of his time, into a consistent literary display of light and color phenomena. The painterly effects, enjoyed in themselves, are at the same time forced to accord with the overall novelistic (narrational) intent of the writer as has been suggested herein and which will be implied throughout this study. Ultimately, the light and color fields are returned to literature by being transformed into metaphors, being pushed as much in the direction of Mallarmé as is possible for prose art, especially the novel. Finally, the metaphors are frequently pressed into purely abstract light and color fields which may go beyond impressionism into a symbolic expressionism.

In trying to bridge approximately one hundred years of literary evolution in France, the process perhaps can be reduced to a formula which we hope is not too simplistic: Lyric feeling is transformed into light and color constructions which in turn undergo metamorphoses.

4

CHAPTER III

IMPRESSIONISTIC MODES

I. *Impressions of the City*

A great love for the ambiance of Paris (1) is expressed in Zola's correspondence and newspaper articles, and Paris is a dominating presence in eleven of the twenty volumes of the *Rougon-Macquart*. Zola had written in an article of 1872:

> ... J'aime d'amour les horizons de la grande cité. Selon moi, il y a là toute une mine féconde, tout un art moderne à créer. Les boulevards grouillent au soleil, les squares étalent leurs verdures et leur petit monde d'enfants; les quais allongent leurs berges pittoresques...; les carrefours dressent leurs hautes maisons, avec les notes joyeuses des tentes, la vie des ténèbres. Et selon qu'un rayon de soleil égaie Paris, ou qu'un ciel sombre le fasse rêver, la ville a des émotions diverses, devient un poème de joie ou de mélancolie (2).

---

(1) The best thematic study of the role of Paris in the work of Zola is Nathan Kranowski, *Paris dans les Romans d'Emile Zola* (Paris, 1968). Kranowski not only studies Zola's Paris from the perspective of sociology, but also does some metaphorical and symbolic analysis. This book's major asset is the comparison made with other literary manifestations of Paris, particularly the romantic. See also, Stefan Max, *Les Métamorphoses de la grande ville dans les Rougon-Macquart* (Paris, 1966).

(2) Article in *La Cloche*, January 24, 1872, cited by Mitterand, Volume I of the Pléiade edition of *Les Rougon-Macquart*, 1614.

This lyric feeling should be understood within the spirit of modernity (3) which is fundamental to an understanding of the impressionistic modes which this chapter will treat. Commitment to the spirit of their time unites writers and painters in a common effort to seize the moment, the hustle and bustle, the movement of city life. The modern writer, starting with the prose of Flaubert and the poetry of Baudelaire (4), will be acutely sensitive to the ever-increasing, on-going activities of modern man. Zola competes with the painter in creating impressions of light and color, especially in movement. Furthermore, he will attempt to capture the nuances of change in a stable object, creating with literary means a series of impressionistic paintings much in the manner of Monet's cathedrals, lily ponds, and bridges. Capturing the rapid tempo of the modern world gives rise to a particular mode of viewing in the *Rougon-Macquart,* the recording of the part for the whole, and sometimes the whole for the part, an impressionistic synecdoche. And Zola will attempt to go beyond the painter with his development of olfactory and sound impressionism. The *Rougon-Macquart* finally will display a symbolic style of movement which seems to form the ideological basis for his specific type of impressionism. So viewed, impressionism

---

Similar ideas are expressed in another Zola article, «Causerie du dimanche,» *Le Corsaire, December* 3, 1872.

(3) Zola endlessly reiterates the idea of being of one's time, and of the necessity of artistic renewal. Among the many documents which could be cited is an article in *La Cloche* of May 5, 1872, entitled «Lettres Parisiennes—Sur la prostitution de l'art dramatique en France. Le grand mouvement naturaliste régénérera le théâtre,» and an article on the evolution of nineteenth century French theatre in *Le Bien public* of September 4, 1876. In both, Zola calls for theatrical renewal under the rubric of modernity. Here he is doing for the second half of the century what Stendhal had done in the first half with his *Racine et Shakespeare.* Zola so loathes the decayed romantic theatre of his time that he makes a strong case for Racine. Most critics have commented on Zola's modernism, but Guy Robert says it best: «S'il ne veut pas répéter inutilement les oeuvres des âges passés, l'artiste doit se tourner vers le sien et lui demander son inspiration. Sinon, il se condamne à manquer à son premier devoir: être original.», Robert, *Principes,* 12.

(4) One very startling romantic vision of the world, anticipating the modern one, is the image of an almost surrealistic locomotive in Alfred de Vigny's poem «La Maison du berger».

means the movement of modern life. Contemporaneity is the key to this modern art. The sense of modern Paris is felt across the *Rougon-Macquart* (5). It is a Paris subject to transformations as science makes it the city of lights: «A l'horizon, une grande fumée blanche flottait, mettait Paris dormant dans la buée lumineuse de toutes ces flammes» (*Ventre*, 605). For those who know Zola's novels well, the lights, flames and fires of Paris are sometimes real, but more often than not metaphorical, symbolic in intent. Verhaeren, poet of *Les Villes tentaculaires,* said that Paris is the real protagonist of the *Rougon-Macquart* (6), and Zola certainly approximates the Belgian poet in his descriptions of the foundry workers in *L'Assommoir.* It is, however, the feel for the lights and the sounds and the movement of the great city which characterizes the novels of Zola. In the following passage where Count Muffat awaits Nana in the passage des Panoramas, we note the unique light and color impressions as found only in a great metropolis, clustering within a restricted area multiple shops with diverse activities, various shapes and sounds. Here it is mainly inundations of light and color. Elsewhere, other dimensions, olfactory ones, will be added:

> La soirée était très douce, une averse venait d'emplir le passage d'un flot de monde. Il y avait là une cohue, un défilé penible et lent, resserré entre

---

(5) A concise analysis of the meaning of contemporaneity for writers and painters alike is found in: Linda Nochlin, *Realism* (Baltimore, 1971), especially page 28. Baudelaire seems to be the very first example of the spirit of modernity in French literature, the *Tableaux parisiens* revealing the «... sensibilitié d'homme des villes.», Pierre Citron, *La Poésie de Paris dans la littérature française de Rousseau à Baudelaire* (Paris, 1961), 332. See also Martin Turnell, *Baudelaire: A Study of his Poetry* (Norfolk, Connecticut, 1954), 176-177, and the very fine study of Marcia Joan Weiss, «The Paris Motif in the Prose Poems of Charles Baudelaire,» (Master of Arts dissertation, The George Washington University, 1971). All of these studies, especially that of Marcia Weiss, insist upon Baudelaire's desire and ability to capture the ephemeral, the fleeting aspects of Paris in his poetry. The similarity to Zola's prose descriptions of the city is evident.

(6) Jean-Albert Bédé, preface to Kranowski, *Paris dans les Romans de Zola,* v.

les boutiques. C'était, sous les vitres blanchies de reflets, un violent éclairage, une coulée de clartés, des globes blancs, des lanternes rouges, des transparents bleus, des rampes de gaz, des montres et des éventails géants en traits de flamme, brûlant en l'air; et le bariolage des étalages, l'or des bijoutiers, les cristaux des confiseurs, les soies claires des modistes, flambaient, derrière la pureté des glaces, dans le coup de lumière crue des réflecteurs; ... (*Nana*, 1259).

Throughout the novels Zola speaks of the «ardent» life of the city as in «... on voyait passer la vie ardente des boulevards, qui grouillaient et flambaient sous la belle nuit d'avril» (*Nana*, 1096). The intent is to blend the lyricism of nature, here, an early spring night, with the idea of modern man in his modern city. This is to be captured by depicting the agitation of a confused mass, with a spirit of liveliness, being translated into color as fire: «... la nuit épaissie du boulevard se piquait de feux, dans le vague d'une foule toujours en marche» (*Nana*, 1099). Zola and the impressionist painters are city dwellers, and impressionism is a city art. Even when the writers and the painters go to the country they will take with them the sensibilities of the city (7).

Light and movement frequently mean the triumph of modern life. *Pot-Bouille* and *Au Bonheur des dames* both illustrate the triumph of the here and the now, the present, over older traditions which try in vain to perpetuate themselves into the contemporary scene. Older ideas and institutions are characterized by shadows, darkness, silence and immobility. In *Pot-Bouille,* Zola contrasts the new idea of big business, taking advantage of new concepts of mercantilism, management systems and advertising, with the small merchants who remain in an earlier time, refusing to change. Not of the epoch, their stores are dark and immobile. without customers. This is an old idea in Zola, going back to the first volume with the descriptions of the sleepy aristocratic quarter of Plassans not in tune with the times, or the contrast between the animated and illuminated *hôtel* Saccard, and the dark, traditional

---

(7) Hauser, *Social History of Art*, II, 871.

bourgeois home of Renée's father in *La Curée*. *Au Bonheur des dames* contrasts the expanding department store with the shops of the little merchants, particularly that of Denise's Uncle Baudu. Modern Paris is an endless motif in the *Rougon-Macquart* of which these examples give only a small idea. As we discuss other impressionistic modes, other aspects of the Paris motif will be implied if not formally discussed.

II. *Stable Object Subject to Change*

> A chaque heure, les jeux de lumière changeaient ainsi les profils des Halles, depuis les bleuissements du matin et les ombres noires de midi, jusqu'à l'incendie du soleil couchant, s'éteignant dans la cendre grise du crépuscule (*Ventre*, 730).

A striking resemblance between impressionistic procedure and the literary art of Zola is found in the repeated creation of a constant object. That Zola is trying to rival the painters is undeniable; stable object subject to change, however, will also serve novelistic ends. Color and light effects and movement must be evaluated in terms of the compositional requirements of the novelistic form. The single elements of light, color and movement can be viewed in a purely lyrical manner, or as spontaneous, haphazard, formless rendering. Yet to say only this would distort the novelistic artefact seen in its totality. As Monet frames each subject, so the novelistic frame must be considered (8). The analogy cautions us, however, to ponder the relationship between impressionistic effect and novelistic goals. This means that the descriptive art of Zola must be seen in its literary geometry which is multi-layered. Impressionism in the novel must be seen within the context of recognizable geometric lines, surfaces, and solids found within the line of narration.

The literary utilization of an impressionistic cityscape is illustrated by Zola's painting of the *Boulevard des Italiens* as

---

(8) It can be useful to the literary critic to study the descriptions made by the art historians of the formal geometries of painting. See William C. Seitz, *Claude Monet* (New York, n. d.), 27-28.

seen from the café Riche in *La Curée,* a painting which in many ways resembles Monet's *Boulevard des Capucines* (1873) painted two years after the Zola text, or the well-known boulevard work of Pissaro. These views will be related by Zola to the drama of seduction being played out in the private dining room between Renée and Maxime. There are three impressions of the *Boulevard,* corresponding to three soul states of Renée: anticipation of seduction, precipitation, and post-coïtal shame and guilt. The impressionistic descriptions are joined to a symbolic intent in the constant of the ambulating prostitutes, and both techniques therefore serve the over-all novelistic goal. Here the insistence is simply upon the fact that Zola sees description as central to his art, and such description with him will be impressionistic. This is made apparent in studying the preparatory notes for this novel:

> *Il faut qu'une description du boul, tienne tout le chapitre et suive le drame* — [underlining by Zola]. Je puis mettre ma scène entre Renée et Maxime au Café Anglais. ... Aspect du boulevard vers minuit vu d'une fenêtre. Ce qui frappe avant tout, c'est la ligne éclairée des Kiosques: enseignes coloriées, vertes, rouges, jaunes. Pas de lumière épandue. D'énormes lanternes chinoises ou vénitiennes. Les arbres font deux lignes sombres dont les têtes se détachent finement en noir sur le ciel bleu, des deux côtés. En dessous, sur le boulevard, un roulement continu de voitures, des yeux qui filent. L'omnibus de la Madeleine. Pas d'équipages, des fiacres — Sur les trottoirs, les boutiques fermées (nommer quelques boutiques). Les cafés ouverts projetant une grande lueur. Consommateurs plus rares aux tables. Le va-et-vient des promeneurs, dans l'ombre, puis éclairés. Effet de cette promenade lente. Des yeux s'arrêtent. Les filles allant de café en café. Une isolée en toilette de toile femme que Renée verra avant et qu'elle retrouvera, toujours lente et en quête. Le brouhaha qui monte (9).

---

(9) Emile Zola, *Manuscrit* 10282, *feuillet* 228, *Nouvelles acquisitions françaises* (Paris: *Bibliothèque Nationale*). Hereafter abbreviated *Fr. Nouv. Acq.*

We note immediately the strong emphasis by Zola on light, sharply contrasted with shadow, insistence upon the idea of line, with strong compositional elements of planes. In addition there are impresssions of ceaseless movement and increasing noise. Three sharp divisions are made: The first painting is that of the boulevard just before midnight accompanied by a description of the seated prostitute. The second painting is a little later with a description of a prostitute waiting at a street corner. The third painting is very late with again the element of the waiting prostitute. The presence of the strolling prostitute, but particularly of the seated one, seems like a more elegant version of Degas' *L'Absinthe* (1876) although the Zola text is five years earlier. At least from the point of view of subject matter the Zola text deserves some comparison with the Degas painting:

> Renée en remarqua particulièrement une, seule à une table, vêtue d'un costume d'un bleu dur, garni d'une guipure blanche; elle achevait, à petits coups, un verre de bière, renversée à demi, *les mains sur le ventre, d'un air d'attente lourde et résignée* (*Curée*, 450).

The first painting presents an animated street scene. Light, color, contrast, movement and sound are presented in nominal style with subject placed in terminal position as psychological predicate:

> En bas, sur le boulevard, Paris grondait, prolongeait la journée ardente, avant de se décider à gagner son lit. Les files d'arbres marquaient, d'une ligne confuse, les blancheurs des trottoirs et le noir vague de la chaussée, où passaient le roulement et les lanternes rapides des voitures. Aux deux bords de cette bande obscure, les kiosques des marchands de journaux, de place en place, s'allumaient, pareils à de grandes lanternes vénitiennes, hautes et bizarrement bariolées, posées régulièrement à terre, pour quelque illumination colossale. Mais, à cette heure, leur éclat assourdi se perdait dans le flamboiement des devantures voisines. Pas un volet n'était mis, les trottoirs s'allongeaient sans une raie d'ombre, sous une pluie de rayons qui les éclairait d'une poussière

d'or, de la clarté chaude et éclatante du plein jour. Maxime montra à Renée, en face d'eux, le café Anglais, dont les fenêtres luisaient. ... C'était un va-et-vient continu; des promeneurs passaient par groupes, des filles, deux à deux, traînaient leurs jupes, qu'elles relevaient de temps à autre, d'un mouvement alangui, en jetant autour d'elles des regards las et souriants (*Curée*, 449-450).

The description continues for almost another page, always gaining in intensity, accompanied by metaphorical transformations. The second tableau is less animated, there are more shadows.

> Elle se pencha de nouveau. Au milieu, sur la chaussée, les fiacres et les omnibus croisaient toujours leurs yeux de couleur, plus rares et plus rapides. Mais, sur les côtés, le long des trottoirs, de grands trous d'ombre s'étaient, creusés, devant les boutiques fermées. Les cafés seuls flambaient encore, rayant l'asphalte de nappes lumineuses. De la rue Drouot à la rue du Helder, elle apercevait ainsi une longue file de carrés blancs et de carrés noirs, dans lesquels les derniers promeneurs surgissaient et s'évanouissaient d'une étrange façon. Les filles surtout, avec la traîne de leur robe, tour à tour crûment éclairées et noyées dans l'ombre, prenaient un air d'apparition, de marionnettes blafardes, traversant le rayon électrique de quelque féerie (*Curée*, 453).

The third tableau, after the seduction, is characterized by shadows accompanied by sentiments of solitude. Only from the café Anglais does there yet come light and laughter. Symmetrical patches of red and green are seen, but ever so faintly, enough light to produce color, but not enough to illuminate:

> Elle alla à la fenêtre, tira les rideaux, s'accouda. L'orchestre était mort; la faute s'était commise dans le dernier frisson des basses et le chant lointain des violons, vague sourdine du boulevard endormi et rêvant d'amour. En bas, la chaussée et les trottoirs s'enfonçaient, s'allongeaient, au milieu d'une solitude grise. Toutes ces roues grondantes de fiacres

semblaient s'en être allées, en emportant les clartés
et la foule. Sous la fenêtre, le café Riche était fermé,
pas un filet de lumière ne glissait des volets. De
l'autre côté de l'avenue, des lueurs braisillantes
allumaient seules encore la façade du café Anglais,
une croisée entre autres, entrouverte, et d'où sortaient des rires affaiblis. Et, tout le long de ce
ruban d'ombre, du coude de la rue Drouot à l'autre
extrémité, aussi loin que ses regards pouvaient aller,
elle ne voyait plus que les taches symétriques des
kiosques rougissant et verdissant la nuit, sans l'éclairer, semblables à des veilleuses espacées dans un
dortoir géant. Elle leva la tête. Les arbres décou-
paient leurs branches hautes sur un ciel clair, tandis
que la ligne irrégulière des maisons se perdait avec
les amoncellements d'une côte rocheuse, au bord
d'une mer bleuâtre. Mais cette bande de ciel l'attristait davantage, et c'était dans les ténèbres du boulevard qu'elle trouvait quelque consolation. Ce qui
restait au ras de l'avenue déserte, du bruit et du
vice de la soirée, l'excusait (*Curée*, 457).

This must be called literary impressionism, all three of these
paintings rendering light, color, movement and sound through
impressionistic grammatical modes, complemented by figurative
structures. The topography is delineated, and the descriptions
are constantly made referential to the basic narrational structure
rendered in the *passé simple*. Flaubert was the first perhaps
to put an impressionistic heroine into a description (10) with
Emma's reactions at the ball at La Vaubeyssard. This becomes
conventional in Zola, with impressionistic heros and heroines
reacting strongly to impressionistic landscapes. This is a highly
condensed and vital form of the pathetic fallacy which becomes
commonplace in Zola while remaining a minimal unit in the
overall art of Flaubert. The great scenes of Flaubert have a
different basis. Consider, for example, the *comices agricoles*
of *Madame Bovary*. As here, it is a question of seduction,
but Flaubert settles for ironical contrast. Rodolfe, using his
romantic dictionary to seduce Emma, contrasts with the banal

(10) See Helmut A. Hatzfeld, *Initiation à l'explication de textes
français* (Munich: Max Hueber, 4ème édition augmentée de cinq
textes nouveaux, 1975), 121.

speeches of the agricultural fair. Here the cityscape extends out into space Renée's feelings. Nevertheless, there is something almost gratuitous about these tableaux; they well might be considered as independent and well-done boulevard scenes. Zola's intent is to render indirectly a seduction scene by putting the psychological effect into the three tableaux, but there is little feeling that Renée, except in the last tableau, is receiving these impressions in the manner of Emma Bovary at the ball. Light and movement, therefore, only become effective psychological units when conjoined to the idea of stressed sexuality as seen in the persistent presence of the prostitutes.

The novel par excellence for impressionistic tableaux remains, of course, *Le Ventre de Paris*, Zola depicting the great market at various times of the day and subject to diverse atmospheric conditions. While these reactions to the market are designed to be the impressions of either the painter, Claude Lantier, or the revolutionary Florent, we know that Zola himself had strong reactions to it. In a very early study based partly in interview, Robert Sherard relates Alexis' anecdote of Zola's visit to Les Halles:

> ... as they were leaving the *Cloche* together, Zola would insist on his accompanying him to the Halles, which are quite close by, and would repeat over and over again, 'What a grand book there is to be written about this monster monument!' Together the two friends used to wander about the market-place in every direction. One day as they were walking home up the rue Montmartre, Zola turns round and points and cries, 'Look, look, I say!' The effect, writes Alexis, was marvelous. The Halles seen in the dusk looked like palaces of Babylon rising one above the other. Zola was at once out with his note-book and set to work to write down a description of this scene. Afterwards visiting it at all times of the day and in all kinds of weather, he filled the same note-book with penpictures of its varying aspects, under rain, under snow, at early morning, at noon when the mighty heart is lying still, and at night when it is already beginning to prepare for the labours of the following morning (11).

_____
(11) Sherard, *Zola*, 104.

Le Ventre de Paris exhibits every possible characteristic of
literary impressionism. The play of light and color on fixed
object is of course the principle factor, and the preparatory
notes give abundant evidence of this: «La charcuterie dans le
soleil levant»; «Les Halles, le soir, rappel», «Les Halles l'après-
midi; pendant les grands froids et les grandes chaleurs» (12);
«Pour que le tableau des Halles soit vivant, il faut que j'y
mette cet affamé, en disant un mot de la faim. Mais je ne
conte pas son histoire qui viendra plus tard» (13). This last
note reveals the necessity for Zola of having an impressionistic
spectator. The notes so continue: «Dernier tableau des légumes.
Le soleil sur les légumes. Flamboiement.»; «La charcuterie.
Description de la devanture dans le soleil. Lisa sur la porte.» (14); «Un coucher de soleil dans les Halles, vu par Florent.» (15). Moreover the market with its modern architecture
of soaring iron provides an adequate geometry of line, surface
and volume to give solid spaces in which to place the light and
color. Solids and light, however, are not fused in the manner
of the Monet paintings of the end of the century. Additional
features are movement, sound, and olfactory impressionism, an
analogous impressionism from music, and similitudes of form
in the cheese symphony.

That Zola has treated Les Halles much in the same manner
as Monet treated the Rouen cathedral has been amply demonstrated by Silas Robert Powell (16) who has extracted a series
of paintings from the novel which are as follows: Les Halles
before sunrise; Les Halles at sunrise; Les Halles at midday;
Les Halles at sunset; Les Halles «par les soirées de flamme»;
Les Halles on cold nights; Les Halles on nights when the moon
is not visible; Les Halles «par les nuits limpides.» Further-

---

(12) *Fr. Nouv. Acq.* 10338, *feuillet* 3.
(13) *Fr. Nouv. Acq.* 10338, *feuillet* 10.
(14) *Fr. Nouv. Acq.* 10338, *feuillet* 16.
(15) *Fr. Nouv. Acq.* 10338, *feuillet* 33.
(16) Silas Robert Powell, «Impressionistic Art in *Le Ventre de
Paris* of Emile Zola,» (Master of Arts dissertation, The George
Washington University, 1967). This excellent work develops many
of the ideas which are central to this study. While we now know
more about the role of the verb in literary impressionism, Powell's
analysis of the great tableaux of *Le Ventre de Paris* remains
convincing.

more, he has established a narrational parallel which is as follows: Florent arriving at Les Halles; Florent joining the society of Les Halles; Florent rejecting the society of Les Halles; Florent being rejected by Lisa, «La Reine des Halles;» Florent being rejected by Les Halles; Florent being expelled from Les Halles. (17) What is striking in these tableaux is the combination of light and color with either stated geometric forms or metaphorical transformations which suggest these forms. Thus in the description of the market before sunrise, emphasis is placed on its colossal size which seems to be growing: «... de gigantesques pavillons, dont les toits superposés lui semblaient grandir, s'étendre, se perdre, au fond d'un poudroiement de lueurs» (Ventre, 609). Again we see form increasing and then disappearing, being lost in an abstract powder of light. Emphasis on form is more strongly stated in the sunrise scene:

> Elles se solidifiaient, d'un gris verdâtre, plus géantes encore, avec leur mâture prodigieuse, supportant les nappes sans fin de leurs toits. Elles entassaient leurs masses géométriques; et, quand toutes les clartés intérieures furent éteintes, qu'elles baignèrent dans le jour levant, carrées, uniformes, elles apparurent comme une machine moderne... quelque chaudière destinée à la digestion d'un peuple, gigantesque ventre de métal, boulonné, rivé, fait de bois, de verre et de fonte, d'une élégance et d'une puissance de moteur mécanique, fonctionnant là, avec la chaleur du chauffage, l'étourdissement, le branle furieux des roues (Ventre, 626).

The procedure is very literary, combining liquid light with an equal insistence on hard and solid form through metaphorical expression. Without the light elements the description begins to look like a primitive Léger industrial painting. This procedure is sharply delineated in the description of Les Halles at midday. Claude perceives «... un coin du géant de fonte. C'étaient des échappées brusques, des architectures imprévues, le même horizon s'offrant sans cesse sous des aspects divers»

---

(17) Powell, 93-95 and 87-89.

(*Ventre,* 781). These architectures are then transformed into fanciful literary images:

> ... des profils de maisons et de palais superposés, une *babylone de métal,* d'une *légèreté hindoue,* traversée par des *terrasses suspendues,* des *couloirs aériens,* des *ponts volants* jetés sur le vide (*Ventre,* 781).

Solid forms are set into motion, a sense of the aerial movement of this modern gothic is conveyed through the three form-images, adjectively reinforced, terraces, corridors, bridges.

If, historically, the impressionists first made their discovery of the movement of light by observing its reflections on water, the use of the sea motif to describe the market might be considered as Zola's metaphorical rendering of what was for the painters a prime discovery in real water. Thus the roofs of the market spreading out their «... nappes grises» is followed by a series of water descriptions with luminous qualifications: «... des lacs endormis...» with «... reflet furtif de quelque vitre allumait la lueur argentée d'un flot.»; «... la visión vague d'un bord de mer...» with «les eaux mortes et ardoisées d'une baie...» (*Ventre,* 713). If the categories established by Powell have been analyzed in some detail, it is to insist upon the presence of form in these vast fields of light. Yet the two domains are not fused, light dominates. Therefore, we can agree with Powell's conclusion that «... symmetrical form has been reduced to a vibrating surface of color spots bathed in light.» (18).

Literary impressionism can refer to the changes of light on a given object at just one moment. The various stages of a single sunset can be followed:

> Le soleil pâlissait, la poussière d'or rouge n'était plus qu'une lueur blonde, dont l'adieu se mourait dans la soie des tentures et les panneaux des meubles (*Bonheur,* 458).

Gold red dust (the intense moment of the sunset) is softened to blond (in sense of light) «lueur», finally seen in the palest of reflected light in the textures and furniture of the apartment.

---

(18) Powell, 95.

And it should not be forgotten that the recording of fixed object at various moments of the day need not be impressionistic. This is illustrated by the various depictions of the department store in *Au Bonheur des dames,* before opening, after opening, at midday, at closing, in the evening, in the rain. These are simply efforts to capture the meaning of the store, and in this novel are achieved through the metaphorical fields of monster and heating machine.

A unified field of multiple impressions is found in the description of Claude Lantier's painting of La Cité in *L'Oeuvre* (231-32); «A toutes les heures, par tous les temps, la Cité se leva devant lui...» This means viewing la Cité under snow, impressionistically:

> Sous une tombée de neige tardive, il la vit *fourrée d'hermine,* au-dessus de l'eau *couleur de boue,* se détachant sur un ciel d'*ardoise claire.*

In the first spring sun, it is presented lyrically but not impressionistically: «... aux premiers soleils, s'essuyer de l'hiver, retrouver une enfance, avec les pousses vertes des grands arbres du terre-plein». Simile creates a fairyland atmosphere on a foggy day: «... un jour de fin brouillard, se reculer, s'évaporer, *légère* et *tremblante* comme un palais des songes». Images of collapse reinforced with hard coloration reveal the Cité subject to rain and storm:

> ... ce furent des pluies battantes qui la submergeaient, la cachaient derrière l'immense rideau tiré du ciel à la terre; des orages, dont les éclairs la montraient *fauve,* d'une *lumière louche de coupe-gorge,* à demi-détruite par l'écroulement des grands *nuages de cuivre.* ...

Subjected to wind storms, the Cité is tossed about in a blue sky which pales in the movement of the air: «... des vents qui la balayaient d'une tempête, aiguisant les angles, la découpant sèchement, nue et flagellée, dans le bleu pâli de l'air.» Under an ardent sun it is bathed in a diffuse light, which has the brilliancy of a fine piece of jewelry:

> ... quand le soleil se brisait en poussière parmi les vapeurs de la Seine, elle baignait au fond de cette

clarté diffuse, sans une ombre, également éclairée partout, d'une délicatesse charmante de bijou taillé en plein or fin.

There is an impressionistic sunrise:

Il voulut la voir sous le soleil levant, se dégageant des brumes matinales, lorsque le quai de l'Horloge *rougeoie* et que le quai des Orfèvres reste appesanti de ténèbres, toute vivante déjà dans le ciel rose par le réveil éclatant de ses tours et de ses flèches, tandis que, lentement, la nuit descend des édifices, ainsi qu'un manteau qui tombe.

The sharp, metallike qualities of the noonday sun are described:

... sous le soleil frappant d'aplomb, mangée de clarté crue, décolorée et muette comme une ville morte...

In the best tradition of lyrical romanticism the series of paintings concludes with a sunset, always Zola's preference, but rendered with the new assets of impressionistic language:

... gardant aux arêtes des monuments les franges de braise d'un charbon près de s'éteindre, avec de *derniers incendies qui se rallumaient dans des fenêtres*, de *brusques flambées de vitres qui lançaient des flammèches et trouaient les façades.*

A total of nine consecutive impressions of the *Ile de la Cité*, but Zola states that Claude actually saw twenty, and a tenth is added, Claude's favorite, the transparent air of a September evening:

... il en revenait toujours à la Cité qu'il avait vue la première fois, vers quatre heures, un beau soir de septembre, cette Cité sereine sous le vent léger, ce coeur de Paris battant dans la transparence de l'air, comme élargi par le ciel immense, que traversait un vol de petits nuages (*L'Oeuvre*, 232).

Throughout these variations there are greater and lesser degrees of literary impressionism seen in effervescent light fields found

5

in spaces which are ever expanding and opening up. The technical achievement is the expression of a deep emotional enthusiasm for the Parisian atmosphere.

The emotional basis for Zola's impressionism is to be found in a series of sunsets recorded in Chapter IV of *L'Oeuvre*. The description opens with a passage of pure lyricism, the description of Claude and Christine's promenades through the capital, accompanied by the sun as they walk, like all young people in love, along the *quais* of the Seine, poking into little shops, surrounded by flowers and caged birds. Zola himself is forced to exclamation:

> Ah! que de beaux couchers de soleil ils eurent, pendant ces flâneries de chaque semaine. Le soleil les accompagnait dans cette gaieté vibrante des quais, la vie de la Seine, la danse des reflets au fil du courant, l'amusement des boutiques chaudes comme des serres, et les fleurs en pot des graine-tiers, et les cages assourdissantes des oiseliers, tout ce tapage de sons et de couleurs qui fait du bord de l'eau l'éternelle jeunesse des villes (*L'Oeuvre*, 104).

These impressionistic walks across Paris are accompanied by dense metaphorical descriptions of various sunsets:

1. Tandis qu'ils avançaient, la braise ardente du couchant s'empourprait à leur gauche, au-dessus de la ligne sombre des maisons; et l'astre sem-blait les attendre, s'inclinait à mesure, roulait lentement vers les toits lointains, dès qu'ils avaient dépassé le pont Notre-Dame, en face du fleuve élargi (104).
2. Dans aucune futaie séculaire, sur aucune route de montagne, par les prairies d'aucune plaine, il n'y aura jamais des fins de jour aussi triom-phales que derrière la coupole de l'Institut (104).
3. A chacune de leurs promenades, l'incendie chan-geait, des fournaises nouvelles ajoutaient leurs brasiers à cette couronne de flammes (104).
4. ... le soleil, reparaissant derrière la pluie, alluma la nuée tout entière, et il n'y eut plus sur leurs têtes que cette poussière d'eau embrasée, qui s'irisait de bleu et de rose (104).
5. Les jours de ciel pur ... le soleil, pareil à une

boule de feu, descendait majestueusement dans un lac de saphir tranquille; un instant, la coupole noire de l'Institut l'écornait, comme une lune à son déclin; puis, la boule se violaçait, se noyait au fond du lac devenu sanglant (104-105).

6. Dès février, elle agrandit sa courbe, elle tomba droit dans la Seine, qui semblait bouillonner à l'horizon, sous l'approche de ce fer rouge (105).

7. Mais les grands décors, les grandes féeries de l'espacc ne flambaient que les soirs de nuages. Alors, suivant le caprice du vent, c'étaient des mers de soufre battant des rochers de corail, c'étaient des palais et des tours, des architectures entassées, brûlant, s'écroulant, lâchant par leurs brèches des torrents de lave... (105).

8. ... ou encore, tout d'un coup, l'astre, disparu déjà, couché derrière un voile de vapeurs, perçait ce rempart d'une telle poussée de lumière, que des traits d'étincelles jaillissaient, partaient d'un bout du ciel à l'autre, visibles, ainsi qu'une volée de flèches d'or (105).

Following these eight variations, the passage concludes with the same affirmation of lyric joy with which it began:

Et le crépuscule se faisait, et ils se quittaient avec ce dernier éblouissement dans les yeux, ils sentaient ce Paris triomphal complice de la joie qu'ils ne pouvaient épuiser, à toujours recommencer ensemble cette promenade, le long des vieux parapets de pierre (105).

Impressionism means seizing nature's transitory moments. Claude and Christine seem assured that the sun will rise again tomorrow, to provide another spectacular show at the end of each day. These eight descriptions well summarize Zola's intent and method, a lyrical feeling rendered with new prose techniques which rival the work of the painters. In two pages sunsets are recorded across months, seasons, and atmospheric conditions. A precise topology is presented with the cathedral and the Institute as markers. There is a scientific rendering (number six), poetically, of the earth's proximity to the sun. There are rich fields of luminosity, especially number four which presents the shimmering of light on the water as the sun is perceived through the rain. Number two expresses hyperbolically the triumph of the cityscape (impressionism as a city art) over any bucolic romantic setting. The whole passage abounds with movement announcing the triumph of Paris, a triumph seen in her royal sunsets (*triomphale, couronne de flammes, majestueusement*).

The repeated presentation of a single object can have functions which may have little to do with literary impressionism. The sea which serves as a backdrop in *La Joie de vivre* is not presented in an impressionistic manner. It acts more like a motif, with no precise meaning, but hovering around concepts of man's impermanence, the eternity of nature, somewhat in the manner of the poetry of Victor Hugo. The seascapes of this novel can be seen as paintings presenting various aspects of the physical sea, but these would not be impressionistic ones, but half-romantic, half-realistic. The same can be said of other constants, the wheat fields of *La Terre,* the plain of *Germinal.* While impressionistic elements are present in greater and lesser degrees, the basic thrust is that of motif.

III. *Parts for Whole: Impressionistic Synecdoche*

Impressionism means the artistic elaboration of the science of optics as it was developed in the nineteenth century. Even without the science it is apparent from the texts that modern writers are developing a special manner of viewing concrete reality. This may be a purely psychological posture and it may imply with Zola the additional painterly aspect. Whatever the cause, Zola has a unique vision of reality. Both he and his characters frequently transform objective reality by exaggeration and by metaphorical mutations of the raw material. Most striking in this regard is the development of a literary mode of perception, which seems to have no exact equivalent in the world of painting, namely the use of synecdochic constructions.

It is now common knowledge that Flaubert had a keen predilection for viewing parts rather than wholes. This is a type of psychological impressionism where the eye receives percepts and the literary artist refuses, for the moment at least, to organize the parts into a logical whole. Flaubert as an adolescent writer exhibits such traits. A young romantic, he falls in love with love and not with a woman. Thus in describing a woman who is attractive to him, he describes not an essence called a woman, but parts of the woman: her ankle, foot, arm, eyes, hair. While having peculiarly romantic traits with Flaubert, such a procedure has some precedence in the west, particularly in the emblematic love poetry of the Middle Ages and the Renaissance. With the young Flaubert, however, it looks more like Romantic fetish, somewhat akin to Emma Bovary's cry «J'ai un amant,» fixing on *amant* (instead of «I am in love with Rodolphe») as she also fixes on *adultère*, or as the young Flaubert concentrated the idea of womanhood in *actrice* and *maîtresse*. The works of Flaubert's youth are filled with such cases, especially the *Mémoires d'un Fou* (1838) in which is recorded the first «impression» the hero receives of Elisa Schlésinger on the beaches of Trouville, the sensations of a form of woman (dripping wet from the ocean) running past the young man. The passage in intent is impressionistic, expressing an intensified romantic sentiment:

> Et puis, quand elle revenait et qu'elle passait près de moi, que j'entendais l'eau tomber de ses habits et le frôlement de sa marche, mon coeur battait avec violence; je baissais les yeux, le sang me montait à la tête, j'étouffais. Je sentais ce corps de femme à moitié nu passer près de moi avec le parfum de la vague. Sourd et aveugle, j'aurais deviné sa présence, car il y avait en moi quelque chose d'intime et de doux, qui se noyait en extases et en gracieuses pensées, quand elle passait ainsi.
> Je crois voir encore la place où j'étais fixé sur le rivage; je vois les vagues accourir de toutes parts, se briser, s'étendre; je vois la plage festonnée d'écume, j'entends le bruit des voix confuses des baigneurs parlant entre eux, j'entends le bruit de ses pas, j'entends son haleine, quand elle passait près de moi (19).

The wedding scene of *Madame Bovary* provides several examples of this type of focalization, but still not yet of the

---

(19) Gustave Flaubert, *Oeuvres complètes*, I (Paris: Aux Editions du Seuil, 1964), 237.

variety found in Zola. The arrival of the wedding guests is presented through a sound impressionism, hearing but not seeing the arrival: «De temps à autre, on entendait des coups de fouet *derrière la haie*; bientôt la barrière s'ouvrait: c'était une carriole qui entrait.» (*Madame Bovary*, 24). In the paragraphs which follow concentration is given to impressions of body parts and articles of clothing. It is almost as if personality has been effaced. Guests descend from a carriage:

> Galopant jusqu'à la première marche du perron, elle s'y arrêtait court, et vidait son monde, qui sortait par tous les côtés, en se frottant les genoux et en s'étirant les bras. (*Madame Bovary*, 24-25).

Who are these people? Relatives and friends no doubt, but they will remain faceless. Instead, simple impressions of the movements of wedding guests are recorded. We join Flaubert as a casual and impersonal observer, fascinated not by the person, but by the dress. Anonymity emanates from the syntactically impressionistic presentation of a young girl in her first communion dress, for she is just *any* fourteen or sixteen year old:

> ... et l'on voyait à côté d'eux, ne soufflant mot, dans la robe blanche de sa première communion rallongée pour la circonstance, quelque grande fillette de quatorze ou seize ans, leur cousine ou leur soeur aînée sans doute, rougeaude, ahurie, les cheveux gras de pommade à la rose, et ayant bien peur de salir ses gants. (*Madame Bovary*, 25).

Such reporting, in which impressionistic detail dominates over individual characterization, produces a stance of detachment and a spirit of alienation. The scene continues with humanity swallowed up in its garments:

> ... ils avaient des habits, des redingotes, des vestes, des habits-vestes; — bons habits, entourés de toute la considération d'une famille, et qui ne sortaient de l'armoire que pour les solennités; redingotes à grandes basques flottant au vent, à collet cylindrique, à poches larges comme des sacs; vestes de gros drap, qui accompagnaient ordinairement quel-

que casquette cerclée de cuivre à sa visière; habits-vestes très courts, ayant dans le dos deux boutons rapprochés comme une paire d'yeux, et dont les pans semblaient avoir été coupés à même un seul bloc la hache du charpentier. (*Ibid.*).

This is the photographic eye, since it catches detail which the analytical or editing eye (for the mind makes automatic choices over which perceptions it will receive and those which will be ignored) will not record. Flaubert and Zola have an eye which seizes the small, the minute detail, which seems in itself a contradiction to the different views of impressionism. This is a uniquely modern sensibility and mode of perception in literature. It means attention to the parts, to the small detail, to modifications of objective forms, exaggerations.

The opening paragraph of *Le Ventre de Paris* offers a fine example of the concentration on a part and the nuance of slight detail which could not be perceived by the average viewer:

> Un bec de gaz, au sortir d'une nappe d'ombre, éclairait les clous d'un soulier, la manche bleue d'une blouse, le bout d'une casquette... (*Ventre*, 603).

A unique and original mode of vision is being presented in such a descriptive passage: a gas light which *spotlights* the nails of a shoe, the blue sleeve of a blouse, the end of a cap. This is delightful to us; for Florent, a psychological victim of impressionism, it can be terrifying:

> Il lui sembla que les becs de gaz, avec leur oeil unique, couraient à droite et à gauche, en emportant la route; il trébucha, dans ce tournoiement; il s'affaissa comme une masse sur les pavés (*Ventre*, 607).

But what is the eye which perceives the blue sleeve of a blouse? Why not the sleeve of a blue blouse? Simply because Zola's art has a new mode of perception. Color will be seen, but only in the spotlighting of the object. Across the *Rougon-Macquart* the phenomenon of recording the part for the whole, the movement of limbs and clothing, a haphazard and confusing array of heads and arms is seen in many variations.

At the most realistic level just parts may be presented because they have indeed been detached from the whole. This is the rough reality of the amputations which take place in the military hospitals of *La Débâcle*: «... des jambes et des bras coupés s'entassaient...» (*Débâcle*, 673). Partial perception may be caused by impairment of vision, such as Deloche, who, eating in the basement canteen of the department store, can only perceive the passing pedestrians through the *soupirail*:

> ... et sa récréation, tous les jours, après le déjeuner, était de regarder ainsi les pieds des passants qui filaient vite au ras du trottoir, des pieds coupés aux chevilles, gros souliers, bottes élégantes, fines bottines de femme, un va-et-vient continu de pieds vivants, sans corps et sans tête (*Bonheur*, 550).

Or the perception of the headless woman running in the rain:

> ... le grand manteau de velours, garni de renard argenté, mettait le profil cambré d'une femme sans tête, qui courait par l'averse à quelque fête, dans l'inconnu des ténèbres de Paris (*Bonheur*, 414).

It is striking how similar this last passage is, psychologically, to the Flaubert materials. The observer detached from the observed, psychological anonymity, the impressionistic reporter watching and intuiting mission or intent.

The process can at a basic level of affectivity be seen as quite literary and normal. Thus the happy atmosphere of a wedding reception will concentrate on the smiling faces:

> Un murmure de paroles aimables montait, des visages continuellement souriaient autour de la mariée: des faces épaisses de pères et de mères, des profils maigres de fillettes, des têtes fines et compatissantes de jeunes femmes (*P. B.*, 152).

Yet Zola's camera will, with a zoom lens, turn only to these faces seen across the reception hall as «visages,» «faces,» «profils,» and «têtes.» As with Flaubert, individuality is unimportant. These are the faces not of the fathers and mothers (*des*) but any fathers, mothers, any little girls (*de*). The parts are being stressed in an impersonal manner. While the following simply means: «The women gathered around each other,» the presentation becomes highly animated and pictorial when recorded as: «Les jupes se rapprochèrent» (*Conquête*, 1023).

Nouns and verbs of movement commonly activate the inanimate parts. *Flot* and its variables constitute a regular substantive field in Zola: «... derrière le flot des habits noirs.» (*P. B.*, 81); «... le flot envahissant des jupes...» (*Nana*, 1300); «... un flot dans lequel apparut la jupe de la femme, une veste d'homme, des cheveux blanc hérissés...» (*Débâcle*, 633); «... un galop de gros souliers...» (*Joie*, 986); «... on ne voyait plus ... que le remuement des hanches et des gorges, au milieu d'une confusion de bras.» (*Germinal*, 1268); «... un fourmillement de redingotes...» (*Argent*, 23). *L'Assommoir* provides an example of impressionistic synecdoche in which the autonomy of things in motion is seen in a very concentrated manner:

> C'était un envahissement du trottoir, de la chaussée, des ruisseaux, un flot paresseux coulant des portes ouvertes, s'arrêtant au milieu des voitures, faisant une traînée de blouses, de bourgerons et de vieux paletots, toute pâlie et déteinte sous la nappe de lumière blonde qui enfilait la rue (409).

It is the verb, however, which alone can give life to the parts, endowing them not only with spirit, but almost with personality: clothing overflows: «... deux flots épais d'habits noirs débordaient...» (*P. B.*, 81); bonnets lean forard to watch a spectacle: «... des bonnets de femme se penchaient, avec leurs brides envolées par le vent» (*Son Excellence*, 86). Parasols participate in an impressionistic color riot: «... des ombrelles voyantes, tendues comme des miroirs, mettaient des rondeurs d'astre au milieu du bariolage des jupes et des paletots.» (*Ibid.*); white surplices disappear behind green trees: «... les surplis du prêtre et de l'enfant de choeur disparaissaient entre les arbres verts...» (*Oeuvre*, 362); shirts pile up: «Peu à peu, les blouses s'amassaient à l'angle du trottoir...» (*Assommoir*, 407); fans bat with increasing tempo: «... mais les éventails battaient plus nerveusement...» (*Curée*, 541).

If the same technique cannot be found in painting, there are at least some parallels which should be commented. The impressionistic painting wants to create a harmony between the object and the light surrounding it. Portraits blend into the light field. Moreover, as we note these parts in movement, the examples are making it clear that light and color fields usually surround the parts. In a descriptive tableau from *La Curée,* for example, the guests at table are seen as part of the general composition. They have become an interesting painting; individual traits and psychologies are missing. For the moment, there is no anecdote as we simply observe the black and white contrast, the men acting as impressionistic shadow patches, the women as light fields:

> *Les épaules nues,* étoilées de diamants, flanquées d'habits noirs qui en *faisaient ressortir* la pâleur, ajoutèrent leurs *blancheurs laiteuses* au *rayonnement* de la table (*Curée,* 339).

Or similarly where the milk-white shoulders of the women (paleness), crushing against the black suits of the men (blackness or shadow), are illuminated under the chandeliers:

> ... dans les salons où les épaules nues s'écrasaient parmi les habits noirs, sous la clarté ardente des lustres...» (*Argent,* 258).

Parts are also seen as geometric arrangements. Three circular planes of skirts form a painting in *La Conquête de Plassans*: «L'abbé s'étant assis, un triple cercle de jupes l'entoura» (1021).

While noting the motion of these objects, at the same time a curious kind of personification takes place, the objects chatting, smiling, fleeing, shoulders shrugging: «La galerie était pleine d'habits noirs, debout, causant à demi-voix, et de jupes, étalées largement le long des causeuses.» (*Curée,* 350); «... souvent il apercevait des coins de redingote qui fuyaient.» (*Curée,* 466); «... des habits noirs inquiets se haussaient à la porte.» (*Curée,* 558). The objects sometimes receive collective human labels: «... noyé dans ce peuple d'épaules...» (*Curée,* 555); «Cependant, la foule des bonnets blancs, des caracos noirs, des blouses bleues, emplissait les étroits sentiers, entre les tas» (*Ventre,* 628). Similarly, there is the transformation of a person into a part, in the form of simile or metaphor, or the part will come to represent the psychological whole. Madame Chanteau is spotted at a distance on the beach: «De l'autre côté, sur la plage, Mme Chanteau faisait la tache noire et perdue d'un insecte» (*Joie,* 871). Even more interesting from the same novel is Pauline's viewing from her room, with a certain amount of jealousy, the beach stroll of Lazare and Louise: «Mais Pauline, surtout, s'intéressait au veston blanc de Lazare et à la robe rose de Louise, qui éclataient au soleil» (*Joie,* 936). Still more impressionistic is this viewing by Pauline two pages later:

> ... Pauline, absorbée, suivait jusqu'au soir à l'horizon, la robe bleue de Louise et le veston blanc de Lazare, au milieu des taches sombres des ouvriers (*Joie,* 938).

Fragmentation of the human body blends well with moral novelistic intent in a brief description of half-naked actresses backstage:

> Le long du couloir, par les fentes, on apercevait des coins de nudité, des blancheurs de peau, des pâleurs de linge (*Nana,* 1222).

What can possibly explain these impressionistic synecdoches? A partial answer is found in the very flamboyancy of the Second Empire where men, usually attired in formal black, as in the Zola examples, form a contrast with the ornamentation, the draping of the female form in expensive materials, rich and brilliant color, unique hair colorings, and resplendent jewelry (20). Zola, in these fragmented sequences which are principally constructed from articles of clothing, is emphasizing the importance of accoutrements and costume in manner similar to that of the painters, and not necessarily restricted to the impressionists. A study of academic, realistic, and official painting of the period will confirm this. The pale white effect

---

(20) Joanna Richardson, *La Vie Parisienne, 1852-1870* (New York, 1971). This is probably the most interesting if not best cultural history of the Second Empire. Her historical research has substantiated many of the stylistic traits discussed in this study. Her discussion of the extravagant hair tints of the day (248) may explain the exaggerated hair lights which we find in so many of Zola's descriptions.

of exposed shoulders which keeps occurring in the specimens we have been citing exists in such paintings as the portrait of Mademoiselle Duvergier made in 1853 by Jean-Léon Gérome (1824-1904), or in the 1854 portrait of the Empress Eugénie by Edouard Dubufe. Zola's equivalent in the world of painting, at least from the viewpoint of contextual emphasis on rich clothing, textures and radiancy of public interiors, is found in the paintings of James Jacques Joseph Tissot (1836-1902), especially his *Woman of Fashion (La Mondaine)*, 1885, reproduced in *The Neglected Nineteenth Century* (21) and forming part of his series «Pictures of Parisian Life.» A whole series of official paintings convey the same spirit which we have been discussing in this section: The Winterhalter painting, *Au rendez-vous des grisettes: the Empress and her ladies-in-waiting*; especially the splendid illumination, costume and movement of *A gala ball at the Tuileries in 1867* by Tetar van Elven; the very fine costuming in Guérard's color lithograph *La vie du boulevard: the scene outside Tortoni's*; and the painting of Henri Baron, *Souper aux Tuileries,* 1867, which, if studied closely, would explicate many of the examples from Zola which we have been discussing.

If any painting comes close to Zola's animated parts for the whole, it is *Le tout Paris by the sea. The Empress Eugénie on the beach at Trouville,* by Eugène Boudin, 1864. The principal grouping in this scene is the rapid movement of eight women in multi-colored dresses, carrying parasols, moving across the beach. It is the collective rhythmic movement of the group which counts, the parts, dresses and parasols conveying the movement, the individuals without importance. Contrary to the Zola technique, a compositional whole is implied in all the paintings, academic or innovative, while Zola's procedure syntactically does efface the whole.

A flamboyant age is captured by the writer and the painter in different manners. Synecdochic representation of people in movement is a discernible trend in the novel form. The emphasis in painting upon costume is also a realistic awareness of the importance of the parts as they may add up to a new whole of changing light patterns. When Zola's fragmented parts

---

(21) The H. Shickman Gallery (New York, 1970).

are fused with light, he must be seen as paralleling in literature the work of the painters.

There are other modes of impressionism in the *Rougon-Macquart,* the next, that of olfactory impressionism, being one to which the painter would like to aspire in the atmospheres of his landscapes (especially country and farm scenes), but which the writer is better equipped to handle.

IV. *Olfactory Impressionism*

Literary olfaction was rather new when Zola was writing, having no more history than its subtle use in *Madame Bovary* and its daring exploitation in the *Fleurs du mal.* In Baudelaire olfactory sensations are based in the theory of *correspondances,* and its best use in Zola is also when it mixes with other perceptions, as called for in Baudelaire's sonnet. Isolated and concentrated olfactory perception is concentrated in a few novels, *Le Ventre de Paris* and *La Faute de l'Abbé Mouret.* It discreetly blends with other sense perceptions in the other novels, as in this rich description of the arrival of the royal procession into the dining room:

> C'était une approche presque tendre, une arrivée gourmande dans un milieu de luxe, de lumière et de tiédeur, comme un bain sensuel où les odeurs musquées des toilettes se mêlaient à un léger fumet de gibier, relevé d'un filet de citron (*Son Excellence,* 160).

What strikes the mind is the fusion of odour with light, odours themselves delineated and contrasted, crowned with a descriptive field suggesting outrageous materialism.

Zola and the inhabitants of the *Rougon-Macquart* are very susceptible to olfactory sensation. His narrational style falls back on animalistic, instinctive, erotic behaviour based in olfactory perceptions. Napoleon III is talking with Clorinde in whom he seems to have an interest and Zola writes of «... l'appétit sensuel des hommes que *grise l'odeur de la femme*» (*Son Excellence,* 295). In the Théâtre des Variétés, the narrator seems as conscious of distinct smells as poor Comte Muffat:

> Quand on ouvrait la porte de ce trou à charbon,

un souffle violent d'alcool en sortait, qui se mêlait
à l'odeur de graillon de la loge et au parfum péné-
trant des bouquets laissés sur la table (*Nana*, 1204).

Zola seems to share Octave Mouret's subtle olfactory ability.
Octave has been seducing (commercially) the women of high
society at Henriette's tea with his display of silks. He remains
a conqueror in spite of the troubling odours which emanate
from their hair. He drinks some more tea which seems to
mitigate the hidden but active sexual odour, «fauve,» (i.e. of
wild animals) of these refined and elegant women:

> Il continuait à boire, entre chaque phrase, une petite
> gorgée de thé, dont le parfum attiédissait ces odeurs
> plus âpres, où il y avait une pointe de fauve (*Bon-
> heur*, 464).

Odour has, of course, ideological implications within Zola's
system. The natural odours of man and beast are contrasted
with the bad and corrupting odours of perfumes and cosmetics
(immoral sexuality) or with the rich incense odour of Catholic
ritual. Thus nature takes some revenge on abbé Mouret's poor
country church: «Une odeur forte de basse-cour venait par la
porte ouverte, soufflant comme un ferment d'éclosion dans
l'église, dans le soleil chaud qui gagnait l'autel» (*Faute*, 1225).

Technically, olfactory descriptions start off as simple narrational listings, but nonetheless, the impressionistic word order,
rendering sensation as sweetness, sourness and intensity with
consistent adjectival modification, looks as if the intent is
beyond a simple abstract narration. Thus Mathilde's herb shop:
«... le sucre fade des mauves, l'âpreté du sureau, l'amertume
de la rhubarbe, mais surtout la flamme de la menthe poivrée...»
(*L'Oeuvre*, 71). A more interesting example, very Baudelairian,
is found in Count Muffat's olfactory perceptions in le passage
des Panoramas:

> Toutes les boutiques lui étaient connues, il en
> retrouvait les odeurs, dans l'air chargé de gaz, des
> senteurs rudes de cuir de Russie, des parfums de
> vanille montant du sous-sol d'un chocolatier, des
> haleines de musc soufflées par les portes ouvertes
> des parfumeurs (*Nana*, 1260-1261).

Odour is also rendered through simile and metaphor. Lise the hard-working peasant woman is seen as «... cette femme à quatre pattes, *suante, odorante* ainsi qu'une bête en folie» (*Terre*, 467). Octave Mouret's department store has become a temple to the vanity and egoism of the Parisian social butterflies. Zola records the various odours related to products destined for purchase by this consuming society in a rich field of impressions received by Madame Desforges as she closes her eyes and feels the store about her:

> Mais ce qui la surprenait surtout, dans la fatigue de ses yeux aveuglés par le pêle-mêle éclatant des couleurs, c'était, lorsqu'elle fermait les paupières, de sentir davantage la foule, à son bruit sourd de marée montante et à la chaleur humaine qu'elle exhalait. Une fine poussière s'élevait des planchers, chargée de l'odeur de la femme, l'odeur de son linge et de sa nuque, de ses jupes et de sa chevelure, une odeur pénétrante, envahissante, qui semblait être l'encens de ce temple élevé au culte de son corps (*Bonheur*, 631).

Metaphorically Zola underlines his loathing for illicit sexual relationships: «... l'odeur de la fornication...» (*Germinal*, 1432) which is a rich literary abstract impressionism with approximately the same value as «... le lit chaud encore de l'adultère...» (*Germinal*, 1431). Fundamentally, olfactory impressionism seems to revolve about concepts of sexuality and *gourmandise*. The lesbian prostitute Satin seems to sense out bedroom odours on humid nights in Paris, sending her into the streets in quest of clients:

> Satin surtout avait le nez. Les soirs humides, lorsque Paris mouillé exhalait une *odeur fade de grande alcove mal tenue*, elle savait que ce temps mou, cette fétidité des coins louches enrageaient les hommes (*Nana*, 1313).

In the creation of *grands tableaux* three novels remain outstanding for odour descriptions, *Au Bonheur des dames*, *La Faute de l'abbé Mouret* and *Le Ventre de Paris*. *Au Bonheur des dames* should be the equivalent of les Halles of *Le Ventre de Paris*, but it is not. The representation of smell in the cologne and perfume counter is weak by comparison with the other novels. There is rather a concentration on refined flowery smells faintly indicated: «... odeur pénétrante de sachet enfermé, qui embaumait la galerie.» (788); «Une senteur exquise s'épandait alentour, les dames en passant trempaient leurs mouchoirs» (789). Apart from incorporation into the great tableau which terminates the novel, odour impressionism is scattered in small segments across the novel.

The celebrated *symphonie des fromages* of *Le Ventre de Paris* must be considered the most successful olfactory literary impressionism of the entire series, especially since it is mostly free of thesis, unlike the olfactory fields of either *La Curée* or *La Faute de l'abbé Mouret*. Found in Chapter V of the novel, it is very cleverly interpolated and contrasted, ironically and with humour, with the gossip of Mademoiselle Saget and Madame Lecoeur about Florent's revolutionary background. The whole passage undergoes degrees of gradation sharply delineated from each other in the following manner: (1) the description opens with a presentation of butter, eggs and cheese somewhat in terms of their odour but mainly concentrating on light and form impressionism; (2) followed by a consistent effort to render smell through a variety of literary means, and again accompanied by light and color effects; (3) reaches an intensification similar to that found in gradated literary building structures, such as the finale of the description of the Pension Vauquer at the beginning of *Le Père Goriot* or the culmination of the «comices agricoles» in the *Bovary*. Furthermore it integrates the narrational plot, spelling out the «cheesy» implications of the gossip for Florent. The elements of each section, isolated from the body of the text, look like this: the odour of the cheeses is stated, followed by form and light evocations of the dairy products: Breton butters overfill their containers: «... les beurres de Bretagne, dans des paniers, débordaient;» (826); butters from Normandy are described by analogy to first drafts of a sculptor: «... les beurres de Normandie... ressemblaient à des ébauches de ventres, sur lesquelles un sculpteur aurait jeté des linges mouillés;» (826); others resemble rocky peaks in a very extended simile:

> ... d'autres mottes, entamées, taillées par les larges couteaux en rochers à pic, pleines de vallons et de

cassures, étaient comme des cimes éboulées, dorées par la pâleur d'un soir d'automne (827).

Eggs have stressed their «... blancheur de craie;» (827). In a syntax becoming more and more heavily impressionistic, is presented an array of diverse cheeses, some in movement, in which geometric form is suggested through analogy to wheels, a child's fist roundness, density of craniums, ancient disks; textures are nuanced. The extended moon figuration is perhaps the most delightful of the passage, suggesting states of ripeness through analogy to the moon in its various quarters:

> Mais c'était surtout sur la table que les fromages s'empilaient. Là, à côté des pains de beurre à la livre, dans des feuilles de poirée, s'élargissait un cantal géant, comme fendu à coups de hache; puis venaient un chester, couleur d'or, un gruyère, pareil à une roue tombée de quelque char barbare, des hollande, ronds comme des têtes coupées, barbouillées de sang séché, avec cette dureté de crâne vide qui les fait nommer têtes-de-mort. ... Trois brie, sur des planches rondes, avaient des mélancolies de lunes éteintes; deux, très secs, étaient dans leur plein; le troisième dans son deuxième quartier, coulait, se vidait d'une crème blanche, étalée en lac, ravageant les minces planchettes, à l'aide desquelles on avait vainement essayé de le contenir. Des port-salut, semblables à des disques antiques. ... Les roquefort... prenaient des mines princières, des faces marbrées et grasses, veinées de bleu et de jaune, comme attaqués d'une maladie honteuse de gens riches qui ont trop mangé de truffes; tandis que... des fromages de chèvre, gros comme un poing d'enfant, durs et grisâtres, rappelaient les cailloux que les boucs, menant leur troupeau, font rouler aux coudes des sentiers pierreux (827).

This is impressionistic virtuosity at practically its highest point in literature. The passage retains at its base a fundamental placement in reality, dairy products in a specific market. It then proceeds to give exactly descriptive qualification of sizes, shapes, textures, and does this through a dazzling inventory of very creative similes, especially recalling the Balzacian mode, with the moon metaphor and above all the analogy to human

6

kind («maladie honteuse de gens riches») and to the male goat, procedures so typical of the author of the *Comédie Humaine.*

Part II divides the cheese odours into six distinct renderings in one sentence divided by semi-colons:

1. *les mont-d'or*: simply characterized by their light yellow color with an «... odeur douceâtre;» (827).
2. *les troyes*: size: «épais»; edging: «meurtris»; taste: «âpreté», «forte», objective enough but followed by an olfactory metaphor; *«ajoutant une fétidité de cave humide;»* (827).
3. *les camembert*: by analogy only, the smoky quality of wild game: «... d'un fumet de gibier trop faisandé;» (827).
4. *les neufchâtel, les limbourg, les marolles, les pont-l'évêque*: size indicated and followed by a *correspondance,* better still a synesthesia which crosses smell with musical accent, inducing nausea: ... mettant chacun leur note aiguë et particulière dans cette phrase rude jusqu'à la nausée; ... (827-28).
5. *les livarot*: color and taste are qualified, as they produce «... une vapeur de soufre...» (828) in the throat.
6. *les olivet*: the most terrible of all, spotlighted through syntactical delay of subject and reinforced with the ghastly image of peasants burying *charognes* in a steaming field under a burning sun: «... puis enfin, par-dessus tous les autres, les olivet, enveloppés de feuilles de noyer, ainsi que ces charognes que les paysans couvrent de branches, au bord d'un champ, fumantes au soleil» (828).

Balzac's literary gradations seem heavily dependent upon accumulation, exaggeration and hyperbole. Zola's gradations, while similar, also take advantage of nominal style. Thus the clause of the *olivet* is written without verb (verb only appearing in the simile). The cheese is simply there, with its horrible stench.

The third part is delayed by some narrational paragraphs of Mademoiselle Saget's gossip with Madame Lecoeur. This is a very clever device, allowing the passage of time to move the sun higher in the sky, intensifying its heat and light. Then Zola deftly inserts across the conversation, markings of the cheeses, which become stronger in odour, wafts of nauseating smells coming to their noses. The pervading odours are translated into a symphony of smells: «Le soleil oblique entrait sous le pavillon, les fromages puaient plus fort» (829); «... des râles de limbourg arrivèrent entre les trois femmes, aigres et amers, comme soufflés par des gorges de mourants» (829); «Et, comme elles soufflaient un peu, ce fut le camembert qu'elles sentirent surtout.» (830):

> Cependant, au milieu de cette phrase vigoureuse, le parmesan jetait par moments un filet mince de flûte champêtre; tandis que les brie y mettaient des douceurs fades de tambourins humides. Il y eut une reprise suffocante du livarot. Et cette symphonie se tint un moment sur une note aiguë du géromé anisé, prolongée en point d'orgue (830).

This particular olfactory impressionism is unique to Zola. In analyzing the passage, it is apparent that the three parts are held together by a literary art which refuses no analogy. Within each section, there is an increasing gradation, each section becoming more intense than its predecessor. Parts I and II divorced from III would indicate a pure literary impressionism. Part III, however, insists upon moving the materials into the narrational structure. As the women gossip about Florent, their anxiety and fears of revolution and upheaval increase. The reader might think, nonetheless, that their psychological nausea is being produced by the odours and the visions of the running cheese swimming in the hot sun. To the contrary, their sickness is being induced by visions of revolution:

> Madame Lecoeur en fut malade; elle voyait les Halles flamber, une nuit que Florent et ses complices se seraient cachés au fond des caves, pour s'élancer de là sur Paris (830).

The narrator's voice concludes the tableau with a subjective commentary on the real «odours» of les Halles: «Cependant, il semblait que c'étaient les paroles mauvaises de Mme Lecoeur et de Mlle Saget qui puaient si fort» (833).

Two modes of olfactory presentation form part of the basic structure of *La Faute de l'abbé Mouret*. The *Paradou*, the great natural garden, acts as accomplice to the love of Albine and Serge. Consequently, all of nature calls out to them: the plants, the herbs and the flowers with their rich scents, which hardly veil their erotic invitation to the young couple:

> Ce n'était plus l'heureuse langueur des plantes aromatiques, le musc du thym, l'encens de la lavande. Ils écrasaient des herbes puantes: l'absinthe, d'une griserie amère; la rue, d'une odeur de chair fétide; la valériane brûlante, toute trempée de sa sueur aphrodisiaque. Des mandragores, des ciguës, des hellébores, des belladones, montait un vertige à leurs tempes, un assoupissement, qui les faisait chanceler aux bras l'un de l'autre, le coeur sur les lèvres (*Faute*, 1387).

Another impressionistic mode is invading this odiferous field, namely animism, which pervades the entire novel. Father Mouret's psyche is invaded by all the forces of nature which vaunt the procreative processes and the joys of sexual union. This process is built in exactly the same manner for Florent reacting to Les Halles. Here the invading forces of nature, represented as strong smells, are enumerated, contrasted and summarized as the odour of the desirable young girl:

> ... c'étaient, plus près, les sueurs humaines que l'air apportait des Artaud, les senteurs fades du cimetière, les odeurs d'encens de l'église, perverties par des odeurs de filles aux chevelures grasses; c'étaient encore des vapeurs de fumier, la buée de la basse-cour, les fermentations suffocantes des germes (*Faute*, 1310-11).

Vegetable life is an innocent accomplice of the loves of Silvère and Miette in *La Fortune des Rougon*. The strong odours of plant life form a part of a larger animistic scheme in both *La Curée*, where Renée and Maxime act out their incestuous love in the hot-house, and in *La Faute de l'abbé Mouret,* where the lovers are invited to love, death, and for Albine at least, a rather ridiculous transfiguration, the supreme effect of olfactory penetration being found in her suicide, effected by asphyxiation from the scent emanation of the thousands of flowers she has placed around her bed.

Albine's metamorphosis into a lovely scented flower, built out of the dung heaps and other natural fertilizers, is part of a vast philosophical system in Zola which has been adequately discussed by many critics. Zola's fuzzy naturism, further clouded by an unworthy sentimentalism, imposes a thesis on this novel which limits the free functioning of the impressionistic modes. Thesis in *La Faute de l'abbé Mouret* is the most intrusive of the entire series. Whether or not Serge Mouret is living an unnatural life as a celibate priest is problematic. Imposition of narrow problem into the novel form inhibits its natural freedom. In this case *La Faute de l'abbé Mouret* becomes unfortunately just a part of the bitter quarrel in the nineteenth century between arch-conservative, even regressive prelates, and anti-clerical liberals, such as Zola. Such is not always the case with Zola. The impressionistic mode sucessfully complements the enormous existential struggle of *Le Ventre de Paris* which explodes into multiple levels of meaning. The same can be said of a great novel like *Nana* where the «mouche d'or» legend, the golden fly born on the dung heaps of Paris (an exact parallel to Albine, the flower of the *Paradou*), is successfully blended into the tense narration of moral corruption during the Second Empire.

V. *Sound Impressionism*

Working mainly with a visual impressionism, Zola complements it with olfactory, sound, animistic and movement modes. If Dr. Deberle's garden is a post-impressionist Bonnard painting, it has the added dimension of music, that of the *orgues de Barbarie* from the rue Vineuse (*Page,* 952). A brief look at the third Paris tableau in *Une Page d'amour* shows how successfully Zola blends various impressionistic modes, moving from the visual to other sense perceptions, almost in the sense of the synethesia suggested by Baudelaire and Rimbaud. Very refined atmospheres are presented, abstractly rendered, but truly felt, of heat and freshness, heat from the roofs of Paris, freshness from the river, crisscrossed with sound:

... des sons montaient encore, affaiblis et distincts,

un brusque roulement d'omnibus sur le quai, le sifflement d'un train traversant le pont du Point-du-Jour; et la Seine... passait très large avec la respiration forte d'un être vivant. ... Une odeur chaude fumait des toits encore brûlants, tandis que la rivière, dans cette exhalaison lente des ardeurs de la journée, mettait de petites haleines fraîches (*Page*, 965).

Zola's literary antecedents can be easily traced. Rousseau achieved gradations and contrasts in the *Cinquième promenade* where he contrasts pastoral music and the noise of the city: «... à se recueillir dans un silence que ne trouble aucun autre bruit que le cris des aigles, le ramage entrecoupé de quelques oiseaux, et le roulement des torrens qui tombent de la montagne» (Rousseau, *Cinquième promenade*, 1040). Chateaubriand's careful arrangement of syllabic groups, moving with solemn verbal transmutations in the preterite from abstract to specific term, creates a total silence in which the single sound of thunder can be heard prolonging itself across great distances:

Les voix de la solitude s'éteignirent, le désert fit silence, et les forêts demeurèrent dans un calme universel. Bientôt les roulements d'un tonnerre lointain, se prolongeant dans ces bois aussi vieux que le monde, en firent sortir des bruits sublimes (22).

It is Flaubert, however, who truly masters the technique of impressionism (23), and his use of auditory impressionism shows for what literary ends it can be successfully employed. Emma visits the abbé Bournissien seeking counsel for the troubles of her romantic heart. Rejected, she turns to return home, more anxious and troubled than before. It is at this point that Flaubert creates an auditory impressionism with the

---

(22) François-René de Chateaubriand, *Atala, René, Les Aventures du dernier Abencérage* (Paris: Classiques Garnier, 1958), 88. Hereafter all citations from Chateaubriand will refer to this edition, and page number will be given immediately following the text.

(23) Hatzfeld, *Initiation*, 117-124, explains the nature of Flaubert's impressionism. The discussion of auditory impressionism in *Madame Bovary* is also derived from Professor Hatzfeld.

sounds of the catechism class coming to the ears and confused mind of Emma:

> Mais la grosse voix du curé, la voix claire des gamins arrivaient encore à son oreille et continuaient derrière elle:
> —Etes-vous chrétien?
> —Oui, je suis chrétien.
> —Qu'est-ce qu'un chrétien?
> —C'est celui qui, étant baptisé..., baptisé..., baptisé (*Madame Bovary*, 107).

The most literary and least impressionistic mode for sound is the analogy to music. Thus light is seen synesthetically from a chandelier: «Les clartés du lustre... chantaient une symphonie en jaune mineur...» (*Curée,* 350).

The onomatopoetic procedure is more effective and fairly typical: «Les écrevisses passaient toujours, on entendait les petits *craquements* des *carapaces,* pendant que la conversation tombait sur la politique» (*Germinal,* 1314). The following evocation of mealtime in the company canteen is evidence of the high degree to which Zola can bring this art:

> C'étaient un cliquetis grandissant de fourchettes, des glouglous de bouteilles qu'on vidait, des chocs de verres reposés trop vivement, le bruit de meule de cinq cents mâchoires solides broyant avec énergie (*Bonheur,* 665).

Zola the realist is an impressionist. The smallest impression is recorded. It is always something seen, heard, smelled *à travers un tempérament.*

Sound is usually recorded by simple statement within the narration: «Gueulin, la voix couverte par les bruits de ferraille du vieux fiacre...» (*P. B.,* 130). More sophisticated procedures, however, can be observed. There is the isolation of a single sound heard by someone: «Le *frôlement* de sa soutane sur les marches avertissait Mouret...» (*Conquête,* 965); Octave hears the return of the Josserands: «... il était encore sur le palier, lorsqu'il entendit un *bruit* de robes de *soie frôlant* les marches.» (*P. B.,* 20); the Baudu family eats the noonday meal: «Les Baudu déjeunaient, on entendait le *bruit des fourchettes...*»

(*Bonheur,* 607). Sound effect is frequently constructed to show increasing intensity or diminution. Claude Lantier is bombarded with the derisive laughter of the crowd looking at his painting:

> ... Claude, resté en arrière, entendait toujours monter les rires, une clameur grandissante, le roulement d'une marée qui allait battre son plein (*L'Oeuvre,* 126).

Onomatopoetically, and with alliteration, we hear the approach of as yet an unseen train: «On entendit le train... s'approcher avec un grondement qui grandissait» (*Bête,* 1029).

For the literary artist, metaphor is a normal device to indicate any perception. Thus, the adverse reaction of the crowd sounds to Claude like the roar of the ocean:

> Alors, Claude, de tout ce tumulte, n'entendit au loin que *le bruit de mer,* le grondement du public roulant en haut, dans les salles (*L'Oeuvre,* 300).

The enumeration of small details can be a means of indicating the vibrancy of a total life. Zola animates the cathedral of *Le Rêve* and sound impressions play a major role in the whisper of a low mass in Latin, the sound a woman kneeling down, a faintly articulated prayer:

> Toujours la vie frémissait en elle: des bruits perdus, le murmure d'une messe basse, l'agenouillement léger d'une femme, un frisson à peine deviné, rien que l'ardeur dévote d'une prière, dite sans paroles, bouche close (*Rêve,* 863).

Sound may also be put in relief by a preparatory silence. The acute voices of women speaking is joined by the ringing of spoons in glasses, interrupted by a short period of silence, not unlike the silence of the sea between the arrival of waves on the shore. This allows a single sound, a saucer returned to a small salon table, to reach definition within the vacuum during a ladies' afternoon tea reception:

> Ces dames prenaient par moments des voix aiguës, que le léger tintement des cuillers dans les tasses

de Chine accompagnait; et l'on entendait de temps
à autre, au milieu d'un court silence, le bruit d'une
soucoupe trop vivement reposée sur le marbre du
guéridon (*Bonheur*, 454).

Converserly, intense sound as a background may accompany
the slightest single auditory line imaginable. During a sea
storm, Lazare is busy writing: «Dans le grondement de la
tempête, on n'entendait que la plume de Lazare» (*Joie*, 821).
The delineated nuances of a series of sounds is an indication
of the refined senses of the impressionist generation bringing
to an ultimateness the tentatives of Chateaubriand. Etienne
hides deep in a mine. In total darkness, with visual perception
destroyed, his impressionistic ear seizes every nuance of sound:
«Le silence bourdonnait à ses oreilles, il n'entendait que la fuite
d'une bande de rats, le craquement des vieux boisages, le bruit
d'une araignée filant sa toile» (*Germinal*, 1460). The seizing
of a theatrical atmosphere through the recording of sound as
it could be perceived by any acoustically sensitive person, is a
high point of the art of Zola and shows how much he can
compete with a science, that of sound recording, which as yet
did not exist:

> Et, au milieu de cet air étouffé, de ces piétinements
> et de ces chuchotements, la voix des acteurs en scène
> arrivait étrange, assourdie, une voix dont la fausseté
> surprenait. Puis, c'était, plus loin, au-delà des bruits
> confus de l'orchestre, comme une immense haleine,
> la salle qui respirait et dont le souffle se gonflait
> parfois, éclatant en rumeurs, en rires, en applaudis-
> sements. On sentait le public sans le voir, même
> dans ses silences (*Nana*, 1217).

The most striking bit of auditory impressionism, however,
is to be found in *Germinal*. Here Zola joins sound with the
visual arts and anticipates the geometric and then expressionist
art of the twentieth century. The miners on strike hold an
illegal meeting in the dark of the night. Their collective hope
for victory is expressed in the singing of the *Marseillaise* which
seems a confused bellowing from the thousands of voices,
although in the role of omniscient author, Zola, as if hidden
behind the trees, hears this, and records at the same time the
sound of their *sabots* on the frozen winter earth:

... on voyait seulement les trous des bouches noires, chantant la *Marseillaise,* dont les strophes se perdaient en un mugissement confus, accompagné par *le claquement des sabots* sur la terre dure» (*Germinal,* 1436).

Auditory impressionism is a minor but consistent and important aspect of the on-going, changing, moving style of the *Rougon-Macquart.* Zola proceeds from quite conventional literary modes to report, and then to duplicate, as far as the form will permit, auditory impressions.

The impulsion to duplicate the exterior world, first realistically and then abstractly, is an expansion of the seeds of modern sensibility planted by Rousseau, the implications of which are seen in the radical transformations of art and literature at the end of the nineteenth century. It is most discernable in Mallarmé's poetry and rapidly evolves in painting from the time of theoretical and practical impressionism. Zola's boyhood friend, Cézanne, represents this evolution, moving from light theories into concern over geometric form, sharper and harder colors, as will be seen in post-impressionistic trends. Over one hundred years elapse in the evolution of literary and artistic styles which may have as their basis a strong subjective feeling for the exterior world first realized by Rousseau and the following romantics, who had as yet no full vocabulary, literary or artistic, to capture the light, color and form of their true feelings. This is not to deny the technical advances of the Barbizon school or of Corot where impressionistic and *plein air* methods are implied, if not realized. The impressionists perhaps solved the technical problems of how to make concrete Rousseau's feeling. But the world is composed of more than light; the forms too must be recorded in their essence, objectively, with abstraction. What Mallarmé attempted in the poem is ultimately achieved in painting as it moves from impressionism into the succeeding geometrical and formal movements which carry on to today, always with a solid and consistent substratum of lyricism as the unifying atom.

Closely studying catalogues of impressionist painting, it is obvious that the main concern is light and movement. Yet, in the mind's eye, as we do with the literary text, is not sound also evoked? Literature has the words for sound, painting does not, but dynamic commitment to expressing all vital aspects of modern life surely implies the sound element also. The 1877 Gare Saint-Lazare picture of Monet evidently implied sound as well as color and movement for Georges Rivière, the editor of *L'Impressionniste,* who saw in the Saint-Lazare series not only light and color but the multiple sounds of a great station (24). The dazzling light and color impressionism of Monet's *Rue Montorgueil Decked out with flags,* 1878, in its composition also presents the staccato sounds of a Bastille day parade.

If we return to the Zola painting of the miners singing the *Marseillaise,* with its parallel audition of wooden shoes striking the hard earth, we find a very modern and almost abstract compositional feature: «... on voyait seulement *les trous des bouches noires...*» (*Germinal,* 1436). We should recall at the same time the shrimp eating clerks of Mouret's department store, those «... cinq cents mâchoires solides broyant avec énergie» (*Bonheur,* 665). Do such descriptions have implications for romantic and modern art? The protruding, gaping black holes of mouths in *Germinal* and the munching jaws of *Au Bonheur des dames* recall at one and the same time the satires of the Daumier lithographs, especially of lawyers, cartoons which insist upon strong formal linear depiction of human beings in desperate or inauthentic situations which bloat and distort the features, giving priority to segmented parts of the human anatomy. Light and color simply are not sufficient or adequate for either literature or painting. If the first step out of the abstract lyricism of Rousseau is the descriptive techniques found in the romantic novelists, poets, and painters, culminating in the light and color of Zola and the impressionists, then why not another step?. Is impressionism just a first step, the first formal expresssion of the meaning of Jean-Jacques Rousseau? The literary and artistic parallels are close in the evolutionary sense, if not in chronology.

Zola's attempt at auditory impressionism indicates that his literary art was already breaking away from the strict boundaries of impressionistic light, forcing the literary medium to do other things. That is precisely what is involved in the mouths of his striking miners, singing their mute *Marseillaise*

(24) Seitz, *Monet,* 106.

across the cold winter's night. It is a painting which wants to sing. The same can be said of Toulouse-Lautrec's *Singer with Open Mouth,* or the Norwegian, Edward Munch's auditory painting, *The Scream* (1893), or Van Dongen's *Modjesko Soprano Singer* (1908). Is Zola's auditory mode, like these paintings, on the road to Expressionism?

VI. *Dynamization*

Animism, the quickening of brute matter (25), has fascinated nineteenth century novelists who study «natures» without the presence of man or agent. It is not that these «thing» pictures have no relationship with man; on the contrary, he is influenced by this «thing» world which would minimize, if not dehumanize him.

A world of animated forms, moving, changing, growing, appearing, disappearing, contorting, can be a thing of delight, a joy in nature, but it is impossible to be certain that Zola's literary animism does not have sinister overtones, especially if one is inclined to view the modern technological world with a certain amount of fear. Such seems to be the impressions of many of Zola's heros and heroines, Florent, Hélène, Gervaise, among others. The opening sentence of *Le Ventre de Paris* depicts the autonomy of things with human beings effaced from the scene:

> «Au milieu du grand silence, et dans le désert de l'avenue, les voitures de maraîchers montaient vers Paris, avec les cahots rythmés de leurs roues, dont les échos battaient les façades des maisons, endormies aux deux bords, derrière les lignes confuses des ormes» (603).

We are struck by the absence of human beings; this is not the arrival of the *maraîchers,* but of their vehicles. As the market wagons converge at various intersections, on their way

---

(25) The Dangelser study of 1938 was probably the first to comment in detail on this aspect of Zola, and since then many critics have worked in this area, particularly worthwhile being the study of Alfred C. Proulx, *Aspects épiques des Rougon-Macquart de Zola* (The Hague, 1966), and the work of Philip Walker.

to Les Halles, no impression is given of workers bringing produce to the market. It is rather the idea of gigantic vegetables invading the sleeping city. It is, as Zola notes: «... cette nourriture qui passait» (*Ibid.*).

Zola's animistic natures are derived from conventional literary practice, the idea of the «sleeping» city, for example. The aristocratic section of Plassans is so considered, for these aristocrats with their attachment to the Church and old manners are out of touch with the times. The same slight animistic quality is attributed to the home of Renée's father in *La Curée,* to the shops of the small merchants in *Au Bonheur des dames,* or any peaceful-looking facade: «... la façade dormait, haute et noire, d'une mélancolie de couvent...» (*Nana,* 1144). Bourgeois interiors are usually asleep. It may be the apartment house of *Pot-Bouille* or simply a late night scene as in the opening pages of *Une Page d'amour*: «La veilleuse dormait, les meubles dormaient» (801).

As might be expected, light is frequently the most dynamic of forces. Technically, its source is found in Flaubert where light movement is used with discretion. In Zola, it is overdone: «Et les bouteilles de Champagne... allumaient autour de la table l'éclair de leurs casques d'argent» (*Page,* 896). In *La Faute de l'abbé Mouret,* light is used to reinforce the anti-clerical thesis, the sun sending its rays into the church, destroying the pale candlelight:

> ... le soleil enflammait l'autel, blanchissait les pan-neaux de faux marbre, mangeait les clartés des deux cierges, dont les courtes mèches ne faisaient plus que deux taches sombres (*Faute,* 1226).

Dynamic and vitalized thing life is created in a variety of manners for a multitude of things: a giant tree tries to look into the church of Father Mouret: «... un gros sorbier *se haussait, jetant* des branches par les carreaux cassés, *allongeant* ses bourgeons, comme pour regarder à l'intérieur» (*Faute,* 1222); haystacks, which can hardly be in movement, nonetheless seem so against the flat plain of *La Beauce*: «Seules, des ombres de meules *bossuaient* cette nudité morne» (*Terre,* 619); a dessert spreads out: «... au milieu de la nappe, s'étalaient des oeufs à la neige dans un saladier» (*Assommoir,* 456); Dr. Pascal's documents need no assistance as they leave the *armoire,* spread out on a table and then return to form a pile again: «Et les dossiers *défilaient, étalaient* leurs documents, *retournaient s'empiler* dans l'armoire» (*Pascal,* 1009); two piles of plates act as a frame for the centering of a large loaf of bread pierced by a knife, its handle soaring into the air: «Des piles d'assiettes de rechange se dressaient à chaque extrémité; tandis que, au milieu, s'allongeait un gros pain, percé d'un couteau, le manche en l'air» (*Bonheur,* 544); peasants assessing damage to their crops caused by a hailstorm are turned into lanterns: «... les lanternes sortaient... se multipliaient, couraient et dansaient» (*Terre,* 461); department store merchandise is personified: «... les pièces de draps.. respiraient, soufflaient...» (*Bonheur,* 402).

Machine life is at the center of animistic creation in the *Rougon-Macquart.* In *Germinal, La Bête humaine* and *L'Assommoir,* the mine, the locomotive and the *alambic* take on symbolic proportions, and are viewed by author and reader with a certain awe. The steam machine has a voice of its own which only Zola can hear:

> ... tandis que la machine à vapeur, allant son train, sans repos ni trêve, semblait hausser la voix, vibrante, ronflante, emplissant l'immense salle. Mais pas une des femmes ne l'entendait... (*L'Assommoir,* 391).

The dynamic movement of things involves three verbal fields: (1) verbs of unfolding and display, (2) verbs of penetration, and (3) verbs of ambulation, seen in terms of human limbs. This last field attracts related concepts of breathing, snoring, spitting, coughing and the like. It is no wonder that these novels seem populated by horrible monsters about to devour. There is danger near, in and around: «Les robinets crachaient, les seaux jetaient des flaquées...» (*L'Assommoir,* 401-402). The animated foundry of *L'Assommoir* reveals a poetry of things similar to the verse of Verhaeren or the paintings of Léger:

> ... les cisailles mécaniques... mangeaient des barres de fer, croquant un bout à chaque coup de dents, crachant les bouts par derrière... (536).

The small merchant Bourras faces not only bankruptcy, but physical danger from the department store:

La petite maison de Bourras, serrée entre le *Bonheur des Dames* et l'hôtel Duvillard... semblait devoir être écrasée du coup, le jour où le magasin envahirait l'hôtel, et ce jour était venu, le colosse tournait le faible obstacle, le ceignait de son entassement de marchandises, menaçait de l'engloutir, de l'absorber par la seule force de son aspiration géante (*Bonheur*, 580).

The radical dynamization of object in Zola can be measured by contrasting it with the life of things found in Balzac: the *Turgotine* of *Les Chouans*, the antique shop in *La Peau de Chagrin*, the Pension Vauquer of *Le Père Goriot*. The world of things has become quite sinister toward the end of the century.

Monster-object, however, while the most striking of thing animism, is only a part of a general system of attributing life to things. Zola consistently effaces human *wholes*, as in the pleasant race track scene in *Nana* which is filled with activity (of human beings) but not a single person is seen. A fiesta of movement and sound asks and answers a series of impressionistic questions: What were they doing and where? — eating lunch here and there and everywhere, spreading out cold meats, baskets of champagne passed around by the hands of invisible valets. Not a human being present and yet by its dynamic style, the very vibrancy of human pleasure is conveyed to the reader:

A ce moment, la pelouse s'animait davantage. Des lunchs s'organisaient en plein air, en attendant le Grand Prix. On mangeait, on buvait plus encore, un peu partout, sur l'herbe, sur les banquettes élevées des *four-in-hand*, et des *mail-coaches*, dans les victorias, les coupés, les landaus. C'était un étalage de viandes froides, une débandade de paniers de champagne, qui sortaient des caissons, aux mains des valets de pied. Les bouchons partaient avec de faibles détonations, emportées par le vent; des plaisanteries se répondaient, des bruits de verres qui se brisaient mettaient des notes fêlées dans cette gaieté nerveuse (*Nana*, 1388).

VII. *Movement Impressionism*

In all the modes examined so far the basic unit is movement, expressed in diverse ways, change, flux, multiplication, dimunition, creation, destruction. Seizing the modern city means capturing the ever-changing facets of a metropolis. The single object is subject to barometric pressures, atmospheric conditions, daily and seasonal quality changes in light; a whole person or object is placed in a light or a movement which allows only for the fragmentary and momentary perception of it as a part. Odours arrive only to disappear. Man is bombarded by the noise of the modern world, occasionally silenced to permit the perception of a single, interesting and often aesthetic sound. The inanimate world awakens and moves under strange and curious lights and colors. Such are the modes of Emile Zola's *Les Rougon-Macquart*. The unifying principle is movement.

The increasing tempo of movement across time is complemented by a literary camera which moves about all possible space, capturing whatever may be in motion. Thus Saccard observes the *Bourse*:

> Et Saccard, dont les regards retournaient sans cesse au dehors, voyait aussi la place se remplir peu à peu, les voitures et les piétons affluer; tandis que, sur les marches de la Bourse, éclatantes de soleil, des taches noires, des hommes se montraient déjà, un à un (*Argent*, 14).

The rural setting also presents moving paintings of increasing numbers:

> Depuis le déjeuner, le nombre des semeurs semblait y avoir grandi... ils se multipliaient, pullulaient comme de noires fourmis laborieuses... (*Terre*, 377).

These two descriptions prove that Zola can imitate the techniques of the painter and also maintain conventional literary procedure. The painterly effect of brilliant sunlight on the steps of the *bourse* contrasts with the individuals represented as black brush strokes. In the passage from *La Terre*, the simile of the black ants approximates the *taches noires* of *L'Argent*.

Combining the vividly descriptive imperfect reinforced by present participles, Zola conveys to the reader the feeling of accelerating movement:

> Mais le train venait d'entrer dans le tunnel, l'effroyable grondement approchait, ébranlant la terre d'un souffle de tempête, tandis que l'étoile était devenue un oeil énorme, toujours grandissant, jaillissant comme de l'orbite des ténèbres (*Bête*, 1273).

The *Rougon-Macquart* describes great arrivals and departures, the march of the insurgents (*Fortune*), the strikers (*Germinal*), the arrival of market wagons (*Ventre*), workers going to the factory (*Assommoir*), troop movements and retreats (*Débâcle*). There are smaller scenes of people in restaurants, theatres, at exhibitions and expositions, innumerable traffic jams, the fury of the stock exchange, the activity of a newspaper room, a continual and increasing coming and going, back and forth activities, batting doors, slamming windows, the chaos of the modern world.

The fever and intensity of modern life is often described in terms of the extreme velocity involved. Thus the lusting stage-door Johnnies are impressed by the rapid back-stage movement of the actresses, not one of whom can be identified:

> Ces messieurs clignaient les paupières, ahuris par cette dégringolade de jupes tourbillonnant au pied de l'étroit escalier, désespérés d'attendre depuis si longtemps, pour les voir ainsi s'envoler toutes, sans en reconnaître une seule (*Nana*, 1226).

Similarly, mounting mental anxiety is accompanied by multiple physical movement and the almost physical «gallop of fear» in an evacuation scene of *La Débâcle*:

> ... les populations, gagnées par la panique montante, croyaient entendre le lointain roulement de l'invasion, grondant plus haut de minute en minute, et déjà, des charrettes s'emplissaient de meubles, des maisons se vidaient, des familles se sauvaient, à la file par les chemins, où passait le galop d'épouvante (422).

7

Balzac and Flaubert both knew that the constant activity of Paris was a prime attraction to the young heros of their novels. Neither has captured this sense of the city as intensely as Zola:

> Claude vécut ces premiers mois dans une excitation croissante. Les courses au milieu des rues tumultueuses, les visites chez les camarades enfiévrées de discussions, toutes les colères, toutes les idées chaudes qu'il rapportait ainsi du dehors... (*Oeuvre*, 202).

While intensity of movement is not confined to Paris, it is there that the vibrancy of life is most felt. The confusion of a newspaper office is depicted: «... le travail fiévreux du journal, le galop des rédacteurs, le va-et-vient de la copie, au milieu des battements de porte et des coups de sonnette» (*L'Argent*, 270). *La Bête humaine* records the constant activity of the station, the moving trains, the anonymous voyagers ceaselessly traveling: «Sous eux, toujours, les petites machines de manoeuvre allaient et venaient sans repos» (*Bête*, 1010).

These few samples give some idea of the scope of movement in the *Rougon-Macquart*, verbs and nouns of filling, showing, growing, multiplying, overflowing, spreading out, dispersing, turning, flying, coming, going, arriving, departing, throwing, walking, not ceasing, not stopping. Movement is basic to the psychology and thus to the language of Zola.

CHAPTER IV

STRUCTURES OF MOVEMENT AND DECAY

There is no doubt that Zola was always drawn to the writing of a vast synthetic opus which would give directions to the secular city of the future, an ultimate and scientific solution to modern man's pursuit of happiness as proclaimed by Rousseau and the new spirit of the concluding eighteenth century. This is evident in the young «romantic» Zola planning a vast literary recapitulation of the progress of mankind, somewhat along the lines established by Hugo in *La Légende des siècles* and the preface of *Cromwell.* Given this proclivity, it is no wonder that much critical activity has been devoted to the so-called epic and mythic structure in Zola. Whether or not this fusion of the spirit of Hugo and that of Auguste Comte has been successful is a matter of debate.

Whatever his intent, the world of the *Rougon-Macquart* is not one of peace, harmony, and fellowship among men. Rather it is a world in motion, and often violent and destructive. Instability and disintegration are its marks. Creative activity is aborted. The brave new world of the future must await the obvious thesis novels to be written at the end of his life.

I. *Through Space and Time: Augmentations and Diminutions*

The basic element of instability in the *Rougon-Macquart* is found in its structure of movement. Movement need not be seen as necessarily destructive. There is the idea of voyage as quest and discovery. For the modern world, however, movement can mean the great displacement of people which starts with the Industrial Revolution. The ultimate of the dromedary syndrome, the wandering about in quest of stability, is seized by Maurice Barrès in *Les Déracinés* (1897) and is clearly opposed to the spirit of flux advocated by Gide.

These aspects of movement are found in Zola, but without any apparent awareness of their significance. If Jean Macquart wants to establish roots with Françoise in *La Terre,* with Henriette in *La Débâcle,* he finally so does in *Le Docteur Pascal.* But Jean is the healthy exception. For the most part we have the wanderers, those who leave the country (Plassans) hoping for a better life in Paris —Gervaise or Octave Mouret; and those in Paris who flee the proletarian foyer— Nana, seeking stability in the world of the *nouveaux riches.* Zola's novels exploit more radically than those of Balzac, the on-the-go aspect of modern life. The next step has to be the move west in the depression years novels of John Steinbeck, or the new *picaros* of Kerouak.

Patterns of movement are discernible from the first novel and sometimes are simply formal modes for expressing young love and lyric joy. The best examples remain *La Fortune des Rougon* and *La Faute de l'abbé Mouret,* the latter somewhat spoiled by the inability of the thesis to integrate itself into the novel.

La Fortune des Rougon utilizes spatial expansion as a geometry of the development of love. Here Zola establishes himself within the tradition of the novel, which has historically projected the development of love onto a geometric plane. Chapter V joins Chapter I in narrating the adventures of Silvère and Miette as they join the march on Paris. But much as Zola has utilized the intervening chapters to give us the necessary introductory background of the Rougon and the Macquart, so he also uses Chapter V to explain the development of the love of Silvère and Miette. Spatial expansion is his primary mode. Their love is born when their reflections fuse in the *puits mitoyen* (176). As the love develops, they need to come into more direct proximity than simply that of their reflection; Silvère takes the forbidden key and joins the two properties for «... Miette et Silvère se lassaient un peu de n'apercevoir que leur ombre» (186). As their love develops, so also does their need to expand out into space. Thus they meet in the

Saint-Mittre (192), which also becomes too confining (198). As the seasons pass and their love grows stronger, they walk farther into the countryside, and finally engage in nude swimming innocently. Reaching the limits of time and horizon, Zola forces them back to the point of departure:

> Cependant, la campagne libre, les longues marches en plein air, les lassaient parfois. Ils revenaient toujours à l'aire Sainte-Mittre, à l'allée étroite, d'où les avaient chassés, les soirées d'été bruyantes, les odeurs trop fortes des herbes... (206).

Time, but more importantly, space, restricted and expanded, are Zola's means of describing this developing love:

> Et ce fut ainsi que, pendant près de deux années, ils s'aimèrent *dans l'allée étroite, dans la campagne large* (208).

The same spatial-temporal expansion is used in *La Faute de l'abbé Mouret,* but in a more formal manner. In addition, the idyll of Serge and Albine in the *Paradou* is central to the narration, while Silvère and Miette's adventure is subordinate to a larger frame. In both instances, the naturalistic *carte de tendre* is denied. The quest for pure love seems impossible either for theological or romantic reasons. Did Zola know the difference? In any case, the walk of love seems to be a basic pattern with Zola, proven by its reappearance in Volume XII, *La Joie de vivre,* and Volume XX, *Le Docteur Pascal.* During the convalescence of Monsieur Chanteau, Pauline and Lazare venture outdoors. At first they restrain themselves to the terrace (840), then they venture into the courtyard, then the vegetable garden (841). Through a door they arrive at the cliffs of the sea (841). After exploring the churchyard and the village, they finally walk, under the cliffs, along the sea, where free from curious eyes, they enjoy, as did Silvère and Miette, the joys of bathing in the nude (842).

When old Dr. Pascal and his niece Clotilde first fall in love, they remain at home, then venture into the garden, from which they go around the entire property. The idea of spatial expansion is meant to convey the growth of their love:

> Lentement, leur amour avait eu un besoin d'élargis-

> sement et d'espace, d'abord hors de la chambre,
> puis hors de la maison, maintenant hors du jardin,
> dans la ville, dans l'horizon vaste (*Pascal*, 1076).
> Cependant, Pascal et Clotilde élargissaient encore
> leur domaine, allongeaient chaque jour leurs pro-
> menades, les poussaient à présent en dehors de la
> ville, dans la campagne vaste (*Pascal*, 1081).

Movement, structurally, seems characteristic of the nineteenth century novel. With the early romantics it seems to be
mainly the wandering of the hero meditating his destiny,
prototypically found in Chateaubriand's *René,* but also
illustrated by the various solitary mountain climbers, Senancour's *Obermann,* or the solitary country walks of Lamartine,
Hugo and De Musset. In these instances it is a question of
the unique individual trying to work out his destiny in a
physical space. Starting with Balzac, the wanderer seems
confined to a more compact area, the city. Man's fate seems
tied up with the metropolis; the city seems to dictate behavior.
Balzac's Rastignac, ambitiously running from one *hôtel particu-
lier* to another sets the mode. The early romantic hero is
replaced by the proletarian romantic, who during his walks,
meditates the human condition, seeing himself as social leader.
Such is the condition of Etienne during what Zola calls his
«... continuelles promenades» (*Germinal,* 1515). A parallel
case is that of Florent as he wanders through the vastness of
Les Halles. Paris provides pleasures for the modern voyager
as he discovers new and artificial paradises in which to
experience sensation. The various expositions of merchandise
arranged by Octave Mouret provide veritable trips through
enchanting lands. The *exposition des ombrelles* is constructed
by Zola as a voyage through a fairyland for the materialistic
customer, Mme Marty, who goes from counter to counter
making purchases:

> Mme Marty cherchait une phrase pour dire son
> ravissement, et elle ne trouva que cette exclamation:
> —C'est féerique!
> Puis, tâchant de *s'orienter*:
> —Voyons, le lacet est à la mercerie... J'achète
> mon lacet et *je me sauve.*
> Je vous *accompagne*, dit Mme de Boves. N'est-ce

pas, Blanche, *nous traversons les magasins,* pas davantage? (*Bonheur,* 619-620).

Claude Lantier is Zola's most restless hero. After some years in the country with Christine, he is back in Paris, happy to be again part of its tumultuous movement and life: «Lorsqu'il se retrouva sur le pavé de Paris, Claude fut pris d'une fièvre de vacarme et de mouvement...» (*L'Oeuvre,* 168).

In an age without rapid means of communication, the necessity to move about a vast space such as Paris can provide a unifying element for the narrational structure of the novel. Such is the case with Chapter XV of *Pot-Bouille* in which Auguste, seeking revenge for the adultery of his wife Berthe with Octave, sets out in the morning to locate his brother-in-law Duveyrier, to be a witness in his duel with Octave. The pattern seems to be derived from Flaubert (Emma and Léon in the carriage in Rouen) with, however, a humorous mocking of bourgeois *moeurs* almost exactly as it can be found in the theatre of Feydeau or Courteline. The passage extends over fourteen pages (299-313) and is composed of the following elements: (1) a rambling trip across Paris in search of someone who might know the correct address of Duveyrier's mistress Clarisse. The carriage makes four stops, each of which underlines the lack of self-knowledge on the part of these bourgeois. The first stop is at the apartment of the teen-age mistress of Uncle Bachelard where we see a quarrel provoked by his discovery that the little girl has slept with his nephew. The second stop is at the office of Trublot who knows the street but not the number. The third stop is *chez* Clarisse, and a fourth, at a restaurant. All are ironic, for seeking help to avenge an adulterous wrong, Auguste has made three encounters where adultery and fornication are considered as norms, and a fourth where the sin of gluttony is added, as Bachelard orders Rabelaisian quantities of food and wine. (2) Zola pays close attention to the time element, recording impatience and delays as the day advances. (3) Auguste's mental attitudes are added as another dimension, for as the day wears on, he is less inclined to engage in a duel which he truly fears. (4) At each stop, the number of persons in the *fiacre* increases, making for an uncomfortable ride. (5) The *fiacre* itself is consistently described in a Balzacian manner; it is old and cumbersome and takes on human qualities: «... cette voiture *lamentable* l'attristait» (*P. B.*, 300); «... le fiacre roula *péniblement*.» (305); «Le grand cheval blanc fumait sans avancer, le cou cassé dans une salutation *douloureuse*...» (307); «... dans les cahots *laborieux* du fiacre...» (312). (6) Over the whole scene is felt the presence of the coachman, complaining about all this movement:

> Le cocher jura. Rue d'Assas, ah! malheur! en voilà des paroissiens qui aimaient la promenade! Enfin, on arriverait quand on arriverait (*P. B.*, 307).

A symbolic thrust is added when Trublot decides to bring food from the restaurant to the *cocher* for whom he expresses a certain «sympathie», «... car ... il avait, à certains détails, flairé un ancien prêtre» (313). This is a ride through a bourgeois hell of adulterers seeking revenge, driven by a defrocked priest who cannot forgive their sins.

Spatial horizons are seen as expanding, especially when the characters seem to be on the road to discovery and self-fulfillment. Dr. Deberle's garden is an expanding space for Hélène as her love for the doctor develops. Actually, it is a small garden. As Father Mouret discovers life, the *Paradou* increases its dimensions: «Je ne sais plus. C'était tout petit, et voilà que ça grandit toujours...» (*Faute,* 1330). The market of Paris is an ever-expanding universe for Claude Lantier who will create from it «... des natures mortes colossales, des tableaux extraordinaires» (*Ventre,* 623).

On the other hand, space can move about a person to create feelings of suffocation and claustrophobia. *Pot-Bouille* presents stuffy interiors, stench-ridden interior courts where there is never a breath of fresh air. Gervaise is very much aware that she is a prisoner of tight spaces (1).

Gervaise's claustrophobia separates her from the great crowds of the Second Empire who seem unaware of the ephemeral nature of their liaisons. *Nana* provides the best examples of over-crowding as a structure suggestive of instabil-

---

(1) Lewis Kamm, «The Structural and Functional Manifestation of Space in Zola's *Rougon-Macquart*,» *Nineteenth-Century French Studies,* 3 (nos. 3-4, 1975), 224-236.

ity. The personages are groups of soulless insects, anonymous beings thrown here and there in Paris society, with instant gratification the only goal. In Chapter VI we follow the increasing numbers of men who come to the country in pursuit of Nana. Her loge is always overpacked: «... la loge était trop petite pour tout ce monde. Il fallut s'entasser» (1210). Lecherous admirers fill her dressing room. At Nana's dinner party we see the arrival of uninvited guests (1170); by page 1176 they number thirty-eight; on page 1189 eleven more arrive. This chapter ((IV) stresses character instability, random behavior, alienation, in ways similar to that found in Chapter III of *L'Assommoir* (Gervaise's wedding), and the tempo of increasing numbers seems to be the backbone of the structure, creating a physical and a moral overcrowding. Crowding of space reinforces the feeling that everything is temporary, that tomorrow it will all disappear. Nothing belongs to Nana, the silverware and china are rented, the food is brought in by caterers. The spirit of Nana infects the house of Muffat, where we witness an overcrowded reception:

> C'était une folie d'empiler cinq cents personnes dans un appartement où l'on aurait tenu deux cents à peine. Alors, pourquoi ne pas signer le contrat sur la place du Carrousel? (*Nana*, 1426).

Formal preoccupation with time parallels the spatial structures of these novels. *La Terre* follows the seasons like motifs in terms of planting, growth and harvest. After the spring of their budding love and the summer of their full love, Serge and Albine arrive at autumn which signals the end of all living things. Zola has a true penchant for cyclic markings, and Dangelzer notes that the seasons and the hours of the day were to indicate not only progressions in Serge's rebirth (learning to walk, first steps into the sunlight and so on) and maturation, but also the hours of the day were to indicate the movement of the love of Serge and Albine: «9 heures. —Au verger. De purs enfants. Pas un mot d'amour ... 10 heures. —Les prairies. Deux amoureux de douze ans ... jouant à l'amourette ... 12 heures. —La forêt. Le premier amour, l'adolescence encore discrète. Les rougeurs ... 2 heures. —Les rochers. La flamme éclate ... Nature ardente. Ils se perdent et se retrouvent avec un baiser brûlant qui leur donne un frisson.» (2). In a less formal manner Zola treats the sexual education of Comte Muffat under the tutelage of Nana. In his Catholic marriage, Muffat seems to have missed a normal adolescence. With Nana, he truly becomes a teenager again:

> C'était sa jeunesse qui s'éveillait enfin, une puberté goulue d'adolescent, brûlant tout à coup dans sa froideur de catholique... (*Nana*, 1227).

The return to childhood and start of a new life is approved by Zola in the case of Serge, for to him, priestly celibacy is a perversion. But he cannot approve the return to adolescence of Muffat, for he wishes to paint Nana as a destructive force. What is the difference between Nana and Albine?

Movement in time can also mean an increased tempo of activity. The pattern can be one of aimless wandering, such as that of Lazare after the death of his mother (*La Joie de vivre*), the last days of Gervaise with the walks across Paris to visit Coupeau at the *hôpital* Sainte-Anne, or her wanderings through the *quartier*, starving, encountering her own past in hallucinations. The next to last chapter of *Nana* (XIII) provides us with a true pathology of intensity and movement. Nana the destroyer rides through Paris destroying others, destroying herself, sleeping with as many men and women as possible, trying to find in this sexual proliferation some meaning to life, or perhaps a way to end it.

Zola establishes patterns of acceleration which reach a maximum intensity, and then end in collapse. In terms of human relationships, the high point is followed by death, usually in the form of murder. Nana's pursuit of pleasure in the final days of her life is equivalent to the lustful tracking of Françoise by Buteau. Her rape is followed by death at the hands of her sister.

Increases in numbers may be simply a means of advancing a scene, a lyrical expression of youthful exuberance and ambition. Claude and Sandoz enjoy walks across Paris, and they

---

(2) Dangelser, *Description du milieu*, 208, cites the commentaries of Maurice Le Blond on *La Faute de l'abbé Mouret*.

are frequently joined by friends also intent on the literary and artistic conquest of the capital:

> C'était l'*expansion habituelle,* la bande peu à peu accrue des camarades racolés en chemin, la marche libre d'une horde partie en guerre. Ces gaillards... prenaient possession du pavé (*L'Oeuvre,* 72).

The day of the *Ducasse* in *Germinal* provides the miners with relaxation as they stroll from *estaminet* to *estaminet,* greeting each other, accepting drinks, their numbers always increasing, all recorded with delightful intrusions of *style indirect libre*:

> En chemin, sur le pavé il fallut entrer au débit Casimir, puis à l'estaminet du *Progrès.* Des camarades les appelaient par les portes ouvertes: pas moyen de dire non. ... Ils restaient là dix minutes, ils échangeaient quatre paroles, et ils recommençaient plus loin, très raisonnables, connaissant la bière, dont ils pouvaient s'emplir, sans autre ennui que de la pisser trop vite, au fur et à mesure, claire, comme de l'eau de roche. A l'estaminet Lenfant, ils tombèrent droit sur Pierron qui achevait sa deuxième chope, et qui, pour ne pas refuser de trinquer, en avala une troisième. Eux, burent naturellement la leur. Maintenant, ils étaient quatre, ils sortirent avec le projet de voir si Zacharie ne serait pas à l'estaminet Tison (*Germinal,* 1264).

The whole narrative progression of *Au Bonheur des dames* and of *L'Argent* is spaced by announcement of increases in capital, value of stocks, the increasing size of each sale, increase in the number of customers, increase in the number of employees:

> Toujours ils s'engraissaient, ils étaient maintenant mille employés, ils annonçaient vingt-huit rayons (*Bonheur,* 591). Le personnel venait d'être augmenté encore, il dépassait quatre cents employés; (*L'Argent,* 229).

As Capital increases material commodities, it finds a ready-made market which is anxious to consume these goods. It may be out of love, as is the case with Dr. Pascal who cannot resist making gifts to his child-mistress Clotilde:

> Après les bijoux, ce furent des robes, des chiffons, des objets de toilette. La chambre s'encombrait, les tiroirs allaient déborder (*Pascal*, 1071:

or it may be simply the compulsive buying, across the novel, of Mme Marty (*Bonheur*, 637). Such augmentations accord well with ostentatious consumption during the Second Empire, but patterns of increase seem also derived from the novelist. He is interested in expanding and reducing systems. What is seen above as an example of a consuming society has its parallel in the death of Albine at the conclusion of *La Faute de l'abbé Mouret*. Her death is not simple: she gathers vast quantities of flowers from the *Paradou,* piling them up in her room, roses, violets, lilies, and so on, a floral harvest of the entire park it would seem, and surrounded by these flowers, she dies asphyxiated (*Faute,* Chapter XIV).

The biographies of Zola attest to his numbers compulsion. This probably is the personal explanation of the calendar and number fixations found in the *Rougon-Macquart.* Nevertheless they are very effective devices. Counting thus must be considered as part of the structure of movement in his novels. Outstanding examples are the day by day, month by month reportings of troop movements, battles, and progress of the war in *La Débâcle,* and the tension created in *Germinal* as the days of the strike are enumerated, or the number of days the miners are trapped in the mine is calculated.

Neurosis aside, the *Rougon-Macquart* presents contrasts of expanding and diminishing structures. Zola has rendered aesthetically the economic poles of the Second Empire which make some men fat, others thin. It is probably true that Emma Bovary, the last romantic, died of her debts (3). Yet the mannequin, the dehumanized Renée, died without essence, probably without any idea of her debt to the hairdresser Worms, a bill accumulating across her entire existence: «La note de Worms se montait à deux cent cinquante-sept mille francs» (*Curée,* 599). Zola calls this a «... rage de dépense...» (*P. B.,* 187). *Pot-Bouille* is the novel of the consuming society, ever eating and drinking and buying. Uncle Bachelard is the

---

(3) See the analysis of Marjorie Bonwit, *Gustave Flaubert et le principe d'impassibilité* (Berkeley, 1950).

prime example. In the restaurant is he gourmet or gourmand, or simply bourgeois?

> ... il exigeait tout ce qu'il y avait de *plus cher*, des curiosités gastronomiques, *même immangeables*... (*P. B.*, 187).

Bachelard is not interested in the quality, but the quantity of the food which he orders (4), its exotic labels and its cost, the ostentation alone has value (*P. B.*, 188).

As Bachelard consumes, others starve. Food is turned into a primary motif in *Germinal*. As with invasion in *La Conquête de Plassans*, the many levels of eating, or not eating, swallowing, and taking in, are here exploited by Zola. The basic naturalistic level is the desperate condition of the miners. Food is of primary importance — to stay alive, to keep from dying, or just enough food so that one cannot die when death would be desired. On the naturalistic level we are asked to contrast those without food and those with food. On a symbolic level, the mine is seen as a giant feeding off the workers; the workers thus must destroy the thing which is eating at them. The novel concludes with an image of April hope, a grain which will grow and feed independent and dignified workers.

The principal interior scenes of the novel are constructed around eating, especially that of the rich. A great scene in this regard is a victory celebration where, as the dinner progresses, there is produced an increasing state of euphoria, produced by the consumption of much rich food, and by the idea that the strike has been crushed (*Germinal*, 1522). *La Fortune des Rougon* utilizes approximately the same structure as *Germinal*. The concluding pages of each novel alternate between scenes of the victors celebrating over their dinners while the miners starve and the insurgents die. The victory celebration of the Rougon family is marked by the progression of the meal:

> ... le soir, *au dessert*, des rires montaient dans la buée de la table... (*Fortune*, 314).

---

(4) Zola's interpretation of Second Empire eating habits is correct according to what is reported in Christian Guy, *De la Société gourmande au XIXe siècle* (Paris, 1971).

La Maheude's child dies of hunger: «Elle est morte de faim, ta sacrée gamine» (*Germinal*, 1478). Zola well knows that some augment at the expense of the diminution of others. The well-meaning Grégoire family crosses the line of angry miners and their wives, confident that they are loved by the people:

> ... et ils semblaient si paisibles, ils avaient si bien l'air de croire à une pure plaisanterie de la part de leurs braves mineurs, dont la *résignation les nourrissait* depuis un siècle... (*Germinal*, 1443).

With food we increase or at least stabilize; without it there is death. Thus it can represent, as it does in *Le Ventre de Paris*, the struggle between the poor and the rich, the fat and the thin, the thinking and the unthinking, the loving and the unloving. Food is almost existential in Zola.

II. *Invasion, Violence and Collapse*

Some worlds expand in space and time; others diminish. The old nobility was replaced by the new Napoleonic aristocracy. Both these worlds will disappear under the domination of the new crowd of 1851. Such a contrast is seen in the mournful, cloister-like description of the aristocratic *quartier* of Plassans in *La Fortune des Rougon,* sleepy old-timers passed by the march of history. In *La Curée,* Renée's garish and modern townhouse near the parc Monceau shines and glitters obscenely in the new right bank Paris, while her father's respectable *hôtel* sits somberly on the Ile Saint-Louis.

The implications of change during the Second Empire are more widespread, however, than mere contrast of a social caste. French society has been in turmoil, confusion and change since the revolution of 1789; the Second Empire, fully unleashing a capitalistic vigor, destroys more than an aristocratic minority. New ways destroy old and individual ways. Bourgeois thrift, altruism are out of fashion as each person seeks to spend to the limit, or to rob his neighbor. It is a world which would be uncomfortable either for Père Grandet or his daughter Eugénie.

As augmentations have been noticed, so are now seen the decreases. Small merchants cannot survive against the price wars waged by Octave Mouret's department store. The small store of Denise's uncle disappears into its dark and other century shadows:

> A mesure que le *Bonheur des Dames* s'élargissait, il semblait que le *Vieil Elbeuf* diminuât (*Bonheur,* 588).

If impressionism, not as a technique, but as a feeling or attitude of instability is correct, then it is more accurate for describing Zola than is naturalism. In the *Rougon-Macquart,* we contrast not only the old and new mercantilism, the aristocracy and the new bourgeoisie, but the constant building of the new Paris which sits side by side with the slums of *L'Assommoir.* This novel presents a constant negative, and pessimistic drawing of milieu in terms of dirt, rust, disorder, decay, disintegration and death. What is happening to the buildings also happens to the characters. The description of the stairwell to the Lorilleux apartment is representative (415). The «naturalistic» landscape of *L'Assommoir* is equated with Hélène's psychological perception of Paris in the final tableau. If not impressionistic in procedure, the intent could be so, a Paris in decay, the decay of Gervaise's *quartier* spreading out over the entire city:

> Les maisons sortaient toutes noires des masses blanches où elles dormaient, comme *moisies* par des siècles d'humidité. Des rues entières semblaient *ruinées, dévorées de salpêtre,* les toitures près de *fléchir,* les fenêtres *enfoncées* déjà (*Page,* 1087-88).

Quick and easy and transitory fortunes are amassed by the new speculators, while honest and altruistic individuals find their modest *rentes* progressively reduced. In *La Joie de vivre* Pauline lends money to Lazare for his sea factory. Progressively, her money is used for additional projects and daily support of the family. In *L'Oeuvre,* Claude and Christine are gradually reduced to poverty, as Claude takes from his principal. When Saccard's bank is declared bankrupt (*L'Argent*), thousands of small *rentiers* see their lives ruined — rural priests planning a modest retirement, impoverished nobility hoping to make decent alliances for unmarriageable daughters.

Zola's sense of the meaning of these financial difficulties

is translated into a mode of seeing. In the *Rougon-Macquart*, properties are seized, appropriated. The next step is the diminution of the human being himself. Death is the final decrease. Fouan spends an old age besieged by disrespect and violence from his children and is finally murdered by Buteau. At the interment, Jean Macquart watches the descent of the coffin:

> Pourtant, dans la terre, il distingua le cercueil, *diminué* encore, avec son étroit couvercle de sapin, de la couleur blonde du blé; ... il ne voyait plus qu'une tache pâle... (*Terre*, 805).

Fouan as a recognizable human form shrinks before the very eyes of Jean as the casket is lowered, the blond wood becoming nothing more than an impressionistic «tache pâle», similar to the wheat fields of *La Beauce*. A return to nature? This must be Zola's intent, but the *Rougon-Macquart* leaves us with the uneasy feeling that mankind is being diminished, dehumanized. Zola's naive belief in a brave new world, composed of the work ethic and scientific progress clashes dramatically with the burial of Claude Lantier at the conclusion of *L'Oeuvre*. Sandoz (Zola) proclaims to Bongrand:

> Nous ne sommes pas une fin, mais une transition, un commencement d'autre chose... Cela me calme, cela me fait du bien, de croire que nous marchons à la raison et à la solidité de la science... (*L'Oeuvre*, 360).

And Sandoz utters the last words of the novel: «Allons travailler.» (*L'Oeuvre*, 363), a banality comparable to Voltaire's «cultivons notre jardin.» However, the atmosphere of this burial accords perfectly with the dismal forecast for humanity seen throughout the *Rougon-Macquart*. The individual is being annihilated. Not even romantic eternal sleep will be possible for Claude, as the cemetery must burn up old caskets, making way for the new dead:

> ... dans ce coin du champ, ce qu'on brûlait ainsi, c'étaient les planches pourries des bières, un bûcher énorme de planches fendues, brisées, mangées par la terre... (*L'Oeuvre*, 359).

Furthermore, a railway (Zola's hope for the road to the future) encircles the cemetery (*L'Oeuvre*, 361). Zola's descriptive art, his intuitive grasp of the reality of the Second Empire as the first step towards twentieth century dehumanization, contradicts his superficial thesis of human progress. Flaubert had understood this problem in the first *Education sentimentale*.

Movement translated into the concept of invasion becomes a structural motif of the *Rougon-Macquart*. On one level this is nothing more than man's eternal battle with the elements, the invading sea of Bonneville:

> On sentait que la mer avait *galopé* jusqu'à la route, qu'elle était là maintenant, *gonflée, hurlante* (*Joie*, 828);

or the water-filled mines of *Germinal*. Natural invasions of a major and minor degree are manifest throughout the series. More serious is the envy and covetousness displayed by the Rougon-Macquart clan. A major structure in the first volume is the repeated depiction of Félicité, sitting in her *salon jaune* and looking out of her window of envy onto the proximate aristocratic quarter, especially the home of M. Peirotte. In the end, she triumphs, and from the window she can see the funeral candle burning next to M. Peirotte's body (*Fortune*, 315). Greed pushes the seemingly refined Josserand girls into rough and brutal actions. Each year at Uncle Bachelard's anniversary party, the girls try to get from the old man a twenty franc piece. To this end they get him drunk. Berthe does succeed in extracting the coin:

> Leurs mains frémissaient, toutes deux devenaient brutales, elles auraient giflé l'oncle. Mais Berthe eut une exclamation de victoire... (*P. B.*, 43).

La Conquête de Plassans exploits on multiple levels the idea of invasion. It is, of course, thematically the consolidation of the triumph of the Rougon family in Plassans. Structurally, it is the negative invasion of the Mouret household by the abbé Faujas and his mother, and in the second half of the novel, there is the second invasion with the arrival of the priest's sister and brother-in-law. The idea of invasion and conquest

— 113 —

8

is reiterated at many levels in this novel, four of which are outstanding.

First there are the turns in the narration, as psychological stances are put in opposition and relief. The procedure here is somewhat akin to what we find in *Madame Bovary*. Emma's downward path at times seems to be abetted by random remarks. It is suggested that horseback riding would be good for her health. This provides the setting for the seduction by Rodolphe in the woods. It is also suggested that going to the theatre in Rouen would be a healthy diversion for her. Ironically, the discussion between Homais and Bournissien on the morality of the theatre proves Bournissien to be right, for it is at the theatre that Léon is refound, and Emma experiences a final degradation before her suicide. Now in similar manner, Zola has the priest Faujas introduced into the Mouret household against the will of Marthe. Gradually she comes under his influence, attends church and engages in charitable activities. Olympe and Trouche arrive in Plassans, and Marthe is looking for someone to supervise the new day-care center for poor girls. She is speaking to the abbé about the position:

> Vous comprenez, il faut un homme d'une moralité parfaite, avec toutes ces jeunes filles... Mais du moment qu'il s'agit d'un de vos parents... (*Conquête*, 1003).

It then seems only reasonable to Marthe that the priest's relatives should lodge at the house:

> Et vous ne savez pas ce qu'il faut faire? Il y a deux chambres dont vous ne vous servez pas, en haut. Pourquoi votre soeur et son mari ne logeraient-ils pas là? (*Ibid.*);

with the reply of the priest:

> J'avais en effet pensé un instant à leur donner ces deux chambres; seulement, *j'ai eu peur de vous contrarier, en introduisant tout ce monde chez vous* (*Ibid.*).

Rose the servant, like Marthe, is gradually won over to the priest. The justice of peace pays a call on Faujas, and Faujas starts to lead him up to his quarters, but the servant opens the door to the seldom used Mouret salon, furthering the conquest of the house:

> Entrez donc, disait-elle. Est-ce que vous n'êtes pas chez vous, ici? (1029).

These examples are typical of the psychological turns in this novel, with Marthe, unknowingly, encouraging and arranging the progressive appropriaton of her home.

Zola also underlines this idea of invasion through his presentation of the abbé Faujas in terms of darkness (emanating first simply from his cassock), a darkness which destroys the happiness of the family. From the very first pages the figure of the priest creates «... une tache de deuil sur la gaieté du mur blanchi...» (*Conquête,* 906). The idea of darkness becomes structurally very pertinent at the end of the novel when, Mouret, insane, returns to set fire to his house. He recalls with lucidity the arrival of Faujas; his fire will end forever the shadows which have invaded his home:

> Qui donc lui avait changé sa maison. ... Il ne voyait que des ombres se glisser le long du corridor: deux ombres noires d'abord, pauvres, polies, s'effaçant; puis deux ombres grises et louches, qui ricanaient. ... les ombres grandissaient, s'allongeaient contre les murs, montaient dans la cage de l'escalier, emplissaient, dévoraient la maison entière (*Conquête,* 1194).

This is a high art representing invasion. The alienated mind of Mouret has correctly assessed the meaning of the shadows of the first chapter. Zola's style makes the invasion all encompassing, down to the basic structure of the house. As with *L'Assommoir* and *Une Page d'amour,* the idea of physical decay and collapse is an added dimension.

Across the novel the insinuations of covetousness are judiciously placed as narrational markers. Their cumulative effect (similar to Balzac's manner of piling up multiple tiny details, all of which move toward a single theme), in a chilling manner, describes the invasion of the Mouret household. Here are some samples extracted from across the text showing that the structural thesis is verified by the microstructure of the style:

> Elle s'était avancée jusqu'à la porte de la cuisine, en avait inspecté les quatre murs; puis, revenant sur le perron, elle avait lentement, d'un regard, *pris possession du jardin* (908).
>
> ... elle achevait son inspection, avec l'aisance tranquille d'une personne qui *visite une propriété à vendre* (909).
>
> On est très bien ici... (910).
>
> Vous ne me dérangez nullement... je vous assure. ... Je sais que les propriétaires aiment à se rendre compte. ... Je vous en prie, examinez tout en détail. ... *La maison est à vous* (927).
>
> Il resta un instant debout, à regarder les joueurs; en réalité, il examinait les tentures, le tapis, le meuble (950).
>
> Le jardin de Mouret lui appartenait maintenant (1027-1028).
>
> Mon paradis reste ouvert (1062).

As a contrast Zola builds up progressively the reactions of Mouret to this invasion, statements which made Mouret a prophet of his own doom:

> ... la maison est au pillage (991).
>
> La maison peut bien me tomber sur la tête... (997).
>
> On n'est plus chez soi... (1000).
>
> Ce sera heureux, si l'on ne nous met pas à la porte nous-mêmes (1011).

Lastly, it is the gradual occupation of the entire house which corroborates this structure. The Faujas give up eating alone and come to the Mouret table. Soon it is impossible to decide who owns the butter and who the cream. Rose finally prepares only foods which the abbé enjoys. Such sequences, especially in the concluding section, with the invasion of Trouche and Olympe, form part of this basic aesthetic structure which makes *La Conquête de Plassans,* if not one of the most read of the series, certainly one of the finest constructions of Zola.

The immoral invading force makes itself at home. Nana finds herself accepted by high society; she is invited to the engagement party of Count Muffat's daughter. But why not? After all, she was responsible in her own perverse way for the wedding.

Invasion carries with it the idea of destruction. The invaders not only want to possess but often also have a need to destroy. There is a spirit of revenge in them. Rastignac had looked over Paris from Père-la-Chaise, and then descended to conquer it. The abbé Faujas would violently destroy Plassans:

> L'abbé Faujas tendit les bras d'un air de défi iro-nique, comme s'il voulait prendre Plassans pour l'étouffer d'un effort contre sa poitrine robuste: Il murmura: 'Et ces imbéciles qui souriaient, ce soir, en me voyant traverser leurs rues!' (*Conquête*, 916).

Destruction also means simple change, in the sense that time and event destroy familiar milieu. We learn in the final volume that the *Paradou* of Serge and Albine has been divided up into lots (*Pascal*, 960), destroying any physical remembrances of their romantic love. This is not too far removed from Hugo's return to the forest of love in the «Tristesse d'Olympio» — all is effaced by time and often by man.

Zola's destructive forces do not seem psychologically or even linguistically too far removed from the processes of the romantics. It is basic to his system to have natural forces of invasion and destruction as a background to the personal and societal destructions of the series. In at least one instance, it looks like nothing more than a late nineteenth century pathetic fallacy. As Clothilde is preparing to leave Pascal to join Maxime in Paris, a mistral rages about the house. This famous wind is worthy of epic description, but should it be seen as a sign of imminent death?

> Des branches cassaient, disparaissaient, des toitures étaient soulevées, charriées si loin, qu'on ne les retrouvait plus. Pourquoi le mistral *ne les prenait-il pas ensemble, les jetant là-bas, au pays inconnu, où l'on est heureux?* (*Pascal*, 1149).

It is difficult in the text to determine if this is the voice of Zola, Clotilde or Pascal. In any case, the separation is painful for the couple, and someone is giving in to pathetic fallacy. The destructive storm immediately calls to mind high romantic literature, the passionate leave taking of the lovers across the grand canal of Venice in Madame de Stäel's *Corinne,* but better yet, the cry of Chateaubriand's René to the elements:

> Levez-vous vite, orages désirés, qui devez emporter René dans les espaces d'une autre vie! Ainsi disant, je marchais à grands pas, le visage enflammé, le vent sifflant dans ma chevelure, ne sentant ni pluie ni frimas, enchanté, tourmenté, et comme possédé par le démon de mon coeur (*René,* 214).

Pascal escorting Clotilde to the Plassans railroad station looks a bit like a latter-day René, much older, more scientific, and certainly, more sentimental:

> Et, pareil aux arbres échevelés, Pascal tenait bon, avec ses vêtements qui avaient des claquements de drapeaux, avec sa barbe et ses cheveux emportés, fouettés de tempête (*Pascal,* 1155).

Destruction in one form or another is a basic element of the *Rougon-Macquart.* The tearing down of Paris is alluded to many times; there are specific demolitions in *La Curée* and *Au Bonheur des dames* where »watchers» evaluate the significance of this destruction. Zola's attitude, like that of Denise of *Au Bonheur,* is ambivalent. He seems to see some value, an idea of progress. For Gervaise, visiting Coupeau all the way across Paris, or wandering in her final agony, the new landscape only adds to her bewilderment and alienation. Hélène's apocalyptic visions of Paris being destroyed record her own psychology, but accord also with what was truly happening.

Many critics have noted the unusual number of conflagrations. The outstanding examples are the fires of *La Conquête,* the fire in the mine of *Germinal,* burning for centuries, a Dantean hell as Zola describes it, very close to this earth. The burning of Paris during the *commune* is one of the major descriptive feats of Zola. He sees destruction, especially by fire, as a sort of purification and preparation for a new age of creativity, sharing somewhat the philosophy of some of his more radical arsonists.

Destruction is also manifest in the number of riots and

insurrections depicted. The first volume opens with the march of the insurgents. As with the marches of the miners in *Germinal,* unanimistic spirit takes hold, carrying the group forward in what often turns out to be a destructive urge. The directionless crowds of the Paris *commune* show the relativity of political and moral positions which can occur in mob psychology. It demonstrates what can happen when the spirit of 1789 filters into the collective. As with *Les Mains sales* of Sartre, today's victim may be tomorrow's persecutor. The mindless movement of the crowd will lead to the destruction of property on a grand scale, the destruction of mine equipment in *Germinal* being a prime example. In *La Bête humaine,* the train rushes out of control down the last pages of the novel. Will it lead to a future of creation or destruction is the question again asked by Zola, with the naive, almost ridiculous, suggestion that it will lead to a brave new world.

Above all, the *Rougon-Macquart,* is a novel of murders, wanton neglect of the sick and dying, and suicides. Very few are exempt. *La Bête humaine* could be classified as a *roman policier*: *La Terre* must lead the list in number of calculated and spontaneous murders. Zola has a penchant for bringing all things to an end. Thus death is a necessary element even in the fairy tale novel *Le Rêve*. The usual path, however, is bloody death and suicide: the murder of Silvère in *La Fortune des Rougon,* the deaths of Marthe, Mouret, Faujas, Mme Faujas, Trouche and Olympe at the conclusion of *La Conquête de Plassans,* the death of Coupeau in his delirium tremens and Gervaise in her despair in *L'Assommoir,* the hideous smallpox death of Nana. *La Joie de vivre* is the paradoxical novel of death and life in the Zola system. It is useless to even start counting the deaths of *Germinal.* Of all the attempted and effected suicides, that of Claude Lantier in *L'Oeuvre* remains the chilling example.

Many of the inhabitants of Zola's world are prone to destructive violence. Claude Lantier, despairing of his genius, is frequently seen slashing his paintings. Nana remains, however, the prototypical avenger and destroyer. Her destructive urge at the end of the novel is the equal of Renée's pathology of spending at the conclusion of *La Curée.* Nana is also a compulsive buyer and receiver: «Elle ne pouvait voir quelque chose de très cher sans en avoir envie...» (*Nana,* 1433). In

Chapter XIII, Zola insists upon two points through his repeated commentary: Nana sullies and destroys all with which she comes into contact, objet or person:

> Rien ne lui restait aux mains; elle cassait tout, ça se fanait, ça salissait entre ses petits doigts blancs; une jonchée de débris sans nom, de lambeaux tordus, de loques boueuses, la suivait et marquait son passage (*Nana*, 1433).

Philippe brings Nana a gift of an antique porcelain candy container:

> —Prends garde, murmura-t-il, c'est fragile.
> Mais elle haussa les épaules. Il lui croyait donc des mains de portefaix! Et, tout à coup, la charnière lui resta aux doigts, le couvercle tomba et se brisa. Elle demeurait stupéfaite, les yeux sur les morceaux, disant:
> —Oh! il est cassé! (*Nana*, 1435).

As an individual psychotic case, Nana's destructiveness should be measured as a pathology, but it does seem that she is a mythical force of destruction set loose upon the Second Empire:

> Elle avait saisi un éventail, tirant sur les branches et la soie se déchira en deux. Cela parut l'exciter. Pour faire voir qu'elle se moquait des autres cadeaux, du moment où elle venait d'abîmer le sien, elle se donna le régal d'un massacre, tapant les objets, prouvant qu'il n'y en avait pas un de solide en les détruisant tous (*Nana*, 1436).

Zola's descriptive reinforcement of her destructive urge reiterates itself across many pages:

> Elle apportait d'instinct la rage d'avilir. Il ne lui suffisait pas de détruire les choses, elle les salissait. Ses mains si fines laissaient des traces abominables, *décomposaient* d'elles-mêmes tout ce qu'elles avaient cassé (*Nana*, 1460).

Coupled to this field is the general atmosphere of doomsday collapses of any environment touched by Nana. Choosing just one page to stress the word area corresponding to the structure of destruction and doom, we find a noun and verb field of extreme collapse which is representative of the milieu as depicted throughout the concluding pages:

> L'hôtel semblait bâti sur un gouffre, les hommes... s'y *engloutissaient,* sans laisser la trace d'un peu de poussière... tout ce qui peut hâter la *ruine,* dans une maison *dévorée...* en haut, chez Madame, la *débâcle* soufflait plus fort... (*Nana,* 1433).

One of the most salient features of the *Rougon-Macquart* is the transformation of individual defeat into a general system of cosmic collapse. Lazare arrives at a philosophy of total destruction because of his fear of death: «Il voulait supprimer la vie afin de supprimer la peur» (*Joie,* 1057). He awaits the imminent destruction of the universe:

> Avec un ami, sa conversation tombait tout de suite sur les embêtements de l'existence, sur la rude chance de ceux qui engraissaient les pissenlits, au cimetière. Les sujets lugubres l'obsédaient, il se frappa de l'article d'un astronome fantaisiste annon-çant la venue d'une comète, dont la queue devait balayer la terre comme un grain de sable: ne fallait-il pas y voir la catastrophe cosmique attendue, la cartouche colossale qui allait faire sauter le monde, ainsi qu'un vieux bateau pourri? (*Joie,* 1058).

Claude Lantier decides that he cannot enter a painting at the *salon*; his nude woman looks dead. His disappointment in his work seizes the extreme vocabulary of Lazare:

> Puis, les ténèbres ont coulé encore, encore: un vertige, un engouffrement, la terre roulée au néant du vide, la fin du monde! Je n'ai plus vu bientôt que son ventre, décroissant comme une lune malade (*L'Oeuvre,* 265).

If the romantic poets insisted that we treat their personal sorrows as phenomena worthy of cosmic appraisal, the *râtés* and the envious of the *Rougon-Macquart* will first inflict violence upon themselves, but then insist upon bringing the

whole world down with them. Flore of *La Bête humaine* is
the key for joining the worlds of personal disappointments to
the organized world of anarchistic destruction. Flore, in her
jealousy of Jacques Lantier and Séverine, plans to kill them
by sabotaging the railroad tracks. The thought that such action
brings death to others does not bother her. Since she cannot
be happy, no one else should be:

> ... sous un besoin grandissant de l'anéantissement
> de tout. Puisqu'il ne restait personne qui l'aimât, les
> autres pouvaient bien partir avec sa mère. Des
> morts, il y en aurait encore, et encore, et on les
> emporterait tous d'un coup (*Bête,* 1252).

In *Germinal,* Zola questions the *bonne volonté* or *mauvaise
foi* of the socialist Etienne. The example of Flore in *La Bête
humaine* may be the link between personal motive for destruc-
tion and its ultimate elaboration into an anarchistic theory.
We find many professional exterminators in the *Rougon-
Macquart.* Canon, the friend of Jésus-Christ, is an itinerant
prophet of revolution, ruin and death in *La Terre* (643).
Sigismond, the Marxist, makes similar predictions: «... tout
se supprime, tout se transforme et disparaît» (*Argent,* 285).
Maurice is converted to anarchism towards the end of *La
Débâcle*: «Le sombre besoin de destruction montait en lui...»
(*Débâcle,* 875). The prototype for these extremists is Souvarine
of *Germinal.* He is not only a man of his word, but exis-
tentially dedicated to the cult of destruction, for he does blow
up the mine. But we cannot help but wonder if the motivation
is not similar to that of Flore. Did it not all start back in
Moscow the day he saw his mistress hanged?

Finally, only one point needs to be made. Hostilities,
violences, destructions occur on all levels in the work of
Zola. These final examples show dramatic events of worlds
collapsing. But are not these ultimate fulfillments based in the
petty day-to-day hostilities of the small people of the *Rougon-
Macquart*? That is, the countless repetitions of sociological
venial sins, do they not finally lead to the mortal ones? In
many of the novels we note silly rivalries, the competition
between Lise and La Belle Normande in *Le Ventre de Paris,*
the competition among department store clerks: «La guerre
de la lingerie et des confections en prit une violence nouvelle...»

(*Bonheur,* 519), the petty fights between neighbors lodged in the *SNCF* quarters in Le Havre: «La rivalité, de plus en plus envenimée entre les Lebleu et les Roubaud...» (*Bête,* 1064); «... cette guerre des deux logements» (1065). In Zola's world, these trivial quarrels, while often humourous, are the first links in a chain leading to violence, war, destruction and collapse of entire systems.

III. *Man Subject to his Milieu*

Baroque man filled his architecture with metaphysical fears best expressed in Pascal's statement on vast spaces. Newtonian physics for a short time reassured man that he had a proper and regulated occupation of space as can be ascertained in the paintings of Watteau and Fragonard. The pathetic fallacy which is observed in France for the first time in the writings of Rousseau insists on a precarious balance of happiness, but also confusion, as the romantic hero wanders through vast natures, less and less sure of his role in the universe. French romanticism, unlike its English counterpart, has few moments of exhaltation in nature's spaces (Wordsworth). Man wanders, trembling, unsure of his destiny.

By the end of the century, man seems not only lost, but swallowed up by his environment. Confusion and disorder reign. The novelist records the individual's «impression» of a milieu alive and in movement, making of it a structural mode. This trend seems to start with Flaubert, with Emma's hypersensitivity to her environment, the monotony of life in Tostes and Yonville-l'Abbaye, the excitement of the ball at La Vaubyessard, her visions of what life in Paris could be.

Man reacting to his environment is a basic structure in the novels of Zola. It should first of all be evaluated as a technique for delineation of character, that is, revealing character psychology through the manipulation of milieu as it is perceived by a character whose emotional instability will alter the environment. Three outstanding cases are Florent, abbé Mouret, and the Count Muffat. In all three cases Zola dwells specifically on the effect of odours.

Florent, upon his return, personifies Paris and is convinced that the city is «... fâché de son retour» (*Ventre,* 606). Thus Les Halles becomes to him an invading force, particularly by its smells: «... les odeurs étaient suffocantes» (*Ventre*, 806). According to Zola, abbé Mouret, because of his priestly formation has «... une horreur de la sensation physique» (*Faute*, 1232). He is offended by the smells of Désirée's barnyard, the animality which seems to ascend to the rectory from the village: «Une odeur humaine montait de ce tas de maisons branlantes» (*Faute*, 1272). In the *Paradou* he becomes dizzy with the smells of nature:

> Il le respirait venir avec les parfums qu'il cueillait dans sa course, l'odeur de la terre, l'odeur des bois ombreux, l'odeur des plantes chaudes, l'odeur des bêtes vivantes, tout un bouquet d'odeurs dont la violence allait jusqu'au vertige (*Faute*, 1334).

Chapter V of *Nana* presents Count Muffat as a sort of impressionistic hero. Aside from Zola's own delight in recording the sensory delights of the théâtre des Variétés, the recording of sensation is meant to show Muffat's progressive arousement by Nana. But Nana is only the core of the seduction. All the accessories of the theatre are involved as Muffat makes his tour: the odours of women, soaps, perfumes, cosmetics. He is invaded by smells and sounds:

> Le comte Muffat, pris de sueur, venait de retirer son chapeau; ce qui l'incommodait surtout, c'était *l'etouffement de l'air,* épaissi, surchauffé, où traînait une *odeur forte...* puant le gaz, la *colle* des décors, *la saleté* des coins sombres, les *dessous* douteux des figurantes. Dans le couloir, la *suffocation* augmentait encore; des *aigreurs d'eaux de toilette,* des *parfums de savons, l'empoisonnement des haleines.* ... Il y avait, en haut, des *bruits de cuvette,* des *rires* et des *appels,* un *vacarme de portes* dont les continuels *battements* lâchaient des *senteurs de femme,* le *musc des fards* mêlé à la *rudesse fauve des chevelures* (*Nana*, 1206).

Zola's naturalistic thesis would be something like the irresistible, animalistic call of sex, the odour of woman. Throughout Chapter V (1208, 1222, 1223), Muffat's reactions to erotic detail are presented impressionistically. He is hypersensitive to a milieu which he tries to flee.

These are three examples of threat conveyed by specific sensory reaction. It can be, however, a general phychological stance, an irrational response to object and person. Throughout *L'Assommoir*, Gervaise seems menaced, first, by the general environment, caught between the hospital and the slaughter-house (5), but threatened from the start by the proximity of the Lorilleux: «... le voisinage des Lorrilleux, porte à porte, l'effrayait beaucoup» (464); the long-sought revenge of Virginie, and the terrible past which lurks into the present with the return of Lantier. Chapter VI explores the menace of Lantier, seen finally as a spatial progression. For more than seven years Gervaise had not even heard his name. Renewed friendship with Virginie brings him back into her life, and Zola records this as the past invading the present: «... son passé, à cette heure, allait droit à son présent» (549). Gervaise then develops a fear psychology; she senses that Lantier is in the *quartier*, that he is spying, waiting to seize her. This psychology continues into the following chapter. A tone of imminent rape or even murder is established. At the end of Chapter VII, she still has the feeling of being hunted, but she cannot precisely situate the enemy. Structurally, the process is striking. During the *noce* given by Gervaise, the door is open to the street, and we see Lantier, standing across the street looking at the celebration. He is finally invited in, and to the table. The party is at its height, the crowd inebriated; Gervaise is not exactly sure what is going on. Zola concludes the chapter by revealing Gervaise's anxiety through her confusion: what is this breath of air which she feels on her neck?

> ... quant à Lantier, il *avait dû rester* jusqu'à la fin, elle sentait même encore un souffle dans ses cheveux, à un moment, mais elle ne pouvait pas dire si ce souffle venait de Lantier ou de la nuit chaude. (595).

Threats, real or imagined, can be more directly sensed. In *La Joie de vivre* the ailing Madame Chanteau is convinced that Pauline is poisoning her soup, and Tante Phasie of *La*

---

(5) Kamm, «The Structural and Functional Manifestation of Space in Zola's *Rougon-Macquart*,» 224.

Bête humaine knows that her husband is trying to kill her in order to get her money. The *Rougon-Macquart* is filled with perpetual cat-and-mouse games; old Fouan hiding his *rente* documents from his sons, Aunt Phasie's husband hunting day and night for the poor woman's small fortune.

Fears of the environment are exploited as hallucinatory states. Metamorphosis of the environment may be attributed to effects of alcohol, such as the delirium tremens of Coupeau:

> C'étaient les boules qui devenaient des rats. Ces sales animaux grossissaient, passaient à travers le filet, sautaient sur le matelas où ils s'évaporaient (*Assommoir*, 788).

All of nature is transformed into invading sexual symbols in the mind of Father Mouret. In the first part of the novel, Serge, in his sentimental devotion to the Virgin actually sees her advance towards him. To Zola there probably is not much difference between the visions of Coupeau and those of abbé Mouret:

> ... et il la (Mary) voyait s'avancer vers lui, pleine de grâce ... il jetait son coeur à ses pieds, pour qu'elle marchât dessus... (*Faute*, 1290).

The most important transformations of nature are those of Hélène, where the five tableaux, progressively seen as negative and destructive spaces, reveal her developing sentiments, and the transformations of Les Halles in the mind of Florent, who, returning from captivity, is like a shell-shocked war veteran. Many of the descriptions in *Le Ventre de Paris* are presented through his distorted and frequently hallucinatory viewing of things. Escaping from Guyenne, Florent suffers from a hydrophobia which transforms the market into bodies of water (*Ventre*, 867).

The *Rougon-Macquart* also makes cultural evaluations of man's reaction to life in the metropolis. Octave Mouret is a modern impressionistic hero. He is the link back to several generations of young men who start coming to Paris in the novels of Balzac. The modern conqueror of the city must have the necessary appetites, to use Zola's word: «... il le sentait (Paris) publiquement ouvert aux appétits des gaillards solides» (*P. B.*, 3).

Different from any preceding literary method is Zola's depiction of the impressionable hero and heroine reacting to the pandemonium of modern life. Octave arrives in Paris:

> Les jurons des cochers tapant sur les chevaux qui s'ébrouaient, les coudoiements sans fin des trottoirs, la file pressée des boutiques débordantes de commis et de clients, l'étourdissaient (*P. B.*, 3).

Denise arrives in Paris with her brothers: «... effarés et perdus au milieu du vaste Paris» (*Bonheur*, 389). Reporting for work at the department store, she does not recognize the entrance: «... elle était restée saisie...» (*Bonheur*, 472), and with reason, for since her last visit, it has been transformed into an oriental salon for another sales event. Octave is an impressionistic magician. As a modern capitalist, he uses color in a flamboyant and disordered way in order to disorient the customer, who will make irrational choices, buying unnecessary items. Mouret puts colors together in order to create: «... mal aux yeux» (*Bonheur*, 434). The clients will react much as the public did upon first seeing the impressionist paintings, rubbing their eyes and taking distances. That he has been successful in this can be seen in the reactions of Mme Desforges as she crosses the store:

> Mais ce qui la surprenait surtout, dans la fatigue de ses yeux aveuglés par le pêle-mêle éclatant des couleurs, c'était, lorsqu'elle fermait les paupières, de sentir davantage la foule, à son bruit sourd de marée montante et à la chaleur humaine qu'elle exhalait. Une fine poussière s'élevait des planchers, chargée de l'odeur de la femme ... une odeur ... envahissante, qui semblaient être l'encens de ce temple élevé au culte de son corps (*Bonheur*, 631).

Zola's dimension here, however, remains primarily literary, never restrained to the optical. The description of sense impression moves quickly from the visual, to delineated nuances of odour, directed back to the abstract concept of «woman», ending in a purely metaphorical, that is, literary summation of the meaning of the impressions received by the customer.

Unlike the impressionistic painters, the ultimate goal is to make reactions to the environment serve novelistic goal:

> Cinq heures sonnaient, lorsqu'elle se trouva sur le trottoir de la place Gaillon, étourdie, au milieu des fiacres et de la foule (*Bonheur*, 560).

Seen out of context, this citation might seem to be simply a reaction to the movement of the carriages and the crowds. Contextually, however, the *étourdissement* of Denise is provoked not simply by the movement, but also because she has just been dismissed from her position. The psychological state will explain the confusion just as much as the chaotic ambiance:

> ... seule d'une minute à l'autre, perdue dans cette grande ville inconnue, sans appui, sans ressources! (*Bonheur*, 562).

The musings of Octave show how literary psychology and reaction to modern milieu fuse in the work of Zola. Octave has just had an interview with Mme Hédouin whom he would like to seduce. His thought fuses with his perception of the city:

> Dans la rue, *assourdi par les fiacres, bousculé par les passants*, le jeune homme ne put s'empêcher de faire remarquer que cette dame était très belle, mais qu'elle n'avait pas l'air aimable (*P. B.*, 17).

The atmosphere acting on the person seems essential to artistic and literary impressionism. Hatzfeld has called this: «... *refined response to nature*» (6). This modern response to environment seems to be derived from Rousseau. Hélène passively receives the Paris twilight into her soul:

> Elle *goûtait le charme du crépuscule*, l'effacement dernier des choses, l'assoupissement des bruits. Une lueur de veilleuse brûlait à la pointe des flèches et des tours: Saint-Augustin s'éteignit d'abord, le Panthéon, un instant, garda une lueur bleuâtre, le dôme

---

(6) Hatzfeld, *Literature Through Art*, 169.

éclatant des Invalides se coucha comme une lune dans une marée montante de nuages (*Page*, 965).

Rousseau's boatride in the *Cinquième Promenade* is like a forerunner of Hélène's sensation in her posture:

> ... je m'esquivois et j'allois me jeter seul dans un bateau que je conduisois au milieu du lac quand l'eau était calme, et là, m'étendant tout de mon long dans le bateau les yeux tournés vers le ciel, *je me laissois aller et dériver lentement au gré de l'eau,* quelquefois pendant plusieurs heures, plongé dans mille rêveries confuses mais délicieuses, et qui sans avoir aucun objet bien déterminé ni constant ne laissoient pas d'être à mon gré cent fois préférables à tout ce que j'avois trouvé de plus doux dans ce qu'on appelle les plaisirs de la vie (1044).

There is not too much difference between these two texts of the late eighteenth and nineteenth centuries. Zola's text shows the evolution toward physical and visual precision of the sentiments of Hélène, translated into details of diminishing sounds and lights. Rousseau's text remains abstract and general; otherwise, both show two fundamental points of joining: passivity and solitude, the receptacles of strong sensations. The refined response to nature of which Hatzfeld speaks is joined by the idea of man being acted upon, what Arnold Hauser has called the «... fundamentally passive outlook on life...» (7), that is, allowing the atmosphere to infiltrate the essence. And not surprisingly, as Hauser has again revealed, the super populations of the big cities, with their constant movements, produce not a sentiment of solidarity, but one of solitude (8), if not alienation. At the end of *Une Page d'amour,* Hélène is totally alienated from the city of Paris. Man is seen as more and more detached from the very environment which acts so powerfully upon him. Lazare of *La Joie de vivre* is a late nineteenth century reincarnation of Jean-Jacques Rousseau. The *rêverie* of the modern hero, however, contemplating either the cityscape or the celestial skies, leads to more un-

---

(7) *Social History of Art,* II, 873.
(8) *Ibid.,* 878.

9

certainty, solitude, and finality. Lazare, beset by the idea of death, leaves the house and wanders about the countryside. The vision described is not that of a real landscape acting upon the character to produce a meditation on human destiny. It is rather the landscape of the mind, of a future world in constant movement, a world in which Lazare will not exist:

> Comme Pauline lisait un soir le journal à son oncle, Lazare était sorti, bouleversé d'avoir entendu la fantaisie d'un conteur, qui montrait le ciel du vingtième siècle empli par des vols de ballons, promenant des voyageurs d'un continent à l'autre: il ne serait plus là, ces ballons qu'il ne verrait pas, disparaissaient au fond de ce néant des siècles futurs, dont le cours en dehors de son être l'emplissait d'angoisse (*Joie*, 885).

The fundamental modern problem of time, with its implications of change, meaning ultimately death, was introduced by romanticism. In the late nineteenth century this produces drastic soul states of passivity, solitude and alienation.

If modern man is increasingly pessimistic (which may account for the neurotic compulsion to derive instantaneous pleasure from the moment) with the evidence of his transiency and the permanence of nature, he suffers from a threat which was unknown to the romantic generation, the danger of losing his human identity. In Zola's world, man seems dominated and controlled by things. This explains the role of aggressive and destroying objects, the personification and *chosification* of the material world, the *alambic* of *L'Assommoir*, the monster mine of *Germinal*, the train of *La Bête humaine*. Starting with *Au Bonheur des dames*, this idea becomes preeminent to Zola. The department store is seen as a machine to which the workers must sacrifice their individuality and personality; they are all «... emportés par le branle de la machine, abdiquant leur personnalité...» (*Bonheur*, 516). Denise, ambivalent in her attitude toward the new concept of mercantilism, senses that the store is indeed a powerful machine which may be controlling lives: «... à se sentir si peu de chose, dans cette grande machine qui l'écraserait avec sa tranquille indifférence» (*Bonheur*, 536). The machine-department store manipulates its customers:

L'heure était venue du branle formidable de l'après-midi, quand la machine, surchauffée menait la danse des clientes... (*Bonheur*, 491-492).

The chef in the company canteen works with the regularity of a robot: «... prêt à remplir de nouveau les assiettes, de son mouvement rythmique d'horloge bien réglée» (*Bonheur*, 550). Modeling a coat, Denise senses that she has become a mannequin, but her sense of self still is able to interpret this as a nakedness (*Bonheur*, 498), for she has not as yet been dehumanized. But dehumanization is what is implied by Zola in such structures. It is picturesque in *L'Assommoir* to see Gervaise swallowed up by her laundry:

> ... elle disparaissait entre les chemises et les jupons ... et, là-dedans, au milieu de cette mare grandissante, elle gardait ses bras nus, son cou nu, avec ses mèches de petits cheveux blonds collés à ses tempes, plus rose et plus alanguie (*Assommoir*, 508).

But the unanimistic opening of *L'Assommoir* bespeaks a frightening world of isolated souls, in no communication with each other, on their way to the daily and meaningless task, swallowed up by a force which they do not understand:

> Par moments, un ouvrier s'arrêtait, rallumait sa pipe, tandis qu'autour de lui les autres marchaient toujours, *sans un rire, sans une parole dite à un camarade*, les joues terreuses, la face tendue vers Paris, qui, un à un, les dévorait, par la rue béante du Faubourg-Poissonnière. (*Assommoir*, 378).

Zola sensed that life was becoming impersonal, that a world was forming in which all is in movement, but without any sense or identification. He has grasped the ultimate meaning of romanticism. Lamartine, in poems such as «L'Isolement» concentrates on the image of a river which carries in its flow our lives. The problem is simply stated in terms of time. Zola renders more drastically the river of time. The Seine River (real as opposed to Lamartine's allegory) carries away (*charrier*) the physical evidence of man's fall and loss of dignity:

Et il semblait, la nuit, lorsqu'on passait les ponts,

> que la Seine *charriât,* au milieu de la ville endormie, les ordures de la cité, miettes tombées de la table, nœuds de dentelle laissés sur les divans, chevelures oubliées dans les fiacres, billets de banque glissés des corsages, tout ce que la brutalité du désir et le contentement immédiat de l'instinct jettent à la rue, après l'avoir brisé et souillé (*Curée,* 435).

The *Rougon-Macquart* captures man in his last stage of humanity, when, in the *débordement* as Zola would say, of his *appétits,* he has become almost an animal. The next step, which Zola perceived correctly, is the creation of a technology which will satisfy every momentary craving of animal-man. Technology can insure instant luxury, pleasure, to such an extent that it becomes routine and meaningless. This is the final message of Zola's art, even if he himself did not understand it. Aunt Phasie on her deathbed finds an anonymous world arriving in her house because of a train wreck. Who these people are and why they are there, she does not know. But *philosophe* in a way, she understands the meaning of movement, the idea of a modern world constantly on the go, where no one stays put. Earlier in the novel, she merely speculates on the passing trains:

> Souvent, elle croyait reconnaître des visages, celui d'un monsieur à barbe blonde, un Anglais sans doute, qui faisait chaque semaine le voyage de Paris, celui d'une petite dame brune, passant régulièrement le mercredi et le samedi. Mais l'éclair les emportait, elle n'était pas bien sûre de les avoir vus, toutes les faces se noyaient, se confondaient, comme semblables, disparaissant les unes dans les autres (*Bête,* 1032).

Later, convinced more and more that she is being poisoned by her husband, she wonders how these people who pass by can be unaware of her predicament. How can life be so indifferent?

> ... tante Phasie, de son lit de malade, regardait. C'était donc là ce monde, qu'elle aussi voyait passer dans un coup de foudre, depuis un an bientôt qu'elle se traînait de son matelas à sa chaise. ... elle vivait

... clouée là, les yeux sur la fenêtre, sans autre
compagnie que ces trains qui filaient si vite. Toujours elle s'était plainte de ce pays de loups, où
l'on n'avait jamais une visite; et voilà qu'une vraie
troupe débarquait de l'inconnu. Dire que, là-dedans,
parmi ces gens pressés de courir à leurs affaires,
pas un ne se doutait de la chose, de cette saleté
qu'on lui avait mise dans son sel! ... Enfin, il
passait pourtant assez de foule devant chez eux,
des milliers et des milliers de gens; mais tout ça
galopait, ... Et tante Phasie les regardait les uns
après les autres, ces *gens tombés de la lune*, en
réfléchissant que, lorsqu'on est si occupé, il n'était
pas étonnant de marcher dans des choses malpropres
et de n'en rien savoir (*Bête*, 1183-84).

Zola herein has successfully blended a novelistic goal (Phasie's
concern about being poisoned) into a meditation on the meaning
of rapid transit. This passage is a tribute to his empathetic
vision translated into a superior narrative art. That Zola himself
shares some of her feelings is apparent in the following, a
vision of mankind being pulled back and forth (*apporter* and
remporter) in what may be a meaningless perpetual motion:

Ses grands yeux caves de malade regardaient cette
foule inconnue, ces passants du monde en marche,
qu'elle ne reverrait jamais, apportés par la tempête
et remportés par elle (*Bête*, 1188).

The *Rougon-Macquart* does not offer any explanation of man's
ceaseless movement, indifference and cruelty. Camus' *Mythe
de Sisyphe* will make the commentary on man's dignity and
absurdity. It does show, however, the ultimate place of man
in his environment, man controlled, moved about and dehumanized by his inventions. Moving about in great numbers,
he becomes indifferent to himself and his neighbor. The
American playwright, Leroi Jones, in *Dutchman*, does for the
New York subway what Zola implies in his series. We move
about like phantom ships in the night, unaware of our own
identity and blind to the existence of others. In this respect,
the structure of movement proves to be an excellent means to
show man's solitude and alienation.

IV. *The Collapse of Moral Society*

The last quarter of the twentieth century seems a continuation of the collapse of the traditional western moral code and ethic signalled in the writings of Rousseau, and in the *embourgeoisement* produced by the French revolution. Likewise, the emergence of the individual with Rousseau is characterized almost immediately as the Alceste syndrome, in the sense that Rousseauian individualism and egalitarianism break up the collective stability of classicism as seen in the comedies of Molière; the hero convinced of his superiority, the inferiority of society. In his paranoia, the new romantic hero retreats from society, unable to sustain adequately and in a satisfying way social relationships.

Zola's novels show the next step in this evolution away from classic stability. Anticipating the writers of the twentieth century, the *Rougon-Macquart* reveals life patterns as temporary and contingent. No consistent patterns of behavior can be discerned. Saccard of *La Curée* and *L'Argent* is typical of this here-today, gone-tomorrow psychology, representative of a mobile society without roots, changing residences, buying, spending, always in a state of flux. Saccard gives great dinner parties; yet he cannot pay his butcher. Nana is a vast consumer in a consuming society. She rents everything for her dinner party, for as Zola states: «... Nana n'aurait pas trouvé une douzaine de serviettes au fond des ses armoires...» (*Nana*, 1165).

Psychic instability characterizes the creatures of the *Rougon-Macquart*. Projects are conceived with enthusiasm, and are never realized, usually just fading away into nothingness. This is truly a romantic syndrome. It is the books unread of Loti's *Matelot*, sailing the high seas with dreams of becoming a naval officer, but the books turn yellow and the sailor dies on some oriental shore. Incompletion and frustration, two sentiments with romantic origins are intensified in the late nineteenth century and are best illustrated in the novels of Flaubert and Zola, and in the poetry of Mallarmé. The prototype for the modern, bourgeois failure is Frédéric Moreau of Flaubert's *Education sentimentale*. In Zola, the half-formed, incomplete hero, the failure, is represented by the painter Claude Lantier through a series of aborted, visionary paintings which ultimately reveal only chaos and madness. Sandoz rightfully burns Claude's masterpiece (*L'Oeuvre*, 355). Lazare's instability is the major theme of *La Joie de vivre,* the hero who searches vocational meaning throughout the novel. He would be a writer, musician, journalist and scientist. He fails in all of his undertakings; he cannot stay with any project for any length of time. His emotional life is also in a perpetual state of change. He first loves Pauline, then Louise, then back again to Pauline. Constancy of affection or purpose is not in the character of these people. Mama Coupeau of *L'Assommoir,* Honoré's father in *La Débâcle,* the Fouans of *La Terre,* all exhibit temporary patterns of adhesion and affection, which are easily broken as they move on to new affectional configurations. Zola's novels are filled with petty hostilities and cheap reconciliations. Family relationships in *La Terre* can be described as casual, if not indifferent, in periods of relative calm, but vicious and cruel when in a state of upset. Gervaise effectively disappears from the life of the *quartier* in the concluding pages of the novel. No one is interested in Coupeau's death; there are new interests, new subjects of gossip. We see Gervaise only two times in the last pages, doing a grotesque dance imitation of the final days of Coupeau, and then eating something horrible as part of her total degradation. We are not present for her death; she dies hidden, forgotten, and only her odour recalls her to the story. Nana who should be the centerpiece of her own dinner party, is psychologically absent from it: «Depuis le commencement du souper, elle ne semblait plus chez elle. Tout ce monde l'avait noyée et étourdie...» (*Nana,* 1184). This frightening idea is stressed by Zola in succeeding pages:

> Nana avait disparu. Mais personne ne s'inquiétait de son absence. On se passait parfaitement d'elle, chacun se servant, fouillant dans les tiroirs du buffet, pour chercher des petites cuillers, qui manquaient (*Nana,* 1185).

In a drastic manner *La Terre* underlines the alienation of affections. Jean is never truly loved by his wife Françoise: «... il demeurait un *étranger pour sa femme*» (*Terre,* 737). More striking is alienation when revealed in a psychological viewing: Françoise and Jean arrive in their house after the eviction of Lise and Buteau. Françoise turns and looks at her husband:

> Puis, comme Françoise se retournait, elle resta surprise d'apercevoir Jean. Que faisait-il donc chez eux, cet étranger? (*Terre*, 707).

Ionesco makes comedy of such situations in *La Cantatrice Chauve*; the source of this type of alienation may well be found in the opening pages of Flaubert's *L'Education sentimentale*. Frédéric Moreau is the first incarnation of the last stage of the romantic hero in the nineteenth century, that is, the sentimental bourgeois. Flaubert well analyzes the fluctuations in Frédéric's off-and-on devotion to Mme Arnoux. Discouraged in his pursuit of Mme Arnoux, Frédéric receives the news that his friend, Deslauriers, will arrive in Paris. Rapidly, Flaubert paints the ease with which the young hero can tranfer his affections from Mme Arnoux to his childhood friend: «un pareil homme valait toutes les femmes.» (9). Preparations are made to receive the friend in an elegant manner. But finally comes the invitation so long despaired of, to dine *chez Arnoux*. This invitation rekindles the primary image of Mme Arnoux which dominates until the end of the chapter. Returning home:

> ... il entendit quelqu'un qui ronflait, dans le cabinet noir, près de la chambre. C'était l'*autre*. Il n'y pensait plus (*Education sentimentale*, 50).

Deslauriers has effectively been reduced to a zero in the life of Frédéric. Such superficial transfer of allegiance and affection is a basic structural line in Flaubert's novel. The same pattern goes across the *Rougon-Macquart* but in a less sustained manner. Jacques Lantier looks at his sleeping mistress Séverine, after her confession of participation in the murder of her protector, «... comme s'il ne la connaissait point» (*Bête*, 1208). Because of the murder Séverine and her husband become

---

(9) Gustave Flaubert, *L'Education sentimentale* (Paris: Classiques Garnier, 1958), 43. Future reference to this novel will simply give the page number of this edition following the citation.

strangers to each other, much as Thérèse and Laurent do in *Thérèse Raquin* after the murder of Camille:

> ... passant des journées entières sans échanger une parole, allant et venant côte à côte, comme étrangers désormais, indifférents et solitaires (*Bête*, 1220).

Marcelle Jordan senses estrangement from parents once the solid bourgeois couple give in to the fever of speculation on the stock market:

> ... cette maison cossue où elle avait grandi et où elle croyait ne plus trouver que des étrangers (*Argent*, 272).

Conjugal disunion frequently erupts within the series. Chapter X of *La Conquête de Plassans* is pivotal in showing the culmination of a progressive alienation between husband and wife, caused by the intrusion of the abbé Faujas. Zola writes a final paragraph which sums up well all the psychological factors so carefully and minutely prepared in the preceeding pages. Now we know that all is indeed lost. Marthe, returned to some recognition of reality with the departure of Octave (loss of filial love), cries, and we recall what this family had been before the arrival of the intruders. Husband and wife try to console each other, but now that is impossible. The coveting eyes of the priest's family spy on them:

> Sa voix s'attendrissait, il était près lui-même de sangloter. Marthe, navrée, touchée au coeur par ses dernières paroles, allait se jeter dans ses bras. Mais ils eurent peur d'être vus, ils sentirent comme un obstacle entre eux. Alors, ils se séparèrent; tandis que les yeux d'Olympe luisaient toujours, entre les rideaux rouges (*Conquête*, 1012).

Moral collapse in the novels of Zola is related to mental health, and the very foundation of the family, Tante Dide, is the supreme *aliénée*, whose faulty genetic structure resurfaces here and there in future generations. *La Conquête de Plassans* presents the alienation of husband from wife, but it is also

the progressive insanity of Mouret, provoked by the abbé
Faujas, ending up a «stranger» at his own dinner table
(1086), and the dementia of Marthe who daily sinks deeper
into a fake mysticism:

> Marthe ne semblait pas avoir conscience des bou-
> deries de son mari; il restait parfois une semaine
> silencieux, sans qu'elle s'inquiétât ni se fâchât. Elle
> se détachait chaque jour davantage de ce qui l'en-
> tourait (*Conquête,* 1041).

A major example of conjugal disunion is Chapter X of
Pot-Bouille. The stroke and death of M. Vabre allow Zola
to create a very complex structure in which multiple layers of
the psyche are presented simultaneously in a manner anticipating the high psychological art of the twentieth century novel.
Clotilde sends for her husband whom she knows to be at the
apartment of his mistress. Octave gives Duveyrier the news:
«Votre beau-père se meurt» (*P. B.,* 197). Psychologically, it
is almost impossible for Duveyrier to concentrate on this news,
for his mistress has fled, clearing the apartment of everything.
To the news of his father-in-law's death, Duveyrier poses other
questions to Octave as they return home: «Croyez-vous qu'elle
me pardonne?» (198); «N'est-ce pas? ce que j'ai de mieux à
faire est encore de me remettre avec ma femme, en attendant?»
(*Ibid.*). Clotilde receives from Octave the news of the flight
of the mistress. Her reaction is similar to that of her husband,
thoughts of her dying father are replaced by desperate musings
on what reconciliation with the husband will mean for her,
the resuming of conjugal relations which she loathes:

> Clotilde eut un geste désespéré. ... Ce n'était pas
> assez de perdre son père, il fallait encore que ce
> malheur servît de prétexte à un rapprochement avec
> son mari! ... elle tremblait de ne pouvoir se refuser
> à l'abominable corvée (*P. B.,* 199).

This is the situation of the ultimate bourgeois wife as seen by
Zola, a woman who prefers that her husband have a mistress
so that she may be left alone with her ego. Zola stresses their
solitude:

> Et, en face du vieillard dont le râle emplissait la

chambre d'un frisson, elle et son mari restèrent
seuls (*P. B.,* 200).

In this novel we see Zola successfully engaged in the probing
of the bourgeois psyche. Duveyrier at the death bed of his
father-in-law is seen with a mind filled and occupied with
several matters at the same time: the father-in-law has not left
a will and there is concern over who will inherit; embarrass-
ment that his wife knows about his affair; his need to reconcile
with his wife; but above all, a lingering lust for the lost
mistress. Framed by speech patterns concerning the will, Zola
probes Duveyrier's mind, especially the minute details of his
erotic imagination where he pictures Clarisse undressing. The
scene is perfect in its composition, and Zola is thus able to
transmit to us the inauthenticity of this man of pretended
moral values. His vocalized demand for church rites for the
father-in-law collides with his erotic thoughts:

> Mais Duveyrier, tiré de ses souvenirs sur Clarisse,
> dont il se rappelait justement la façon d'enfiler ses
> bas, une cuisse en l'air, réclama les sacrements avec
> violence (*P. B.,* 208).

The idea of a latent animosity between the sexes is especially evident in *Son Excellence Eugène Rougon.* Rougon
finds total satisfaction in domination of others through politics
while Clorinde mixes sex and politics. The novel is the most
sado-masochistic of the series, sex being used as an instrument
of domination and revenge. Eugène tries to attack Clorinde
sexually. She, however, has a whip in her hand and appears
as a kind of animal tamer:

> L'odeur forte de l'écurie le grisait; l'ombre, chaude
> d'une buée animale, l'encourageait à tout risquer.
> Alors, le jeu changea (*Son Excellence,* 118).

Indeed, the game changes directions throughout the novel, first
Eugène dominating, then Clorinde. This looks like a rough
reworking of *Les Liaisons dangereuses,* with a degree of sadism
unknown in the latter. In Chapter IX, Clorinde burns Eugène's
forehead with a cigarette and threatens to ring and accuse him
of attack: «Clorinde riait d'un air de victoire» (*Son Excellence,*

239). Secretly delighted that Rougon has lost his portfolio, Zola describes her as «... goûtant sans hâte, phrase à phrase, la volupté de se montrer enfin à lui en ennemie implacable et vengée» (*Son Excellence,* 341). It would appear that Clorinde has finally slept with the Emperor. She is seen at a charity ball wearing a real dog collar in black velvet (a gift from the Emperor) with the legend: «*J'appartiens à mon maître*» (*Son Excellence,* 333; the italics are Zola's).

Pot-Bouille is a novel of dominating women. Mme Josserand teaches her daughters that the male is the enemy, an inferior to be manipulated. Nana the avenger reveals her basic hatred for men: «... en mâchant de sourds jurons contre les hommes» (*Nana,* 1136); «Cela l'enchantait de faire poser les hommes» (*Nana,* 1142); «Oh! que les hommes m'embêtent» (*Nana,* 1359). She finds much comfort in lesbian friendship with Satin. In both *Pot-Bouille* and *La Joie de vivre* (Mme Chanteau), Zola creates formidable female war-machines whose physiques alone strike fear into male hearts.

The ultimate of all these steps toward alienation is found in the narcissism of several of the protagonists. Renée and Maxime of *La Curée* are excellent examples, Renée appearing as a little doll only concerned with the adornment of her body which she spends hours admiring. Maxime seems to be inverted; Zola speaks of him as a type of *femme manquée,* too pretty, too refined, too self-centered. Nana is constantly bored, one of her great pleasures is studying her naked body in a mirror. All that gives her pleasure is her beauty. She is an exhibitionist:

> ... elle ne gardait que le souci de sa beauté, un soin continuel de se visiter, de se laver, de se parfumer partout, avec l'orgueil de pouvoir se mettre nue, à chaque instant et devant n'importe qui, sans avoir à rougir (*Nana,* 1358).

These are single atoms whirling about in solitary spaces, coming into contact only with themselves.

If the ideology of the impressionistic thrust has something to do with growth and with decay (10), construction and

---

(10) Hauser, *Social History of Art,* II, 872.

destruction, then it seems an ideal vehicle for Zola to use to show the collapse of moral order during the Second Empire. Count Muffat knows what Nana is doing to him and what this means symbolically:

> Il eut un instant conscience des accidents du mal, il vit la désorganisation apportée par ce ferment, lui empoisonné, sa famille détruite, un coin de société qui craquait et s'effondrait (*Nana*, 1270-1271).

Zola's optimistic and sentimental thesis runs counter-current to the evidence he has presented in the twenty volumes. He wants to tell us not to give up, and to have hope for a better life for man. His great principle as we know is that of life, that life ultimately conquers death through the renewal of the human race. As Albine is being buried, Désirée runs up to her brother, the priest, announcing that «... la vache a fait un veau!» (*Faute*, 1527). As Jeanne is buried, the sun shines bright on an April Paris and «Dans le cimetière, un pinson chantait» (*Page*, 1083). All of the houses of Bonneville have been destroyed by the sea (*Joie*, 1112), but a new sheltered city will be built. Certain characters seem to be prophets of the city of the future: Denise will try to humanize the capitalism of her husband, Octave; Pauline seems to have arrived at some inner peace and understanding of her former love, Lazare, and his wife, Louise, who become like her children at the conclusion of *La Joie de vivre*. Dr. Pascal, the ideal Zola hero, dies, but leaves Clotilde and their child to the future for which they have been prepared because of the education he has given her. The reality which Zola would like to believe in, and which intrudes sometimes through event and person, remains in sharp contrast to the downward movement of the *Rougon-Macquart*. The work is an «impression» of decay, destruction, disintegration as far as the narrative structure is concerned. The process of creativity and becoming seems almost exclusively confined to descriptions of nature, above all the play of light and color. It is to this natural ascendancy that Zola would have us mold human behavior. The narrative modes do not convince us that there is an upward surge. Rather we have the impressions of fugitive moments in disintegrating lives, lives which hardly seem worth living. Movement, destruction, decay, disintegration are reflected also in the language.

CHAPTER V

THE LANGUAGE OF ZOLA

Impressionism in painting is poorly represented by Zola's *L'Oeuvre* which, while exposing many of the theories of that group of painters, more properly should be viewed as eclectic insofar as the novel discusses and fuses in Claude Lantier, many theories of art, some of which have nothing to do with the impressionistic trend. The main obsession of Claude, however, is an impressionistic one, as he seeks the true colors of nature, which are always seen as changing, «decomposing»:

> ... la nature baignait dans de la vraie lumière, sous le jeu des reflets et la continuelle décomposition des couleurs (*Oeuvre,* 204).

Color decomposition, which is scientifically correct, when translated to psychology, means for Claude, the inability to paint, frustration at not realizing the ideal in the work of art: «... il sentait la composition craquer et crouler sous ses doigts» (*Oeuvre,* 234).

Impressionistic color theories are transferred to literature by Zola, and out of them he has created the rich light and color descriptions of the *Rougon-Macquart.* The nuanced, descriptive layers, however, may be seen as a stylistic manifestation of a vast ideological system in which the basic principle is one of change and becoming, states of creation and states of decay. This seems to be the basis of the aesthetic tension found in the twenty novels. Claude's movement is downward; Dr Pascal hopes to reverse that trend through his studies.

Pascal, as Zola's spokesman, sees movement as life's fundamental structure:

> La vie n'est qu'un mouvement, et l'hérédité étant le mouvement communiqué, les cellules, dans leur multiplication les unes des autres, se poussaient, se foulaient, se casaient, en déployant chacune l'effort héréditaire (*Pascal*, 946).

To Pascal, life is composed of perpetual transformations, recyclings, new futures: «Il y avait donc là un perpétuel devenir, une transformation constante dans cet effort communiqué, cette puissance transmise...» (*Pascal*, 947). While some societies might view perpetual motion with apprehension, the good humanitarian doctor exalts in it: «Et l'humanité roule, charriant tout!» (*Pascal*, 1019).

This philosophy translated into literary language means that the fundamental style of Emile Zola is that of movement (of which the light and color patterns are the most manifest descriptive aspects), change, flux, transformation. Verbal language is, of course, by its very nature, movement, but with no other writer of the nineteenth century does it pervade, consistently, and in an extreme manner, the entire structure, from the first volume to the last. Very early in his career Zola found his style; it remains with him, always accelerating, until the end.

I. A Zola Glossary

Movement means, in Zola, two fundamental urges which translate into a language of harmony and creation, and also into a language of violence and destruction.

The language of destruction encompasses the atmospheres of decay and decomposition which fill so many of the novels, especially *L'Assommoir*. It is also the brutal acts performed by the *mâle*, the *bête*, from simple slapping, to wife beating, rape, and on to arson, murder and train wrecks. Destruction includes natural calamity (the hail storm of *La Terre*), insurrections and war. It also means socialist theory and anarchistic upheaval and leveling of the capitalist system (the detonation of the mine in *Germinal*, the burning of Paris in *La Débâcle*).

The language of creation reflects the constant renewal of the earth, the wonder and mystery of human fertility, amazement at the marvel of the new industries, the new machines, or simply the artistic urge (Claude Lantier and Sandoz of *L'Oeuvre*).

This glossary is not all-inclusive but selectively representative, based on an observed frequency across the *Rougon-Macquart*. The idea was to keep the list to a minimum; consequently, nouns have been eliminated when the equivalent verb form is listed and vice-versa. The same applies for adjectives. Color and light nouns, adjectives, and verbs have also been eliminated since their density is apparent from the discussion in Chapter II. The minimal list of adjectives, adverbs, and adverbial expressions should be constantly kept in mind since they so repetitiously combine with the nouns and verbs in single syntactical units. This example from *La Joie de vivre* is typical of the type of modification to be expected: «Mais cet expédient paraissait répugner à la mère *chaque* jour *davantage*» (889).

Furthermore, there are adjectival and adverbial fields which surround the idea of movement, changing the tone, sometimes creatively and optimistically, but more often, indicating rough and drastic qualification. The *Rougon-Macquart,* more often than not, is a cruel world of insensitive peasants, bourgeois, and criminals without conscience. Unified fields of rough and brutal actions are thus found in the adjectives: *rude, vengeur, violent, impitoyable, enragé, éreinté, furieux*; in the adverbs: *violemment, rudement, brutalement.* Nana gets up from a table, but how? «Mais Nana s'était levée brutalement...» (*Nana*, 1184).

It is not to be implied that there is only movement. Movement is central and organic to the work, but other style fields, usually peculiar to the needs of the single novel, are also operative. Technical vocabularies must dominate the more trade-oriented novels. *L'Assommoir* must rely heavily on constructs hammering away at the idea of alcoholism, the style must betray the atmosphere of the slums, the speech of the people.

Selected entries of the glossary will be commented.

Verb: *abattre, aller* plus participle, (*s*) *anéantir, assommer, augmenter, avaler, battre, bombarder, brandir, briser, brutaliser, canonner, (ne pas) cesser, charrier, claquer, commencer, couler, craquer, crever, croiser, croître, culbuter, (ne pas) désemplir, (se) détruire, disparaître, ébranler, échapper, (s') élargir, emplir, empoigner, emporter, enfanter, engouffrer, ensanglanter, envahir, éparpiller, (se) fendre, flotter, grandir, grossir, inonder, jeter, manger, massacrer, (se) multiplier, nettoyer, noyer, pousser, recommencer, renverser, révolutionner, submerger, tomber, trembler, vaincre, (se) venger.*

Noun: *affaissement, assourdissement, battement, bouleversement, bourdonnement, bousculade, branle, changement, clameur, débâcle, déballage, débandade, débauche, débordement, débris, déchéance, dégringolade, déroulement, éblouissement, éboulement, éclaboussement, éclosion, écrasement, écroulement, effondrement, encombrement, entassement, entraînement, étalage, fécondation, flot, flux, fracas, galop, grondement, hurlement, inondation, pullulement, roulement, secousse, va-et-vient.*

Adjective: *chaque, continu, continuel, croissant, englouti, flottant, inépuisable, ininterrompu, intarissable, interminable, successif.*

Adverbial: *davantage, de plus en plus, d'heure en heure, encore, pêle-mêle, peu à peu, toujours.*

Preposition: *sans,* in combinations such as: *sans relâche, sans cesse, sans fin.*

aller plus participle. On-going processes are rendered in the imperfect, then strengthened by the addition of the participle. It can indicate real physical movement or psychological states. Pauline has ordered Louise from the house, creating a tension and sorrow in the inhabitants: «... tous sentaient le déchirement intérieur, la blessure dont ils ne parlaient pas et qui allait en s'agrandissant» (*Joie*, 951).

(s')anéantir. After the departure of Louise the house is plunged into a total silence which seems to swallow up and efface the very structure: «Le silence recommença, un lourd silence où la maison entière semblait s'anéantir» (*Joie*, 947). In the opening pages of *Pot-Bouille* we are introduced to the tyrannical Madame Josserand, a powerful, corpulent *femme forte,* who exercises dictatorial powers over her daughters and meek husband. In some six pages we are presented with a field of destructive movement, the effectiveness of which is heightened by Zola's concentration on her massive vulgarity

— 146 —

joined, ironically, with her concern over her edition of the passive Lamartine:

> Sa femme l'anéantissait, quand elle étalait cette gorge de géante, dont il croyait sentir l'écroulement sur sa nuque (24).
> Et, pour échapper à la nudité terrifiante de sa femme... (*Ibid.*).
> ... elle écrasa magistralement son mari sous un haussement de ses terribles épaules (25).
> ... retourna dans la salle à manger, en tenant son Lamartine étroitement serré sous la chair débordante de son bras (28).
> Elle se leva, s'avança vers lui, en brandissant son Lamartine (30).

assommer. As a typical verb of the *Rougon-Macquart,* it is used in its primary sense: «On trouvait le père et la mère en travers des portes, *assommés* par le calvados...» (*Joie,* 898), and also competes with *abattre*: «... un mari qui assommait sa femme, hurlante...» (*Bête,* 1119). It betrays the aggressive, assaulting actions of men like Saccard pouncing on a passive Paris. The first minister of France, his brother Eugène Rougon knows he must use his fists: «... je suis un homme nouveau, je n'ai que mes poings.» (*Son Excellence,* 77); consequently: «Moi, j'assomme...» «*Ibid.*). It reveals both moral turpitude and physical violence. The word leads, of course, to the motif of *L'Assommoir.*

assourdissement. A noun for sound impression, it is the strongest term possible, beyond *bruit* and *vacarme.* «Maintenant, c'était une polka que sifflait le piston; et, pendant que *l'assourdissement recommençait...*» (*Germinal,* 1270).

augmenter. One of the most frequently used verbs of Zola, for both abstract and physical movement: «... l'indiscipline augmentait...» (*Débâcle,* 505); «... la confusion *augmentait d'heure en heure...*» (*Débâcle,* 494); «Leur nombre *augmentait toujours...*» (*Germinal,* 1396); «... en face de cette neige dont la couche *augmentait toujours...*» (*Bête,* 1166). Sometimes the verb is saying the same thing as the noun subject and the adverb, the three parts all indicating movement: «La bousculade augmentait toujours» (*Oeuvre,* 292).

bourdonnement. Without support, the noun remains simply

descriptive in the literary sense: «... tandis qu'un bourdonnement d'activité agitait les vieux bâtiments de l'auberge» (*Terre*, 505). Surrounded by supporting adverb, adjective and explaining second noun, it gives a high literary impression of confussion and continuity as in this description of the dying Mme Chanteau: «... de la chambre sortait *encore*, le *bourdonnement* confus, le *flux* de paroles *intarissables* de la mourante» (*Joie*, 976).

brutaliser. While brutal actions in themselves may not be necessarily thought of as movement, *brutaliser* combines so frequently with visions of movement that it must be considered part of its constellation. The starving wives of the miners push into Maigrat's store with outstretched arms beseeching food, and he in turn pushes them out: «... il les poussa vers la porte. Comme elles insistaient, suppliantes, il en brutalisa une» (*Germinal*, 1356).

ne pas cesser. The negative affirmation of movement: «Le troupeau ne cessait pas...» (*Débâcle*, 750).

continuel; continuellement. With the conjunction *et*, the adverbs *encore* and *toujours, continuel, continuellement* would form the basis for the decisive parody of the style of Zola. They are used thousands of times in the *Rougon-Macquart*; they are over-used. *Continuel* appears commonly in the affective position and recreates impressions of on-going joy: «... au milieu d'un *continuel* éclat de gaieté» (*Bête*, 998); a distant storm: «... quelque orage devait passer au loin, car l'on entendait un *continuel roulement* de foudre» (*Pascal*, 1002); or disorderly groupings: «... les *continuels* attroupements de foule barrant les trottoirs» (*Débâcle*, 859). Burning gas jets are geometrically spaced («at the back of dark corners, along narrow corridors») through prepositional phrases in the second clause of the following description:

Les soupiraux, de place en place, jetaient une clarté pâle; *et, au fond* des coins noirs, *le long* d'étroits corridors, des becs de gaz brûlaient, continuellement (*Bonheur*, 426).

Uninterrupted activity is stressed by putting the adverb first: «*Continuellement*, du monde entrait et sortait...» (*Débâcle*, 495). It is most effective when a verb of movement is followed by the adverb with the subject left to last: «... d'où s'élevait continuellement une grosse colonne de fumée noire...» (*Débâcle,* 735); «... et c'était là que, depuis le matin, défilaient continuellement des hommes» (*Germinal,* 1287).

craquer. This is a prototypical Zola verb. It can be used in its normal sense, meaning to produce a dry sound: «Seules, les mousses gelées craquaient sous les talons...» (*Germinal,* 1385). Combined with a verb of piling up, it contributes to the style of exaggeration. All purchases in the department store are brought to a central round-up point, and collapse is intimated: «Tout cela *s'empilait* sur la chaise, les paquets *montaient,* faisaient *craquer* le bois...» (*Bonheur,* 637); the flat boats in the Seine seem about to collapse with the weight of yellow apples as they are perceived by Christine and Claude during a lightning storm: «... les toues alignées sur quatre rangs avaient flambé, avec les tas de pommes jaunes dont elles craquaient» (*Oeuvre,* 13); Saccard observes the place de la Bourse in the hot, noonday sun. Is the *craquement* caused by the heat of the sun rays or the fever of speculation?

> La chaleur était accablante, un soleil ardent tombait d'aplomb, blanchissant les marches ... chauffait le péristyle d'un air lourd et embrasé de four; et les chaises vides craquaient dans ces flammes, tandis que les spéculateurs, debout, cherchaient les minces raies d'ombres des colonnes (*Argent,* 195).

The verb is reinforced with simile: «Le vent redoublait de violence, la fenêtre *craquait* comme sous des coups de bélier» (*Débâcle,* 800).

crever. This verb is in approximately the same situation as *craquer,* but also forms part of the metaphorical system of the popular spoken language. In this example it transposes the notion of crowding («There were a lot of people in the cabarets») to a visual impression of swelling, bursting: «... les cabarets crevaient de monde...» (*Germinal,* 1265).

croître, croissant. Variants of *augmenter:* «... la cohue croissante de la ducasse» (*Germinal,* 1264); «... le bruit croissant des conversations...» (*Argent,* 295); «Pauline luttait contre l'asphyxie croissante du petit être misérable...» (*Joie,* 1101); «... un besoin croissant de l'ordure...» (*Argent,* 214); «Pascal resta désarmé, envahi d'une tristesse croissante» (*Pas-*

cal, 984). A description from *La Débâcle* is fashioned like a piece of modern expressionistic photography, a background of general disorder (*bousculade croissante*) becoming a specific mix of concrete and abstract parts (*poings, jurons, larmes*) which may be seen as a foreground of fists, mouths (*jurons*), eyes (*larmes*).

> ... le pitoyable spectacle s'assombrissait,, le nombre des déménageurs et des fuyards devenait plus grand, parmi la bousculade croissante, les poings tendus, les jurons et les larmes (432).

crouler, écroulement. These items are part of the visionary vocabulary of Zola, but they can be used to record something falling: «... le chaume croulait entre les murs fumants» (*Joie,* 1067).

culbuter. Truly a *mot-clé* of the *Rougon-Macquart,* this verb is related to *basculer, dégringoler, tomber.* Françoise, in her jealousy of Jacques Lantier's affair with Séverine plans to «... culbuter le train...» (*Bête,* 1249), with dreams of destroying all life, including her own. In Zola the verb frequently means sexual assault: «... la gamine culbutée dans l'escalier...» (*Argent,* 47); it is obsessively employed in *Germinal*: «... les galants les culbutaient sur les poutres, derrière les bois, dans les berlines» (*Germinal,* 1240), and especially in *La Terre* (442, 443, 456, 476, 504, 565, 589, 614, 621, 631, 642, 675). Saccard ponders the fate of his projected *Banque Universelle* and the collapse of others:

> Quand aux puissantes maisons de crédit qui vous semblent si prospères, attendez qu'une d'elles fasse le saut, et vous les verrez toutes culbuter à la file... (*Argent,* 16).

Saccard's plans, however, are being made in the final days of the Empire. He senses impending doom. Thus, as in the final pages of *La Débâcle,* verbs of movement and collapse are taking on metaphorical tints and whole fields of metaphorical movement join in tight clusters, *culbuter, crouler, emporter, débâcle, appétits,* in which all literal meaning is effaced. The following from *L'Argent* gives some idea of this procedure:

Lui, une fois encore, était par terre: est-ce que cet empire, qui l'avait fait, allait comme lui *culbuter, croulant* tout d'un coup de la destinée la plus haute à la plus misérable? Ah! depuis douze ans, qu'il l'avait aimé et défendu, ce régime où il s'était senti vivre, *pousser, se gorger de sève,* ainsi que l'arbre dont les racines *plongent* dans le terreau qui lui convient! Mais, si son frère voulait l'en *arracher,* si on le retranchait de ceux qui épuisaient le *sol gras des jouissances,* que tout fût donc *emporté, dans la grande débâcle finale des nuits de fête!* (15).

débâcle. Another key word of the *Rougon-Macquart* which utilizes all possible definitions, and confuses them. On at least one occasion the noun is used in its fundamental sense «... rupture de la couche de glace dont les morceaux sont emportés par le courant» (*Le Petit Robert,* 403); «... par la terrifiante débâcle des étangs glacés...» (*Débâcle,* 447). It may indicate the formless remains of a train wreck: «... une débâcle informe de débris» (*Bête,* 1260). In the sense of «fuite soudaine» (*Le Petit Robert,* 403), it indicates the economic apprehensions of Second Empire bourgeois husbands who dread the credit card syndrome of the countless Emma Bovarys to whom they are married. M. Marty fears his wife's extravagances which make him «... assiste à la débâcle de ses appointements, si chèrement gagnés.» (*Bonheur,* 467); or «... la débâcle de ses économies» (*P. B.,* 258). In *La Joie de vivre* the family can purchase the house at Bonneville through «... une occasion pêchée dans la débâcle d'un client insolvable» (822). Lazare never stays long with any one project or idea, always fishing in the sea of human knowledge for his one true vocation, and never finding it: «Un besoin d'ordre persistait, dans cette débâcle de sa vie» (*Joie,* 1043). In its literal meaning *débâcle* does relate to *débandade.* In Zola, the two words seem almost interchangeable. But *débâcle* heightens the idea of movement disorder, disarray, and well serves the purpose of revealing the materialistic, thing oriented, modern world. The department store is a prime symbol of this materialism: «... cette *débâcle* de marchandises qui *tombait* chez lui...» (*Bonheur,* 422). The following example suggests that what may be considered hyperbolic or figurative by the average French speaker is just normal in Zola: Pauline receives her poor for the distribution of alms and medical supplies: «C'était une débâcle de galopins mal mouchés...» (*Joie,* 1002). *Garçon* is not simply changed into the visually picturesque *gamin,* but the verbally derived noun *galopin* (*galoper*). Would not the average person have written *débandade* and not *débâcle?* The confusion is normal to Zola, and in the long run seems overdone. But this example is a highly artistic one of movement. It seems to indicate a kind of lexical synesthesia with Zola in which various types of movement, physical or of the mind, blend; a fusion of semantic function which the dictionary and the analytical mind would want to keep neatly separated. These are not the mental procedures of a thinker, but those of the intuitive artist-writer synthesizing his perceptions of the exterior world.

The next step is to move *débâcle* out of its literal and general figurative connotations into the metaphorical realm. Thus a first menstruation becomes «... la débâcle de cette marée de sang...» (*Joie,* 852); the retreat of the defeated French army, whipped by a metaphorical wind: «... la débâcle d'une armée détruite, fouettée du vent fou de la panique» (*Débâcle,* 452). As with *L'Assommoir,* a word surges up from its literal dictionary meaning and becomes a literary, an aesthetic principle, as title, governing the artistic use of the multiple linguistic parts directed toward it.

déballage. «... on peut s'attendre à un déballage d'histoires fâcheuses...» (*Bête,* 1116). The noun typifies Zola's penchant for the familiar usage over the literal. Thus properly, this example means avowal, confession. With his impulse toward movement, however, does not the primary meaning of the verb find itself operative within the special system of Zola, «sortir et étaler» (*Le Petit Robert,* 403)?

débandade. How do we possibly separate *débâcle, débandade, débauche, débris?* Débris can be the same as *débandade:*

> Et, chez les Rougon, le soir, au dessert, des rires *montaient* dans la buée de la table, toute chaude encore des *débris* du dîner (*Fortune,* 314).

The meanings seem to fuse in Zola's mind, only to be separated at other times, as when *débris* can be seen in a state of *débandade:* «... les *débris* arrivaient *débandés*...» (*Débâcle,* 442). This noun in its strictest definition, «... le fait de se disperser rapidement et en tous sens» (*Le Petit Robert,* 404), exactly represents the chaos and the confusion of the *Rougon-Macquart.* Sprinkled judiciously across the early volumes, this noun with its variations in other parts of speech, starts appearing in noticeable numbers in *Pot-Bouille* and they increase across the remaining ten volumes in a maddening manner. A consistent pattern is the use of the adverbial expression *à la débandade:*

> Le parc avait, dans cet heureux verger, une *gami-nerie* de buissons *s'en allant à la débandade...* (*Faute,* 1366);

the principle is evident, each part of the clause is a single rein-forcement of the other parts, the same idea is restated. Other examples are: «Toute la maison s'en allait à la débandade...» (*Joie,* 811); «Des chaises et des fauteuils antiques traînaient à la débandade» (*Pascal,* 918). The pronominal verb form is also utilized: «Des chaises dépaillées *se débandaient,* parmi des chevalets boiteux» (*Oeuvre,* 22); «... tandis que, sur les plan-ches de l'ancienne fruiterie restées en place, se débandaient quelques moulages d'antiques...» (*Oeuvre,* 66).

The noun can be used to indicate general instability and disorder, either with the definite or the indefinite article: «... la débandade continuait...» (*Débâcle,* 428); «Il y eut une déban-dade, la fosse déserte leur appartint» (*Germinal,* 1423); «Une débandade énorme vida la salle» (*Oeuvre,* 60). It then is subjected to a series of dazzling stylistic manipulations. People, beasts and vehicles are presented in rapid motion:

> Alors, il se produisit une débandade parmi les femmes, toutes couraient... (*Germinal,* 1226).
> ... la débandade de la sortie emplit longuement les corridors (*Bonheur,* 668).
> ... au milieu de cette débandade de filles lâchées à travers les quatre étages...» (*Nana,* 1224).
> ... des troupeaux fermaient la colonne, une déban-dade de grands boeufs piétinant dans un flot de poussière... (*Débâcle,* 463).
> ... c'était une débandade d'autres voitures, isolées, comme échouées sur l'herbe, un pêle-mêle de roues, d'attelages jetés en tous sens, côte à côte, de biais, en travers, tête contre tête (*Nana,* 1381).

These texts have been cited in some detail to give an idea of the extent of these movement fields of which *débandade* seems to be just the precipitating element. The process is to take a single stable element such as *troupeau* and to transform it into an element of velocity, *débandade*.

Débandade sets fragmented wholes in motion: «... la débandade de leurs pieds...» (*Germinal*, 1374); «Il y eut une débandade, un galop de gros souliers» (*Joie*, 986). But the setting in motion of inanimate objects is the most arresting use of *débandade*. Frequently, since many of the scenes describe lavishly decorated tables, with silver, crystal, candles and food, we are close to the art of the still-life. The disarray of chairs and toilet articles leans suspiciously toward what will be German expressionism:

> Une grande psyché faisait face à une toilette de marbre blanc, garnie d'une débandade de flacons et de boîtes de cristal, pour les huiles, les essences et les poudres. (*Nana*, 1207).
> ... il assistait aux détails intimes d'une toilette de femme, dans la débandade des pots et des cuvettes, au milieu de cette odeur si forte et si douce. (*Nana*, 1213).
> ... vingt femmes entassées, une débandade de savons et de bouteilles d'eau de lavande...» (*Nana*, 1223).
> Et Chanteau demeura seul, devant la table encombrée de la débandade du couvert. (*Joie*, 1081).
> ... promenant ses regards sur la vaisselle de la table et la débandade des chaises... (*Joie*, 1094).
> ... une débandade de moulages, disparaissant plus bas sous une forêt de tés et d'équerres, sous un amas de planches à laver, retenues en paquets par des bretelles (*Oeuvre*, 59).

The combination of movement and sound is impressive. The women of the mines, after having castrated Maigrat, are led by the impassioned La Brûlé. Here *débandade* is merely the focusing of movement, which is implied throughout the sentence, accompanied by the howls and screams of the women who seem more like beasts than human beings:

> La Brûlé, alors, planta tout le paquet au bout de son bâton; et, le portant en l'air, le promenant ainsi

qu'un drapeau, elle se lança sur la route, suivie de la débandade hurlante des femmes (*Germinal,* 1453).

Sound is effectively transmitted in the same novel where the rapid movement is accompanied by the tears of the women and the animal-like howlings of their children:

Il faisait presque nuit, et la pluie redoublait, qu'elles emplissaient encore le coron de leurs larmes, au milieu de la débandade glapissante des enfants (*Germinal,* 1292).

Or there may be no sound whatsoever: «... la débandade silencieuse...» (*Débâcle,* 750).

Precipitous movement properly enters the figurative field in *La Débâcle* where the poorly organized French army cannot be explained as a disciplined entity. It is seen as «... une débandade de troupeau mené à l'abattoir» (413), or more pitifully as «... une débandade de gueux, couverts de plaies...» (779).

The past participle form as adjective is frequently used, but not as extensively as the noun.

débauche; déchéance. From physical disorder and randomness as with *débandade,* it is only a step to moral disorder, to *débauche* and *appétit.* From the primary meaning of excess in sensual pleasure there is derived the figurative meaning: «usage déréglé de quelque chose» (*Le Petit Robert,* 404). The literal meaning, of course, dominates (*Argent,* 53, 209; *Bête,* 1016; *Germinal,* 1455), leading into figurative and allegorical fields such as this personification from *L'Argent*:

... il n'y avait pas de soir où la ville en feu n'étincelât sous les étoiles, ainsi qu'un colossal palais au fond duquel la débauche veillait jusqu'à l'aube (253).

The word also means augmentation, increase: «Il y eut une débauche de suppléments...» (*Bonheur,* 552), signifying additional lunch and drink orders in the store's canteen, or *étalage,* as found in this description of the foliage in a hothouse:

Mais, à mesure que leurs regards s'enfonçaient dans

les coins de la serre, l'obscurité s'emplissait d'une débauche de feuilles et de tiges plus furieuse (*Curée*, 487).

It is uncanny how purely abstract movements (*déchéance*) which linguistically are evolved from real movements (*déchoir*) will be arranged with strong patterns of rising and falling: «... elle se relevait de cette déchéance en ne le jugeant pas indigne d'elle...» (*Argent*, 163).

déborder; débordement. These forms relate to *débandade* in that they express another aspect of movement, the idea of overflow. Zola's usage is normal, in spite of an abnormal frequency, with both abstract and physical meanings. Furthermore, the diversity of fields covered is unusual. Emotional states are seen as overflowing: indignation (*Germinal*, 1275); hope (*Joie*, 1047); anger (*Débâcle*, 516); tenderness (*Rêve*, 941); love of life ,*Joie*, 856). It also infects typical Zolian thematic fields: success: «Saccard, débordant de son succès...» (*Argent*, 199); sexual excess: «Lui, protégé par ses débordements du quartier latin...» (*Joie*, 869; *Oeuvre*, 69); prostitution: «... le torrent débordé de la prostitution» (*Argent*, 254). «Overflow» meets the central word of the series, *appétit*, in the concluding volume: «... par le débordement des appétits, par cette impulsion essentiellement moderne...» (*Pascal*, 1015).

Débordement animates inanimate objects. There are overflowing trunks, *armoires*, provisions and tables:

> ... elle regardait les malles débordantes, où pas un chiffon d'épouse ni de maîtresse ne traînait... (*Argent*, 374).
> Près de la fenêtre, une vieille armoire normande immense, débordait d'un fouillis d'objets extraordinaires... (*Joie*, 838).
> Des provisions débordaient des râteliers et des armoires (*Germinal*, 1195).
> ... la table débordait de livres de science et de morceaux de musique (*Joie*, 1036).

The surge of people, first caught by Victor Hugo in *Notre-Dame de Paris,* as *fleuve, inondation,* is also found in Zola. A crowded scene at the Bourse: «... les spéculateurs débordaient, s'écrasaient» (*Argent*, 32); a farmer inflates his prices, taking advantage of the famine conditions of war:

> Il vendait sans trop voler, empochait l'argent, livrait la marchandise; si bien que les acheteurs, toujours plus nombreux, le débordant, l'étourdissant... (*Débâcle*, 472).

The terrifying Madame Josserand is seen as an Ionescan growth of overflowing flesh which threatens to invade: «... quand il voyait en face d'elles le visage rigide de leur mère, énorme et débordante dans une vieille robe de soie verte» (*P. B.*, 322).

dégringolade. The figurative and familiar sense dominates (*Argent*, 106, 276, 307). The noun equivalent of the verb effectively conveys downward precipitous movement with sound in *L'Oeuvre*: «La dégringolade assourdie des souliers le long des marches alla en s'affaiblissant...» (89).

dérouler; déroulement. The progressive revelation of a perspective, usually a landscape: «C'était le fleuve se déroulant dans les vastes prairies...» (*Débâcle*, 556); «... le déroulement des prés noirs...» (*Débâcle*, 526). It can signify on-going sound in which specific sound is delineated: «Dans ce déroulement continu du torrent, les insurgés distinguaient des lamentations aigres de tocsin» (*Fortune*, 162). These forms, habitually used with the modern descriptive writers, relate to (*se*)*dresser*, (*s*)*allonger*, (*s*)*élargir*: «La Souleiade ... élargissait son silence nocturne...» (*Pascal*, 994); «... la vaste plaine s'élargissait dans la radieuse lumière...» (*Débâcle*, 571); «A gauche, la plaine s'élargit, immense tapis vert...» (*Fortune*, 162); Claude's dramatic gesture extends his arm to the Place de la Concorde: «Son geste s'élargissait, descendait jusqu'à la place de la Concorde...» (*Oeuvre*, 135).

(*ne pas*) *désemplir*. Intransitive verb used negatively with the sense of being constantly full; see *ne pas cesser*. These negative patterns are common: «... devant un débit de boissons qui ne désemplissait pas» (*Débâcle*, 461).

éboulement. A noun for *Germinal*, of course, but also very effective in *L'Oeuvre*, underlining Christine's initial fright at Claude's studio:

> Mais ce dont elle s'effrayait surtout, c'était des esquisses pendues aux murs, sans cadres, un flot épais d'esquisses qui descendait jusqu'au sol, où il s'amassait en un éboulement de toiles jetées pêle-mêle (23).

ébranler; ébranlement. The *Rougon-Macquart* is filled with the tremblings caused by the new machines, by insurrections, upheavals and wars. Nature trembles in sexual accord with the personnages, Zola's primal unions. Exaggerated movement is recorded in the then considered scandalous mating of the bull and the cow in *La Terre*: «César monta sur la Coliche, d'un saut brusque, avec une lourdeur puissante qui *ébranla le sol*» (374).

éclabousser; éclaboussement. The spilling of liquids. In Zola this usually means blood. Zola's obsessive sexuality, here a fascination with menstrual bleedings, produced this phallic image of assault: «... sa chemise, glissée à terre, semblait avoir reçu l'éclaboussement d'un coup de couteau» (*Joie*, 1043). A crucifix is given movement with the form as adjective-past participle, with rich baroque-like textures of red and gold: «... le Christ en croix, saignant, éclaboussé de soie rouge sur le drap d'or...» (*Rêve*, 897). The symbolic spilling of Silvère's blood in Volume I is recalled by Pascal: «... éclaboussant du sang de Silvère leur fortune commençante...» (*Pascal*, 1009).

écraser; écrasement. With *anéantir, anéantissement*: before entering into Zola's metaphorical field it can indicate physical compression, shock, crush: «... dans l'écrasement des buveurs...» (*Germinal*, 1269). It also indicates thoughts and weather conditions. With a certain amount of scatological humour it betrays the effects of the flatulent art of one of the peasants in *La Terre* (652).

écrouler; écroulement. Indicates a sudden and total collapse of a mass. This can be quite ordinary: «... un mur de la Souleiade fut renversé, qu'on ne put remettre debout, tout un écroulement dont la brèche resta béante» (*Pascal*, 1130). Downward movement or upward movement, idea of display, of *étalage* is apparent, as Zola seeks to put into all kinds of movements the wares of the Second Empire. Along the *quais* of Paris, Claude and Christine admire the «... écroulement de fruits...» (*Oeuvre*, 101). The Au Bonheur des Dames has many *écroulements* of its merchandise such as: «... dans un coin, un écroulement à bon marché, des tapis de Gheurdès...» (*Bonheur*, 471). This verb joins *tomber, abattre, affaisser, crouler, ébouler* as indicators of rough, precipitous, random and sudden movements, sometimes physical, sometimes ideological.

fondre, s'effondrer, effondrement. Real collapses are recorded, especially in *Germinal*: «... le toit s'était effondré sur une dizaine de mètres...» (1296), but figuration dominates over literal meaning: the collapse of life for Lazare upon realizing that his mother is dying (*Joie*, 974), the losses sustained at the stock market (*Argent*, 198), the symbolic burning and collapse of France recorded in *La Débâcle* (815).

emporter. Will be used almost entirely metaphorically and made the equivalent of *charrier*.

encombrement. Of people and vehicles (traffic jams), but it also can be used for any *pêle-mêle* situation:

> ... tandis que le piano se couvrait de poussière et que la table immense disparaissait sous un encombrement de papiers, de livres, de brochures (*Joie*, 941).

This is an excellent coupling of objects (piano, table) with the imperfects covering and effacing them.

entassement. Another type of movement geometry in Zola. «... c'était un entassement de ténèbres...» (*Débâcle*, 526). The physical piling up of the women puts enormous pressure on the department store counter. «... l'entassement de femmes dont *craquaient* les rayons» (*Bonheur*, 626).

envahir; submerger; inonder. Types of invasion, characteristic of the dynamic spirit of the *Rougon-Macquart*. Here Zola truly anticipates Ionesco. Octave Mouret is constantly enlarging his store by buying the little buildings on the block: «... il voyait le *Bonheur des Dames* envahir tout le pâté...» (*Bonheur*, 455); Marcelle's once prudent parents have given in to the vice of financial speculation:

> ... dans cette maison envahie par le jeu, où elle avait vu monter peu à peu le flot des journaux financiers, qui la submergeaient aujourd'hui du rêve grisant de leur publicité (*Argent*, 273).

But invasions are often just that: the increasing distribution of a fatal infection across the body: «... la gangrène envahissante...» (*Débâcle*, 804); collective rush from one area to another: «Des habitués du quartier avaient envahi les tables voisines» (*Oeuvre*, 78).

flot, peuple. *Flot* is the most common noun of movement

in Zola. Basically the movement of water, it should be kept in mind that Zola's sea images fill the entire work; wherever there is movement there is *une mer*. *Flot* has no restrictions: it can refer to emotions, political ideas surging forth, thoughts; light, dust, movements of vehicles and animals; it encompasses individual men and women, social ranks and strata, profession and occupation. It is the vast population of the *Rougon-Macquart* always on the go: «... du flot de paysans...» (*Terre*, 378); «... un flot de gamins...» (*Terre*, 759); «... le flot des derniers spéculateurs...» (*Argent*, 312); «... un flot de gens endimanchés...» (*Pascal*, 1214); «... le flot mondain des promeneurs du Bois» (*Pascal*, 1161); «... au milieu du flot brusque des voyageurs...» (*Bête*, 1105); «... dans le continuel flot de passants qui encombre ce quartier...» (*Bête*, 1120); «... le flot des ouvriers sautait des berlines» (*Germinal*, 1185); «... ce flot d'hommes qui s'écoulait vers la Meuse...» (*Débâcle*, 498); «... tout le flot belge entrait librement» (*Débâcle*, 784); «... le flot des clientes...» (*Bonheur*, 577); «Un flot de foule envahit les collatéraux...» (*Rêve*, 922); «... flot de femmes...» (*Curée*, 557).

Peuple, related to *flot*, usually indicates movement, and like *flot* requires backup from precise, specific nouns indicating class, type: «... ce peuple de clientes...» (*Bonheur*, 631); «... au milieu de son peuple de coquettes» (*Bonheur*, 631); «... son peuple de femmes» (*Bonheur*, 796). There are «... peuple de figures saintes» (*Rêve*, 896), «... peuple des peintres...» (*Oeuvre*, 283), even trees: «... le peuple paisible des arbres...» (*Faute*, 1382). While capable of indicating movement, like *flot,* it is less a question of movement and more that of establishing psychological nations within the universe of the *Rougon-Macquart*.

galop, galoper. More vivid than *flot,* less common, but still very frequently used: «... avec leurs lampes dansantes, qui éclairaient mal ce galop d'hommes noirs...» (*Germinal*, 1296); «... un interminable galop...» (*Argent*, 139). Biblical echoes to the four horsemen invite Zola to utilize this form for apocalyptic visions even at the simple level of simile and metaphor: a storm at the moment of the death of Mouche: «On aurait dit le galop d'une armée dévastatrice...» (*Terre*, 459); «... *le* galop de cauchemar, le défilé de tous ces fantômes...» (*Pascal*, 1035).

grandir, grandissant. These forms prove very effective in seizing on-going movement in the series. The verb supports striking visualizations of measurable change. Two trees in *Germinal* are put into movement by extending the concept of *pousser* into the similitude of grandir: «... deux arbres poussaient, un sorbier et un platane, qui semblaient grandir du fond de la terre» (1366). As night comes on, a hat seems to grow: «La nuit augmentait, le chapeau semblait grandir dans cette ombre» (*Terre*, 418). Zola will repeatedly use the present participle form as adjective: «... le succès grandissant...» (*Argent*, 275); «... sa passion grandissante...» (*Bête*, 1159).

grondement. «... le grondement des roues» (*Germinal*, 1396); «La foule grondait toujours...» (*Débâcle*, 871). Often the basic sound movement (*grondement*) will be supported by another verb of movement and a metaphor:

> Alors, Claude, de tout ce tumulte, n'entendit au loin que le bruit de mer, le grondement du public roulant en haut, dans les salles (*Oeuvre*, 300).

grossir, a variation of *grandir*: «Saccard, à son pilier, voyait grossir autour de lui la cohue de ses flatteurs et de ses clients» (*Argent*, 300); «... vers les fumées grossissantes...» (*Débâcle*, 464).

inépuisable, ininterrompu, interminable. Adjectival equivalent of the negative verb: «... au milieu de l'inépuisable déballage des marchandises» (*Bonheur*, 636); «... sa fécondité inépuisable...» (*Joie*, 1120); «... un cortège ininterrompu» (*Débâcle*, 432); «... un roulement ininterrompu de foudre» (*Débâcle*, 517); «... une file ininterrompue...» (*Débâcle*, 526); «... des flots ininterrompus de voitures coulaient...» (*Argent*, 22); «... des files d'hommes interminables...» (*Fortune*, 163); «... devant l'interminable flot qui passait...» (*Débâcle*, 423); «... on apercevait l'interminable queue» (*Débâcle*, 463).

manger. This verb is found in the figurative speech of the spoken French language. It is part of Zola's narrational voice; it is found in the speech of his characters. The priest of Bonneville speaks of the sea: «Voici plus de cinq cents ans que la mer les mange...» (*Joie*, 896). The colorful speech of the people works into the *parole* of Zola where it will be vivified, intensified, densified and finally metaphorized.

massacre, massacrer. These forms are attached to the field of crude and brutal movements. The wedding banquet of Lise and Buteau provides a dazzling display of rough movement of the eating peasants:

> Alors, ce fut un massacre, un engloutissement: les poulets, las lapins, les viandes défilèrent, disparurent, au milieu d'un terrible bruit de mâchoires (*Terre*, 525).

nettoyer. A first cousin of *balayer*, its use is almost entirely metaphorical.

noyer. «... une fin de quadrille noyait le bal dans une poussière rousse» (*Germinal*, 1269). A very interesting movement in which sound (music) is transformed into invading liquid (*noyer*) which in turn becomes colored semi-matter (*poussière rousse*).

pulluler, pullulement. «... un pullulement de bêtes sans cesse...» (*Faute*, 1273).

roulement. «... le roulement continu des pieds» (*Oeuvre*, 283).

révolutionner. Used usually in the metaphorical sense. In this example, however, it means a rapid tidying up of the house and the preparation of lunch with the unexpected arrival of Sandoz at the country house of Claude and Christine: «Claude garda Sandoz dans la salle, pendant que Christine révolutionnait la maison pour le déjeuner» (*Oeuvre*, 159).

sans. This preposition serves the same function as the negative verbs listed and the prefix in *-in*: «... en voyant les devis augmenter sans cesse» (*Joie*, 865); «... un flot sans cesse accru de soldats...» (*Débâcle*, 524); «... on montait quand même, on montait sans cesse...» (*Argent*, 293); «... des attentes sans fin...» (*Débâcle*, 520); «... en battant la province sans relâche, pour le placement de ses idées» (*Germinal*, 1344).

se succéder; successif. Indications of progressions: «... le détraquement successif de tous les organes...» (*Joie*, 964). This example from *Le Rêve* shows the verb engendering another verb of movement:

> Cela n'en finissait plus, les cierges se succédaient, se multipliaient, le grand séminaire, les paroisses, la

cathédrale, les chantres attaquant l'antienne, les chanoines en pluviaux blancs (922).

toujours. The adverb of *Les Rougon-Macquart,* the adverb of Zola. «Les voitures n'avançaient toujours pas» (*Curée,* 320); «Les commis entraient toujours» (*Bonheur,* 416); «... un travail lent s'opérait, elle lisait toujours...» (*Joie,* 867); «Des femmes arrivaient toujours, pour rejoindre et emmener leurs hommes» (*Germinal,* 1271); «... en une ligne toujours grandissante» (*Germinal,* 1405); «... ils la regardaient croître, toujours, toujours» (*Germinal,* 1572); «Mais des paysans entraient toujours...» (*Terre,* 559); «Sous la marquise, les becs de gaz brûlaient toujours...» (*Bête,* 1053); «Mais on marchait, on marchait toujours, péniblement...» (*Débâcle,* 508); «La route montait toujours...» (*Débâcle,* 509); «... les cuirassiers passaient, passaient toujours...» (*Débâcle,* 527). Related to *toujours* is *maintenant.*

II. *Nominal Style*

The decisive trait of nineteenth century French prose is the increasing use of nominal style. The phenomenon has more than adequately been treated, the best work being that of Bally, Moser (especially her analysis of the journal entries of the Goncourt brothers, certainly derived from the earlier syntactical study of Georg Lösch) and the comparative work of Helmut Hatzfeld (1).

Nominal style aims at the total elimination of the verb. Such radical restructuring is often achieved by the Goncourt brothers in their journal, with main verb eliminated (2). This

---

(1) Charles Bally, «Impressionnisme et grammaire,» in *Mélanges Bernard Bouvier* (Geneva, 1920); Ruth Moser, *L'Impressionnisme français* (Geneva, 1952); Georg Lösch, *Die impressionistische Syntax der Goncourt* (Nurnberg, 1919); Helmut A. Hatzfeld, *Literature Through Art,* especially 169-170. For more complete bibliographical information consult Karl Vossler, Leo Spitzer and Helmut A. Hatzfeld, *Introducción a la Estilística Romance* (Buenos Aires, 1932); Helmut A. Hatzfeld, *A Critical Bibliography of the New Stylistics 1900-1952* (Chapel Hill, 1953); Helmut A. Hatzfeld and Yves Le Hir, *Essai de Bibliographie critique de stylistique française et romane 1955-1960* (Paris, 1961).

(2) Moser, 126.

elliptic or telegraphic style is well suited to diary entries, but presents problems in narrative sequences. Nevertheless such a style does permeate the novels of the Goncourts and of Pierre Loti. Likewise, the hermetic narratives of Mallarmé's sonnets use an impressionistic nominal style through a variety of grammatical manipulations, not least among them being a penchant for pronominal constructions and infinitives (3).

Zola follows the nominal trend. There is a minimization of the role of the verb with a concomitant increase of pale verbs, such as *avoir, être* and related forms, without, as Hatzfeld would say, «clarifying» verbs (4). Intransitive verbs, revealing isolated and static groupings, are preferred to the transitive forms.

The dramatic and stately nominal sentence which opens *Salammbô*: «C'était à Mégara, faubourg de Carthage, dans les jardins d'Hamilcar» (Flaubert, *Salammbô,* 1) is approximated many times by Zola:

> C'était rue Véron, à Montmartre, dans un petit logement, au quatrième étage (*Nana,* 1287).
> C'était dans la grande chambre à coucher de la Croix-de-Maufras, la chambre tendue de damas rouge, dont les deux hautes fenêtres donnaient sur la ligne du chemin de fer, à quelques mètres» (*Bête,* 1275).

The opening sentence of *La Débâcle* is constructed in a similar manner: «A deux kilomètres de Mulhouse, vers le Rhin, au milieu de la plaine fertile, le camp était dressé» (401). Flaubert's sentence is purer, Zola's tends to proliferate and conclude with weak verb. But he can construct without any verb at all: «Une mer de verdure, en face, à droite, à gauche, partout» (*Faute,* 1327).

But, as Zola's theories on painting are eclectic and hardly a true description of the impressionist tendency in painting (5),

---

(3) John Andrew Frey, *Motif Symbolism in the Disciples of Mallarmé* (Washington, 1957), 65.

(4) Hatzfeld, *Literature Through Art,* 169.

(5) Two works have clarified the thorny question of Zola's relationship with the impressionists, and, above all, the rupture with Cézanne: Robert Judson Niess, *Zola, Cézanne and Manet, A Study of 'L'Oeuvre'* (Ann Arbor, 1968); Patrick Brady, *'L'Oeuvre' de*

so also his style is never purely impressionistic in the sense that Moser and Hatzfeld attribute impressionism to the Goncourt brothers and to Loti. His style is filled with more movement than impressionism can tolerate. While impressionism depicts the subtle changes of shimmering light, Zola's feverish and at times frantic style of movement is betraying a symbolism. His nervous and tense style reveals an omniscient narrator, telling, explaining, pointing out, in a quite verbal manner. The nominal sentences are perhaps pauses, periods of calm, respites from the verbal assault. Zola is capable of creating, with intransitive verbs, patches of glistening impressionistic light, but this technique is at odds with his strong transitive verbal mode which seems incompatible with literary impressionism. The verb is highly operative in Zola, frequently assuming highly concrete qualities; abstract verbs are avoided, and the verb, noun-like, presents a highly visual and symbolic expression of objects: «... des tombes *bossuaient* les champs...» (*Débâcle*, 848); «... du visage, que les cheveux blonds ... *nimbaient* d'or» (*Rêve*, 841); «... la cavalerie *sabrait* toujours les fuyards...» (*Fortune*, 219).

Nominal style in Zola is being restricted by his strong narrative voice (Flaubert was naturally on the road to impressionism, if only by the effacement of the author as a basic principle of his work). Yet nominal style is there, as in this *tableau* of Claude at the official exhibition:

> Cette fois, ne pouvant avancer, il reconnut des peintres, le peuple des peintres, chez lui ce jour-là, et qui faisait les honneurs de la maison: un surtout, un ancien ami de l'atelier Bouton jeune, dévoré d'un besoin de publicité, travaillant pour la médaille, racolant tous les visiteurs de quelque influence et les amenant de force voir ses tableaux; puis, le peintre célèbre, riche, qui recevait devant son oeuvre, un sourire de triomphe aux lèvres, d'une galanterie affichante avec les femmes, dont il avait une cour sans cesse renouvelée; puis, les autres, les rivaux qui s'exècrent en se criant à pleine voix des éloges,

---

Emile Zola (Geneva, 1968). Professor Brady's work contains a kind of glossary to the light and color fields of *L'Oeuvre* which can supplement the glossary of this chapter.

les farouches guettant d'une porte les succès des camarades, les timides qu'on ne ferait pas pour un empire passer dans leurs salles, les blagueurs cachant sous un mot drôle la plaie saignante de leur défaite, les sincères absorbés, tâchant de comprendre, distribuant déjà les médailles; et il y avait aussi les familles des peintres, une jeune femme, charmante, accompagnée d'un enfant coquettement pomponné, une bourgeoise revêche, maigre, flanquée de deux laiderons en noir, une grosse mère, échouée sur une banquette au milieu de toute une tribu de mioches mal mouchés, une dame mûre, belle encore, qui regardait avec sa grande fille, passer une gueuse, la maîtresse du père, toutes deux au courant, très calmes, échangeant un sourire; et il y avait encore les modéles, des femmes qui se tiraient par les bras, qui se montraient leurs corps les unes aux autres, dans les nudités des tableaux, parlant haut, habillées sans goût, gâtant leurs chairs superbes sous de telles robes, qu'elles semblaient bossues, à côté des poupées bien mises, des Parisiennes dont rien ne serait resté, au déballage (*Oeuvre*, 283-284).

This long sentence reveals a style in which verbal quality is being submerged by noun and adjective, where existing verb is mainly the impersonal mode of the present participle, with past participles used as adjectives. This is a single, coordinate sentence divided into five tableaux or viewings as Claude, unable to move in the crowded room, observes successively the various scenes. This is accomplished through a series of adverbial *puis,* and the verbal stamp *il y avait.* Syntax as a logically organizing principle is restrained to the opening verb in the *passé simple,* followed by a descriptive imperfect bordering on the picturesque. Five groupings of persons are seen by putting into syntactical relief their substantive aspects and reducing their movements to prototypical gestures and gaits which are representative of their mental sets (the contrast between the ambitious painter and the *arriviste* rich painter). The former friend of Bouton *jeune* is portrayed in a manner which wants to be nominal. A series of clauses introduced first by the past participle (*dévoré*) and followed by a string of present participles moves from mental state, «travaillant pour la médaille», to posture or action (*racolant, amenant*);

that is, forcing potentially influential visitors to view his work. Here Zola is visualizing psychology, and this is effected through the unity of the suite of participles. If the style were not impressionistic, but ordered and analytical, the arrangement might look something like this:

> *Un ancien ami de l'atelier Bouton jeune qui était dévoré d'un besoin de publicité travaillait pour obtenir la médaille: aussi racolait-il tous les visiteurs et les amenait-il de force voir ses tableaux.*

Zola then photographs the successful painter. The opening and concluding clauses indicate a habitual pose, receiving group after group of admiring young ladies. There is no need to trace various mental attitudes. He has arrived: his attitude needs no verb, nominal style sums up the picture: triumphant smile on the lips, hypnotic and pleasing manner. The scene overflows with a series of snapshots catching characteristic poses rendered through participles: «... les farouches *guettant* d'une porte...», «les blageurs *cachant*...», «... les sincères *absorbés, tâchant...*, *distribuant...*». The passage concludes effectively with the impersonal *il y a* which merely posits a thing or a person as existing, as being there. It has become a coinage like *voilà*.

Nominal style can co-exist with narrative verbal style:

> Cette nuit-là par cette bise aigre de novembre qui soufflait au travers de leur chambre et du vaste ateliers, ils se couchèrent à près de trois heures (*Oeuvre*, 341).

The narration is reserved to the final clause. The next step back in the narration is the subordinate clause in the imperfect, the blowing of the breeze. Dominating the verbal situation are nominal effects achieved by placing *nuit* and *bise aigre de novembre* in primary position in the sentence, extending the noun field through two prepositional phrases which extend the substantive viewing. The psychological intent might be rendered as follows in English: «That night, with a biting November wind blowing across the room and the large studio, they went to bed around three». Similarly, with a description of the cemetery toward the end of the novel:

> En effet, sous le ciel gris de cette matinée de novem-
> bre, dans le frisson pénétrant de la bise, les tombes
> basses, chargées de guirlandes et de couronnes de
> perles, prenaient des tons très fins, d'une délicatesse
> charmante (*Oeuvre*, 357).

Here there are two noun fields introduced prepositionally,
with heavy adjectival qualification. The third item, the tombs,
is presented as a dominating «thing», followed by a dense
description, leaving the verb in a weak, terminal position.
Etre, avoir, et compagnie are at the verbal base of nominal
style:

> C'était un grand cimetière plat, jeune encore, tiré
> au cordeau dans ce terrain vide de banlieue, coupé
> en damier par de larges allées symétriques (*Oeuvre*,
> 356).

This procedure is derived from Flaubert, and Zola sprinkles
it generously throughout the *Rougon-Macquart*. To be effective
it should be accompanied by dominant noun fields, iconic
blocks, and adjectives:

> La joie avait gagné de maison en maison, les rues
> étaient une ivresse, un nuage de vapeurs fauves, la
> fumée des festins, la sueur des accouplements, s'en
> allait à l'horizon, roulait au-dessus des toits la nuit
> des Sodome, des Babylone et des Ninive (*Argent*,
> 253-54).

Time, voice and number revelations of the paradigm ideally
should be eliminated:

> Grande ouverte, cette immense armoire de chêne
> sculpté, aux fortes et belles ferrures, datant du
> dernier siècle, montrait sur ses planches, dans la
> profondeur de ses flancs, un amas extraordinaire
> de *papiers*, de *dossiers*, de *manuscrits*, *s'entassant*,
> *débordant*, *pêle-mêle* (*Pascal*, 917).

In this example, the final two participles and the adverb form
a complementary group of three to the three nouns, each group
having equal artistic force. Grammatical function and distinction have been diminished.

III. *The Imperfect Tense*

The imperfect, a true attribute of the Romance literatures as they opt from the eighteenth century on, for the genre novel, is the descriptive tense *par excellence*. The Hatzfeldian formula to describe the rush toward impressionism after 1850, the «Triumph of Description over Narration» (6), means that descriptive art, carried to its highest degree, becomes impressionism. Furthermore, this tense becomes the ideal vehicle for transmitting continuing psychological states, first observed externally, but leading ineluctably to the interiorizations found in the imperfects of Proust and in the *monologue intérieur* of Valery Larbaud, Mauriac and others. Using this tense to reveal immediate and particular moments of psychological stress and change, Zola has perhaps surpassed Flaubert. His psychological imperfects look so natural that it is hard to believe that they were innovative just a generation earlier.

The imperfect as a vehicle for movement, beginnings, endings, increases and decreases is regularly used in Zola's novels. This is the old Flaubertian pattern, but applied now to unique situations. The description of lights appearing over Paris in the third tableau of *Une Page d'amour,* where we are able to enjoy one of the rare appearances of *naître* in the imperfect, shows the normal interplay of *passé simple* and *imparfait* with truly heightened aesthetic intent:

> Et, une à une, d'autres étincelles parurent. Elles naissaient dans la nuit avec un brusque sursaut, tout d'un coup, et restaient fixes, scintillantes comme des étoiles. Il semblait que ce fût un nouveau lever d'astres, à la surface d'un lac sombre. Bientôt elles dessinèrent une double ligne, qui partait du Trocadéro et s'en allait vers Paris (*Page*, 969).

The on-going process of the description is witnessed in small scenes across the work: the slowly dying camp fire of the army in *La Débâcle*: «... il ne resta, sur la terre nue, que les feux des cuisines qui achevaient de s'éteindre» (421); in the twilight sun, the stained-glass windows of the cathedral slowly

---

(6) Hatzfeld, *Literature Through Art,* 165.

bring out of the shadows the legend of St. George: «Dès le crépuscule, la légende renaissait de l'ombre, lumineuse, comme une apparition» (*Rêve*, 864); the attempted suicide of Mazaud leaves bloodstains on the floor which slowly move and increase in size: «Il y avait par terre une large tache qui s'élargissait» (*Argent*, 358-359); *Macquart*, marinated by a lifetime of drinking is slowly consumed by fire; the next day Dr. Pascal will find nothing but a pile of ashes: «Mais elle grandissait, s'élargissait rapidement, et la peau se fendait, et la graisse commençait à se fondre» (*Pascal*, 1093). Zola, attentive to small detail, fixes his camera upon a flower found on the floor: «Mme Bron venait de distribuer les derniers bouquets, seule une rose tombée se fanait, près de la chatte noire» (*Nana*, 1219). There is nothing static in all of these descriptions; they are alive, filled with movement, processes, change. The idea is not to tell what happened, but to give the sense of what is taking place.

More interesting for the art of the novel is the continuation of the Flaubertian psychological imperfect. It can begin measuring growth as in this rather poetic temporality where we feel the days and years passing, changing Pauline from little girl into mature woman, measured against the daily tide changes of the sea:

> La mer, cependant, battait deux fois par jour Bonneville de l'éternel balancement de sa houle, et Pauline grandissait dans le spectacle de l'immense horizon (*Joie*, 847).

As clock time ticks away, speech and events take place in *temps,* and the imperfect renders the psychological *durée.* Denise receives temporary shelter at her uncle's, whose business is being destroyed by the great department store. The family expresses its anger to Denise, but already her mind is being pulled to the family's enemy: «... dont le désir d'être au *Bonheur des Dames* grandissait, au milieu de toute cette passion» (*Bonheur*, 410). Etienne sits down and a feeling of sadness slowly overcomes him: «Etienne, à son tour, vint s'asseoir sur la poutre. Sa tristesse augmentait sans qu'il sût pourquoi» (*Germinal*, 1241). Slowly the miners are convinced by Etienne's radical ideas: «Et les idées semées par Etienne poussaient, s'élargissaient dans ce cri de révolte» (*Germinal*, 1292). The sad Chanteau household is being transformed by the joyful presence of Pauline: «Un lien nouveau était créé, et il naissait une espérance au milieu de leur ruine, sans qu'on sût au juste laquelle» (*Joie*, 833); «... une vie nouvelle chassait le deuil de la maison...» (*Joie*, 997). These imperfects particularly record changing emotions in relationships. The central idea of *La Joie de vivre* revolves around the precarious situation of Pauline who loves Lazare. He, in his immaturity, sometimes treats her as a brother or «copain»; afterwards, he desires her. This situation persists throughout the novel, and the following is a subtle one-sentence rendering of the predicament: «La femme, qu'ils oubliaient tous deux, se réveillait dans sa chair...» (*Joie*, 867). Developing tenderness and love surprise Maurice who cannot understand his growing affection for Jean Macquart: «Maurice resta surpris de la grande tendresse qui l'attachait déjà à ce garçon» (*Débâcle*, 491); marriage seems to have destroyed the love between Christine and Claude: «L'épouse diminuait l'amante, cette formalité du mariage semblait avoir tué l'amour» (*Oeuvre*, 230).

The theme of possessing, conquering is fundamental to the *Rougon-Macquart* series, and a whole array of verbs in the imperfect exploits the psychological nuances of this theme. The basic verb of *La Conquête de Plassans* is *appartenir*. Marthe, usually indifferent to religious questions, has been exposed to spiritual conversations with the hypocritical priest. As he takes over her house, he now takes over her soul: «Alors elle lui appartenait, il aurait fait d'elle ce qu'il aurait voulu» (*Conquête*, 974). Octave's plan to conquer Paris means first conquering Mme Hédouin. This slow process, which will lead to the opening of the department store, starts in *Pot-Bouille* and we have many reiterations of the following: «Il devenait son maître» (*P. B.*, 340). Saccard, out of power since *La Curée*, ambitiously starts some new schemes in *L'Argent*: «... heureux de sentir sous ses talons ce pavé de Paris, qu'il reconquérait» (108). Rachel the servant, like one of the *Bonnes* of Genet, slowly dominates her mistress Berthe:

> Rachel, qui acceptait sans révolte les plus dures besognes, accompagnées de pain sec, prenait possession du ménage, les yeux ouverts, la bouche

serrée, en servante de flair attendant l'heure fatale
et prévue où madame n'aurait rien à lui refuser
(*P. B.*, 226).

Perhaps no writer before the introspective novelists of
the twentieth century could depict the neurosis of love as
well as Emile Zola. The *Rougon-Macquart* is a confused and
perverse world where normalcy is easily deranged. Intimate
love and sexual relationships are hard to disentangle: mistresses
and wives who play many roles, the mistress as mother, the
lover as son or even girl friend. No novel perhaps exploits
these themes so much as *Nana,* and the character of Count
Muffat must be considered one of Zola's greatest psychological
creations. Its success is in part due to the incessant imperfect,
indicating the possession of Muffat's body and soul by *la
mouche d'or.* Count Muffat's temptation is a Second Empire
perversion of the young Flaubert's intoxication with theatres
and actresses. Muffat is first seduced by atmospheres, the
original temptation coming in the form of the theatrical
performance in which Nana appears naked on the stage. The
théâtre des variétés with all of its many contrasts to Muffat's
bourgeois *hôtel* is an extension of Nana's sensuality (Bordenave
does call it his bordello), and going back stage there, or in
Nana's bedroom, Muffat experiences suffocation, claustrophobia, vertigo: «Au troisième étage, Muffat s'abandonna à
la griserie qui l'envahissait» (1222); «... dans cette chambre,
un vertige le grisait» (1459); «Et toujours, malgré les luttes
de sa raison, cette chambre de Nana le *frappait de folie*» (*Ibid.*).
The imperfects render the conquest of Muffat, like an insistent
motif:

> Tout son être se révoltait, la lente possession dont
> Nana l'envahissait depuis quelque temps l'effrayait
> (1213).
> Lorsqu'elle ferma l'oeil droit et qu'elle passa le
> pinceau, il comprit qu'il lui appartenait (1214).
> Mais un sourd travail s'opérait et Nana le recon-
> quérait lentement, par les souvenirs, par les lâchetés
> de sa chair, par des sentiments nouveaux, exclusifs,
> attendris, presque paternels (1331).
> La femme le possédait avec le despotisme jaloux
> d'un Dieu de colère... (1459).

Zola uses the same processes to describe Muffat's return to religion:

> Chaque jour, la religion le reprenait davantage. Il pratiquait de nouveau, se confessait, et communiait... (1448).

A decisive *passé simple* indicates an abrupt change of pattern in this psychology. Surprising Nana in *flagrant délit* with the old debauchee, the marquis de Chouard, and learning of the infidelity of his wife Sabine, Muffat meekly returns to the Church; he is immediately under the power of Father Venot: «M. Venot l'emmena comme un enfant. Dès lors, il lui appartint tout entier» (1464). Muffat's final religious conversion recalls the religiosity of Emma Bovary, for Zola knows that the bourgeoisie of the Second Empire has been infected by Emma's romantic pathology:

> Au fond des églises, les genoux glacés par les dalles, il retrouvait ses jouissances d'autrefois, les spasmes de ses muscles et les ébranlements délicieux de son intelligence, dans une même satisfaction des obscurs besoins de son être (1465).

The imperfect in Zola, as in Flaubert, is becoming a very complicated instrument for rendering psychological states. Unless the reader is very attentive a misreading of the text is quite possible. This comes about because of the use of the tense to create a scene which is at one and the same time habitual, that is, representative of a soul state which can occur on multiple occasions, but at the same time is recorded with specific detail which would seem to belong to a single occasion. The dissipation of Emma's marriage with Charles is maybe the protoplast for this type of construction. Emma had the habit of taking her greyhound dog on walks and Flaubert writes:

> Sa pensée, sans but d'abord, vagabondait au hasard, comme sa levrette, qui faisait des cercles dans la campagne, jappait après les papillons jaunes, donnait la chasse aux musaraignes en mordillant les coquelicots sur le bord d'une pièce de blé. Puis ses idées peu à peu se fixaient et, assise sur le gazon,

qu'elle fouillait à petits coups avec le bout de son
ombrelle, Emma se répétait:
—Pourquoi, mon Dieu, me suis-je mariée? (*Madame Bovary*, 41, 42).

The point is simple enough. We know that on each and every
one of these walks, Emma's dog did not chase a specific
musaraigne or bite at poppies; nor on each occasion could a
parallel be drawn between the dog running in circles, quieting
down, and Emma's thoughts doing the same thing. It is a
representative scene, and Flaubert is the first major exploiter
of the imperfect in this manner. Zola has equally complex
structures of the imperfect. A stormy confrontation between
Nana and Count Muffat mingles imperfects which transmit
his psychological anguish (caught between her infidelity and
his family's indifference to him), habitual quarrelsome encounters between Muffat and Nana which at first glance seem
to be a single scene (but which have taken place many times
in the recent past), and interpolated *style indirect libre*:

Elle était allée ouvrir la porte. Il ne sortit pas.
Maintenant, c'était sa façon de l'attacher davantage;
pour un rien, à la moindre querelle, elle lui mettait
le marché en main, avec des réflexions abominables.
Ah bien! elle trouverait toujours mieux que lui, elle
avait l'embarras du choix: on ramassait des hommes dehors, tant qu'on en voulait, et des hommes
moins godiches, dont le sang bouillait dans les
veines. Il baissait la tête, il attendait des heures plus
douces, lorsqu'elle avait un besoin d'argent; alors,
elle se faisait caressante; et il oubliait, une nuit de
tendresse compensait les tortures de toute la semaine. Son rapprochement avec sa femme lui avait
rendu son intérieur insupportable. La comtesse,
lâchée par Fauchery ... s'étourdissait à d'autres
amours. ... Estelle, depuis son mariage, ne voyait
plus son père; chez cette fille, plate et insignifiante,
une femme d'une volonté de fer avait brusquement
paru, si absolue, que Daguenet tremblait devant elle;
maintenant, il l'accompagnait à la messe, converti,
furieux contre son beau-père qui les ruinait avec
une créature (*Nana*, 1448-1449).

The passage is preceded by some short paragraphs in which

Muffat discovers Nana's infidelity. A specific incident, seeing Foucarmont leave Nana's apartment, provokes a confrontation between Nana and Muffat which is properly recorded in the *passé simple*; it is a single incident. The same paragraph records other incidents, recorded in the pluperfect. The final sentence expresses Nana's fatigue with these constant scenes and is recorded in the imperfect. Seizing the essential elements, it looks like the following. *passé simple*: «... il vit sortir Foucarmont...»; «... il lui fit une scène»; «... elle se fâcha...» (1448); pluperfect: «... plusieurs fois, elle s'était montrée gentille»; «... le soir où il l'avait surprise avec Georges...»; «... elle était revenue la première avouant ses torts...» (*Ibid.*); imperfect: «... à la fin, il l'assommait avec son entêtement...» (*Ibid.*). This indirect verbal manipulation is followed by the direct and taunting speech of Nana: «Eh bien, oui, j'ai couché avec Foucarmont. Après? ... Hein? ça te défrise, mon petit mufe» (*Ibid.*).

All of this is a rapid and subtle preparation for the imperfects which follow. In a brilliant sentence, Zola puts Muffat's reactions in the imperfect, contrasting with Nana's movements in the *passé simple*: «Il restait suffoqué par la carrure de son aveu; et, comme il serrait les poings, elle marcha vers lui, le regarda en face» (*Ibid.*). In the pivotal transitional paragraph to the one under analysis, Nana informs Muffat that he may get out if he will not tolerate her manner of living. She opens the door and he does not leave, recorded in the pluperfect and the preterite. We see then that the key word is the adverb *maintenant* which creates the habitual, representational scene which follows in the text, but which has been elaborated from a specific moment in time when Nana asks him to accept her as she is or to leave. The passage continues with delicate manipulations of the imperfect. There is *style indirect libre* in the conditional, and the imperfect reports the speech and the thoughts of Nana. Starting with, *Il baissait la tête...,* we have the physical and mental reactions of Count Muffat. Translating the passage into English shows the difficulties involved: «He would lower his head, he would wait for sweeter hours when she would have a need for money; then she would be more caressing.» These are the repeated, habitual thought modes of the Count recorded as speech patterns. The imperfect then shifts from Muffat to the recording imperfect of Zola: «And he was forgetting, a night of tenderness always compensated for the tortures of an entire week.» Zola's voice continues a bit before a transition is made to Muffat's situation at home with wife, daughter, and son-in-law. But be this Zola's voice or not, these mental images of the family are also torturing the soul of the Count. The very end of the narrative of Daguenet's evaluation of his father-in-law, while still the narrative imperfect of Zola, is budding on *style indirect libre* because the phrase could only belong to the son-in-law: «... furieux contre son beau-père qui *les ruinait avec une créature*» («qui nous ruine avec une créature»), «who is destroying us with a creature.»

The aesthetic manipulation of tenses, particularly the imperfect, was really unknown before the second decade of the twentieth century. It was Eugen Lerch who upset the idea of a standard imperfect and who made the discovery of the «picturesque» imperfect in the major French novelists of the nineteenth century (7).

The picturesque imperfect consists mainly of a living and vital representative scene which sums up a number of similar events which probably occur in the fictional time of the novel, but which cannot be rendered in their countless manifestations without making the novel repetitious. Consequently, a single scene is meant to represent all of them.

Balzac's *Eugénie Grandet* of 1833 gives us one of the

---

(7) «Das Imperfectum als Ausdruck der lebhaften Vorstellung,» in *Zeitschrift für Romanische Philologie*, XLII (1922), 311 ff. and 388 ff. For an illuminating discussion of the stylistic manipulations of the tenses see Hatzfeld, *Critical Bibliography of the New Stylistics*. Hatzfeld points out the continuation of Lerch's work in the United States by Anna Granville Hatcher, the work of Louis Bru-Laloire in France, «L'Imparfait de l'indicatif est-il un tens?,» *Revue de Philologie française et de littérature*, XLI (1929), 56-89, in which we have this telling statement: «Ce n'est plus un 'tens'..., mais une simultanéité immobilisée avec une durée immobile.», 72, cited by Hatzfeld, 233-234. A seminal work in this whole discussion is that of the late Tatiana Fotitch, *The Narrative Tenses in Chrétien de Troyes* (Washington, 1950), in which some of the stylistic questions of tense interplay have been resolved. The importance of Lerch's work is amply discussed by Professor Hatzfeld in his bibliography, stressing the relationship between grammatical and stylistic categories.

earliest examples. Cousin Charles finds consolation and pleasure in the company of his cousin and his aunt. Their daily lyrical encounters are recorded by Balzac as a single scene:

> Il aimait cette maison, dont les moeurs ne lui semblèrent plus si ridicules. Il descendait dès le matin, afin de pouvoir causer avec Eugénie quelques moments avant que Grandet vînt donner les provisions; et, quand les pas du bonhomme retentissaient dans les escaliers, il se sauvait au jardin ... Charles demeurait entre la mère et la fille, éprouvant des délices inconnues à leur prêter les mains pour dévider du fil, à les voir travaillant, à les entendre jaser (8).

That this aesthetic technique was being absorbed into the literary language is proven by its appearance in the first *Education sentimentale* of Flaubert where we find a parallel passage to the Balzac, a single scene, with specific detail, summing up the young love of Henry and Emilie:

> Henry descendait au jardin pour lire, et il trouvait Mme Emilie qui y était venue par hasard; ou bien Mme Emilie prenait son ouvrage pour aller coudre sous la tonnelle, et Henry, tout à coup, sortant de derrière un arbre, la faisait tressaillir. Ces petits événements étaient pour eux de grandes aventures (9).

Now as we saw from the *Nana* passage, the picturesque imperfect can be used for less than picturesque purposes towards the end of the century, especially in the hands of Zola. The instances of this mode in Zola deserve some attention. *La Joie de vivre* presents a classical case. Pauline and Lazare are in love, and working together at their sea experiments. Surprisingly enough, Zola gives a clue, with his *parfois* which regulates all the following material in a way not to be found with his predecessors. We thus know that the scene is just representative:

---

(8) Honoré de Balzac, *La Comédie humaine*, III (Paris: Bibliothèque de la Pléiade, 1955), 587.

(9) Gustave Flaubert, *Oeuvres complètes*, I (Paris: Aux Editions du Seuil, 1964), 314.

12

Parfois, cependant, au milieu de la grande chambre encombrée, ils se prenaient les mains, ils riaient d'un air tendre. C'était un traité de Phycologie qu'ils feuilletaient ensemble et qui rapprochait leurs chevelures; ou bien, en examinant un flacon pourpré de brome, un échantillon violâtre d'iode, ils s'appuyaient un instant l'un à l'autre; ou encore, elle se penchait près de lui, au-dessus des instruments qui encombraient la table et le piano, elle l'appelait pour qu'il la soulevât jusqu'à la plus haute planche de l'armoire (876).

While admiring the infusion of color into the scene, and while admitting that Zola is classically reproducing the new form in the imperfect, nevertheless, by comparison with the texts of Balzac and Flaubert, disappointment is felt by the presence of the adverbial temporal markings (*parfois, bien, encore*), the conjunctive semi-colons, the conjunction *ou*, all of which tend to make separate temporal units out of what was fused in earlier texts. But already we are anticipating the hallmarks of the Zola sentence. The description of the country idyll of Christine and Claude also has stylistic limitations:

Le soleil ayant reparu, des journées adorables se suivirent, des mois coulèrent dans une félicité monotone. Jamais ils ne savaient la date, et ils confondaient tous les jours de la semaine. Le matin, ils s'oubliaient très tard au lit, malgré les rayons qui ensanglantaient les murs blanchis de la chambre, à travers les fentes des volets. Puis, après le déjeuner, c'étaient des flâneries sans fin, de grandes courses sur le plateau planté de pommiers, par des chemins herbus de campagne, des promenades le long de la Seine, au milieu des prés, jusqu'à la Roche-Guyon, des explorations plus lointaines, de véritables voyages de l'autre côté de l'eau, dans les champs de blé de Bonnières et de Jeufosse (*Oeuvre*, 146).

In spite of the lyrical spirit of Zola, manifest in his affective *adorable,* the temporal lyric in the *passé simple* looks much like the style of the romantics. His narrative voice dominates.

As the second sentence moves into the imperfect, there are still analytical markings which inhibit the lyrical force of the imperfects, namely, *le matin,* implying that this is a sequence: «mornings they would do so and so», plus the indications that they took walks and not a single walk. The passage concludes with such reporter observations on geographical location that we could be tempted to believe in the traditional realism.

During a *veillée* in *La Terre* is recounted a «... histoire dramatisée du paysan, avant et après la Révolution...» (*Terre,* 428), entitled *Les Malheurs et le triomphe de Jacques Bonhomme.* While not exactly falling into the category of picturesque imperfect, the entire story is recounted in the imperfect, a literary equivalent perhaps of the historical present in French. It has to be seen as a lyrical dramatizing of past events. From the viewpoint of strict grammar, the tense would be hard to justify. The implications of Lerch's original discoveries on the picturesque imperfect have yet to be fully realized in the history of modern French literature. The examples from Zola would not indicate any greater degree of sophistication than what is found in Balzac or Flaubert.

In no instance does Zola seem innovative in the use of the imperfect. He amplifies what he has inherited from Flaubert. Zola, with the flamboyancy characteristic of his style, takes from Flaubert, takes from the literary impressionism surrounding him, takes from the conversations of the painters he knows, and from all of this perhaps overdoes natural evolutions in literature and painting. Yet, he produces a whole society which lives and breathes. Some of the historical critics may yet be correct in calling him a romantic. The specific style elements seem borrowed and overdone. There is no writer, however, who has produced such a vital, on-going process in his artistic language as we shall see from an examination of his syntax, and then his sentence.

IV. *The Zola Sentence*

There is no way to evaluate properly the style of Zola without measuring it in terms of the evolution of modern French prose out of the writings of Jean-Jacques Rousseau. Zola's sentence must also be measured in terms of what Hatzfeld has called the triumph of description over narration, especially after 1850 (10). The interplay of narrational and descriptive modes, changing the very structure of the novel, will necessarily fashion the basic sentence in fresh and innovative manners.

The question of *cursus* or prose rhythm cannot be ignored, although this work will only touch upon it in the most general way. How have rhythmic preoccupations on the part of writers driven them to new creations which influence our reception of the printed word? The basic drive here is the development of two tendencies in the nineteenth century. There is the almost impossible achievement of Ciceronian *cursus* (of a French already lyricized by Rousseau and not measurable with the yardstick of Bossuet's prose) by Chateaubriand in a language which by its fixed stress is antithetical to such procedures, and there is, in a contrary vein, the impulsion of the modern Stendhal, rejecting poetry and ornamentation as indicative of earlier literary periods, and opting for the simple and matter-of-fact Senecan sentence which reaches its peak in the *ordres du jour* of Napoleon I, the ideal for Stendhal (11).

The question of author voice is also part of the discussion. This again starts with Rousseau (12). As Hatzfeld has well demonstrated, it is Rousseau who destroys the brittle and witty *esprit* of Rococo conversational style, creating a lyrically modified, modern classical-baroque oratorical style, but one which has been put on a new type of syllable count not

---

(10) «After 1850 art turns to a new concept of life, which, even before the technical consequences are fully realized, can be called impressionism.», Hatzfeld, *Literature Through Art*, 165. This should not exclude, however, the enormous development of descriptive art wrought by Chateaubriand at the very beginning of the century.

(11) The best and most formal discussion of this problem is by Jean Mourot in *Le Génie d'un style, Chateaubriand, Rythme et sonorité dans les Mémoires d'Outre-Tombe* (Paris, 1960). Mourot makes it clear that Chateaubriand's pattern, while Ciceronian, is at times also derived from Seneca (327). The battle of romanticism, which Stendhal lost to Victor Hugo, means not simply the survival of poetry and a new renaissance for it, but also the development of modern prose style which is elaborate and ornamental in its figures and in its rhythms.

(12) The opening sentence of the first *Rêverie* is evidence that we are witnessing the birth of a new style: «Me voici donc seul sur la terre, n'ayant plus de frère, de prochain, d'ami, de société

assimilable to any traditional *cursus* (13). Rousseau's transformations of French prose pass through Chateaubriand and reach a high point, before Proust, in Flaubert, where formal style problems are paramount. Flaubert seems essential in two ways, first by continuing, and consciously, the investigation of the *cursus* of modern French, seeking harmony between the written and the spoken word, and then by the elaboration of the principle that the writer must not be present in his creation (14).

* * *

To this point the general tendencies of nineteenth century prose have been considered: nominal style as the basic high-art tendency of this prose, with the dominating pattern of the imperfect as a verbal aspect in the modern novel. Yet there remains what can be called the typical Zola sentence, a sentence of violent movement, seen verbally, adverbially, prepositionally, This seems to be the unique aspect of Zola's sentence. Such a sentence, however, must be evaluated against the correcting principle of the simple narrative sentence.

If psychology and description have forced artistic imperfect modes upon the narration, if impulsion toward tableau composition has speeded the process of nominal style, nevertheless, the basic pattern of the novel is narrative. Here is not meant the commenting narrative voice, but the motor voice of the author who still needs the simple sentence to change direction,

---

que moi-même. Le plus sociable et le plus aimant des humains en a été proscrit par un accord unanime» (995).

(13) See Helmut A. Hatzfeld, *The Rococo: Eroticism, Wit, and Elegance in European Literature* (New York, 1972), particularly the concluding chapter, «Rousseau's Romanticism, Destroyer of the Rococo.» Hatzfeld speaks of Rousseau's «... radically different concept of love and his flight from the curt Rococo style into a new period style comparable, in its rhetorical flights, to the Romantic *néo-grécisme* in architecture and painting...» (247).

(14) The celebrated letters to Louise Colet during the elaboration and writing of *Madame Bovary*, especially the letter of December 9, 1852 concerning the non-intervention of the novelist in the world he has created. See also the letter of October 12, 1853. While valid for Flaubert, this point of view became unfortunately a generalized ideal for the novel, thanks to critics like Percy Lubbock, *The Craft of Fiction.*

or simply to tell us what happens next. This means that none of the processes described can be considered as exclusive.

The simple narrative sentence seems more typical of the early novels. Toward the end of the series, simple narration is rarer, Zola's long, heavy-breathed, movement sentences gaining dominance. The simple matter-of-fact sentence, however, never dies. Narrational sentences so typical of *La Fortune des Rougon*: «Les jeunes gens traversèrent le faubourg endormi sans échanger une parole» (19); «La lutte fut cruelle» (49); «Pascal, dès lors, fut jugé» (67); «Félicité referma la porte» (105), sentences in which actions or states are marked in recognizable time units, continue across the series, and the following examples are illustrative: «La Teuse, en entrant, posa son balai et son plumeau contre l'autel» (*Faute,* 1215). This is an action-packed sentence, having almost theatrical quality about it. Description is not necessarily seen as having a long and complex development, it may be very simple: «La lune se levait, derrière les Garrigues» (*Faute,* 1307), wherein the only subjective pause is found in the affective role of the comma. Narrational sentences frequently open novels, setting the narrational clock in motion: «Gervaise avait attendu Lantier jusqu'à deux heures du matin» (*Assommoir,* 375). Habitual action may be recorded along the time line: «Les après-midi où Coupeau s'ennuyait, il montait chez les Lorilleux» (*Assommoir,* 489). These sentences tell briefly, succinctly, what had happened, what conditions were like: «Hélène n'avait pas dormi de la nuit» (*Page,* 987); «A neuf heures, la salle du théâtre des Variétés était encore vide» (*Nana,* 1095); «Alors, Nana se mit à rire» (*Nana,* 1190). Narrative sentence structure, simple in its elements, forms an important and basic aspect of novelistic structure. While it may be obvious, it could be overlooked in the light of the attention given to more complicated aesthetic patterns.

* * *

Zola consistenly arranges his syntax in such a manner as to destroy the traditional, organized and logical exposition of thought processes as they are ordered by the analytical mind, substituting for this process a word order which reflects the way the senses perceive the reality offered by the exterior world; the order is natural. One critic has referred to this as the «dislocation» of impressionism (15).

While this procedure has been recognized by a large number of critics, its full literary implications have never been stated so clearly as by Helmut Hatzfeld in his analysis of impressionistic word order in Chapter VIII of part I of *Madame Bovary*, «Le Bal à la Vaubyessard» (16). The sentence analyzed by Hatzfeld:

> Cependant, au haut bout de la table, seul parmi toutes ces femmes, courbé sur son assiette remplie, et la serviette nouée dans le dos comme un enfant, un vieillard mangeait, laissant tomber de sa bouche des gouttes de sauce. Il avait les yeux éraillés et portait une petite queue enroulée d'un ruban noir. C'était le beau-père du marquis, le vieux duc de Laverdière (*Madame Bovary*, 46).

This Flaubertian pattern is continued by Zola and receives some modifications. What are the implications? The syntactical procedure in general is to place frequently the adjective in the affective position, to place the subject of the sentence in the final position, as the psychological predicate, in the terminology of E. Lerch, and to minimize the role of the verb along the nominal lines, to the profit of the noun. The accumulation of detail, often rendering the whole by the part, can also strongly deny person, if subject, any essential role in

---

(15) Alexis François, *Histoire de la langue française cultivée*, II (Geneva, 1959), 238. In a very brief chapter, François seeks to summarize the situation, the development of the logically constructed sentence unit from the time of the seventeenth century, its animation in the nineteenth, and also its destruction then, starting with Michelet and going on to the Goncourt brothers and Daudet. There is no mention of Zola, but then the very title of the work would exclude him for obvious reasons. François' work, highly subjective, still distinguishes between an impressionistic and a naturalistic style (237-47).

(16) Without repeating Hatzfeld's analysis, his essential definition should be stated: «La phrase la plus impressionniste est celle où les éléments, sans aucune intervention de logique ou d'arrangement, sont énumérés exactement dans la suite que les yeux ou les oreilles les perçoivent.», *Initiation*, 120.

the order of things, person being just one more detail in the general accumulation.

Renée, for example, as an impressionistic observer will receive fragmentary percepts of a reality:

> Et, dans ce rayon, la jeune femme, clignant les yeux, voyait par instants se détacher le chignon blond d'une femme, le dos noir d'un laquais, la crinière blanche d'un cheval (*Curée*, 593).

wherein the parts, seen with their color attributes, precede the real subject. *Le Ventre de Paris* is filled with such constructions as in Zola's description of the *Marché des fleurs coupées* where we see «... les panachures vives des marguerites, le rouge saignant des dahlias, le bleuissement des violettes, les chairs vivantes des roses» (*Ventre*, 622), *panachures* being a fine variation on our regular *tache*, followed by nuanced adjective, adjective turned into noun, with a final kinesthetic impression in the manner of Baudelaire.

The Flaubertian manner, piling up of detail in a chaotic fashion and delaying subject, is noticed in Zola from the very beginning of the *Rougon-Macquart* series. The farmers are arriving at Les Halles:

> En haut, sur la charge des légumes, allongés à plat ventre, couverts de leur limousine à petites raies noires et grises, les charretiers sommeillaient, les guides aux poignets (*Ventre*, 603).

Flaubert consistently uses a complementary explanatory sentence, usually opening with *C'était*. Zola usually will just insert the subject normally at the end of the sentence. The opening paragraph of *Le Ventre de Paris* is probably the densest field of independent, impressionistic syntactical patterns in the entire work of Zola. The description of the *canotiers* in *Son Excellence Eugène Rougon* follows the same procedure:

> Au-delà du pont, au milieu de la nappe élargie de la rivière, très bleue, moirée de vert à la rencontre des deux bras, une équipe de canotiers en vareuses rouges ramaient, pour maintenir leur canot à la hauteur du Port-aux-Fruits (*Excellence*, 87).

Sometimes a series of independent clauses is created in which the first part follows regular subject-predicate syntactical arrangement, while the second is impressionistic, with subject last, the whole more or less syllabically balanced:

> Louise Violaine, descendue de son panier, avait rejoint Caroline Héquet; et, à leurs pieds, dans le gazon, des messieurs installaient une buvette, où venaient boire... (*Nana*, 1388).

Downplay of the verb usually accompanies the pattern of placing the subject last. In this example, there is only one verb, and it is found in the culminating seventh clause:

> Au milieu du salon, en satin bleu, d'un luxe neuf et déjà taché de graisse, une des soeurs, la plus petite, assise sur le tapis, torchait une casserole apportée de la cuisine (*P. B.*, 308).

It is apparent that clause follows clause, continually explaining, complementing, or giving additional impressionistic aspects. In the following sentence it is as if a photographer is looking down on the crowded store. As the sentence begins, the customers have become part of Zola's traditional impressionistic «mass» —the literary impressionistic «sea», —which turns into multi-colored and vivid hats, with finally the real detail of hair. In reading the sentence it is somewhat like moving back from an impressionistic painting in a gallery:

> Et cette mer, ces chapeaux bariolés, ces cheveux nus, blonds ou noirs, roulaient d'un bout de la galerie à l'autre, confus et décolorés au milieu de l'éclat vibrant des étoffes (*Bonheur*, 627).

This syntax will prevail even though the individual elements have nothing formally impressionistic about them, that is, in terms of light and forms. The basic syntactical elements in themselves may be logically ordered, as in this example from *La Joie de vivre,* where organizing principles, like the use of the possessive adjective, are at work:

> De l'autre côté, abrité contre le mur de *son* jardin, dans la crainte que le vent ne fendît *sa* soutane, l'abbé Horteur regardait aussi (*Joie*, 984).

In the following example the balancing of the parts is striking. If we consider the third clause as a kind of main clause, because of the presence of the verb, then we have an arrangement of two clauses introducing the verbal clause, followed by two closing clauses which, while balancing 1 and 2, also go on to create new units, the clauses of past participle with which the sentence closes:

> Contre un mur, sur des planches de bois blanc, étaient rangés un millier de volumes, des livres classiques, des ouvrages dépareillés, découverts au fond d'un grenier de Caen et apportés à Bonneville (*Joie*, 838).

	(1) contre un mur ⟷	(4) livres classiques
(3) millier de ↗ volumes	(2) sur des ⟷ planches	(5) ouvrages dépareillés ↕
		(6) découverts
		(7) apportés

The past participle of clause 5 engenders the past participle in 6 and 7, and is the logical continuation of a rhetorical «snowball» style which seems to have its origins in the bombast of the romantic theatre and in the persuasive style of George Sand (17). This is a fine example of impressionistic syntax, a literary mode of assembling reality, in this instance, subject with very pale verb, prepositional topography, noun fields, and static past participles.

The number of clauses varies in Zola, but four seems to be fairly typical. In this example from *Le Rêve,* four clauses are presented, the first three concentrating on a variety of

---

(17) Nancy Wall, «The Persuasive Style of the Young Sand,» (doctoral dissertation, The George Washington University, 1974). See especially the last chapter which gives a very impressive stylistic analysis of the Sandian sentence, characterized by patterns of self-propagation induced by specific parts of speech, present and past participles, possessive and demonstrative adjectives and pronouns, and so on.

impressions, (a) shadows which (b) are turning blue the snow-flakes in which (c) are found a contourless form which (d) turns out to be a little girl:

> Dans les ténèbres, que bleuissait la chute lente et entêtée des flocons, seule une forme indécise vivait, une fillette de neuf ans... (*Rêve*, 815).

The Zola sentence is basically composed of impressionistic units in dense descriptive fields in the imperfect. But the constellation is more complicated than the analysis to this point would have us believe. There is also the sentence of movement, with a coordinate over subordinate structure, relying heavily on conjunction, adverbial clause and phrase, prepositional phrase. All of this means at times a highly verbal style asserting itself in the face of the nominal style. Examining the sentence of movement as the unique and typical Zola structure, the question of its adherence to a general impressionism will perhaps remain open to debate.

* * *

The basic pattern of movement in the Zola sentence is one where a series of actions is reported, detail being added to detail, creating a sequence of descriptive photographs. The standard narrational pattern of the novel, usually felt with the verb in the *passé simple* in a simple sentence, is the point of departure. These patterns are best isolated in the more heavily narrative novels such as *Son Excellence Eugène Rougon*. Therein, chapters are frequently joined by simple sentences in the preterite: «Des semaines se passèrent» (*Son Excellence,* 185); or action-reaction patterns are created: «L'empereur ayant gagné, Rougon demanda une revanche» (*Son Excellence,* 169). Or simple narration may be modified through subordination: «Il glissa ses deux bras autour du bel embonpoint de Mme Correur, qui lui sourit» (*Son Excellence,* 95). The transition to the more ordinary Zola process, however, is found when Zola employs neither simple sentence nor subordinate clause. Rather it is through the route of added clause modifying the original statement: «Trois mois plus tard, un soir de décembre, le comte Muffat se promenait dans le passage des Panoramas»

(*Nana,* 1259). This sentence illustrates how Zola has pushed the mania for descriptive art to the ultimate limits possible for the nineteenth century. The simple narration of the promenade of Muffat is delayed until two preceding clauses narrow down the temporal field, the second clause being more precise than the first. Following the gradation which is being established here, it can be shown that the next step for Zola will be to insist upon the accumulative description as having more novel-istic importance than the simple narration. In fact it is the accumulation of detail, usually presented nominally, which gives importance to any action.. Eugène Rougon arrives in the salon of Clorinde. The arrival contrasts sharply with what Eugène sees, at least as Zola has (re)constructed the picture:

> Lui, difficile d'ordinaire à décontenancer, *resta* un instant sur le seuil, timidement. Devant le vieux piano qu'il tapait avec furie, pour en tirer des sons moins grêles, se tenait le chevalier Rusconi, le légat d'Italie, un beau brun, diplomate grave à ses heures (*Son Excellence,* 62).

Not only is the sentence impressionistic with the anticipating subject pronoun *il* only identified at the end of the third clause, and also filled with movement, but Rusconi himself has his vocational, physical and psychological portrait drawn within the same sentence.

Zola seems bent on rapid scene creation, a series of actions and movements impelled by conjunctions and prepositions:

> Un jour, au crépuscule, comme elle était sortie à pied pour aller voir son père, qui n'aimait pas à sa porte le bruit des voitures, elle s'aperçut, au retour, sur le quai Saint-Paul, qu'elle était suivie par un jeune homme (*Curée,* 423).

The rapidity of this sentence is astonishing. A single sentence takes Renée out of her carriage some distance from the house of her father, the visit to the father (a primary narrational goal in the more traditional novels) is totally effaced from the sentence, lost somewhere inside the first subordinate clause, the second series of coordinate clauses («returning», «on the Saint Paul quai»,) have her realizing that she is being followed.

The sentence isolates and puts into relief a series of movements with time and place elements added.

The verbs, usually in the imperfect, frequently record a series of movements or details: «Rougon, paisiblement, donnait des réponses, expliquait les retards, descendait dans les détails les plus minutieux» (*Son Excellence,* 56); «Les laveuses avaient mangé leur pain, bu leur vin, et elles tapaient plus dur, les faces allumées, égayées par le coup de torchon de Gervaise et de Virginie» (*Assommoir,* 401); «Le prêtre baisait la nappe, joignait les mains, multipliait les signes de croix sur l'hostie et sur le calice» (*Faute,* 1223). What is accomplished by accumulation of verb and past participle can also be achieved by noun repetition: «Les voix, les rires, les mots gras se mêlaient dans le grand gargouillement de l'eau» (*Assommoir,* 401). *L'Assommoir* provides many examples of Zola's sentences of detail accumulation and movement, showing how early he had mastered this technique:

> Quand elle allongeait la tête, en camisole blanche, les bras nus, ses cheveux blonds envolés dans le feu du travail, elle jetait un regard à gauche, un regard à droite, aux deux bouts, pour prendre d'un trait les passants, les maisons, le pavé et le ciel... (*Assommoir,* 500).

Quand elle allongeait la tête,
1. en camisole blanche,
2. les bras nus,
3. ses cheveux blonds envolés dans le feu du travail.

elle jetait
1. un regard à gauche,
2. un regard à droite,
3. aux deux bouts,

pour prendre d'un trait,
1. les passants,
2. les maisons,
3. le pavé et le ciel,

No matter how small the scene, Zola insists upon adding detail onto detail, and almost always by way of coordinate clause, coordination going hand in hand with nominal tendency:

> Nana et Pauline marchaient les premières, le paroissien à la main, retenant leurs voiles que le vent gonflait; et elles ne causaient pas, crevant de plaisir à voir les gens sortir des boutiques, faisant une moue dévote pour entendre dire sur leur passage qu'elles étaient bien gentilles (*Assommoir*, 680).

Zola's style has minimal subordination. The *Rougon-Macquart* achieves its message through illustrative tableaux. If the procedure is based in narrative style, at its highest, the verb seems to be submerged by noun detail, controlled by conjunction, preposition and adverb. The following description or rather confusing (from the analytical view) evocation of high society enjoying an afternoon in the Bois de Boulogne places the verb squarely in the middle of the sentence where it is lost amid the photo montages surrounding it:

> Au milieu des taches unies, de teinte sombre, que faisait la longue file des coupés, fort nombreux au Bois par cette après-midi d'automne, *brillaient* le coin d'une glace, le mors d'un cheval, la poignée argentée d'une lanterne, les galons d'un laquais haut placé sur son siège (*Curée*, 320).

With nominal phrases dominating, Zola looks more and more like a painter of Second Empire life. It may be the highly nuanced and qualified description of a window as in:

> Devant les deux larges fenêtres, des rideaux de calicot, soigneusement tirés, éclairaient la chambre de la blancheur tamisée du petit jour (*Faute*, 1316);

or this very accurate description of a valet performing door service:

> Dans le vestibule du petit hôtel, Pierre se tenait debout, en habit et en cravate blanche, ouvrant la porte à chaque roulement de voiture (*Page*, 889).

And like Zola, his creatures are presented as engaging in impressionistic perception. Comte Muffat, through a half-open doorway sees a servant washing herself, and reacts sexually:

> Un jour, *en passant*, il avait aperçu, par une *porte
> entrebaîllée,* une servante qui se débarbouillait; et
> c'était l'unique souvenir qui l'eût troublé de la pu-
> berté, à son mariage (*Nana,* 1213).

Frequently, the recall of the past on the part of a person is
stylistically reported through the enumerative sentence pattern
we have been examining here. Florent's introspections on the
year he has spent at Les Halles are seen in the construction of
four clauses, each with a *mot-thème* corresponding to the
principal idea of the first clause, *année mauvaise: persécution,
nausées, indigestion, hostilité*:

> Et il revit l'année mauvaise qu'il venait de passer,
> la persécution des poissonnières, les nausées des
> journées humides, l'indigestion continue de son es-
> tomac de maigre, la sourde hostilité qu'il sentait
> grandir autour de lui (*Ventre,* 867).

Evaluating the past ten years of her life with Saccard, Renée
comes to certain fundamental truths about her own self-
deception, but also to a realization of the true nature of her
husband as a man coveting, working day and night for money.
Not surprisingly, her recall of the past takes the form of a
prolonged and action filled metaphor, for her perception and
Zola's are the same:

> Depuis dix ans, elle le voyait dans la forge, dans les
> éclats du métal rougi, la chair brûlée, haletant,
> tapant toujours, soulevant des marteaux vingt fois
> trop lourds pour ses bras, au risque de s'écraser
> lui-même (*Curée,* 574).

Etienne, listening to the anarchist Souvarine, allows his mind
to duplicate, through a series of vivid flashbacks, exactly the
same material which Zola has already reported:

> Saisi de peur, l'autre le regardait, songeait aux his-
> toires dont il avait reçu la vague confidence, des
> mines chargées sous les palais du tzar, des chefs
> de la police abattus à coups de couteau ainsi que
> des sangliers, une maîtresse à lui, la seule femme
> qu'il eût aimée, pendue à Moscou, un matin de pluie,

> pendant que, dans la foule, il la baisait des yeux, une
> dernière fois (*Germinal*, 1343).

This sentence is illustrative of Zola's constructions for it successfully blends narration (the first three clauses) with the nominal visual listings. Stylistically the passage achieves an aesthetic unity through the past participle constructions, found first in the narration, and then in two staccato-like visualizations of Souvarine's violence. The last vision, that of the hanging of the mistress, is impressive precisely because of the addition of isolated detail in successive clauses: «hanged in Moscow, on a rainy morning, kissing her through the crowd with his eyes», and the pathetic, «for the last time».

A fundamental procedure is the metamorphosis, explanation, extension, or repetition, in succeeding clauses, of a postulation made in the first. Zola approaches the same topic from various angles, always getting closer to the truth or reality as he perceives it. Pierre Rougon, through the events of the coup d'état is transformed into a «... terrible monsieur».

> Ce fut ainsi que ce grotesque, ce bourgeois ventru,
> mou et blême, devint, en une nuit, un terrible mon-
> sieur dont personne n'osa plus rire (*Fortune*, 289).

Curée is amplified, in a tripartite structure into evocations of sound and light:

> C'était l'heure où la curée ardente emplit un coin
> de forêt de l'aboiement des chiens, du claquement
> des fouets, du flamboiement des torches (*Curée*, 435).

Noise is heard near the *paradou* and five clauses differentiate the sounds:

> Des bruits venaient du parc, des frôlements d'ailes,
> des frissons de feuilles, des bonds furtifs cassant
> les branches, de grands soupirs ployant les jeunes
> pousses, toute une haleine de vie roulant sur les
> cimes d'un peuple d'arbres (*Faute*, 1255).

This explanatory style is not just movement, but a manner with Zola. In *La Faute de l'abbé Mouret*, three sentences repeat the same idea, that Albine and Serge are truly masters of *le paradou*:

> Cependant, à cette heure, le parc entier était à eux. Ils en avaient pris possession, souverainement. Pas un coin de terre qui ne leur appartînt (*Faute*, 1390).

The idea of possession is reiterated constantly in the following sentences, turning the original idea into a motif: «... leur royaume...» (*Ibid.*); «Ils possédaient la forêt...» (*Ibid.*); «Ils régnaient partout...» (1391); «... ils étaient les maîtres...» (*Ibid.*). Nana disappears from Paris, adding to her mythic status. Zola's narrational voice transforms the departure into a *plongeon* becoming a *fugue* becoming an *envolée*:

> Nana, brusquement, disparut; un nouveau plongeon, une fugue, une envolée dans des pays baroques (*Nana*, 1471).

She herself, in one sentence becomes *femme chic, rentière, marquise*:

> Alors, Nana devint une femme chic, rentière de la bêtise et de l'ordure des mâles, marquise des hauts trottoirs (*Nana*, 1346).

Marjolin and Cadine are the true children of Les Halles. Zola, with his typical proliferation, announces that the market is their *volière, étable, mangeoire*. With his usual eye and ear for harmonious and rhythmic balancings he complements the tripartite nomenclature of the market with three verbs and with three nouns. We note also the rhythmic transformation of the possessive adjective into definite article:

> Ils en vinrent tous deux à ne plus quitter les Halles. Ce fut leur volière, leur étable, la mangeoire colossale où ils dormaient, s'aimaient, vivaient, sur un lit immense de viandes, de beurres et de légumes (*Ventre*, 772).

The *service de la réception* in the department store is described as an area which constantly swallows up materials:

— 193 —

13

> Tous les arrivages entraient par cette trappe béante;
> c'était un engouffrement continu, une chute d'étoffes
> qui tombait avec un ronflement de rivière (*Bonheur*,
> 422).

The arrival of spring to the mining town is recorded in a very
long sentence in which we can hear the ardent rhythm of
Zola's voice, as he too rejoices in the renewal of the earth,
particularly in the strong *ne jamais aucun* negation which forms
the contrast of the concluding clause:

> Le printemps était venu. Etienne, un jour, au sortir
> du puits, avait reçu à la face cette bouffée tiède
> d'avril, une bonne odeur de terre jeune, de verdure
> tendre, de grand air pur; et, maintenant, à chaque
> sortie, le printemps sentait meilleur ... après ses
> dix heures de travail dans l'éternel hiver du fond,
> au milieu de ces ténèbres humides que jamais ne dis-
> sipait aucun été (*Germinal*, 1251).

The successive piling up of harmonious traits can convince us
that Dr. Pascal is a young man in spite of the fact that he is
almost sixty:

> Lui-même, dans cette clarté d'aube, apparaissait,
> avec sa barbe et ses cheveux de neige, d'une solidité
> vigoureuse bien qu'il approchât de la soixantaine,
> la face si frâiche, les traits si fins, les yeux restés
> limpides, d'une telle enfance, qu'on l'aurait pris,
> serré dans son veston de velours marron, pour un
> jeune homme aux boucles poudrées (*Pascal*, 917).

The message is clear, the single term will not suffice; there
is no real predilection for the simple sentence. A train is
arriving, but it is not just a train but an express: «On entendit
le train, un express, caché par une courbe...» (*Bête*, 1029).

From the rhetorical style of the romantics, particularly
George Sand, Zola has inherited the tendency to repeat the
same word twice, in other words to use an echo-apposition:
«L'ennui était au fond des tristesses de Lazare, un ennui
lourd...» (*Joie*, 1014); «Angélique ... sentit le rire, le bon rire
lui remonter des flancs...» (*Rêve*, 877); «Des heures, des heures
passaient...» (*Page*, 1034). In the same manner he will repeat

parts of speech, preposition, interrogative and demonstrative adjectives, definite article. In the longer sentences such repetitions are accompanied by artful variations of the prepositions. He combines threefold anaphoras with triads of substantives in the same case:

> Quelle fresque immense à peindre, quelle comédie et quelle tragédie humaines colossales à écrire, avec l'hérédité, qui est la Genèse même des familles, des sociétés et du monde! (*Pascal*, 1008).
> Elle le comprenait maintenant; il lui apparaissait grandi par cet effort surhumain, par cette coquinerie énorme, cette idée fixe d'une immense fortune immédiate (*Curée*, 574).
> Elle, au contraire, d'une indifférence de fille grandie en serre chaude, ne semblait aimer de l'amour coupable que les sorties furtives, les cadeaux, les plaisirs défendus, les heures chères passées en voiture, au théâtre, dans les restaurants (*P. B.*, 258).

The lively and animated sentences of Zola, however, are truly explained through categories of grammar. It is the manipulation of past and present participles, conjunctions, adverbs and prepositions, adverbial and prepositional phrases which accounts for a style marked by great movement both in time and space. Past participles introducing successive clauses modify and explain an opening narrational clause:

> Et ils entraient peu à peu dans un état de béatitude particulier, bercés par toutes ces idées charnelles qu'ils remuaient, chatouillés par de petits désirs qui ne se formulaient pas (*Curée*, 429).

The past participle can interact with the present participle:

> Eclairée d'une seule lampe, brûlant sur l'autel de la Vierge, au milieu des verdures, l'église s'emplissait, aux deux bouts, de grandes ombres flottantes (*Faute*, 1285).

It is the present participle, however, which gives true dynamization to the Zola sentence. Marjolin and Cadine cross a street in a nonchalant manner:

> Ils y arrivaient, bras dessus, bras dessous, *traversant*
> les rues avec des rires, au milieu des voitures, sans
> avoir peur d'être écrasés (*Ventre*, 765).

This is particularly effective when there is an accumulation of
clauses, introduced by the present participle, to indicate the
idea of constant movement. Two descriptions of the *aire*
Saint-Mittre are illustrative of this process: a description of
the bohemians who periodically inhabit it:

> Ce monde vit sans honte, en plein air, devant tous,
> faisant bouillir leur marmite, mangeant des choses
> sans nom, étalant leurs nippes trouées, dormant,
> se battant, s'embrassant, puant la saleté et la misère
> (*Fortune*, 8).

Or daily activity:

> Le matin et l'après-midi, quand le soleil est tiède,
> le terrain entier grouille, et au-dessus de toute cette
> turbulence, au-dessus des galopins jouant parmi les
> pièces de bois et des bohémiens attisant le feu sous
> leur marmite, la silhouette sèche du scieur de long
> monté sur sa poutre se détache en plein ciel, allant
> et venant avec un mouvement régulier de balancier,
> comme pour régler la vie ardente et nouvelle qui a
> poussé dans cet ancien champ d'éternel repos (*For-*
> *tune*, 9).

In addition to creating a feeling of sound and movement
through the use of the participles, like under a magnifying
lens, stressing a moment within the flux of finite verbs, the
repetition of the prepositions achieves a graphic gradation,
establishing a vertical hierarchy, always ascending: the first
layer indicating turbulence, the second, the children running
among the gypsies at their fires, putting in relief the woodsman
who seems symbolic. What is seen here, in the very first
pages of the series, is an increased tempo of movement which
will become characteristic of the entire work.

Present participles effectively translate Lantier's actions
upon his return to the apartment of Gervaise, and are blended
with a direct reporting of his speech:

> Il surveillait maman Coupeau, exigeant les biftecks très cuits, pareils à des semelles de soulier, ajoutant de l'ail partout, se fâchant si l'on coupait de la fourniture dans la salade, des mauvaises herbes, criait-il, parmi lesquelles pouvait bien se glisser du poison (*Assommoir*, 609).

The present participle is an essential element of the Zola sentence. Like the imperfect, it instills a lively and animated «reality» on the materials, convincing us of the authenticity of what we are reading.

While frequently used, the present participle, however, cannot be seen as fundamental to the Zola sentence. It is necessary to isolate those elements which appear consistently across the *Rougon-Macquart*. The following is a typical Zola sentence and we should answer the question as to why it is so described:

> Après le déjeuner, lorsqu'elle revint donner un regard, Angélique se désespéra: la lessive entière menaçait de s'envoler, tellement les coups de vent devenaient forts, dans le ciel bleu, d'une limpidité vive, comme épuré par ces grands souffles; et, déjà, un drap avait filé, des serviettes étaient allées se plaquer contre les branches d'un saule (*Rêve*, 878).

The sentence is very long; Zola wishes to enclose as much information, as many perspectives and nuances as possible within the basic syntactical unit. There are three grammatical units which account for the fundamental sentence construction in Zola: (1) the Zola sentence proliferates clauses, usually coordinate ones. The basic techniques of coordination are employed: a series of clauses are joined by the simple comma, indicating a short pause for each element. There is a consistent use of the colon to introduce an explanation or an enumeration; the semi-colon is used to separate but not to isolate or detach the parts. The basic connective is the conjunction of co-ordination, *et*. This simple coordinate enables Zola to join together multiple parts of his discourse, with each additional clause having the same function of expressing an added feature, a relationship, or an approximation. *Et* pulls into its orbit related conjunctions such as *tandis que, à mesure que, cepen-*

dant, lorsque, quand, comme, pendant que, expressing various relationships between the parts, progression, simultaneity; (2) the conjunctions are complemented by nouns indicating time units, usually qualified by definite and indefinite articles and indefinite adjectives, and adverbs marking movement in time, such as *alors, puis, dès lors,* even adverbs of location, *en haut*; (3) the sentences abound with prepositional markings of place and time: *avant, après, entre, dans, sur, sous, le long de, au milieu de, derrière, jusqu'à, contre, autour de, à, pendant.* Thus the basic pattern of the Zola sentence is one of coordination of multiple elements distinguished in time and space.

The most simple grouping is the prolongation of the original idea through coordination achieved by *et.* Shirts are first perceived as a mass, but through the conjunction, followed by the prepositions *depuis* and *jusqu'à,* nuances of color are discerned. Finally, within the same sentence, the shirts are contrasted with the round and white bonnets:

> Parmi la masse des blouses, confuse et de tous les bleus, depuis le bleu dur de la toile neuve, jusqu'au bleu pâle des toiles déteintes par vingt lavages, on ne voyait que les taches rondes et blanches des petits bonnets (*Terre,* 508).

In the two opening clauses of the first sentence of *Le Ventre de Paris,* the conjunction merely serves as an equalizer of two clauses which are saying more or less the same thing: «Au milieu du grand silence, et dans le désert de l'avenue...» (*Ventre,* 603). The two parts approximate each other in syllabic count, and recall similar harmonies in Chateaubriand where successive clauses state the same idea, as in the storm description in *Atala*: «Les voix de la solitude s'éteignirent, le désert fit silence, et les forêts demeurèrent dans un calme universel» (*Atala,* 88). The opening sentence of *L'Oeuvre* illustrates the progressive nature of the coordinate sentence structure. Three actions are recorded as simultaneous, and this is achieved through the use of two conjunctions:

> Claude passait devant l'Hôtel de ville, *et* deux heures du matin sonnaient à l'horloge, *quand* l'orage éclata (11).

The very long sentences are usually divided, almost in half, by a semi-colon, followed by *et*. In the following example it is interesting to note how subject and verb cluster very close to the semi-colon on both sides of the division, while the extremities of the sentence, beginning and end, accumulate accessory detail:

> Tout le long des marbres et des glaces, accrochés aux barres à dents de loup, des porcs et des bandes de lard à piquer pendaient; *et* le profil de Lisa, avec sa forte encolure, ses lignes rondes, sa gorge qui avançait, mettait une effigie de reine empâtée, au milieu de ce lard et de ces chairs crues (*Ventre*, 667).

The description of the procession into the royal dining room at Compiègne is a fine illustration of the careful and balanced construction achieved by Zola in his long and elaborate coordinate clauses. The sentence divides into three parts: the first part, divided into four, describes the movements and psychological stance of the men; the second part, equally divided into four, describes the costuming and beauty of the women; the third part concentrates on objects, the rug, the trains of the skirts, and concludes with a subordinate clause:

> Les hommes se penchaient, disaient un mot, puis se redressaient, dans le secret chatouillement de vanité de cette marche triomphale; les dames, les épaules nues, trempées de clartés, avaient une douceur ravie; *et,* sur les tapis, les jupes traînantes, espaçant les couples, donnaient une majesté de plus au défilé, qu'elles accompagnaient de leur murmure d'étoffes riches (*Son Excellence,* 160).

The semi-colon and the conjunction serve to underline stylistically an important structure of *L'Assommoir.* In the opening page, Gervaise is awaiting the return of Lantier who has been out all night. The first half of the sentence records her impression of perhaps having seen her common-law husband enter the Grand-Balcon. It would appear that he had gone there with Adèle; fearing to be seen together in the light of the doorway, they separated before entering, just as they are separated in the sentence by the semi-colon. Only

Gervaise's analytical mind can put the two parts (Lantier and Adèle) together:

> Ce soir-là, pendant qu'elle guettait son retour, elle croyait l'avoir vu entrer au bal du Grand-Balcon, dont les dix fenêtres flambantes éclairaient d'une nappe d'incendie la coulée noire des boulevards extérieurs; *et*, derrière lui, elle avait aperçu la petite Adèle, une brunisseuse qui dînait à leur restaurant, marchant à cinq ou six pas, les mains ballantes comme si elle venait de lui quitter le bras pour ne pas passer ensemble sous la clarté crue des globes de la porte (*Assommoir*, 375).

Such connectives enable Zola to group a great quantity of clauses within a single sentence. In the following, Zola's observing eye, fusing with that of the painter Claude Lantier, makes a panoramic sweep of the crowd at the official salon:

> Des espaces restaient vides, des groupes se formaient, s'émiettaient, allaient se reformer plus loin; toutes les têtes étaient levées, les hommes avaient des cannes, des paletots sur le bras, les femmes marchaient doucement, s'arrêtaient en profil perdu; et son oeil de peintre était surtout accroché par les fleurs de leurs chapeaux, très aiguës de ton, parmi les vagues sombres des hauts chapeaux de soie noire (*Oeuvre*, 283).

The conjunction seems to provoke the remainder of the sentence to proliferate its parts, one part of speech doubling, in order to produce linguistic couplets, as in this sentence from *Le Docteur Pascal,* only with more factual differentiation:

> Le canal récent, dont les eaux d'irrigation devaient transformer le pays mourant de soif, n'arrosait point encore ce quartier; et les terres rougeâtres, les terres jaunâtres s'étalaient à l'infini, dans le morne écrasement du soleil, plantées seulement d'amandiers grêles, d'oliviers nains, continuellement taillés et rabattus, dont les branches se contournent, se déjettent, en des attitudes de souffrance et de révolte (957).

Following the semi-colon is to be found the ever-expanding explanation by Zola, with intense visualization, as his camera moves across the terrain, the main clause of the first part of the sentence: «Le canal ... n'arrosait point encore ce quartier». A series of couplings is created which looks like this:

les terres rougeâtres ⟷ les terres jaunâtres
s'étalaient à l'infini

dans le morne écrasement du soleil
plantées seulement — amandiers — oliviers
continuellement taillés — rabattus
se contournent — se déjettent
souffrance — révolte

Perhaps most characteristic of Zola is his habit of beginning a sentence with the conjunction *et*. At times it seems to be his means of forcing the sentence to coordinate and join with sentences before it. Studying a two-page description of Lisa's *charcuterie* in *Le Ventre de Paris,* leading up to the final sentence beginning with the conjunction *et,* we can see that the conjunction serves as the last term of a gradation, the apotheosis of the store as a *chapelle du ventre.* Zola begins his description of the display of Lisa's delicacies. Only the first part of each sentence, or part after semi-colon is indicated:

Puis, dans ce cadre.	(636)	adverb
Il était posé sur ...	(636)	nominal; preposition
par endroits	(636)	preposition
C'était un monde ...	(636)	nominal
D'abord	(636)	adverbial locution
il y avait	(636)	nominal
Les jambonneaux ... venaient au-des-sus	(636)	nominal; preposition
Ensuite	(636)	adverb
Il y avait encore ...	(637)	nominal; adverb
Entre les assiettes.	(637)	preposition
Une caisse ... étaient posées, aux deux coins, négligem-		

ment ... ...   (637)   nominal; preposition;
                                 adverb
... tandis que, der-
     rière ... ...   (637)   adverb; preposition

Thus the field leading into the sentence under discussion is limited to nominal verbal presentation and adverbial and prepositional fields. The eye is being directed up and down, back and forth, around and about. Finally one object is to be put into relief:

> *Et* là, *sur* le dernier gradin de cette chapelle du ventre, *au milieu* des bouts de la crépine, *entre* deux bouquets de glaïeuls pourpres, le reposoir se couronnait d'un aquarium carré, garni de rocailles, où deux poissons rouges nageaient, continuellement (*Ventre,* 637).

The purpose of the introductory conjunction *et,* which almost has the meaning of a startling *mais,* is to put into relief some part of a description; it is a means of spotlighting salient features. Claude views the *salon,* the usual prepositional wandering and markings are indicated and then:

> Et, au milieu de cette nudité de halle mal soignée, les murs surtout tiraient l'oeil, alignant en haut, sur des étagères, une débandade de moulages, disparaissant plus bas sous une forêt de tés et d'équerres, sous un amas de planches à laver, retenues en paquets par des bretelles (*Oeuvre,* 59).

The introductory conjunction also serves as a means of joining an interrupted narration. In Part V, Chapter III of *Germinal* there is a description of the rampaging miners moving about the countryside destroying mine equipment. Chaval and Catherine are captured by the miners and forced to participate in the activities. Zola finishes photographing the miners with: «Aux fosses! à bas les traîtres! plus de travail!» (*Germinal,* 1416), which are the screams of the crowd. Then a concluding paragraph describes Deneulin surveying the damage done to his mine, speculating on his impending ruin. Zola opens Chapter IV by again describing the march of the miners. The *et* is simply picking up the material cropped in the preceding chapter:

> Et la bande, par la plaine rase, toute blanche de gelée, sous le pâle soleil d'hiver, s'en allait, débordait de la route, au travers des champs de betteraves (*Germinal*, 1417).

The *et,* is creating, therefore, a sort of continuity. The intensification of movement produced by these coordinate constructions can serve as an appropriate backdrop for character analysis. At the beginning of *L'Argent,* Saccard, down on his luck, but anxious to reconquer Paris, is having lunch in a restaurant near the stock exchange. Zola cleverly joins Saccard's interior attitude with his description of the noisy exterior of the restaurant, and finally,again through the conjunction unifies the exterior scene outside the restaurant with the first idea. It works as follows:

> Dans son incertitude de la route à prendre, de sa vie à refaire, il les traitait tous de filous, ceux qui étaient là (other business men having lunch). Ah! si on l'y forçait, comme il les traquerait, comme il les tondrait, les Moser trembleurs, les Pillerault vantards, et ces Salmon plus creux que des courges, et ces Amadieu dont le succès a fait le génie! (*Argent*, 19-20).

This passage, echoing Saccard's thoughts of revenge, is then joined to a description of the noise in the restaurant. The noise and movement are interpreted in terms of a haste to finish eating and to get back to the stock market, for everyone's fate is dependent upon the right decision concerning Suez stocks, to buy or to sell:

> Le bruit des assiettes et des verres avait repris, les voix s'enrouaient, les portes battaient plus fort, dans la hâte qui les dévorait tous d'être là-bas, au jeu, si une débâcle devait se produire sur le Suez (*Argent*, 20).

With this preparation, the final sentence of the paragraph, introduced with the famous *et,* has Saccard surveying, through the restaurant window, the steps leading up to the Bourse. The purpose of this sentence, filled with the intense movement provoked by laissez-faire capitalism, is to show the world which Saccard must conquer. He will have to be quicker and more intelligent than all those whom he is surveying. Thus the importance of the *et,* joining this description to the two previous passages, a world in movement, symbolic of that which Saccard hopes to dominate:

> Et, par la fenêtre, au milieu de la place sillonnée de fiacres, encombrée de piétons, il voyait les marches ensoleillées de la Bourse comme mouchetées maintenant d'une montée continue d'insectes humains, des hommes correctement vêtus de noir, qui peu à peu garnissaient la colonnade; pendant que, derrière les grilles, apparaissaient quelques femmes, vagues, rôdant sous les marronniers (*Argent,* 20).

A gratuitous scene? Not at all, for it blends into the narration, but nevertheless, Zola seems to enjoy these Paris scenes for their own sake.

In the concluding volumes of *Les Rougon-Macquart,* the introductory conjunction becomes more frequent. More and more it seems to be a vocalization of fear, prophetic warnings of impending doom, on the part of the French people, victims of the collapse of the Second Empire, as in:

> Et tous croyaient entendre grossir le grondement de l'invasion, ce roulement sourd de fleuve débordé qui, maintenant, à chaque nouveau village, s'aggravait d'un nouvel effroi, au milieu des clameurs et des lamentations. (*Débâcle,* 431);

or the voice of Zola himself as journalist on the war front, sketching an abandoned French village:

> Et pourtant la ville aurait encore eu à peu près son aspect de tous les jours, sans les boutiques aux volets clos, sans les façades mortes, où pas une persienne ne s'ouvrait (*Débâcle,* 620).

Even without the serious events of wars and the destructions of nations, the voice of Zola is moving into prophecy, and the last volumes announce the messianic voice of the post-*Rougon-Macquart* series. Such is the tone of *Le Docteur Pascal*. In his own way, in spite of all his scientific pretentions, Zola is starting to take natural phenomena much too seriously. The conjunctive summary of a mistral storm in the south of France has parallels with what Victor Hugo did in «Les Djinns» from *Les Orientales*:

> Et c'était une rage, une trombe furieuse, continue, qui flagellait la maison, l'ébranlait des caves aux greniers, pendant des jours, pendant des nuits, sans un arrêt (*Pascal*, 1147).

If the very mature Zola is often a prophet of doom, he balances this with a message of hope. Such is the meaning of the very last sentence of *Les Rougon-Macquart*:

> Et, dans le tiède silence, dans la paix solitaire de la salle de travail, Clotilde souriait à l'enfant, qui tétait toujours, son petit bras en l'air, tout droit, dressé comme un drapeau d'appel à la vie (*Pascal*, 1220).

In this case, the conjunction *et,* while grammatically relating to the preceding sentence, really looks forward to the blank page beyond. *And,* the future, what will it bring? It is on this note of hope that Zola concludes the twenty volumes.

Other conjunctions serve to stimulate the sentence to linguistic reproductivity. Simultaneity is expressed through *tandis que,* and Zola, in the following example, balances the thought and the action of Octave Mouret against the reiterated reflexion of Mme Desforges:

> Tandis qu'il la complimentait et qu'il faisait quelques pas près d'elle, en maître de maison galant, elle réfléchissait, elle se demandait comment le convaincre de sa trahison (*Bonheur*, 640) .

Conjunctions such as *tandis que, cependant, lorsque, à mesure que, comme,* form a dense field within the novels, and are only dominated by *et. Cependant* looks very traditional, the sort of narrative connective which Flaubert still believed in when he wrote *Madame Bovary,* and which he tried to eliminate from *L'Education sentimentale* (18). Zola's ever-flowing narrative, and his voice, cannot imagine a sentence without the connectives:

> Cependant, M. de Boves et Vallagnosc, qui marchaient en avant avec Mme Guibal, arrivaient au rayon des dentelles (*Bonheur*, 640).

The preposition also has great status in the Zola sentence. Its principle function is to give the precision of life and movement to the scenes. Acting as qualifier it makes the scene more vivid with exact definition and localization. No statistical count is necessary to verify the dominating presence of the preposition in the work of Zola. The reader may casually turn to almost any page and the prepositions stand out, perhaps more than in any other writer of the nineteenth century:

> ... *pour* finir d'étourdir leur journée, *avec* leur notion pervertie de l'argent, *dans* les restaurants et les théâtres, les soirées mondaines et les alcôves galantes (*Argent*, 313).
> Et, *au milieu de* l'église ardente, débordante de clergé et de peuple, *sous* les voûtes élancées... (*Rêve*, 925).
> ... *dans* le plein air, *au milieu* du vert jaune des pampres... (*Terre*, 663).
> ... *contre* les cimaises de toutes les salles, *autour de la* galerie extérieure, partout enfin, *jusque* sur les parquets ... *entre* lesquelles ... filant *le long* des cadres ... *sous* le flot... (*Oeuvre*, 279-280).
> *Dans* des coins de boudoir, *aux* dîners de gala, *derrière* les jardinières en fleur, *à* l'heure tardive du thé, *jusqu'au fond* des alcôves... (*Argent*, 233).

---

(18) Edouard Maynial's listing of the variants shows how Flaubert was consistently eliminating the connectives. For example: «Il demanda au garçon de lettres s'il pouvait le présenter chez Arnoux» (33). Maynial's footnote 102 (435) shows the original as: «Alors il demanda...». Maynial notes: «Remarquer la fréquence des conjonctions ou adverbes éliminés par Flaubert» (*Ibid.*). The connectives, of course, as reminders of the presence of the narrator, are not desired by Flaubert. With Zola, they are a witness to his presence within the text.

... *dans* un verre de couleur ... *à* droite du tabernacle, *contre* le mur (*Faute*, 1219).
Dans les rues ... *le long des* maisons ... *sur* une seule file... (*Fortune*, 224).
Dans la plaine rase, *sous* la nuit *sans* étoiles ... *à travers* les champs de betteraves (*Germinal*, 1133).
... le marquis de Chouard installé *entre* les deux toilettes, *sur* une chaise (*Nana*, 1223).
... en l'accusant d'aller les regarder *par* le trou de la serrure, *dans* leurs chambres, quand elles se couchaient (*P. B.*, 250).
A l'autre bout, *aux* deux côtés du poêle, l'abbé Faujas et Marthe étaient comme seuls (*Conquête*, 969).
La veilleuse, *dans* un cornet bleuâtre ... *derrière* un livre... (*Page*, 801).

Zola is equally concerned with time, its passage, and sequence of events. To this end he will use the old Flaubertian formula (typical of so many of the chapter openings of *Madame Bovary*), time markers such as *le lendemain, un après-midi, ce jour-là, chaque soir*. Adverbial temporal connectives run throughout the work: «*Alors,* sous cette poussée formidable de publicité...» (*Argent*, 232); «*Puis,* la belle charcutière se pencha...» (*Ventre*, 667); «*Puis,* ennuyées d'avoir été déshabillées ainsi...» (*P. B.*, 250); «*Puis,* le long des routes...» (*Débâcle*, 422). The adverbial marking of time usually joins with related elements to prolong the sentence, with each grammatical element hammering away at the same idea. The abbé Faujas and his mother are slowly taking possession of the Mouret household. Zola insists upon this scheme in a tripartite structure which starts with an adverbial expression, repeated as an indefinite adjective which turns into an adverb: «*Dès lors, chaque jour, régulièrement,* les Faujas descendirent passer la soirée avec les Mouret» (*Conquête*, 969).

The description of a train wreck in a snowstorm is a fitting example with which to close this discussion of the sentence of Zola. It contains most of the elements considered:

Quelques glaces furent baissées, des têtes apparurent: une dame très forte, avec deux jeunes filles blondes, charmantes, ses filles sans doute, toutes trois Anglaises à coup sûr; et, plus loin, une jeune femme brune, très jolie, qu'un monsieur âgé forçait à rentrer; tandis que deux hommes, un jeune, un vieux, causaient d'une voiture à l'autre, le buste à moitié sorti des portières (*Bête,* 1168).

This is a style of coordination with nominal tendencies. It is characterized by excessive use of conjunctions, prepositions, adverbs and adverbial and prepositional phrases. Its purpose is to add detail and nuance, the original term sometimes being repeated or transformed into something similar, all serving to produce sentences marked by great movement and sequential impressions of observed reality. This gives a unique cast to the narrational style of Emile Zola. In the above example from *La Bête humaine* we have a finely honed specimen showing Zola's moving eye recording a series of impressions, with each succeeding clause getting closer to the reality. Heads which appear through the opened windows of the train are slowly identified as belonging to a rather formidable woman accompanied by two blond girls, and Zola observes them to be charming. His impressions are slowly being analytically organized: these must be the daughters of the woman (*sans doute*), and Zola can wager (*à coup sûr*) that they are all English. Jumping over the semi-colon, Zola's roving eye is moved by the conjunction and the adverb to distinguish a young brunette, who also receives his admiration, and she is related to the older gentleman as the little girls are to the «dame forte.» The final adverbial connective presents the third aspect of the tableau, the conversation, between coaches, of a young and an older man. The whole has the movement of a rolling movie camera. As the glossary has tried to demonstrate that the basic Zola vocabulary is one of movement, so this section has insisted that the syntax of Zola produces dazzling self-propagating sentences which remain central to his style.

V. *The Subjective Narrative Voice of Zola*

If we were to accept as basic to the novel the idea of a «story» being told by a «story teller,» which fits in perfectly with any historical consideration from the medieval romances up to Zola, we would not be upset to find that Zola's voice has indeed permeated the entire structure of his work. From the perspective of omniscient «story teller,» Zola's procedure is absolutely orthodox. This would mean that the endeavor of Flaubert to create a distance between himself and the «autonomous narration,» as Lubbock would put it, the critical preference for the story which is not told but which tells itself, is out of the main stream of the genre as we can describe it historically, and Zola, in spite of his desire to be modern, and sociologically or scientifically objective, is within the tradition. It is curious to see Flaubert as the exception, especially when criticism has been telling students for years that he is the estimable model. The serious aesthetic ponderings of Flaubert and Proust, with the evidence of their superior art, could easily convince us, of course, that they were on the right, the only road.

While Zola has profited from the work of Flaubert, in other ways he writes as if Flaubert had never existed. In his omniscience he most resembles Balzac. If in Chateaubriand the heros and heroines all look alike (idealized romantic beauty), and if furthermore they all speak in the same manner (*style noble*), there are parallel situations in Zola, if not of the same order. His metaphors, similes and vocabulary regularly repeat across the twenty volumes. His narrative voice applies the same basic linguistic, syntactical and metaphorical pattern to all situations; they relate less to theme and more to the man himself. At times Zola uses the language of his creatures; at times they use his, and in many instances we cannot distinguish, nor is it important that we do so. Flaubertian differentiated point of view, as twentieth century criticism has described it, seems without importance in Emile Zola. The point of view is his.

It is proposed to discuss the subjective voice of Zola as it appears in the narrative structure of the *Rougon-Macquart*. His discernable timbre, especially in the longer sentences of the final volumes, was suggested in the discussion of the sentence. Now it is time to look at his subjective voice as it appears in his lyrical and moralistic attitudes, and the subjective qualities which emanate from his narration. By definition, all narration is subjective; it was the impossible goal of Flaubert to destroy that subjectivity. Here it is maintained, however, that the main thrust of Zola is not to conceal his presence, but to reveal it at each turn of the phrase.

14

Subjective intrusion into the narration can be noted throughout the work. A simple starting point is Zola's enjoyment of ideal weather conditions, which relates to our discussion of Zola the aesthetic meteorologist. The examples are few but significant as Zola participates in the joy experienced by his characters. Describing the joy of Serge and Albine in *Le Paradou,* as the sunlight fills their chamber, Zola, the sunworshipper, participates actively in their enjoyment (perhaps even more than Serge and Albine), with his exclamation: «Quelle heureuse et tendre journée!» (*Faute,* 1324). Similarly, he is happy to see spring return to Paris, a joy which Gervaise can share with him as all goes well in her laundry: «Quelle heureuse saison! La blanchisseuse soignait d'une façon particulière sa pratique de la rue des Portes-Blanches» (*Assommoir,* 553). The exclamation can, however, be ironic, or intended really to convey the sentiments of the characters, as on the day the Rougon triumph in Plassans: «Quelle journée! Les Rougon en parlent encore, comme d'une bataille glorieuse et décisive» (*Fortune,* 276).

Historical critics have long told us that Balzac usually fell in love with his heroines, especially the innocent French girls victimized by *parvenus* (*Eugénie Grandet*) or by the English bluestockings (*Le Lys dans la vallée*), and that this adoration is revealed in his narrative style. Zola seems to be in a similar but more confusing, for us, situation. How can he reveal a subjective attitude of admiration toward Jeanne of *Une Page d'amour,* whose ego provokes so much guilt in her mother Hélène? Worse yet, how is he attracted to Nana? Yet, the consistent adjective for Jeanne is *adorable,* and it is repeated countlessly across the novel, the following example merely being representative: «Une contraction défigurait le pauvre et *adorable* visage...» (*Page,* 802). Two descriptions of Nana are done in this manner:

> Et les bras nus, les épaules nues, la pointe des seins à l'air, dans son *adorable* jeunesse de blonde grasse... (*Nana,* 1208).
> Et son sourire était *adorable*... (*Nana,* 1225).

The passages clearly indicate the voice of Zola, and they mean involvement. In the case of Jeanne, the explanation is simple.

Zola, like Victor Hugo, adores children, all of them, and his voice reveals this. He treats the child-woman heroine of *Le Rêve* in a similar manner. The case of Nana is more complicated. At first one is tempted to say that there is, as with Count Muffat, an attraction-repulsion syndrome operative. More likely, the subjective style reveals Zola's peculiar sexual-material syndrome: he believes in and exalts the beauty of the human body; his dilemma is Nana's degradation in Second Empire France. In all three novels it is Zola's visual admiration of physical grace (of little girls or Empire sirens) which gives *adorable* its exaggerated or emphatic meaning, of *aimable, gracieux, charmant, exquis.*

As the heroines are formed more and more in the likeness of their creator, the subjective admiration increases. There are three women in the *Rougon-Macquart* who share Zola's outlook on life: Denise of *Au Bonheur des dames* who seeks, probably as Zola did, a benevolent capitalism working for the people; Pauline of *La Joie de vivre* who learns how to accept life in all its joys and sorrows, a type of materialistic mystic if such an expression could be used; and Clotilde, Dr. Pascal's disciple and «child-bride.» All three of these heroines are presented under the sympathetic eye of the novelist, their physical and spiritual qualities constantly being stressed by the author. Denise is perhaps the best example. A metaphorical field of royalty, regal posture, mature ideas and attitudes, benevolence, surround her. She is goodness triumphant at the end of the novel, her marriage to Octave Mouret will insure a quasi-socialistic ambiance for the department store employees. Her humble origins are controverted by her royal behaviour. And her physical appearance reveals purity, as in the following description, following a rather unpleasant encounter with a nasty shopper:

> Denise avait entendu. Elle leva ses grands yeux purs sur cette dame qui la blessait ainsi et qu'elle ne connaissait pas. Sans doute, c'était la personne dont on lui avait parlé, cette amie que le patron voyait au-dehors. Dans le regard qu'elles échangèrent, Denise eut alors une dignité si triste, une telle franchise d'innocence, qu'Henriette resta gênée (*Bonheur,* 636).

Balzac is seen as a severe critic of Restoration France (19), and many pages of his novels pass judgment, such as the opening pages of *Eugénie Grandet* where he regrets the decline of moral values in France:

> La maison, pleine de mélancolie, où se sont accomplis les événements de cette histoire, était précisément un de ces logis, restes vénérables d'un siècle où les choses et les hommes avaient ce caractère de simplicité que les moeurs françaises perdent de jour en jour (20).

Such criticisms, Flaubert wanted to avoid, but we are all aware of the celebrated lapsus during the agricultural fair when the old peasant woman is awarded twenty-five francs for fifty-four years of service:

> Ainsi se tenait, devant ces bourgeois épanouis, ce demi-siècle de servitude (*Madame Bovary*, 141).

Zola chooses to be a severe judge of Second Empire France. The earliest volume to reveal this strongly is *La Curée*. It is seen in the content, the characters becoming for us their own judges as we see them engaged in the most supercilious of actions. Laure d'Aurigny must dye her red hair which is so offensive to her latest love (*Curée*, 319). Zola describes the ostentation of the Hôtel Saccard in terms which leave no doubt as to his opinion: «... cette grande bâtisse ... avait ... l'importance riche et sotte d'une parvenue» (*Curée*, 332). While adjudging the architecture simply because it is of the period Napoléon III, he correctly assesses the mixture of styles so prevalent in the nineteenth century:

> C'était une réduction du nouveau Louvre, un des

---

(19) See Bernard Guyon, *La Pensée politique et sociale de Balzac* (Paris, 1947). For an appreciation of Balzac as almost a Marxist critic of his society, *sans le savoir*, the works of Georg Lukács on European realism are essential. The critical edition of *Les Paysans* by J. H. Donnard (Paris, 1964) complements the above studies.

(20) Honoré de Balzac, *La Comédie humaine*, III (Paris: Bibliothèque de la Pléiade, 1955), 483.

échantillons les plus caractéristiques du style Napoléon III, ce bâtard opulent de tous les styles (*Ibid.*).

High society is seen as «... des Parisiens de la décadence...» (*Curée*, 348), as speculators upsetting any standard moral system:

> L'Empire allait faire de Paris le mauvais lieu de l'Europe. Il fallait à cette poignée d'aventuriers qui venaient de voler un trône, un règne d'aventures, d'affaires véreuses, de consciences vendues, de femmes achetées, de soûlerie furieuse et universelle (*Curée*, 367).

Zola's moral outrage expresses itself mainly about money and sexual affairs, which seem interlaced in the twenty volumes, particularly in *Nana*, *Pot-Bouille* and *L'Argent*. He finds it difficult to understand a public attracted to the obscene théâtre des variétés; even the dignified and aristocratic Count Muffat assists at Nana's presentation. Only Zola seems shocked and he lets the reader know it:

> On saisissait les allusions, on ajoutait des obscénités, les mots inoffensifs étaient détournés de leur sens par les exclamations de l'orchestre. Depuis longtemps, au théâtre, le public ne s'était vautré dans de la bêtise plus irrespectueuse. Cela le reposait (*Nana*, 1112).

Pot-Bouille is a novel which claims to unmask bourgeois hypocrisy. If on the one hand Zola loathes their double sexual standard, on the other he resents their pretention to having more than they have: Adèle is the only cook the Josserand family has been able to retain, says Zola, «... dans cette misère vaniteuse de bourgeois...» (*P. B.*, 27). He seems even to share the sentiments of the conservative parents of *Son Excellence Eugène Rougon* who, in a sort of *style indirect libre* pass judgment on the times:

> Et, discrètement, le père et la mère déplorèrent les nécessités de notre abominable époque qui empêchent les fils de grandir dans la religion de leurs parents (*Son Excellence*, 211).

In the *Rougon-Macquart* an acute observer could find many examples which would demonstrate Zola's subjective attitudes, not just about the Second Empire, but about society and social types in general. The style reveals attitudes and prejudices which are not too different from those of Balzac. *La Terre* reveals an attitude which could be taken from *Les Paysans*: «Au fond de tout paysan, même du plus honnête, il y a un braconnier» (639).

Zola's subjective and dogmatic attitude, however, enters more directly into his narration. Is this caused by the rather naive deterministic thesis, or is it derived from an absolutism ingrained in the mentality of Zola and perhaps distorted by the pseudo-science of which he was a victim? The latter seems to be the case. Zola tends to see human beings in terms of an extreme spectrum of vice and virtue. Some people are by nature good, and others bad. Here again he approximates Balzac, but with the added dimension of late nineteenth century Tainian positivism and scientism. On the one hand he looks like Cesare Lombroso, the Italian doctor and criminologist, (1835-1909), seeing the criminal as formed by society; on the other, his narrative voice would make us believe in instinctive urges toward good and evil. His description of Trouche, the brother-in-law of the abbé Faujas, recalls Balzacian physiologies, but in a more sinister manner:

> Sa face, toute couturée, suant le vice, était comme allumée par deux petits yeux noirs, qui roulaient sans cesse sur les gens, sur les choses, d'un air de convoitise et d'effarement (*Conquête*, 1006).

The *déchéance* of Coupeau and Gervaise is observed and controlled by Zola's narrative voice in such a manner as to allow no liberty of interpretation of motive on the part of the reader. Zola is there commenting. In Chapter V, Coupeau, half-drunk, arrives at the laundry, and, after publicly fondling the breasts of Gervaise, kisses her. Zola sees this indecency and informs the reader that this is the first step downhill to decay:

> Et le gros baiser qu'ils échangèrent à pleine bouche, au milieu des saletés du métier, était comme une première chute, dans le lent avachissement de leur vie (*Assommoir*, 509).

Even the choice of one of his key words, *avachissement,* is criticism of the strongest kind. The Lombrosian point of view is explicitly stated concerning Coupeau's drinking problems: «Et, vraiment, il n'y avait pas à le traiter de père sans moralité, car la boisson lui ôtait toute conscience du bien et du mal» (*Assommoir,* 744).

Ultimately, however, the deterministic thesis is less important than the fact that Zola is a moral absolutist, more rigid and puritanical than the religions he attacks. As Balzac believed in absolute types, Parisians and provincials, male and female, Catholic and Protestant, French and foreigner, vice and virtue, similar systems are at work in Zola and revealed in the narration. He is a pseudo-scientist using the traditional moral vocabulary, clouding the issues with a fake sociology and science. In *Pot-Bouille,* he makes his point about the vice of the maids and the cooks. His disapproval of their conduct is reinforced by the chain reaction description of their habits, with a strong physiological portrait at the conclusion, explaining the meaning of their vice:

> Elles s'entendaient bien ensemble, soignant leurs vices, la femme de chambre cachant l'ivrognerie de la cuisinière, et la cuisinière facilitant les sorties de la femme de chambre, d'où celle-ci revenait morte, les reins cassés, les paupières bleues (*Pot-Bouille,* 104-105).

Zola's moral absolutism then, means a style which reduces man to types which are seen as universally functioning in a certain manner, much like his description of the peasants in *La Terre.* The loss for Gervaise occurs when she loses her sense of «womanly pride»: «Naturellement, lorsqu'on se décatit à ce point, *tout l'orgueil de la femme s'en va*» (*Assommoir,* 729). Séverine's visit to the minister M. Camy-Lamotte is part of her effort to cover up a horrible crime, the murder of her protector. Zola explains her behavior in terms of an absolute rule of criminal conduct as he sees it:

> Mais, sous cette demande, qui servirait tout au moins à expliquer la visite, *il y avait un motif plus impérieux,* un besoin cuisant et insatiable de savoir, ce besoin qui *pousse le criminel à se livrer plutôt que d'ignorer* (*Bête,* 1107).

During the same visit M. Camy-Lamotte reacts to the gentle, helpless tone of Séverine through which both he and Zola see. Zola describes her attitude as belonging to the general category called feminine hypocrisy:

> M. Camy-Lamotte ne put alors que la faire asseoir, d'un geste, car cela était dit sur un ton parfait, sans exagération d'humilité ni de chagrin, avec *un art inné de l'hypocrisie féminine* (*Bête*, 1110).

To explain the sudden attacks of violence of Jacques Lantier, Zola has recourse to an anthropomorphic theory of violence, passed down from one male to another, across generations, back to pre-historic times. That Zola was a victim of pseudo-scientific theories which infiltrate the *Rougon-Macquart* is evident throughout the work, such as the internal combustion death of Old Macquart in *Le Docteur Pascal*. What is important here is that Zola's narrative voice reiterates over and over that this is indeed his belief:

> Des mains qui lui viendraient d'un autre, des mains léguées par quelque ancêtre, au temps où l'homme, dans les bois, étranglait les bêtes! (*Bête*, 1207).

Thus to the very end of the series, strong moral and equivocal scientific attitudes express themselves overtly in the *Rougon-Macquart*. In no way should his art be seen as coldly objective or clinical.

As Zola the man exhibits paternal affection for all children, and displays male admiration for feminine pulchritude, Zola the thinker reveals himself increasingly as the *Rougon-Macquart* series concludes with a dramatic crescendo. Ideological preaching becomes a discernible characteristic of Zola at least from the time of *L'Oeuvre,* with the writer Sandoz manifestly representing Zola (with an uncanny rivalry of fiction with reality as Sandoz explains to Claude Lantier the plan of the *Rougon-Macquart*), and Lantier partly Cézanne. In the creation of Pauline of *La Joie de vivre,* and Dr. Pascal (the name assumed by Zola during his London exile), there is no doubt that characterization is being used to fit ideology, and is not being derived from any «realistic» observation of life about him, save observation of the self. Furthermore, the increasing catastrophes of the final days of the Empire compel Zola into a narration in which he cannot exclude his own Greek chorus-like commentary. Zola's voice becomes more and more evident in the second half of the series as can be ascertained by Professor Mitterand's notes to the Pléaide edition, notes which show a positive accord between Zola's beliefs and the truisms of his characters. This is especially true when Zola comments on life attitudes, such as the philosophy of Pauline, who gives her fiancé to her rival, and ends up as mother-confessor and surrogate mother to the *foyer* she has established against her own sentiments. Pauline has arrived at a comprehension of the meaning of life. Zola's narrative, especially with its modern emphasis on «sound mind in sound body», betrays his accord with Pauline's position:

> C'était la vie acceptée, la vie aimée dans ses fonctions, sans dégoût ni peur, et saluée par la chanson triomphante de la santé (*Joie*, 857).

Likewise, the coupling of old Pascal and young Clotilde, designed to produce the child of the future, is observed and recounted by Zola, witness at the naturalistic wedding, godfather of the child of the positivistic future:

> N'était-ce pas la mystique vaincue, la réalité consentie, la vie glorifiée, avec l'amour enfin connu et satisfait? (*Pascal*, 1062).

The messianic interpretation of the industrial revolution and budding technology, with its roots in romanticism, infects the last novels of the series and becomes *idée fixe*. *Les Trois Villes* creates a vast panorama of symbolic cities of the past and the future. Zola opts for the future. Across the *Rougon-Macquart* he has tried, as a socialist-oriented bourgeois, to assess positively the meaning of modern industry, mass merchandising and transportation. The train becomes a specific symbol with him. If Zola regrets the hospital trains which take so many people to Lourdes in a reaffirmation of faith repugnant to his positivistic commitment, he also affirms his faith in the train of the future, which will lead to Paris, a city of lights, illuminated with hope for mankind. The final two pages of *La Bête humaine* betray this belief. The voice can only belong to Zola;

since Jacques and Pecqueux are dead, only the narrator is about. Although there is an urgency and concern on his part for the soldiers on the train being led to the ultimate defeat of Sedan, nevertheless the train will travel beyond that defeat to join with the trains of the post-*Rougon-Macquart,* to lead mankind into the city of the future. Sedan seems to be a necessary purgation to create a brave new world.

> Qu'importaient les victimes que la machine écrasait en chemin! N'allait-elle pas quand même à l'avenir, insoucieuse du sang répandu? (*Bête,* 1331).

Aside from this ideology which is questionable, we also detect Zola, the sensitive and concerned Frenchman, who cannot record impassibly the events of the Franco-Prussian war. Across *La Débâcle,* in a voice only equal to that of Victor Hugo of *Les Châtiments,* Zola ponders the fate of France invaded, its troops fleeing in shameful defeat. The anxiety of the French army is translated into a mournful sound crossing the land-scape. The narrator questions himself as to what this could mean:

> Sous le ciel sombre, à ce moment, un grand cri douloureux passa. Etait-ce la plainte d'un oiseau de nuit? Etait-ce une voix du mystère, venue de loin, chargée de larmes? (*Débâcle,* 415).

The question asked is not unlike the series of interrogations of Napoléon in Hugo's «Expiation.» In this case, the sound in the plain points to Sedan, seen as the final cleansing of a corrupt nation. Zola's anguish betrays itself in a series of exclamations:

> Ah! cette armée de la désespérance, cette armée en perdition qu'on envoyait à un écrasement certain, pour le salut d'une dynastie! Marche, marche, sans regarder en arrière, sous la pluie, dans la boue, à l'extermination! (*Débâcle,* 503).

If this is the voice of the young soldier Maurice, technically it is impossible for us to know so. The conclusion must be that it is the voice of Zola who cannot restrain himself before the spectacle of French defeat. The country has been offered up as victim to the foolish whims of Napoléon III:

> Ah! le bois scélérat, la forêt massacrée, qui, au milieu du sanglot des arbres expirants, s'emplissait peu à peu de la détresse hurlante des blessés (*Débâcle*, 692).

With Zola, the explaining narrator's voice is at its strongest in France since Balzac. This is caused by the imposition on observed reality of his own strong personality, ideology and style. Gifted for seizing essential traits, with the ability to transcribe succinctly those observations to the printed page, Zola cannot nevertheless be seen as an objective reporter. Accuracy of observation does not insure objectivity of interpretation. Zola continues the tradition of subjective narration in the modern French novel.

VI. *The Characters Speak Up*

The *Rougon-Macquart* has multiple and varied nuances of direct speech; the Second Empire is not only seen, it is heard. Speech renders individual and group psychologies through the emotional postures it reveals; through it individual and class outlooks and prejudices come to the fore.

Some of the novels seem more oriented to speech than others. *La Faute de l'abbé Mouret,* for example, opens like an opera before the singers have arrived on stage, with only the rythmic movements of La Teuse cleaning the church in preparation for Serge's morning mass. Yet the first chapter has as its motif the dialogue of the Tridentine mass which contrasts with Zola's descriptive commentary. *Son Excellence Eugène Rougon* is framed with the simple words: «La séance est ouverte.» (*Son Excellence,* 13), that is, the opening and closing chapters take place at the sessions of the legislature, underlining Rougon's in-power-out-of-power role, which is the main theme of the work. The last chapter in particular demonstrates Zola's reliance on speech, recording pro- and anti-government positions among the deputies. At times the speech of the deputies is recorded as it occurs, without any interference from the author:

C'est odieux! c'est intolérable! — Qu'il retire le mot!
— Oui, oui, retirez le mot! (*Son Excellence,* 357);
«—Votre liberté est de la licence! — Ne parlez pas
d'aumône, vous mendiez une popularité malsaine!
—Et vous, ce sont les têtes que vous coupez! (*Son Excellence,* 360-61).

Nana, one of the best of the novels for the representation of direct speech, opens with a description of the hustle and bustle of activity for the opening performance of Nana. The obscene conversations of the men are one of the most striking features of the work; summed up well in the repeated expression of Bordenave, the impressario in Chapter I, «Dites mon bordel.» (*Nana,* 1097, 1098, 1122).

Some of the great characterizations, particularly that of Nana and of Gervaise, are built partly on hearing their voices directly. The many moods of Nana are described by Zola; it is her voice which convinces us—the whole scale of her emotional life, Nana angry, Nana maternal, romantically in love, defending her family from the rue de la Goutte-d'or:

Maman était blanchisseuse, papa se soûlait, et il en est mort. Voilà! Si ça ne vous convient pas, si vous avez honte de ma famille... (*Nana,* 1366).

to a group of rich bourgeois men who dare not contradict her; Nana defending the Emperor, condemning «immoral literature,» speaking against «le peuple,» Nana contrite and compassionate, apologizing to her servant Zoé: «Mais, bête, j'ai dit dinde comme j'aurais dit autre chose. Est-ce que je sais! j'étais en colère. ... Là j'ai eu tort, calme-toi.» (*Nana,* 1371); in brief, all the contradictions of her pathetic character are conveyed to the reader not just by her actions, or by Zola's narrative, but by the direct confrontation with her speaking voice.

Napoléon III remains a mysterious figure throughout the series. We usually see him at a distance, at official ceremonies, staring from a palace window at Compiègne, wandering aimlessly across northern France, sick and bewildered during the Franco-Prussian war. Yet the whole series hints at the sexual exploits of the leader, and in one of his few direct conversational surfacings in the novel, at a royal banquet, his remarks to an American guest in his «voix pâteuse,» seem in character with the composite picture Zola has drawn: «En Amérique, je n'ai jamais vu divorcer que les femmes laides» (*Son Excellence,* 164).

Direct speech, however, is best studied in these novels by social classifications and can be put into two groupings which seem to complement and illuminate each other: the speech of the bourgeoisie versus the speech of the people and the peasants.

The speech of the bourgeoisie, best illustrated by *Pot-Bouille,* reveals fixed and stupid mental sets, an entire dictionary of ready-made phrases, *locutions figées* which support the Empire, family, class status, while disparaging their lessers. In addition, bourgeois speech reveals their lack of freedom, lack of contact with reality. It shows the nefarious effects of romantic thinking when it filters across an entire class which will use the romantic vocabulary to avoid any confrontation with the true nature of their lives. In addition, the bourgeois idiom infects courtesans of proletarian origin, who, installed in material luxury by their bourgeois lovers, will gradually ape bourgeois morality, ironically becoming more and more like the wives of their lovers. All of this speech vividly contrasts with the more direct, honest, and colorful speech of the people.

Madame Josserand will remain the most unforgettable of the pretentious bourgeois of the series. This aggressive, mean and hostile woman has only one drive, to arrive in the world, in spite of the fact that they are living much beyond their economic means. Her whole stance is one of pretense, reiterated across the novel in the form of her favorite expression, the guiding principle of her life:

> Moi, lorsque j'ai eu vingt sous, j'ai toujours dit que j'en avais quarante; car toute la sagesse est là, il vaut mieux faire envie que pitié (*P. B.,* 35).

Madame Josserand arranges every aspect of life, especially seeking advantageous marriages for her daughters. It comes as no surprise, therefore, that young Berthe, shortly after her marriage, turns into a carbon copy of her mother, down to repeating to others the famous expression of the twenty *sous.* She becomes a replay, in her speech, of the family quarrels she had heard as a little girl: «... elle recommençait contre lui (her husband) toutes les querelles de ménage dont on avait bercé sa jeunesse...» (*P. B.,* 226).

Naturally enough Zola has seized the central idea of this bourgeois morality, the expression «comme il faut» which is found everywhere in late nineteenth century literature. It hammers away across *Pot-Bouille*: «Et habitée rien que par des gens comme il faut!» (*P. B.,* 5); «Est-elle assez comme il faut! s'écria Mme Campardon.» (*P. B.,* 78). The concierge of the apartment house, Monsieur Gourd, is very much upset about a woman who comes to the room of a worker. The woman is truly his wife, but the worker is ultimately chased from the building for being immoral:

> Avait-on jamais vu! une créature pareille chez des gens comme il faut, où l'on ne tolérait pas la moindre immoralité (*P. B.,* 100).

Yet the concierge himself accommodates weekly meetings of another man with a woman there, under the guise of scholarship.

L'Oeuvre, while not outstanding in terms of dialogue, does, in one instance, illustrate how formulary can be a guiding principle for human behaviour. In the selection of salon paintings, members of the jury are permitted to select one painting, not on merit, but out of compassion. It is thus that one of Claude's paintings finally hangs in the exhibition. In selecting the painting the jurist repeats this formula: «C'est bon, je le prends pour ma charité» (*Oeuvre,* 281).

Upward mobility in these novels seems to mean prostitute turned kept-woman transformed into a *bourgeoise*. Clarisse, the mistress of Duveyrier, is a first-rate example. As time passes, she puts on weight, and becomes identical to the wife he has neglected. She insists on being called «Madame,» forbids smoking in her presence and takes up piano playing, driving her lover mad, for it was his wife's *soirées musicales* which had driven him out of his own home. Zola speaks of this as Clarisse's «... passion du comme il faut...» (*P. B.,* 309). Her own words best give us the message:

> Vous savez, mon vieux, ajouta-t-elle, si vous venez pour godailler, vous pouvez prendre la porte ...

C'est fini, la vie d'autrefois. A présent, je veux qu'on me respecte (*Ibid.*).

Nana has the same illusions: «Je suis grise, c'est possible. Mais je veux qu'on me respecte» (*Nana*, 1188). During her sojourn in the country (21), she had seen a retired courtesan living on a great estate, living the life of a chatelaine. This becomes Nana's final ideal, to be well-thought of by society. Nana's demands to be so accepted are often cited in the concluding pages of the novel:

> Elle faisait la femme honnête, avec des airs de distinction, pour épater son monde et prouver à ces idiots que, lorsqu'elle voulait, pas une n'avait son chic (*Nana*, 1344).

Not everyone, however, looks ahead to a materialistic future. *La Curée* contains a touching look to the past. Saccard and other speculators are examining a section of Paris which they plan to level and replace with elegant townhouses. A member of the group, an industrialist, dehumanized by his new wealth and the surrender of moral values, is overcome when he recognizes his old humble living quarters:

> La voilà, s'écria-t-il, je la reconnais.
> Quoi donc? demanda le médecin.
> —Ma chambre, parbleu! C'est elle! (*Curée*, 583).

The recall to the past, effected somewhat like Emma's search for moral order during her visit to the abbé Bournissien, triggered by the ringing of the bells of the Angelus and the

---

(21) Chapter VI of *Nana*, the idyll in the country, is an important step in the evolution of romanticism. Nana senses an imminent purification of her spirit in the country air, and she wants to play milkmaid. But there can be no Marie-Antoinette at the end of the nineteenth century, nor is there room for Julie of *La Nouvelle Héloise*. Nana is the last ramification of *La Dame aux camélias*, but with a psychological perversion unknown to the early waves of romanticism. She dresses her young lover Georges in women's clothing; she cannot decide if she is mistress, *amie* to *amie*, or mother to the poor boy. The same role confusion infiltrates her relationship with Count Muffat.

spring nature, engenders in this man, memories of a time when he was young and honest:

> J'y ai passé cinq ans, murmura-t-il. Ça n'allait pas fort dans ce temps-là, mais, c'est égal, j'étais jeune. ... Vous voyez bien l'armoire; c'est là que j'ai économisé trois cents francs, sou à sou. Et le trou du poêle, je me rappelle encore le jour où je l'ai creusé. La chambre n'avait pas de cheminée, il faisait un froid de loup, d'autant plus que nous n'étions pas souvent deux (*Curée*, 584).

The past has been lost, and with it also the young girl he might have married:

> Je me souviens encore d'une repasseuse de la maison d'en face. ... Voyez-vous, le lit était à droite, près de la fenêtre. ... Ah! ma pauvre chambre, comme ils me l'ont arrangée! (*Ibid.*).

The destruction of the old Paris symbolizes also the destruction of moral and sentimental values. The industrialist will never again have his old innocence. To Saccard, refuting these recalls, it is only important to live in a fine house:

> ... ce n'est pas un mal qu'on jette ces vieilles cambuses-là par terre. On va bâtir à la place de belles maisons de pierre de taille. ... Est-ce que vous habiteriez encore un pareil taudis? Tandis que vous pourriez très bien vous loger sur le nouveau boulevard (*Ibid.*).

An opinion, of course, with which the industrialist must agree, for he is no longer the person he was. He must admit that he is also responsible for what is happening, must answer yes to the question of another member of the group: «Allons. ... Vous avez fait vos farces comme les autres (*Ibid.*).

The reign of Zola's particular and peculiar middle-class, without spirit and mind, depends on the subjugation of the working class. This message is repeated over and over in the conversations of these novels. *La Curée* provides a very interesting example, when a discussion of the rebuilding of the right bank under Haussman is seen as not only beneficial to the working man, but good for capital and also for the arts:

> Les travaux de Paris, dit-il, ont fait vivre l'ouvrier.
> —Dites aussi, reprit M. Toutin-Laroche, qu'ils ont
> donné un magnifique élan aux affaires financières
> et industrielles.
> —Et n'oubliez pas le côté artistique; les nouvelles
> voies sont majestueuses, ajouta M. Hupel de la Noue,
> qui se piquait d'avoir du goût.
> —Oui, oui, c'est un beau travail, murmura M. de
> Mareuil, pour dire quelque chose (*Curée*, 343).

The dialogue, given the true nature of the speculations in land during the reconstructions, is an exercise in evasion. Zola's commentary on the empty-head of M. de Mareuil, the *bourgeois gentilhomme* of the nineteenth century, but especially his use of *se piquer*, cannot help but recall to us the famous definition of an *honnête homme* of the seventeenth century by contrast with these *nouveaux riches*. The worker is to be viewed as an animal: «Bah! c'est l'habitude, dit le médecin en reportant son cigare à ses lèvres. Ce sont des brutes» (*Curée*, 583). Adverse opinions of the *peuple* are common. Nana speaks:

> Est-ce qu'on n'était pas heureux, est-ce que l'empe-
> reur n'avait pas tout fait pour le peuple? Une jolie
> ordure, le peuple! (*Nana*, 1369).

M. Gourd expresses the same sentiments:

> Quelle sale chose que le peuple! Il suffisait d'un
> ouvrier dans une maison pour l'empester (*P. B.*, 116).
> Vas-y donc, pourris ta maison avec des ouvriers,
> loge du sale monde qui travaille! ... Quand on a du
> peuple chez soi, monsieur, voilà ce qui vous pend
> au bout du nez (*P. B.*, 255).

Zola, ironically, either through direct or indirect speech, points out the contradictions of middle class thinking. For a group which pretended to support morality and the Church, the positions they take on moral issues is striking. While secretly immoral, they speak of the immorality of the poor. Seeing large poor families they are shocked, and privately insist upon

— 225 —

a program of birth control. Such attitudes pervade not just *Pot-Bouille,* but the naive Grégoire family of *Germinal*:

> Vous n'avez que ces deux-là? demanda Mme Grégoire pour rompre le silence.
> —Oh! Madame, j'en ai sept.
> M. Grégoire, qui s'était remis à lire son journal, eut un sursaut indigné,
> —Sept enfants, mais pourquoi? bon Dieu!
> —C'est imprudent, murmura la vieille dame (*Germinal*, 1211).

M. Grégoire refuses to give La Maheude any money. This scene in *Germinal* provides a very fine contrastive speech pattern, the obstinacy of M. Grégoire reflected in his ready-made formula on the habits of the miners, contrasting with the conciliatory tone of La Maheude, whose discourse gives her a dignity which is only rivalled by that of Gervaise:

> On a du mal en ce monde, c'est bien vrai; mais, ma brave femme, il faut dire aussi que les ouvriers ne sont guère sages. ... Ainsi, au lieu de mettre des sous de côté comme nos paysans, les mineurs boivent, font des dettes, finissent par n'avoir plus de quoi nourrir leur famille (*Germinal*, 1212).
> Oh! ce n'est pas pour me plaindre. Les choses sont ainsi, il faut les accepter; d'autant plus que nous aurions beau nous débattre, nous ne changerions sans doute rien. ... Le mieux encore, n'est-ce pas? Monsieur et Madame, c'est de tâcher de faire honnêtement ses affaires, dans l'endroit où le bon Dieu vous a mis (*Germinal*, 1213).
> Avec de tels sentiments, ma brave femme, on est au-dessus de l'infortune (*Ibid.*).
> Non, ce n'est pas dans nos habitudes. Nous ne pouvons pas (*Ibid.*).

The dialogues of the *Rougon-Macquart* make basic class decisions very clear: suppress the poor, support the Empire. «Law and Order» proverbs are uttered: «... il voterait toujours pour la liberté dans l'ordre et pour l'ordre dans la liberté...» (*Conquête*, 1151); an axiomatic «either or,» or else syllogism is implied:

M. Haffner avait repris d'une voix *sentencieuse*:
Le dévouement à l'empereur est la *seule vertu*, le
seul patriotisme, en ces temps de démocratie inté-
réssée. *Quiconque* aime l'empereur aime la France
(*Curée,* 345).

It may well be that Zola has overstated the double-standard
of the middle class in *Pot-Bouille*. In any case dialogue is the
principle means of making this statement. We listen to these
bourgeois speak and we are appalled. Campardon, who is
sleeping with his sister-in-law while his wife sleeps in a
separate room, doll-like, mechanical, completely unaware of the
situation since she is so wrapped up in herself, is the ultimate
in moral hypocrisy. He is the official architect for the arch-
diocese of Paris, and constantly in the company of the clergy.
He feigns love and devotion for his wife, and we hear him
repeat bourgeois terms of affection to her, such as: «Bonsoir,
mon chat, bonsoir ma cocotte» (*P. B.,* 18); «C'est fini, ma
cocotte... Embrasse ton loup, qui a bien travaillé» (*P. B.,* 179).
Duveyrier is the greatest moral hypocrite of this novel. His
sexuality has been so romanticized that he seems incapable of
distinguishing good from bad. At the very death bed of his
father-in-law, while weeping for the demise of the old man,
his thoughts return to the mistress who has left him. Yet
this same man, a sort of moral schizophrenic, preaches virtue
at every social gathering:

Il y a, messieurs, un fait prouvé qui tranche tout:
la religion moralise le mariage (*P. B.,* 95).
Moralisons le mariage, messieurs, moralisons le
mariage, répétait Duveyrier de son air rigide, avec
son visage enflammé, où Octave voyait maintenant le
sang âcre des vices secrets (*P. B.,* 96).

In all these discussions of morality, attacks are usually made
upon the new literature. This probably means Flaubert's
Madame Bovary. Nana attacks bold and brazen literature,
preferring ennobling and sentimental novels, and Eugène
Rougon leads an attack on those novelists who seem to be
approving adultery. The same Duveyrier, the classic adulterer,
also speaks out against a novel in which this theme is treated:

> Mon Dieu! murmura-t-il enfin, ces auteurs exagèrent, l'adultère est très rare parmi les classes bien élevées ... Une femme, lorsqu'elle est d'une bonne famille, a dans l'âme une fleur (*P. B.*, 95).

The same man, on discovering that his mistress has fled, taking all the furnishings with her, exclaims: «Il n'y a plus d'honnêteté sur terre!» (*P. B.*, 195). Zola was aware of this mentality as a type of romanticism, and so categorizes Nana's thoughts of and Duveyrier's cheap attempt at suicide:

> Nana, toquée d'un baryton de café-concert et quittée par lui, rêva de suicide, dans une *crise de sentimentalité noire...* (*Nana*, 1452).
> Et il sanglotait, il souffrait de la *poésie morte*, de cette petite fleur bleue qu'il ne pouvait cueillir (*P. B.*, 357).

The point is clear. The language of these bourgeois is frozen, filled with clichés, removing them from any knowledge of themselves or reality in general. Zola's dialogues show them as they are. The great unmasking, linguistically, however, must wait for the philologically oriented theatre of Ionesco in the twentieth century. The apartment house of *Pot-Bouille* is mainly seen as facade, the stairwell is always silent. But the main décor is in *faux marbre*. This means there is only the appearance of decency. The kept woman Clarisse can arrange facade, but there is always one lesson not well learned: she serves champagne instead of tea: «Les voix montaient, le champagne compromettait *l'arrangement de décence*, établi par Clarisse» (*P. B.* 135).

Contrasting with the speech of the bourgeoisie is that of the people and the peasants. If the middle class speech is seen as conventional, frozen and evasive, the speech of the people is often very rough, brutal, and always direct to the subject in question. The speech of the people can be seen as a realistic correcting factor to the platitudinal speech of the middle class. *Pot-Bouille* illustrates these contrasts. The masters speak of their servants:

> —Mon Dieu! oui, continua Mme Duveyrier, je suis contente de Clémence, une fille très propre, très vive

—Et votre Hippolyte, demanda Mme Josserand, ne vouliez-vous pas le renvoyer?...
—Nous le gardons. C'est si désagréable, de changer! Vous savez, les domestiques s'habituent ensemble, et je tiens beaucoup à Clémence... (*P. B.*, 88).

The gossipy interchanges of the maids, shouted from window to window across the interior courtyard, contrast in a very rough manner with this bourgeois speech. Their language is obscene as they deride their own and their employers' sexuality:

—Avez-vous entendu, cette nuit, l'autre qui se tor- tillait, avec son mal au ventre? ... Etait-ce agaçant! Heureusement qu'elle part. J'avais envie de lui crier: «Pousse donc et que ça finisse!» (*P. B.*, 267).
—En parlant de farceuse, en voilà une qui m'a l'air de s'en payer! ... Eh! Adèle, pas vrai que ta Mlle Berthe rigolait déjà toute seule, quand tu lavais encore ses jupons? (*P. B.*, 268).
T'as marié ta maîtresse, hier soir, Hein? c'est peut- être toi qui lui apprends à faire les hommes? (*P. B.*, 106).

The direct and indirectly reported speech of this novel is the roughest in the series, but it is rivalled by *La Faute de l'abbé Mouret* and *La Terre*. Continuing and aggravating assault can provoke brutal and intellectually refined linguistic retort. Such is the case in *La Terre* where Françoise is being continually attacked by her brother-in-law Buteau. An aborted rape, with Buteau's semen spilt on the leg of Françoise, justifies the action and the caustic words of Françoise to her sister Lise, the wife of Buteau:

Quand ce fut fini, Françoise, d'une dernière se- cousse, put se dégager, râlante, bégayante.
Cochon! cochon! cochon! ... Tu n'as pas pu, ça ne compte pas ... Je m'en fiche, de ça! jamais tu n'y arriveras, jamais!
Elle triomphait, elle avait pris une poignée d'herbe, et elle s'en essuyait la jambe, dans un tremblement de tout son corps, comme si elle se fût contentée elle-même un peu, à cette obstination de refus. D'un geste de bravade, elle jeta la poignée d'herbe aux pieds de sa soeur.

«Tiens! c'est à toi … Ce n'est pas ta faute si je te le rends (*Terre*, 631).

Such directness is not to be found with the bourgeois tenants of *Pot-Bouille*. Madame Duveyrier fears her husband should leave his mistress; she would be forced into conjugal duties which she sees as «une corvée;» «Ça va donc recommencer, cette abomination» (*P. B.*, 356). And the bourgeois do their best to control their emotions publicly. Hardly ever would they express anger, as does Gervaise, irritated by little Nana's bad habit of sticking out her tongue between her teeth: «—Cache donc ta menteuse! lui criait sa mère.» (*Assommoir*, 709). The people and the peasants express their frustrations and angers, often in highly imaginative language. The peasant fights with the land, «Cette *bougresse* de terre…» (*Terre*, 494); La Grande, in her anger at the damage caused by the hailstorm, addresses herself to the heavens: «Sacré cochon, là haut! Tu ne peux donc pas nous foutre la paix?» (*Terre*, 462).

From the evidence of *Les Rougon-Macquart*, it can be concluded that the language of the people is simple, direct, and very often picturesque. They are able to communicate effectively in language characterized by figuration, marked with meaningful inflection and intonation.

If middle class language seems evasive, so too the language of the church seems ineffective in reaching the «faithful» in *La Faute de l'abbé Mouret*. Abbé Mouret seems out of contact with the reality about him, as he performs the marriage ceremony of Fortuné and Rosalie who have already been blessed with a child:

Ma chère soeur, soyez soumise à votre mari, comme l'Eglise est soumise à Jésus (*Faute*, 1423).

No one seems to understand what Serge is saying:

Que dit-il? demanda Lisa qui entendait mal.
—Pardi! il dit ce qu'on dit toujours, répondit la Rousse. Il a la langue bien pendue, comme tous les curés (*Faute*, 1422).

We are attracted by the speech patterns and rhythms found in the *Rougon-Macquart*, particularly the servants, who seem to emanate from Balzac's *la grande Nanon*: the maids found in *La Conquête de Plassans, La Faute de l'abbé Mouret, La Joie de vivre*; the frankness and the humour which issue forth from such peasant types as Jésus-Christ, la Grande, Jeanbernat, Frère Archangias; or the simplicity of a gentle bourgeois, Monsieur Mouret of *La Conquête*.

Mouret is concerned that his son Serge is coming under the influence of the abbé Faujas. His language is lively, especially his use of *cagot* —a popular expression also found in Rabelais and Molière, with the debasing meaning of *bigot* —and his preference is for Serge to visit prostitutes:

> Tous ces *bobos*-là sont des *frimes* pour se faire *dorloter.* ... je ne veux pas que le curé fasse un *cagot* du petit ... J'aimerais mieux qu'il allât voir les femmes! (*Conquête*, 1038).

Zola's *paysans* are truly *païens,* having little fear of damnation, and not victims of superstitions, although they have their own set of beliefs. Frère Archangias, for example, tries to frighten the boy Vincent away from the cemetery, and the boy replies with a matter of fact *ça* which shows how little he is influenced by the lay brother's remarks:

> ... les morts iront te tirer les pieds, la nuit, si tu marches encore sur eux.
> Oh! je n'ai pas peur, dit-il. Les morts, ça ne bouge plus (*Faute*, 1235).

In spite of the serious implications of his character, Frère Archangias remains one of the most brilliant of Zola's creations from the viewpoint of the use of direct speech. His counterpart is the protector of Albine, old Jeanbernat, the devil incarnate to Archangias. Jeanbernat likewise has no strong feelings for the lay brother:

> Eh! curé, vous promenez donc votre cochon (Archangias) avec vous? (*Faute*, 1443).

The anger, the frustration, and the rage of the lay brother are revealed in a language filled with interjections such as *bonsoir, tiens,* the familiar adverbial *avec,* extended gradations, hyperbole, exclamations. He has not been able to make a single convert in the parish:

> Ils poussent dans l'irréligion, comme leurs pères. Il y a quinze ans que je suis ici, et je n'ai pas encore pu faire un chrétien. Dès qu'ils sortent de mes mains, bonsoir! Ils sont tout à la terre, à leurs vignes, à leurs oliviers. Pas un qui mette le pied à l'église. (*Faute*, 1237).

His misogyny reaches extremes as he sees Albine chasing Serge from *le Paradou*, toward the conclusion of the novel:

> Adieu, la gueuse! Bon voyage! Retourne forniquer avec tes loups ... Ah! tu n'as pas assez d'un saint. Il te faut des reins autrement solides. Il te faut des chênes. Veux-tu mon bâton? Tiens! couche avec! Voilà le gaillard qui te contentera (*Faute*, 1508).

Vivid sexual and scatological imagery seems very characteristic of the peasant speech. Rosalie's father chastises her about her relationship with Fortuné:

> Si je te trouve avec ton mâle, je vous attache ensemble, je vous amène comme ça devant le monde. ... Tu ne veux pas te taire? Attends, coquine! (*Faute*, 1244).

La Teuse is one of Zola's great type creations, and it is the constant representation of her voice, scolding, complaining, demanding attention, which makes her such a vivid personality for us:

> Mais faire lever un prêtre avant le soleil pour s'épouser à une heure où les poules elles-mêmes sont encore couchées, il n'y a pas de bon sens! A votre place, monsieur le curé, j'aurais refusé. ... Pardi! vous n'avez pas assez dormi, vous avez peut-être pris froid dans l'église. C'est ça qui vous a tout retourné. Ajoutez qu'on aimerait mieux marier des bêtes que cette Rosalie et son gueux, avec leur mioche qui a pissé sur une chaise. ... Vous avez tort de ne pas me dire où vous vous sentez mal. Je vous ferais

quelque chose de chaud. ... Hein? monsieur le curé, répondez-moi! (*Faute*, 1430).

The language of the people is very figurative, filled with the colorful imagery of *la langue familière*. It is indicative of linguistic independence, characteristic of active, alert, intelligent if uneducated minds. This of course is the great achievement of Zola in *L'Assommoir,* but it is found throughout the work. It may be just a simple transformation as in the following:

> ... Hein! entendez-vous comme elle *ronfle*! Ça va lui gagner sa journée. Elle sait ce qu'elle fait, allez! —Elle *joue de l'orgue,* reprit la Rousse (*Faute*, 1419).

In *L'Assommoir,* Mme Lérat says something which we would not expect of her, at least as her character has been drawn to this point:

> Eh bien! et moi? reprit la grande veuve, les lèvres pincées. Vous êtes galant. Vous savez, je ne suis pas une chienne, je ne me mets pas les pattes en l'air, quand on siffle! (*Assommoir*, 681).

La Maheude is constantly employing highly figurative language which is a testimony to her intelligence and common sense:

> Souffle la chandelle, je n'ai pas besoin de voir la couleur de mes idées (*Germinal*, 1148).

In *La Terre,* Coelina effectively gets her point across to the abbé Godard who rushes through his Sunday mass in order to be off to his own parish:

> Dites, monsieur le curé, demanda Coelina de sa voix aigre, en l'arrêtant, vous nous en voulez, que vous nous expédiez comme un vrai paquet de guenilles (*Terre*, 410).

Zola's real triumph with speech, however, direct or indirect, is *L'Assommoir.* And at least one thing wrong with much of the literary criticism on this novel is that it has studied its speech from the wrong perspective. This novel has been cited for its use of *argot,* the first novel to use the speech of the people. Glossaries of its vocabulary have been compiled (useful to the modern or foreign reader), and compared with dictionaries of nineteenth century slang. Aesthetically, *argot* in *l'Assommoir* means the voice of the people as protagonist. Very seldom is this effective speech truly offensive, as is the case with some of the other novels. This happens because it is not just *argot* but also what is called *langue populaire, langue familière.* This language is effective because it portrays a warm and sympathetic humanity which perhaps previously had its humanness denied it for the very reason of its language. Zola had the artistic sense to see the positive human values in this speech —humour, wit, *esprit,* compassion, warmth, and above all, naturalness. The language of *L'Assommoir* captivates us by its honesty, by its cutting-through quality, such as Coupeau's response to Gervaise when she inquires as to what they would do if they were married: «Pardi! murmura Coupeau en clignant les yeux, ce que font les autres» (*Assommoir,* 405), Zola achieves with proletarian speech that which Balac sought in the creation of Nanon in *Eugénie Grandet.* Literature just needed the writer who could realize the aesthetic possibilities of proletarian speech. Is Zola «realistically» putting down on paper the very real speech of the people? The answer is no. He has used their vocabulary as his point of departure, he has manipulated the basic idioms of the people, finding their literary and stylistic equivalencies. It might even be wondered whether or not proletarian figuration has replaced metaphor and simile in *L'Assommoir* as the dominant imagistic field.

VII. *Speech as War and Alienation*

Implicit so far is speech reflecting class antagonisms and hostilities. It would be wrong, however, to claim major confrontations of social classes, in any self-conscious manner, in the novels of Zola. He is in no way an early Marxist theoretician. Speech as war and speech as alienation work out of individual encounters in Zola; all can be traced back to the individual psychology. Violent clashes of the human spirit, an ascending vice crushing an established virtue, chaos replacing tranquillity, resulting in a final alienation, such is the pattern often revealed by speech in many of the novels. *La Joie de vivre* is one of the more subtle examples. Speech in this novel is sometimes so strong that it is difficult to comprehend how people who speak of and to each other in such strong terms can then go through the daily formalities of living together, embracing, waiting on each other. Mme Chanteau's discourse in the first pages of Chapter V is a fine example of how Zola can use speech patterns in a gradation, to get deeper and deeper into the psyche of the character. Mme Chanteau had brought the orphaned Pauline to her home. As the years pass, her son Lazare proves to be more and more of a failure in any project undertaken. The situation is aggravated by the fact that the family is using Pauline's money for Lazare's foolish projects and for daily subsistence. This situation provides the background for producing a psychology within Mme Chanteau, one which must defend her son, and evade her own guilt about using Pauline. The path found is to become more and more critical of Pauline, who is innocent. Without analyzing this progression in detail, a few examples taken across the pages illustrate how Zola uses speech to get to the heart of the matter:

> Pauvre enfant, il (Lazare) s'épuise... (*Joie*, 927).
> Et elle plaignait aussi Pauline: la chère petite souffrait beaucoup... (*Ibid*).
> —C'est drôle, cette malheureuse Pauline ne nous a jamais porté bonheur (*Joie*, 928).
> Elle (Pauline) est horriblement avare au fond, et c'est le gaspillage en personne (*Joie*, 929).
> Vois-tu, il y a une chose que je ne le lui pardronne pas, c'est de m'avoir pris mon fils (*Joie*, 930).
> —D'ailleurs, ce n'est guère bon à respirer, l'air de cette chambre (Pauline is ill). Elle pourrait très bien lui (Lazare) donner son mal de gorge. ... Ces jeunes filles qui paraissent si grasses, ont quelquefois toutes sortes de vices dans le sang. Veux-tu que je te le dise? eh bien! moi, je ne la crois pas saine (*Ibid*.).

Speech thus reveals the true and bitter feelings of the woman. Starting as disguise, the words of Mme Chanteau get to the core or her feelings. She resents Pauline, and finally views her as a «vicious» influence on her son.

La Conquête de Plassans is another novel of alienation in which dialogue is an important revealing factor. On the personal level, the conquest means the progressive invasion of the Mouret household by the abbé Faujas, finally driving Mouret out of his own home. In the early pages of the novel, Marthe is seen as a simple person who prefers peace and tranquillity to all else. Her son Octave inquires as to why she does not attend the Thursday concerts: «Vous savez bien, mes enfants, que je n'aime pas sortir. Je suis si tranquille ici» (*Conquête*, 901). Yet, Marthe, under the influence of the priest enters into a pseudo-mystical fervor, neglecting husband and children. It is above all Mouret's disintegration which we follow across the work. Little by little, his will power, his common sense and provençal humor are eroded. The little scene in which Serge announces his intention to become a priest is the first piece of major evidence that Mouret can no longer resist the forces about him. Looking closely at the scene we see how important the speech patterns are in revealing the rapid psychological changes taking place; we hear and sense the last bit of courage leaving the soul of Mouret, we know that all is lost when his sad voice assents to Serge's desire. Zola's commentary shows that Mouret has aged because of what has taken place:

> Mon père, dit Serge, j'ai une grâce à vous demander. Ma mère prétend que vous vous fâcherez, que vous me refuserez une autorisation qui me comblerait de joie...
> Je voudrais entrer au séminaire. ...
> «Toi! toi!» murmura Mouret.
> Et il regarda Marthe, qui détournait la tête. Il n'ajouta rien, alla à la fenêtre, revint s'asseoir au pied du lit, machinalement, comme assommé sous le coup.
> «Mon père, reprit Serge ... j'ai vu Dieu ... j'ai juré d'être à lui. ...
> Mouret ... fit un geste de suprême découragement, en murmurant: «Si j'avais le moindre courage, je mettrais deux chemises dans un mouchoir et je m'en irais.»
> Puis, il se leva, vint battre contre les vitres du bout des doigts. Comme Serge allait l'implorer de nouveau.

«Non, non; c'est entendu, dit-il simplement. Fais-toi curé, mon garçon.» ...
Le lendemain, sans avertir personne, il partit pour Marseille, où il passa huit jours avec son fils Octave. Mais il revint soucieux, vieilli (*Conquête*, 1040).

Conjugal alienation is the sin of the abbé Faujas. Mouret is progressively divorced from his wife and children, and becomes a stranger in his own home (*Conquête,* 1012, 1066, 1071, 1072, 1073). As a last step he enters into a total silence before his removal to the asylum as a true *aliéné*. Marthe herself, in a final confrontation with the abbé Faujas sees clearly what the latter has done to her life:

> Je veux mes enfants. ... Pourquoi me les avez-vous pris? ... Ils s'en sont allés un à un, et la maison m'est devenue comme étrangère (*Conquête,* 1173-1174).

Mouret himself fortunately has enough will and energy left to end the possession of his house by escaping from the asylum and burning it to the ground, bringing to an end the abbé Faujas.

Such will power is missing from the world of *Pot-Bouille.* Mme Josserand truly is responsible for the death of her good husband who can no longer withstand the onslaught of her vigorous and destructive personality. *Pot-Bouille* remains a case study in alienation. Surface order and stability are revealed as sham by Zola. Berthe has only been married for three months and Zola writes: «... une sourde désunion grandissait entre eux (*P. B.,* 225). Madame Josserand preaches across the novel the war of the sexes, teaching her daughters the fundamental rule for survival in marriage, «... ce mépris de l'homme» (*P. B.,* 226). The disharmony of the middle class is revealed collectively in the *soirée musicale* of Mme Duveyrier where the main entertainment is the singing of the *Bénédiction des poignards* from *Les Huguenots.* While filled with humor, at the same time it seems sinister and frightening. There is no harmony, blending or fusing of the voices. Each voice is strident, crying out alone as the inhabitants of the apartment house each live in isolated cells, destinies which only cross superficially. Madame Josserand incarnates best the violence of the novel. Her language betrays it. She is like a general leading her troops into battle, her commands are heard throughout the work: «Marchez!» (*P. B.*, 21); «Prépare-toi, souffla-t-elle à l'oreille de Berthe» (*P. B.*, 49); «Descendons!» (*P. B.*, 81). She hurls insults at her husband: «Manqué! cria Mme Josserand, en se laissant aller sur une chaise» (*P. B.*, 23). This shrew, this *mégère,* in her quarreling voice is constantly destroying basic human relationships. The cascading of bile gives each clause the effect of physical destruction as we almost hear her breath hissing as a backdrop to her vicious statements:

> —Voulez-vous bien marcher! ... Est-ce que je me plains? Est-ce que c'est ma place, d'être dans la rue à cette heure, par un temps pareil? ... Encore si vous aviez un père comme les autres! Mais non, monsieur reste chez lui à se goberger. ... Eh bien! je vous déclare que j'en ai par-dessus la tête. ... Un homme qui m'a trompée sur ses capacités ... en voilà un que je n'épouserais pas, si c'était à refaire (*P. B.*, 23).

One of the most formal constructions of *Pot-Bouille* is the magnificent scene of the gossip of the maids, overhead by Berthe and Octave, who have entered into an adulterous relationship. Its source is the *comices agricoles* of *Madame Bovary,* but there are significant deviations from the Flaubertian pattern which give the basic imprint of Zola. What Flaubert's contrastive irony does for a particular case of romanticism is, in Zola, now seen as a cultural mode widespread in the middle class in France. The speaker at the agricultural fair of Flaubert has no idea of what can be done with his words; Emma and Rodolphe are equally ignorant of the contrast. It has been done by Flaubert for the reader. Berthe and Octave, practically prisoners in the maid's room, scene of their rendez-vous, are forced to hear and to evaluate the words of the maids. And unlike Flaubert, Zola himself makes an analysis of the meaning of the scene. The structure very formally reflects Zola's intent to unmask the lies these bourgeois tell themselves. Structurally, the scene which goes from 266 to 270 is composed of the following elements: (1) a chorus, a cacophony of obscenities shouted from one window to another by the maids; (2) a concomitant layer of ascending and descending narrational fields implying moral and physical *ordure,* garbage; (3) the reactions of Berthe and Octave to what they have heard. This talk makes them see themselves for what they really are, it strips away their romanticism and gives them the desire not to see each other again; (4) a great moral commentary by Zola on what all of this means, metaphorically reinforced, and ending with Zola's exclamation point to underscore its importance. Rearranging the Zola text, according to the above outline, the structure looks as follows, selecting only some examples:

1. Attends! enfant de la borne, je vas te la fourrer quelque part, ta langue!
   —Viens-y donc, vieille soûlarde! dit la petite. Hier encore, je t'ai bien aperçue, quand tu rendais tout dans tes assiettes (*P. B.,* 267).
2. Elle allait être obligée de céder, lorsqu'un flot boueux de gros mots monta de la cour des cuisines (*P. B.,* 266).
   Du coup, le flot d'ordures battit de nouveau les murailles du trou empesté (*P. B.,* 267).
   Les mots ignobles continuaient ... toute une débâcle d'égout, qui, chaque matin, se déversait là (*P. B.,* 269).
   Les bonnes ... jetaient ainsi des débris... (*Ibid.*).
3. ... Berthe, torturée d'une angoisse indicible... balbutia de sa voix douloureuse: «Mon Dieu! Mon Dieu!» (*P. B.,* 268).
   Et une blague ordurière salissait leurs baisers, leurs rendez-vous, tout ce qu'il y avait encore de bon et de délicat dans leurs tendresses (269).
   ... leurs amours, si soigneusement cachés, traînaient au milieu des épluchures et des eaux grasses (*Ibid.*).
   ... leurs yeux s'avouaient l'ordure de leur liaison, l'infirmité des maîtres étalée dans la haine de la domesticité (*Ibid.*).
4. C'était ça leurs amours, cette fornication sous une pluie battante de viande gâtée et de légumes aigres! (*Ibid.*).

VIII. *Speech as Love and Ideal*

In the depressing material just considered, two good people

stood out, François Mouret and M. Josserand. The *Rougon-Macquart* also presents other good people, people we come to respect as we hear them speak. We listen attentively to the words of La Maheude at the conclusion of *Germinal* as she explains to Etienne the life she had wanted, the life we feel that she deserves:

> Moi je rêvassais déjà comme une bête, je voyais une vie de bonne amitié avec tout le monde, j'étais partie en l'air, ma parole! dans les nuages. Et l'on se casse les reins, en retombant dans la crotte. ... Ce n'était pas vrai, il n'y avait rien là-bas des choses qu'on s'imaginait voir. Ce qu'il y avait, c'était encore de la misère, ah! de la misère tant qu'on en veut, et des coups de fusil par-dessus le marché! (1517).

Not at all unlike the ideals of Gervaise, posed at the beginning of *L'Assommoir,* as she is being courted by Coupeau. The passage is introduced by Gervaise's recall of her past in Plassans, drinking with her mother, the beatings from her father, and she recalls her recent past with Lantier. In spite of the odds of this background, Gervaise sees in Coupeau a faint hope for a decent life in the future. This is marked by Zola in her actions: she had started to pick up her basket to leave, but she remains. The pluperfect leads to the imperfect, to a meditation with the present participle:

> Gervaise *avait repris* son panier. Elle ne *se levait* pourtant pas, le *tenait* sur ses genoux, les regards perdus, *rêvant,* comme si les paroles du jeune ouvrier éveillaient en elle des pensées lointaines d'existence. Et elle dit encore, lentement, *sans transition apparente*: (410)

Thus is introduced what may be one of the finest vocal patterns in all of French literature, Gervaise explaining in her own voice her life ideal. It is stated with such directness, simplicity, honesty and dignity that we must say that her speech raises her above her station, giving her the dignity usually reserved to classical heroines:

> —Mon Dieu! je ne suis pas ambitieuse, je ne demande pas grand'chose. ... Mon idéal, ce serait de

travailler tranquille, de manger toujours du pain, d'avoir un trou un peu propre pour dormir, vous savez, un lit, une table et deux chaises, pas davantage. ... Ah! je voudrais aussi élever mes enfants, en faire de bons sujets, si c'était possible. ... Il y a encore un idéal, ce serait de ne pas être battue, si je me remettais jamais en ménage; non, ça ne me plairait pas d'être battue .... Et c'est tout, vous voyez, c'est tout (410-411).

All of this effected without any intervention whatsoever on the part of Zola. Gervaise does speak up, and makes a case which convinces us. And of course, this is exactly the ideal she will not receive, her words giving us the essential of the novel. The elements which appeal to us are the rhythmic markings of her speech: *Mon Dieu, vous savez, Ah, Il y a encore* —these are all tonal supplications: *pas davantage*. We are also impressed by her manner of elaborating the ideal: the idea of not being ambitious is repeated in a most homey and familiar manner: «... je ne demande pas grand'chose...» the ideal household is posited and then explicated as a bed, a table and two chairs. Coupeau approves, Zola approves and we approve. Her ideal is modest, honest, simple and possible. Her voice has convinced us that she merits it. As the passage opened with the frame of her starting to rise from the table in the imperfect, it now concludes with the same verb, but in the preterite:

> Et elle se leva. Coupeau, qui approuvait vivement ses souhaits, était déjà debout, s'inquiétant de l'heure (411).

There is no romanticism here. These simple people have stated their goals. They must now be about other things, Coupeau back to work and Gervaise also. The preterite of leaving, *se leva*, complements a state of affirmation and positive psychology in the early pages of this novel. Unlike the bourgeois of *Pot-Bouille*, the early pages of *L'Assommoir* present us with mentally healthy protagonists for whom the world should hold some promise. Gervaise's cup would be easily filled. If Gervaise is sympathetic to us, it is because her speech reveals mental and moral health. She does not want

16

to be beaten. How unlike Clorinde and Eugène of *Son Excellence Eugène Rougon,* and the other sado-masochistic characters in the *Rougon-Macquart.* The positing of the ideal by Gervaise leads directly to the marriage as can be demonstrated on the very next page of the novel. Coupeau responds to her ideal:

> Et *ne pas être battue,* ajouta Coupeau *gaiement. Mais* je ne vous battrais pas, *moi, si vous vouliez, madame Gervaise.* ... Il n'y a pas de crainte, je ne bois jamais, puis je vous aime trop. ... (412).

We note the digntiy of Coupeau's response, respect and distancing seen in the use of *madame.* At this moment they are pure and lyrical lovers devoid of romantic passion. They have achieved a transcendence of their social status; they are elevated. Gervaise has convinced herself and Coupeau. The marriage does indeed seem worthwhile.

IX. *Modalities of Speech*

Zola has aimed at capturing as many modes of speech as possible. It is not just what the characters say, but how they say it, their intonations, their emphasis. Moreover, speech patterns seem to be integrated into the very structure of the novels. Thus patterns of repetition can express deep emotional feelings. Lazare of *La Joie de vivre* is beset by fears of death and the *néant,* which are intensified during the final illness of his mother. Wandering through his landscapes he ponders final things, summarized in his exclamation, which runs throughout the novel:

> ... les battements de son coeur emportaient ses serments, et le souffle froid glaçait sa chair, et il tendait les mains en poussant son cri: «*Mon Dieu! mon Dieu!*» (*Joie,* 1000).

How far we have moved from Chateaubriand's wandering romantic hero, René. Buteau, upon his expulsion from the farm at Françoise's arrival at maturity and legal rights, at first expresses his rage with a simple «Merde» (*Terre,* 702). Obscenity is replaced by despair, however, in his reiterated shouts from the window: «Je vas me neyer! je vas me neyer!» (*Terre*, 704). An old grandmother rants at the fleeing French army which leaves her alone to face the invading Prussians: «Canailles, brigands! lâches! lâches» (*Débâcle*, 433); the good Frenchman Weiss rails against the Prussians: «Sales bougres, sales bougres!» (*Débâcle*, 583).

Collective speech of the people rythmically intones, a massive chant from the anonymous crowd. The women of *Germinal* march to the store of Maigrat whom they will kill and castrate: «... au chat, au chat...» (*Germinal*, 1451), for because of such types they are starving: «Du pain! du pain!» (*Germinal*, 1423). Their excitement at the castration is expressed through the repetition: «Je l'ai! je l'ai! (*Germinal*, 1453); never again will he be able to molest a woman of the community: «Il ne peut plus! il ne peut plus!» (*Ibid.*). The soldiers of *La Débâcle* have perhaps no idea of the truth of the songs they sing as they are moved across France in boxcars: «A la boucherie! à la boucherie! (*Débâcle*, 437).

Repeated calling of names can have novelistic significance, reinforcing the structure of the narration. In the final pages of *Le Docteur Pascal*, old Félicité is anxious to put in the ground and out of closets those remaining skeletons which could tarnish the name of the family. A primary irritation is old Uncle Macquart. In a chilling sequence, Félicité arrives at his home near the asylum, and cannot locate him. She calls out his name five times within three pages. Combined with Zola's commentary, the isolated calls create a dramatic tension:

> Alors, dans cette solitude, dans cette joie du soleil, elle fut saisie d'un singulier petit frisson, elle appela: «Macquart!... Macquart!... (1091).
> La porte de la bastide, sous les mûriers, était grande ouverte. Mais elle n'osait entrer, cette maison vide, béante ainsi, l'inquiétait. Et elle appela de nouveau: «Macquart!... Macquart!... (*Ibid.*).

She finds him asleep, intoxicated, at his table:

> Macquart! Macquart! Macquart! ... Ah! ouiche! Vous êtes dégoûtant, mon cher! (1092).

Discovering that he is on fire, that «... la peau se fendait, et la graisse commençait à se fondre» (*Pascal*, 1093):

Un cri involontaire jaillit de la gorge de Félicité. «Macquart!... Macquart!» (*Ibid.*).

The cry is repeated for a fifth time, but then ceases, for Félicité stops trying to awaken him and leaves «... sur la pointe des pieds.» (*Ibid.*). She prefers to let him die. What has started off as a cry of inquiry: «Where are you?», which should turn into a cry of alarm, concludes with guilty silence. Dr. Pascal arrives the next day, and after two similar cries (1095), discovers the ashes of his uncle. Zola must have felt this crying out of the human soul in distress to be an effective device in his building of the novel. We hear the voice of little Charles, the illegitimate child of Maxime, a hemophiliac, crying out as he bleeds to death in the presence of Tante Dide at the asylum. Two times he calls out: «Maman! maman!» (*Pascal,* 1103); Tante Dide herself, in her final agony calls out twice: «Le gendarme! le gendarme!» (*Pascal,* 1105), her senile mind returning to the events of long ago when her smuggler lover was killed by the police.

Speech patterns as we have seen elsewhere can effectively serve as contrasts, and are frequently ironic. If the speech patterns of the maids in *Pot-Bouille* put in relief the immoral posture of Berthe and Octave, as auditory receivers, so the final pages of *Nana* try to establish some correspondence between the death of a courtisan and the end of the Second Empire. The last chapter of *Nana* is a detailed wake, the disfigured face of Nana watched over by a group of women, while her lovers remain below, and the whole country prepares for war. The chant of the people, «A Berlin! à Berlin! à Berlin» (1474, 1475, 1477, 1479, 1481, 1482, 1484, 1485), eight times reiterated, is meant by Zola to be joined to the meaning of the *mouche d'or,* Nana, who must symbolize the corruption of the Second Empire. The cry may call for Berlin; because of Nana, the settling of debts will take place at Sedan.

Zola had an ear for patterns of repetition, seeking the song as well as the meaning of the *locution figée.* If on a higher level we appreciate the call to Berlin of the patriotic Parisians, on a lower level, the song of dismissal, as the manager Bourdoncle discharges people from the department store during the slack season, takes our attention with its rhythmic repetition:

Vous étiez assis, monsieur; passez à la caisse!
Vous répondez, je crois: passez à la caisse!
Vos souliers ne sont pas cirés: passez à la caisse!
(*Bonheur,* 534).

Nana herself, a myth in her lifetime, illustrates the speech derivative of the word «myth,» low Latin *mythus,* from the Greek *muthos* roughly translated into modern French and English as *récit, fable, story, word*: «An unproved collective belief that is accepted uncritically and is used to justify a social institution...» (22). That is, myth means what the people are saying, what the people are talking about. *Nana* is the novel par excellence for this sort of speech structure. At the end of the novel, Nana disappears from France. She had last been seen in Paris, but then, rumors have her in Cairo; she had made the conquest of a viceroy, lives in a palace where she reigns over two hundred slaves, whom she has decapitated at her whim. She has had another affair with an enormous black man, she has become the mistress of a prince (1471). Slowly she is transformed into a goddess, a cheap incarnation of a decadent Salammbô (23).

Studying the conversational patterns across *Nana* as they relate to her charm, her centrality in the lives of the men who adore her, we catch bits and ends of conversation which convey the intensity of feeling, the importance of being in her presence. At the theatre we hear nothing but her name repeated over

---

(22) *Random House Dictionary of the English Language,* Unabridged edition, Jen Stein, Editor-in-Chief (New York, 1966), 946.

(23) The relationship between the Nana myth and «decadent» literature at the end of the nineteenth century can be better understood by reading the article of Marilyn Gladdis Rose, «Decadent Prose: the Example of *Salammbô,» Nineteenth-Century French Studies,* 3 (nos. 3-4, 1975), 213-223. While Professor Rose does not consider the Nana material, her comparative appraisal of *Salammbô,* Huysmans' consideration of Moreau's *Salomé* series for the salon of 1876, Villiers de l'Isle-Adam's presentation of Hadaly in *L'Eve future,* plus her astute comments on the American showgirl, Loïe Fuller, and her debut at the Folies-Bergère in 1892 with her dance of the Seven Veils (214) cannot but recall to us Nana's debut in Chapter I at the Théâtre des Variétés. This article certainly clarifies the connection between aesthetic decadence and the atmospheres of the bourgeois theatre.

and over: «le cri: Nana! Nana! avait roulé furieusement» (1120). In Chapter III, in the bourgeois salon of the Countess Muffat, men pass the word back and forth to each other: «Will you be at Nana's tomorrow?»

> C'est pour demain, vous en êtes (1147).
> A minuit chez elle (*Ibid.*).
> On soupe donc chez une femme, demain soir? (1152).
> Ce souper pour demain. ... (1158).
> A minuit, chez Nana (1164).
> A demain, chez Nana (1165).

A high point of Nana's career is found during the race track scene. She has been absent from her court for some minutes. She returns:

> Ah! mes enfants, dit-elle en remontant dans son landau, une blague, leur enceinte du pesage!
> On l'acclamait, on battait des mains autour d'elle: «Bravo! Nana! ... Nana nous est rendue! ...» (1397).

Running throughout the *Rougon-Macquart,* at least starting with the *Nana* novel are whispers, rumors, conversations about the intent of Prussia, whether or not Bismarck is a kind gentleman to be trusted. These conversations serve almost as a leitmotif against which to measure the decadence of the Empire as Zola saw it. There is something ominous about these conversations which instill in the reader a sense of impending doom. Toward the end of *La Terre,* Delhomme is having a casual conversation with Jean: «Dites donc, Caporal, vous savez la nouvelle ... Paraît qu'on va avoir la guerre.»: «La guerre, comment ça?» (*Terre,* 738). The same refrain is picked up in *La Bête humaine:* «Vous savez que nous allons avoir la guerre? —Pas possible! s'écria Philomène. Avec qui donc?» (*Bête,* 1306). Or in *L'Argent*:

> Vous savez ce qu'on dit?...
> On dit que nous aurons la guerre en avril...
> Fichez-moi donc la paix, vous et votre Bismarck!...
> Moi qui vous parle, j'ai causé cinq minutes avec lui, cet été, quand il est venu. Il a l'air très bon garçon...
> Si vous n'êtes pas content, après l'écrasant succès

de l'Exposition, que vous faut-il? Eh! mon cher, l'Europe entière est à nous (*Argent*, 295-296).

The novels of the *Rougon-Macquart* do not unfold chronologically. Zola has deliberately inserted, at calculated intervals, these warnings of war in the conversations of his characters, and they act as a sobering balance to the usual frivolity and fraudulency which are heaped without mercy upon us across the twenty volumes.

Much of the success of the series must be attributed to the very astute capturing of the direct speech of the Second Empire.

X. *Style Indirect Libre* (24)

It is Flaubert's *Madame Bovary* which reintroduces into French prose style the technique known as *style indirect libre.* It can be occasionally noticed before him with other novelists of the nineteenth century; after him, by the time of Zola, it is so absolutely common that it is hard to believe that it had not always been there. Zola uses it in a very normal manner from the very first volume of the series. The device is so common in *L'Assommoir* that we almost get the impression that the novel is telling itself, especially when combined with the direct speech of the characters and Zola's borrowings of the idiom of his creation. This last characteristic often makes it difficult to distinguish the voice of the narrator from the indirectly reported speech. Fundamental to the style of Zola is the close proximity of his narrative voice with the direct and indirect representations of the speech of his characters.

Zola's representation of the new priest in *Germinal,* the abbé Ranvier, a predecessor of the worker-priest of the twentieth century, shows how his narration fuses into indirect reporting. The new priest is sympathetic to the plight of the

---

(24) A very succinct statement on this process is the article by Marcel Cohen, «Le Style indirect libre et l'imparfait en français après 1850,» *Europe,* 77 (1952), 62-69. Cohen pays proper hommage to the work of Bally, Thibaudet and Marguerite Lips, and sums up the situation historically, namely, that this style has always been possible in written French but is little used before 1850. Afterwards it becomes «... un fait conventionnel de la langue écrite» (69).

workers, and he regrets the «deplorable misunderstanding» between the Church and the people. Zola, in his narration, puts the adjective in the affective position, much as it might be in the emotive idiom of the young priest, and the sentence glides gradually and naturally into indirect discourse:

> Il recommença, il parla du déplorable malentendu entre l'Eglise et le peuple. Maintenant, en phrases voilées, il frappait sur les curés des villes, sur les évêques, ... pactisant avec la bourgeoisie libérale, dans l'imbécillité de son aveuglement, sans voir que c'était cette bourgeoisie qui le dépossédait de l'empire du monde (*Germinal*, 1473).

Excellent and very normal examples of *style indirect libre* are found consistently in these novels. The abbé Faujas apologizes for his untimely arrival *chez* Mouret: «Vraiment, il était désolé d'arriver à un pareil moment» (*Conquête*, 906). The same priest, as he infiltrates the society of Plassans, permits himself from time to time to express a political opinion:

> Il donnait même parfois un avis, était pour l'union des esprits honnêtes et religieux. ... Il devait être si facile de s'entendre entre gens de bien, de travailler en commun à la consolidation des grands principes, sans lesquels aucune société ne saurait exister! (*Conquête*, 1131-32).

Serge and Albine hunt in vain for the great tree of the *paradou*: «L'arbre n'existait pas. C'était un conte de nourrice» (*Faute*, 1375). Rougon's puritanical personality rejects the offer of a cigar: «Vous pouvez fumer, dit Clorinde à Rougon. Il remercia; il ne fumait jamais» (*Son Excellence*, 64). Coupeau offers assitance to the overworked Gervaise:

> Et il partit, après lui avoir offert d'aller chercher son lait, si elle ne voulait pas sortir: elle était une belle et brave femme, elle pouvait compter sur lui, le jour où elle serait dans la peine (*Assommoir*, 377-378).

Conservatives complain about the new theories in criminology:

Ces messieurs concluaient contre les nouvelles théories criminalistes; avec cette belle invention de l'irresponsabilité dans certains cas pathologiques, il n'y avait plus de criminels, il n'y avait que des malades (*Nana*, 1372).

Nana is furious at her dinner party, believing that her guests are misbehaving and not showing her the proper respect: «Eh bien! ils allaient voir. Elle avait beau être grise, elle était encore la plus chic et la plus comme il faut» (*Nana*, 1184).

Style indirect libre, like direct speech, becomes most interesting when we are able to distinguish the particular timbre of a voice, or when the speech betrays inventive and imaginative thought processes. The distinctive voice quality always comes through in the great characterizations, La Maheude and Gervaise, for example. As we saw in direct speech the shock of the Grégoire family on learning of the number of childrern in La Maheude's family, her reply in indirect speech impresses us with its common sense and logic:

La Maheude eut un geste vague d'excuse. Que voulez-vous? on n'y songeait point, ça poussait naturellement. Et puis, quand ça grandissait, ça rapportait, ça faisait aller la maison. Ainsi, chez eux, ils auraient vécu, s'ils n'avaient pas eu le grand-père qui devenait tout raide, et si, dans le tas, deux de ses garçons et sa fille aînée seulement avaient l'âge de descendre à la fosse. Fallait quand-même nourrir les petits qui ne fichaient rien (*Germinal*, 1211).

Germinal and *L'Assommoir* both present very vivid picturesque language of the people, a welcome relief from the dreary and monotonous conversations of Zola's bourgeoisie. La Maheude comments on the empty larder:

Quand les hommes et la fille reviendraient de la fosse, il faudrait pourtant manger; car on n'avait pas encore inventé de vivre sans manger, malheureusement (*Germinal*, 1205).

Le père Bonnemort is wise in years and knows that all the

talk of revolution will not much change the conditions of the miners:

> Le père Bonnemort, qui partait pour la fosse, grognait que ces histoires-là ne rendaient pas la soupe meilleure (*Germinal*, 1280).

At the wedding banquet of Gervaise and Coupeau, Mme Putois would like some water:

> Mme Putois ayant demandé de l'eau, le zingueur indigné venait d'enlever lui-même les carafes. ... Elle voulait donc avoir des grenouilles dans l'estomac (*Assommoir*, 579)?

Early in *Germinal*, Catherine, at least for the moment, escapes the sexual advances of Chaval:

> Elle, bonne fille, riait, disait qu'elle monterait la semaine où les enfants ne poussent pas (*Germinal*, 1243).

Gervaise in an even more figurative, popular language, puts off Coupeau's marriage proposal in the following manner:

> Elle savait ce qu'il voulait dire, et elle lui promettait la chose pour la semaine des quatre jeudis (*Assommoir*, 418).

Now not all of these examples are pure indirect free style, but that is without importance. The main thing is that *style indirect libre* is a solid organizing principle of the series, enabling Zola to vary direct reporting and his own narration, by frequently fusing the two. In the battle of styles, the people are always winning out against the middle class, Zola's characters demonstrating a linguistic agility unknown to the serious and romantic middle class, still speaking from Flaubert's *Dictionnaire des idées reçues*.

A final aspect of this style is its use to represent the thoughts of the characters, its final form before turning into the true *monologue intérieur* of the twentieth century novel. From *Au Bonheur des dames* on, Zola seems to be so using this technique with greater frequency. The interior dialogue, however, still remains fashioned on that of speech. Mouret looks at Denise in the department store and wonders if she will become a beautiful woman. His thought is displayed exactly as speech structure:

> Est-ce que cette sauvageonne finirait par devenir une jolie fille? Elle sentait bon de sa course au grand air, elle était charmante avec ses beaux cheveux épeurés sur son front (*Bonheur*, 533).

Denise tries to analyze her relationship with Mouret. In a three-sentence construction, Zola first narrates, then represents Denise's thought, concluding with a commentary on it:

> Deux fois, elle s'était enfoncé les épingles dans les mains, comme aveuglée, les yeux troubles. Etait-il du complot? l'avait-il fait venir, pour se venger de ses refus, en lui montrant que d'autres femmes l'aimaient? Et cette pensée la glaçait, elle ne se souvenait pas... (*Bonheur*, 694).

At times, Zola's narrative voice seems to be pushing beyond the frontiers of *style indirect libre,* into a zone where mental image is not directly translated by the syntax of dialogue. The narrator's voice continues to dominate, but the sentence slides easily into a direct visualization as it is perceived in the mind of the character. This is the case with *La Joie de vivre.* Pauline, confined to bed with an illness, and also not sure as to whether or not Louise is her rival for Lazare, mentally follows their afternoon walks on the beach. Looking at two visualizations within a single paragraph we note the evolution of the Zola narrative:

> Quand elle était seule, ses yeux fixes *semblaient les* (Lazare and Louise) *suivre au loin.* Elle passait les journées à lire, en attendant le retour de ses forces ... Souvent, elle laissait tomber le livre sur ses genoux, une *songerie l'égarait à la suite de son cousin et de son amie. S'ils avaient longé la plage, ils devaient arriver aux grottes, où il faisait bon sur le sable à l'heure frâiche de la marée...* (*Joie*, 935).

The passage clearly starts with Zola's observation of her eyes which he interprets as seeming to follow the walk of Lazare and Louise. He proceeds to inform us of her *songerie* which has her mentally following the couple. The last sentence, however, is ambiguous as to whether or not it is the narration of Zola or the thought of Pauline, which would come out as follows: «if they followed the beach, then by now they must be at the caves.» Representation of Pauline's thoughts continues in a highly detailed and visual manner. Pauline's inquiet soul state, her imagination fired by her jealousy, conjure up such vivid and scrupulous detail, that she seems to be on the beach with Lazare and Louise. This is what she *sees*, in her mind:

> Ses lectures, du reste, l'ennuyaient. Les romans qui traînaient dans la maison ... avaient toujours révolté sa droiture, son besoin de se donner et de ne plus se reprendre. ... Elle repoussait le livre. Maintenant, ses *regards perdus voyaient là-bas, au delà des murs, son cousin qui ramenait son amie, dont il soutenait la marche lasse, l'un contre l'autre, chuchotant avec des rires (Ibid.).*

It is no longer, visually, the hypothetical *si*, the localization of the first part of the paragraph; now Pauline verifies the return posture as proof of the feeling between Lazare and Louise. Suspicion (*songerie*), has been, in her mind (... *ses regards ... voyaient là-bas...*) empirically confirmed.

Again, clearly the narrational voice of Zola, but a high type narration which has penetrated into the visual nuances of Pauline's imagination. Such a device, more typical of the art of Maupassant (*Pierre et Jean*), when coupled with *style indirect libre,* is preparing for the profound psychological art of the twentieth century, mainly that of Proust and Mauriac.

XI. *Fusion of Author and Character Voice*

This discussion of the language of Zola concludes with an examination of novelistic voice, which it is hoped will clarify a problem which has remained clouded for some time, the question of address and point of view, which has unfortunately been too rigorously defined since the time of Flaubert.

We have spoken earlier of Zola's intruding voice, one which is often very sympathetic. A traumatic section of *L'Assommoir* describes the death of little Lalie. Gervaise, while arranging the bedding, sees the torn and emaciated body of the little girl. We then read:

> Ah! Seigneur! quelle misère et quelle pitié! Les pierres auraient pleuré (759).

Knowing Zola it could be his voice. On the other hand the crying stones image fits the character of Gervaise. Some lines down the paragraph we have the following.

> Oh! ce massacre de l'enfance, ces lourdes pattes d'homme écrasant cet amour de quiqui, cette abomination de tant de faiblesse râlant sous une pareille croix! On adore dans les églises des saintes fouettées dont la nudité est moins pure (*Ibid.*).

This is the voice of Zola, Gervaise would not be capable of this type of abstraction. But the following:

> Et Nana avait des hauts et des bas, de vrais coups de baguette, tantôt nippée comme une femme chic, tantôt balayant la crotte comme une souillon. *Ah! elle menait une belle vie!* (743).
> Elle rentrait, ne rentrait pas, pourvu qu'elle ne laissât pas la porte ouverte, ça suffisait. *Mon Dieu! l'habitude use l'honnêteté comme autre chose* (*Ibid.*).

The italicized lines are meant to be the voice of Gervaise and Coupeau, but already we sense the engagement of Zola in the text, for he is involved with the events. Professor Robert J. Niess in a very perceptive article (25) has tried to come to grips with the narrative voice problem implicit in these examples. *L'Assommoir* is a novel built on direct representation of proletarian speech and a dense use of *style indirect libre*, more than any other novel of the nineteenth century with the

---

(25) «Remarks on the Style indirect libre in *L'Assommoir*,» *Nineteenth-Century French Studies*, 3 (nos. 1-2, 174-75), 124-135.

exception of *Les Lauriers sont coupés* (26). Such a use, however, poses in the eyes of Professor Niess, three problems: *style indirect libre* suggests two types of narrative discourse, the author's distinct voice which is «... more or less 'noble', elevated and coherent...» and the voice of the character «... not 'noble' or elevated or necessarily coherent. ...» (27). Given this distinction, Professor Niess proceeds to show that it is often difficult to separate the voice of Zola and that of the character, and that in *L'Assommoir*, while the «... image is clearly the narrator's, ... the language is equally clearly that of Gervaise's world.» (28). Furthermore, the narrator's point of view is often grafted onto the character: «Zola sometimes errs here ... by attributing to the character perceptions he or she could not logically formulate.» (29).

While all of these observations are theoretically and technically correct, I think they miss the point. We have for too long believed in the «reporter» aspect of realistic or naturalistic literature. We should speak of such literature instead in terms of concrete, and sensorial painting, photograph or movie, but not in any sense of author distancing. Flaubert's ideal was to so do, but we should by now accept such an ideal as an impossibility (*Madame Bovary, c'est moi d'après moi*). Then we will no longer be obliged to count his mistakes. Zola did have scientific pretentions; they did not exclude his presence in his work (*vu à travers un tempérament*). Zola's art is not objective, and it was never so intended. This chapter will conclude with a demonstration that not only in the famous *style indirect libre,* but in other narrational modes, Zola indeed has the language of his characters, and more striking, the characters have the language of Zola. These phonomena can be isolated and observed.

A simple manner for Zola is to pick up the vocabulary of the personage and to surround it with citation marks:

> Daguenet était au piano, «à la commode,» comme disait Nana... (*Nana,* 1189).

---

(26) *Ibid.,* 127-128.
(27) *Ibid.,* 125.
(28) *Ibid.,* 130.
(29) *Ibid.,* 129.

We may recall that Nana constantly refers to her «chic.» And we have seen in previous examples that Zola borrows the term, repeats it, and then deliberately, perhaps with as much sorrow as irony, pairs his own high terms of *rentière* and *marquise* with low terms, *de la bêtise, des hauts trottoirs* (*Nana*, 1346).

L'Assommoir remains the battleground for this question of author voice. It seems that the use of familiar language and argot is so central to the basic motif of *L'Assommoir* that there is no way for Zola to avoid using it, even in his own narrative voice, for the consistent hammering away of this «speech» acts as the central unifying force of the novel, giving it backbone and fiber. The best detail example is the death of Coupeau and the description of his convulsions in popular terms.

Only truly great novels such as *L'Assommoir,* novels which can command aesthetic respect, reduce themselves to a few fundamental principles of structure and style. Gervaise's words to Coupeau on her life ideals sum up the novel. Speech is the organizing idea. Zola is doing with speech in this work what Flaubert did with the interior simile in *Madame Bovary,* that is, the simile which does not exist outside the novel, but has point of reference within the novel. The simile of Emma's thoughts about Léon is a good example:

> ... et ses pensées continuellement s'abattaient sur cette maison, comme les pigeons du *Lion d'or* qui venaient tremper là, dans les gouttières, leurs pattes roses et leurs ailes blanches (*Madame Bovary,* 101).

Thus, in passages which are unmistakably the unique voice of Zola, we hear the language of the people. Toward the end of the novel, Coupeau has accepted work in the provinces. Zola uses popular language to explain the advantage of the country air for Coupeau:

> On ne se doute pas combien ça désaltère les po-chards, de quitter l'air de Paris, où il y a dans les rues une vraie fumée d'eau-de-vie et de vin (673).

Coupeau wastes his afternoon. Zola seems to make up a verb:

> Alors, l'après-midi entier, il *flânochait* dans le quartier (516).

Describing the *noce* of Gervaise (VII), he uses a word which Mitterand includes in his glossary of argot, combined with a highly imaginative image:

> Dans un coin de la boutique, le tas des *négresses mortes* grandissait, un *cimetière de bouteilles* sur lequel on poussait les ordures de la nappe (579).

We have previously commented on the highly imaginative language of Catherine resisting the sexual advances of Chaval (she would give in during a week when conception is not possible) or Gervaise refusing Coupeau's offer of marriage (she will marry him the week of the four Thursdays). Zola uses the same formula with another variation. Lalie, a foster mother at eight, is happy to see her little brother and sister happy; it is not often that she is so:

> Elle était toute rose de les voir s'amuser de si bon coeur, elle y prenait même du plaisir pour son compte, *ce qui lui arrivait le trente-six de chaque mois* (692).

Lantier is now spending more time with Virginie than with Gervaise. Contextually this would be the gossip reported. Is this *style indirect libre* or Zola? The latter, Zola *engagé,* although the verbs speak for the gossip reported:

> Seulement, ce qui compliquait la situation, c'était que le quartier, maintenant, *fourrait* Lantier et Virginie dans la même paire de draps. Là encore le quartier se pressait trop. Sans doute, le chapelier *chauffait* la grande brune; et ça se trouvait indiqué, puisqu'elle remplaçait Gervaise en tout et pour tout, dans le logement (675).

Zola admires Gervaise's kindness as much as Goujet or Coupeau:

> Elle était *douce comme un mouton, bonne comme du pain* (502).

The issue, however, is not confined to *L'Assommoir.* An essential contention of this chapter is that Zola's vocabulary should be viewed as *mot-clé*, working back to a system called Zola, and not *mot-thème*. An examination of the metaphorical fields as they relate to narrational voice demonstrates this absolutely. The recurring image in *Germinal* is that of disinterested capital, somewhere way off, probably in Paris, represented as «*Le dieu repu et accroupi...*» (*Germinal*, 1591). Zola uses this image many times throughout the novel, and it is also used by Etienne in his speech to the miners at the Plan-des-Dames:

> ... demanderait des comptes au capital, à ce dieu impersonnel, inconnu de l'ouvrier, accroupi quelque part, dans le mystère de son tabernacle... (1384).

The central image continues to propagate itself across the novel. Deneulin, the small owner, is telling his workers that a strike would put him out of business, that he is not part of big capital. So far it has been used by Zola and Etienne, now Deneulin picks up a variation:

> ... quel beau résultat pour eux, s'ils l'obligeaient à vendre, de passer sous le joug terrible de la Régie! Lui, ne trônait pas au loin, dans un tabernacle ignoré 1392).

An unknown god in his hidden tabernacle against which the workers will build, in the words of the organizer from the *Internationale*, «... l'immense cathédrale du monde futur» (*Germinal*, 1347). Does this image of the hidden idol belong to the fervor of the workers, or is it Zola's word? That it is Zola's can be proven by its use in the very next novel of the series, *L'Oeuvre*. Naudet, the art dealer, states that the best way to attract rich American buyers is to stay home. Zola constructs it in the following manner:

> Quand on voulait avoir les Américains, il fallait savoir rester chez soi, comme *un bon dieu au fond de son tabernacle* (*Oeuvre*, 291).

Just as important to the structure of *Germinal* is the image of the miners bursting forth through the soil to form a new world. Etienne uses it for the first time in one of his speeches:

> Mais, à présent, le mineur s'éveillait au fond, germait dans la terre ainsi qu'une vraie graine, et l'on verrait un matin ce qu'il pousserait au beau milieu des champs (1277).

In another speech he makes a variation on it:

> Mais le mineur n'était plus l'ignorant, la brute écrasée dans les entrailles du sol. Une armée poussait des profondeurs des fosses, une moisson de citoyens dont la semence germait et ferait éclater la terre, un jour de grand soleil (1383).

By the end of the novel, as Etienne walks across the fields, over the miners working beneath him, the image has become a motif. Zola may have heard Etienne's speeches. He knows they are a rich source for a dramatic and poetic conclusion to the novel, rendered in his own voice:

> Des hommes poussaient, une armée noire, vengeresse, qui germait lentement dans les sillons, grandissant pour les récoltes du siècle futur, et dont la germination allait faire bientôt éclater la terre (1591).

Both Etienne and Zola know the meaning of the allegorical title. Thus not only is speech shared, but metaphor also.

Proximity of idea and vocabulary becomes more and more inherent to Zola's novels as the series progresses. If Zola speaks of the innovations in merchandising effected by Octave Mouret as «revolutionary,» if he speaks of the women customers as overwhelmed and seduced by Octave's ideas, Octave himself uses similar language to describe his intentions: «Je veux que dans huit jours le Paris-Bonheur révolutionne la place» (*Bonheur,* 425); that is, Zola's descriptive style parallels the dialogue of Octave.

The final point is that Zola's characters, especially in the last volumes, share Zola's ideology; consequently, we should expect them to share his style. Certain patterns of optimism for the future are discerned in Denise of *Au Bonheur des dames,* in Pauline of *La Joie de vivre,* and in Caroline of *L'Argent.* The latter, while at first an unwilling supporter of Saccard, is truly altruistic in her dreams of a Christian capitalism renewing life in the mid-East. Representing her thoughts, Zola uses a verb which could only be his own:

> «... toute une civilisation, des routes, des usines, des écoles, *fécondant* ce coin mort et sauvage (*Argent*, 397).

Although Zola would have reservations about the anarchistic ideology of the soldier Maurice, nevertheless Maurice's *élan* and interpretation of Paris burning coincides with the messianic vocabulary which we associate with Zola at the end of the series. Zola in some way did see the end of the Empire as a punishment, and a possibility for purification:

> C'était la partie saine de la France, la raisonnable, la pondérée, la paysanne, celle qui était restée le plus près de la terre, qui supprimait la partie folle, exaspérée, gâtée par l'Empire ... Mais le bain de sang était nécessaire, et de sang français, l'abominable holocauste, le sacrifice vivant, au milieu du feu purificateur. Désormais, le calvaire était monté jusqu'à la plus terrifiante des agonies, la nation crucifiée expiait ses fautes et allait renaître (*Débâcle*, 907).

The ideological critics will verify that this is the language of Zola.

By the last volume we have the complete identification of author and character in Dr. Pascal. Anything said by the doctor can be said to represent Zola. His remarks on the human condition seem appropriate to conclude this discussion of narrator voice. Style and content, author and character are totally fused:

> D'ailleurs, n'était-ce pas la vie? Il n'y a pas de mal absolu. Jamais un homme n'est mauvais pour tout le monde, il fait toujours le bonheur de quelqu'un; de sorte que, lorsqu'on ne se met pas à un point de vue unique, on finit par se rendre compte de l'utilité de chaque être (*Pascal*, 1023).

Dr. Pascal's ideas on relativity come from a single, unique point of view which becomes more doctrinaire as the years pass.

This chapter has tried to demonstrate that the fundamental language of Zola is one of movement; it must also be said that a great deal of violence and turbulence is attached to this style. Ultimately, the vocabulary and the syntax, and the point of view must all be traced back to the personality of Zola. It dominates the *Rougon-Macquart,* and is the source of this consistent style across the twenty volumes. The only change is the increased acceleration of this style. This means the movement speeds up and the violence increases. But both elements are there from the very inception.

CHAPTER VI

TOWARDS SYMBOLISM

If it were possible to read Zola out of the historical context of the nineteenth century many of his titles alone would convince the sensitive reader that the fundamental urge is toward allegory. This can be seen in ten of the titles: *La Curée, Le Ventre de Paris, L'Assommoir, Pot-Bouille, Germinal. La Terre, Le Rêve, La Bête humaine, L'Argent, La Débâcle*; in two instances, *La Curée* and *La Débâcle,* it is a case of a repeated thematic word being raised to the level of title. And without making a total inventory, the sensitive reader soon becomes aware that the subtle name symbolization employed by Flaubert in *Madame Bovary* reaches stages of blatant significance in the *Rougon-Macquart.* Allegorical naming is found in almost every volume, sometimes disguised in the familiar locution and argot of the people. For the most idealistic novel of them all, it is fitting that the heroine and hero be named Angélique and Félicien (*Le Rêve*), for the novel revolves about the twin concepts of purity and happiness. Revolutionary ardor baptizes one partisan, La Brûlé (*Germinal*), the prototypes of the earth are first revealed through their labels (*La Grande, Jésus-Christ* of *La Terre*); when great thesis is involved, Zola himself is certainly choosing the names. Albine of *La Faute de l'abbé Mouret* is something of a pure and natural morning flower; Lazare, the death-obsessed hero of *La Joie de vivre,* recalls to us the biblical tale of the resuscitation of Lazarus by Christ. The rough invader and violator of Paris, Saccard, has a name which suggest what he really is, a *saccageur.* The busybody spinster of *Le Ventre de Paris,* Mademoiselle Saget, always seeking more information, feels fulfilled when she knows all; she has arrived at a certain *sagesse.*

In the tradition of Balzac, characters, particularly the secondary ones, are types. This point should not be overstated; it is a tradition of the so-called «realistic» novel, and wends way back, across the *picaresque* tradition to late medieval and renaissance romances. In Zola a catalogue could be established of servant types, political types such as the liberals and the anarchists, polarities of ideologies being a mainstay of his system. Frère Archangias of *La Faute de l'abbé Mouret* stands for a perverted concept of virile Christianity and is opposed by the guardian of Albine, Jeanbernat, champion of the natural life.

Ideologies are commonly reduced to physiologies in the manner of Balzac, and the *Rougon-Macquart* may be viewed as a perpetual war between the social classes, for the economic problem is the very heart of the sociological tension of the series, between conservatives and liberals, dark and moody Catholics and the sun-filled inheritors of the kingdom of Rousseau. Zola's imagination assumes all of this into a vast system which is curiously manifested in the opposition of the fat and the thin. Two favorites of the court of Napoleon III are the obese baron Gouraud and the emaciated M. Toutin-Laroche, two persons and two attitudes on whom Saccard must depend in his speculative schemes (*La Curée,* 395). The bourgeois of *Pot-Bouille* depend upon the physical remedies of their doctor, and occasionally upon the spiritual wisdom of their curate: «... le médecin maigre et nerveux, le vicaire gras et affable» (86). Etienne's zeal for reformation isolates the problems of France with exactly the same imagery:

> ... une idée révolutionnaire du combat ... les maigres mangeant les gras, le peuple fort dévorant la blême bourgeoisie (*Germinal,* 1524).

Some of the soldiers of the French army are characterized by this physical trait: «Ducat petit et gros ... Cabasse grand et sec...» (*La Débâcle,* 512). Fat and thin is the concrete expression of a world of simplistic contrasts in which Zola, in the best of the tradition of the nineteenth century, seems to believe: the rich and the poor, France and Germany, Christian and Jew.

From such a system, however, Zola creates an entirely allegorical novel, *Le Ventre de Paris,* which is «... la bataille des Gras et des Maigres...» (*Ventre,* 804), as Claude explains to Florent. Florent's revolutionary zeal is ultimately explained as personal motivation, «Croyant avoir à venger sa maigreur contre cette ville engraissée...» (*Ventre,* 812), and at Florent's arrest, parts replace wholes in an allegorical thrust:

> Il y eut comme un silence dans la poissonnerie. Les ventres et les gorges énormes retenaient leur haleine, attendant qu'il eût disparu (*Ventre,* 887-888).

Thematic oppositions are useful in exploring Zola's path toward allegorical and symbolic representation, but a systematic study of his language will pinpoint procedural strategy. The point of departure should be a building upon the glossary which was established in Chapter V. Therein it was noted that language is ever moving away from neutral statement, in the dictionary and primary sense of each word. Zola imparts his own particular and at times peculiar affectivity upon the French language. We first observe the neutral use of language. The words then pass into zones of affectivity which become metaphorical, especially as the series rushes to its conclusion. The metaphorical style wants to be symbolic, and the final volumes, especially *La Débâcle,* arrive at an apocalyptic symbolism. Whether or not this symbolism is successful is open to question.

Through a variety of rhetorical and stylistic devices, the acute reader becomes aware of uncanny syntactical combinations in the prose of Zola. Vocabulary seems to be losing its basic semantic thrust, exaggeration and emphasis seem to be at work.

Syntactical clusters appear to be supporting deep and complicated thematic meanings. We sense what Zola means when he refers to Nana as belonging to «... une aristocratie du vice...» (*Nana,* 1347). A deeper layer is suggested, however, by the description of Nana's bed with its exaggerated paradox, as a:

> ... trône assez large pour que Nana pût y étendre

> la *royauté* de ses membres nus, un *autel* d'une
> richesse byzantine, digne de la toute-puissance de
> son sexe, et où elle l'étalait ... découvert dans une
> *religieuse impudeur* d'idole redoutée (*Nana*, 1462).

This short description contains most of the metaphorical
elements which are to be analyzed herein: the crossing of
images of royalty and religion, with the uncomfortable oxymo-
ron of *religieuse impudeur*. That is, terms are being placed
in new and startling configurations. *Son Excellence Eugène
Rougon* treats of the theme of power in politics. At the same
time a parallel structure reveals the sexual competition between
Eugène and Clorinde. Eugène feels helpless out of power, but
we cannot be sure whether or not his *impuissance* is of a
sexual or a political nature, so intertwined are the two within
this novel: «Jamais il n'avait souffert plus cruellement de son
impuissance» (*Son Excellence*, 197). *Pot-Bouille,* desiring to
unmask bourgeois hypocrisy, twists language into striking
stylistic exaggerations, the adjective contradicting the noun:

> Derrière les belles portes d'acajou luisant, il y avait
> comme des *abîmes d'honnêteté* (*P. B.*, 6).
> Il lui sembla plus recueilli, avec ses *portes chastes,*
> ses portes de riche acajou, fermées sur des *alcôves
> honnêtes* (*P. B.*, 20).
> ... sur les trottoirs autorisés des salons bourgeois
> (*P. B.*, 334).

Or an adjective may cling to an unusual noun: «... trois femmes
équivoques...» (*Bonheur*, 525-26). Pot-Bouille abounds in
uncanny, and often ironic, mixtures of physical and abstract
attributes.

> ... la *nudité* froide de la cour, la *paix* recueillie du
> vestibule, les belles *vertus* domestiques des étages
> (*P. B.*, 247).

The basic idea is very simple. From the very beginning, the
language of Zola which has been characterized as a language of
movement, has another level, that of metaphorical transformations. Early in *La Fortune des Rougon,* we see the insurgents

marching to Paris, or rather being carried off to Paris by the forces of destiny, a romantic Marxist reading of the inevitability of the triumph of the working class:

> ... il lui semblait qu'ils ne marchaient plus, qu'ils étaient *charriés* par *la Marseillaise* elle-même (*Fortune*, 32).

This is an early example of unanimism in Zola, and such a concept has transcended any «realistic» rendering. *Charrier* has become metaphorical. Fundamental is the transformation of the basic material; for example, the dressing room of the actresses in *Nana* becomes a «... fournaise empoisonnée de musc...» (*Nana*, 1224).

This procedure emanates from a basic premise of the *Rougon-Macquart*, namely, the idea of *appétit* as the cornerstone of the structure. This is the *mot-clé* of the series, announced in the preface as the main characteristic of the Rougon-Macquart family: «... le débordement des appétits...» (I, 3). While Zola may have believed that his analysis of these appetites was modern and scientific, textual evidence reveals a psychological posture akin to that of a medieval allegorist in the presentation of the struggle between good and evil. In the twenty volumes these appetites are presented as allegories and sometimes as quasi-symbolic structures. The question of appetite is perceived as a moral and not a sociological question. The preparatory notes for the series utilize this word over and over, clearly illustrating the centrality of the idea. We are consequently not surprised to find it used in practically all of the volumes. As the springboard word it engenders related concepts, first of all the idea of the *curée* which becomes titular, the rough devouring of the remains of the hunt, and the organic idea of pleasure in eating. Zola's mind is quite visual and concrete, turning abstractions of good and evil into sensorial depictions of appetites, acts of imbibing, eating, taking-in, of satiation, sometimes with modern existential overtones.

Across the *Fortune* the concepts of desire, instinct, tendency, concupiscence are betrayed by Zola's simple insistence on the *curée*. Mitterand's notes prove how heavily this word figures in Zola's psychological vocabulary between 1868 and

1870 (1). The image of the spoils acts as an allegorical summary of the meaning of the narration of *La Fortune*. The image appears frequently to accompany dishonest action, to depict character trait, and finally blends with the Rougon victory banquet:

> Et, chez les Rougon, le soir, au dessert, des rires montaient dans la *buée* de la table, toute *chaude* encore des *débris* du dîner. Enfin, ils *mordaient* aux plaisirs des riches! Leurs *appétits*, aiguisés par trente ans de désirs contenus, montraient des *dents féroces*. Ces *grands inassouvis*, ces *fauves maigres*, à peine *lâchés* de la veille dans les jouissances, acclamaient l'*Empire naissant*, le règne de la *curée ardente* (*Fortune*, 314; see also 94, 150, 305).

The word appears throughout Volume II, and at one point is developed as a very olfactory motif of the hunt, for the aspiring and anticipating Aristide Saccard:

> Il aspirait ces souffles encore vagues qui montaient de la grande cité, ces souffles de l'Empire naissant, où traînaient déjà des *odeurs* d'*alcôves* et de *tripots financiers*, des *chaleurs de jouissances*. Les *fumets* légers qui lui arrivaient lui disaient qu'il était sur la *bonne piste*, que le *gibier* courait devant lui, que la *grande chasse impériale*, la chasse aux aventures, aux femmes, aux millions, commençait enfin. Ses narines battaient, son *instinct* de *bête affamée* saisissait merveilleusement au passage les moindres indices de la *curée chaude* dont la ville allait être le théâtre (*Curée*, 362).

This single passage shows the synthetic and condensed style of Zola. Focusing on the final image of the *curée*, it brings into play, through its allegorical olfactory impressions, the limited compass points of Zola's world: affective vocabulary will build into allegorical systems centering about appetite, seen as hunting, eating, drinking, conquest, sexuality, and collapse. Basic affective vocabulary items have a way of stretching

---

(1) I, Pléiade, 1534.

themselves across the series. The image of the *curée* reaches
its peak in a real hunting scene. Eugène Rougon watches and
evaluates the conclusion of a royal hunt, the ceremonial of the
curée:

> Les chiens se ruèrent, se vautrèrent sur les débris;
> leurs abois furieux s'apaisaient dans un grognement
> sourd, un tremblement convulsif de jouissance. Des
> os craquaient. Alors, sur le balcon, aux fenêtres, ce
> fut une satisfaction; les dames avaient des sourires
> aigus, en serrant leurs dents blanches; les hommes
> soufflaient, les yeux vifs, les doigts occupés à tordre
> quelque cure-dents apporté de la salle à manger
> (*Son Excellence*, 184-185).

Such a scene puts into relief the *mots-clefs* of preceding volumes: «... appétits de loup...» (*Curée*, 359); «Elle ne se
sentait pas d'indignation contre ces mangeurs de curée» (*Curée*,
595).

The concept of eating and drinking illustrates how Zola's
novels move out of a pretended objective narration into complicated allegorical structures. Viewing the twenty volumes
as an ensemble we cannot but be struck by the number of
eating, drinking and feasting scenes, vast consumption by the
rich contrasted with the poverty and starvation of the poor.
This thematic level is most poignantly expressed in *Germinal*
with the bourgeois dinners of the Grégoire family contrasted
with the starvation of the miners. On the particular level, the
neurotic Rose Campardon of *Pot-Bouille* is seen partly through
her hearty appetite:

> ... Rose, dans sa camisole brodée, au milieu des
> linges garnis de dentelle, mangea d'un gros appé-
> tit ... Oh! l'estomac va bien, ce n'est pas l'estomac
> qui est malade, répétait-elle en trempant ses tartines.
> Deux larmes tombèrent dans son café (*P. B.*, 212).

The next step is to look at the language. Familiar language
has a way of being direct, imaginative and figurative. Véronique
the servant thus uses *dévorer* in counseling Pauline not to let
herself be used by the family: «Ça devient trop bête, d'être
dévorée ainsi...» (*Joie*, 956). The familiar language of Véronique is elevated into a culinary metaphor when Eugène

Rougon advises his brother to be patient and to work for success in Paris:

> Mais, par grâce, attends que la nappe soit mise, et, si tu m'en crois, donne-toi la peine d'aller chercher toi-même ton couvert à l'office (*Curée*, 363).

This pattern then extends into the metaphorical voice of Zola where it is vivified, intensified, spread out in dense fields and finally becomes a sustained metaphor. The rampant materialism of the Empire is described thus, as Zola cites Rougon: «Paris se mettait à table et rêvait gaudriole au dessert» (*Curée*, 367).

The familiar language of *L'Assommoir* presents a very picturesque metaphorical field centering on hunger. There is no food in the house: «En décembre, un soir, on dîna par coeur» (*Assommoir*, 649). Gervaise is gaining weight in spite of having nothing to eat: «... elle grossissait toujours, malgré ses danses devant le buffet vide...» (*Assommoir*, 729). Through figurative repetitions, the narrative insists upon the idea of hunger.

> Les hivers surtout les *nettoyaient*. S'ils mangeaient du pain au beau temps, les *fringales* arrivaient avec la pluie et le froid, les *danses devant le buffet*, les *dîners par coeur*, dans la *petite Sibérie de leur cambuse* (*Assommoir*, 683).

Gervaise joins other poor and hungry women waiting to collect their husbands' wages and Zola says of them all: «Elles logeaient toutes à la même enseigne, chez misère et compagnie» (*Assommoir*, 761).

The sea is a menace to the society of *La Joie*, and Zola depicts it with the verb *manger*: «Voici plus de cinq cents ans que la mer les mange...» (*Joie*, 896); «... le hurlement des misérables mangés par la mer» (*Joie*, 904). Similarly, Eugène Rougon is weakened by the demands of his friends: «... il se rappelait le travail lent de sa bande, ces dents aiguës qui chaque jour mangeaient un peu de sa force» (*Son Excellence*, 344); «... Rougon, en face de la bande gorgée, se trouvait plus petit qu'autrefois...» (345). The summer season is slow in the department store; many employees are discharged: «... en rendant au pavé un bon tiers des commis, les faibles qui se laissaient manger par les forts» (*Bonheur,* 534). The noise of the expanding department store fills the entire quarter, the store becomes the *idée fixe* of the small merchants who are being driven out of business, and they figuratively «drink in» the store in the air they breathe:

> ... tous deux, du matin au soir, ne parlaient ainsi que du magasin, le buvaient à chaque heure dans l'air même qu'ils respiraient (*Bonheur,* 570).

A main idea of *Au Bonheur des dames* is the destruction of the weak by the strong. It is backed up by metaphor which starts off softly enough with Zola's traditional *appétit,* but the store then becomes a gigantic machine with devouring jaws:

> tous n'avaient qu'une idée fixe, déloger le camarade au-dessus de soi pour monter d'un échelon, le *manger* s'il devenait un obstacle; et cette lutte des *appétits,* cette poussée des uns sur les autres, était comme le bon fonctionnement même de la machine, ce qui enrageait la vente et allumait cette flambée du succès dont Paris s'étonnait. Derrière Hutin, il y avait Favier, puis derrière Favier, les autres, à la file. On entendait un gros bruit de *mâchoires* (Bonheur, 542).

In *Le Ventre de Paris* and in *Germinal,* affective vocabulary of ingesting and digesting forms a vast and sustained metaphorical field. In *Le Ventre,* metaphorical gluttony and fasting make the point of the novel. In *Germinal* one of the main images is the mine as a huge eater: «... de boyaux géants capables de digérer un peuple» (1154); «Pendant une demi-heure, le puits en dévora de la sorte, d'une gueule plus ou moins gloutonne...» (*Ibid.*). *Nana* utilizes many unified stylistic fields to create the myth, the two most important being Nana the destroyer and Nana the devourer. Her appetite for men is insatiable: «Nana, en quelques mois, les mangea goulûment, les uns après les autres» (1454). She consumes Steiner, the obese banker: «Il était gros, il était bête, et elle le bousculait, avalant les morceaux doubles, voulant en finir plus vite avec ce Prussien» (*Ibid.*). Particularly vivid is the image of Nana eating up the properties of la Faloise where very specific images of foliage in the sun, ripe wheat fields, vineyards, cows in high grass are created in separate clauses only to be swallowed up by Nana:

> Les feuillages frissonnant sous le soleil, les grands blés mûrs, les vignes dorées en septembre, les herbes hautes où les vaches enfonçaient jusqu'au ventre, tout y passait, dans un engloutissement d'abîme (1455).

Thus the language moves from dictionary sense to figurative sense, and at that point drags in related terms, and as the narration intensifies, the vocabulary becomes more and more drastic. The Comtesse Muffat changes personality and becomes a woman who «... mangeait les restes dédaignés de Nana» (1465).

Language moving constantly into deep subjectivity can easily be discerned if we start with a discussion of *Germinal.* A descriptive language of collapse is natural enough given the subject of this novel, work in dangerous mines, and the destruction of the mines at its conclusion. The description of the destruction is objectively normal: «... tout flambait, l'air s'enflammait...» (*Germinal,* 1555). The objective description is complemented, and with increasing intensity, with subjective descriptive fields: the already noted personification of the mine: «Les cages montaient ... engouffraient toujours des hommes, que la gueule du trou semblait boire» (1158); the vivid and metaphorical imagination of Etienne who comes out of the mines at night and wanders through the countryside:

> C'était en effect, dans le pays entier, un long retentissement de ruines. La nuit, lorsqu'il errait par la campagne noire, ainsi qu'un loup hors de son bois, il croyait entendre les *effondrements des faillites,* d'un bout de la plaine à l'autre. Il ne longeait plus ... que des usines fermées, mortes, dont les bâtiments pourrissaient sous le ciel blafard (1461).

It is obvious here that Zola's own narration is as metaphorical as his reporting of Etienne's thoughts. Zola's final description of the destroyed mines is constructed exactly as the last tableau of *Une Page d'amour,* with the piling up of drastic images of ruin and destruction rendered as: «... la fosse engloutie...,» «... un cloaque...» «... ruines d'une ville abîmée...» (1557).

The expiatory novel *La Débâcle,* given the subject matter of the war and the commune, naturally has vocabulary of destruction and devastation. Zola intends to make of it, however, a symbolic representation of a *châtiment* which will lead to a purification: «Il semblait que la France entière brulât, s'effondrât, au milieu de l'enragée canonnade» (815). «... c'était le 4 septembre, l'effondrement d'un monde, le second Empire emporté dans la débâcle de ses vices et de ses fautes...» (801). Taking just one word from the glossary, *emporter,* and studying its use across *La Débâcle,* it is apparent to what degree this word is used almost exclusively in a metaphorical sense:

> ... la désespérance dont le galop l'emportait parmi ces soldats errants... (426).
> Le Wagon roulait, roulait toujours, emportant sa charge d'hommes... (440).
> Depuis la mort violente de sa femme, emportée dans un affreux drame... (521).
> ... (l') empereur ... pareil à un enfant perdu dans son empire, qu'on emportait comme un inutile paquet, parmi les bagages des troupes (523).
> ... tous ébranlés, emportés sous la même force logique et invicible... (543).
> ... elle fut emportée, sans savoir comment, parmi les troupes qui se repliaient (642).
> ... le reste des troupes venait d'être emporté, au milieu d'une débandade... (857).
> ... sans cesse emporté par l'émotion du moment (860).

Zola's style has the same intensity as that of his most revolutionary heroes. Sigismond, the scholarly revolutionary and friend of Karl Marx in *L'Argent* has a narrow linguistic vision composed of *balayer* (43), *craquer* (44), *sauter* (46), *effondrement* (48) and the like, out of which could be created a very subjective glossary to complement the one already established. What is very striking in this novel is the vision of the future as seen by this dying revolutionary, who dreams of «... la cité de justice et de bonheur...» (392); «... une cité de liberté et de gaieté...» (393). The three ideological camps of *L'Argent,* the communism of Sigismond, the catholicism of Caroline Hammelin and her brother, and the capitalism of Saccard share exactly the same glossary of a world to be destroyed and a world to be made.

Affective vocabulary leading into metaphorical evaluations of reality is not confined to novels of cataclysmic proportions. Zola's perceptions of the world are never limited to objective recording of happening. He imparts message. *La Curée* describes the razing of vast parts of Paris under Baron Hausmann in order to build a new city. Zola will not concentrate on the idea of the new city, however, preferring to impart to the reader the destructive and profit-making energy of Second Empire criminals. We can never be sure in *Pot-Bouille* if Zola is speaking of physical or moral stench, so interrelated are the images. The meaning is literal but there is always a symbolic level.

> ... une pestilence montait de la petite cour obscure, toutes les décompositions cachées des étages semblaient *fondre,* et s'exhaler par cet égout de la maison (384).

Doctor Juillerat of the same novel seems to be a spokesman for Zola when he analyzes for the abbé Mauduit the *malaise* of his patients, these young ladies who have received an «... éducation de poupée...» (*P. B.,* 363). Zola describes his emotion:

> ... dans son emportement de jacobin, sonnait le *glas entêté* d'une classe, la *décomposition* et *l'écroulement* de la bourgeoisie, dont les étais *pourris, craquaient* d'eux-mêmes (*P. B.,* 363).

The idea of revolution is seen at all levels, for instance, the new merchandising methods of Octave Mouret are so described:

> ... le patron était le premier étalagiste de Paris, un étalagiste *révolutionnaire* à la vérité, qui avait fondé *l'école du brutal et du colossal* dans la science de l'étalage (*Bonheur,* 434).

Consequently, this hyperbolic style, which seeks the meaning of the Second Empire in the smallest social details, relates the bankruptcy of the small merchants in the same drastic language used for the collapse of mines, or the total collapse of the Empire itself in the concluding volumes:

> ... c'était la maison de Bourras qui *s'effondrait*, comme minée par les grandes eaux (*Bonheur*, 747).
> ... les Robineau, les Bédoré et soeur, les Vanpouille, *craquaient* et *s'écrasaient* chacun à son tour...» (*Ibid.*).

Mixing the physical and the abstract, it is difficult at times to distinguish in Zola mental attitude from physical description. Thus a rather violent argument at the dinner table *chez Sandoz* begins with an intensification of physical effects, bright candle light, the table on fire in its disarray, which also means the chaos of irrational argument:

> Les bougies de la suspension brûlaient très hautes, les faïences des murs épanouissaient leurs fleurs peintes, la table semblait s'être incendiée avec la débâcle de son couvert, sa violence de causerie, ce saccage qui les enfiévrait là, depuis deux heures (*Oeuvre*, 331).

Impressionistic light in Zola is always balanced by allegorical fires imposed on the physical environment by the eyes of an involved perceiver who puts into the milieu the symbolic perspective of his mind. Zola sets Paris on fire (2) as Saccard walks, imagining a great speculative victory:

> ... en face du palais de la Légion d'honneur, que surmontait une gigantesque croix de feu, braisillant dans le ciel noir, il en prit la résolution hardie, pour le jour où il se sentirait les reins assez forts ... il revint rue Saint-Lazare, au travers de Paris en flammes (*Argent*, 200).

---

(2) For an apt analysis of the «fire» motif see F. W. J. Hemmings, «Fire in Zola's fiction: variations on an elemental theme,» *Yale French Studies*, 42 (1969), 26-37.

18

Paris may burn with success or with failure. Saccard has just been described crossing a Paris in a metaphorical fire of success. Similarly, Caroline looks at the Bourse after the collapse of Saccard's bank:

> Le crépuscule tombait, le ciel d'hiver, chargé de brume, mettait derrière le monument comme une fumée d'incendie, une nuée d'un rouge sombre, qu'on aurait crue faite des flammes et des poussières d'une ville prise d'assaut ... Mais, cette fois, derrière cette fumée rousse de l'horizon, dans les lointains troubles de la ville, il y avait comme un grand craquement sourd, la fin prochaine d'un monde (*Argent*, 360-61).

The meaning is rather clear. For Zola, all happenings, events, all attitudes and psychologies are caught up in the fundamental issue of the Second Empire. At every level we witness war, epidemic sweepings-away, arson, melting, collapse, end-of-world feelings. The whole world is at war. This fundamental idea organizes the *Rougon-Macquart* and gives rise to this recurring subjective, figurative vocabulary. *Nana* remains the novel which most succinctly utilizes figurative level for symbolic effect. The passage of the waltz scene in *Nana* aptly shows how the image of eating and devouring as a principal motif of destruction is joined by the field of light (fire) and movement (the waltz as the perverted movement of Nana across a society) to create a unified field in which objective descriptive materials (a waltz at a night reception) turn Nana into a symbol of Second Empire corruption: what perhaps could have been painted by an impressionist as a happy Second Empire festive occasion is pushed by Zola into the direction of symbol:

> Dans le jardin, une lueur de braise, tombée des lanternes vénitiennes, éclairait d'un lointain reflet d'incendie les ombres noires des promeneurs, cherchant un peu d'air au fond des allées. Et ce tressaillement des murs, cette nuée rouge, étaient comme la flambée dernière, où craquait l'antique honneur brûlant aux quatre coins du logis. Les gaietés timides, alors à peine commençantes, que Fauchery, un soir d'avril, avait entendu sonner

avec le son d'un cristal qui se brise, s'étaient peu à peu enhardies, affolées, jusqu'à cet éclat de fête. Maintenant, la fêlure augmentait; elle lézardait la maison, elle annonçait l'effondrement prochain. Chez les ivrognes des faubourgs, c'est par la misère noire, le buffet sans pain, la folie de l'alcool vidant les matelas, que finissent les familles gâtées. Ici, sur l'écroulement de ces richesses, entassées et allumées d'un coup, la valse sonnait le glas d'une vieille race, pendant que Nana, invisible, épandue au-dessus du bal avec ses membres souples, décomposait ce monde, le pénétrait de son odeur flottant dans l'air chaud, sur le rythme canaille de la musique (*Nana*, 1429-1430).

This extraordinary passage, using as its point of departure, the original idea of the reporter Fauchery —of the *lézarde* in the moral structure of the Muffat household— reiterates at every level possible in the description the idea of corruption and collapse, with the moral implications rendered exclusively physically. But it is no longer possible to speak in terms of a unified glossary moving more and more into affectivity. It is now a question of metaphorical transformations.

Metaphorical descriptions in Zola tend to move away from the objectively perceived reality. The heights of metaphorical vision are found in *La Débâcle* wherein Paris undergoes multiple transformations, but the procedure is present in other novels. The mines of *Germinal* are given many epithets, among which are found «... cette Sodome des entrailles de la terre...» (1395); «... la sale cuisine du diable...» (*Ibid.*); «... en pleine cité maudite» (1397). Similarly, the uncontrolled train at the end of *La Bête humaine*: «... le roulement du monstre ... train fantôme ... bête aveugle» (1331). As the train approaches the tunnel, its headlight is transformed, in a gradation: *Etoile, Oeil, Brasier, Gueule* (*Bête*, 1273). It is more difficult to understand such constructions in novels with less symbolic intent. *L'Oeuvre* is a case in point. From the very first pages, Paris is presented in a mysterious and frightening manner. This is ever so vaguely justified as the fears of the young Christine of a city to which she is new and which she does not yet understand. We must conclude, however, that the real source of these feelings is Zola. He makes the city undergo metamorphoses in a manner similar to Baudelaire. Paris is seen in a violent rainstorm, «... l'apparition violâtre d'une cité fantastique...» (*Oeuvre*, 12). The accompanying descriptive material is sinister: «... la fosse profonde où la Seine coulait à cet endroit, noirâtre...» (*Ibid.*); «D'étranges masses peuplaient l'eau...» (*Ibid.*). On the next page Paris is called «... *la* ville tragique dans un éclaboussement de sang...» (13). Some pages later the same image is amplified:

> ... la cité tragique, cette trouée des quais s'enfonçant dans des rougeoîments de fournaise, ce fossé profond de la rivière roulant des eaux de plomb, encombré de grands corps noirs, de chalands pareils à des baleines mortes, hérissé de grues immobiles, qui allongeaient des bras de potence (*Oeuvre*, 26).

Into the awesome and often terrifying landscape of modern Paris and the world of the Second Empire, a time of birth for the twentieth century, Zola puts the modern idea of unanimism as a psychological principle and personification as a literary mode.

It has long been recognized that Zola is a precursor of Jules Romains. The famous opening pages of *L'Assommoir* with the collective movement of the workers remain the prototypical example, and the collective response of the theatre goers to the performance of Nana (*Nana,* 1220) looks indeed like any passage from Romains. Stylistically the procedure seems to be the opposite of impressionistic synecdoche. It suffices to state here that unanimistic representation is found in the first novel, in the march of the Var insurgents in *La Fortune des Rougon* which works on several levels at the same time: descriptions of nature, overriding, prophetic author voice, unanimistic proportions. Through such devices individual characterization is minimized. The republican insurgents have no individuality, but are presented as a collective force. While not as powerful as the collective scenes of *Germinal,* the idea is the same and shows how natural this method is to Zola. It is striking that Zola uses nature to indicate the hidden support accorded the insurgents, and at first glance nature seems to be singing along with them:

> *La Marseillaise* emplit le ciel, comme soufflée par

> des bouches géantes dans de monstrueuses trompet-
> tes qui la jetaient ... à tous les coins de la vallée
> ... Alors ce ne fut plus seulement la bande qui
> chanta; des bouts de l'horizon, des rochers lointains,
> des pièces de terre labourées ... semblèrent sortir
> des voix humaines ... un peuple invisible et innom-
> brable acclamant les insurgés ... La campagne, dans
> l'ébranlement de l'air et du sol, criait vengeance et
> liberté (*Fortune,* 27-28).

What renders this section highly symbolic is Zola's metamorphosis of individual acts into generic ones, then elevating
individual action to universal significance. The collective surge
is reduced to a stylistic field reiterating solidarity born from
anger: «... une masse compacte, d'une puissance invincible. Il
pouvait y avoir là environ trois mille hommes unis et emportés
d'un bloc par un vent de colère.» (*Fortune,* 28); the individual
becomes a collective seen in abstract general nouns: «Ce rugis-
sement de la révolte, cet appel à la lutte et à la mort...»
(*Fortune,* 32). Similar language, but with more emphasis on
the physical, is found in *Germinal* where the miners assembled
on the Plan-des-Dames are seen as «... la houle des têtes...»
«... une furie de visages...,» «... des yeux luisants...,» «... des
bouches ouvertes...» (*Germinal,* 1380). One noticeable difference between these two novels is the sinister note of *Germinal*
compared with *La Fortune des Rougon*: the added dimension
of hunger has turned the miners of *Germinal* into a ferocious
and ugly force:

> ... la colère, la faim, ces deux mois de souffrance
> et cette débandade enragée au travers des fosses,
> avaient allongé en mâchoires de bêtes fauves les
> faces placides des houilleurs de Montsou (*Germi-
> nal,* 1436).

In all instances, be the collective surge one of social upheaval
or simply the arrival of customers in the department store, the
collective body is moved about passively by forces beyond
the control of the individual:

> ... un enfournement de clientes, entassées devant
> les rayons, étourdies sous les marchandises, puis
> jetées à la caisse (*Bonheur,* 402).

La Bête humaine, exploiting the complex rail lines of modern France, provokes in Zola a unanimistic simile of the lines as a giant body stretching from Paris to Le Havre:

> C'était comme un grand corps, un être géant couché en travers de la terre, la tête à Paris, les vertèbres tout le long de la ligne, les membres s'élargissant avec les embranchements, les pieds et les mains au Havre et dans les autres villes d'arrivée (*Bête,* 1035).

Likewise, Zola's use of personification has been more than amply commented by critics since the seminal work of Dangelser. The personification of the French nation is a particular characteristic of *Son Excellence Eugène Rougon.* The Baptism of the imperial prince assembles «... la grande famille française...» (25), for the child is indeed, in the words of a deputy, «... L'Enfant de France...» (26). Chapter IX, however, describing a mild reign of terror inaugurated by Rougon, uses personification in a very concrete and visual manner, France seen as physically at the whim and fancy of Rougon. France begins outside Rougon's office:

> Au dehors, la France, peureuse, se taisait (217).
> Le pays tremblait, dans la terreur qui sortait, comme une fumée d'orage, du cabinet de velours vert, où Rougon riait tout seul, en s'étirant les bras (218).
> Quand il marchait, il enfonçait son tapis à coups de talon, pour qu'on entendît la lourdeur de son pas aux quatre coins de la France (*Ibid.*).
> Son désir était de ne pouvoir poser son verre vide sur une console, jeter sa plume, faire un mouvement, sans donner une secousse au pays (*Ibid.*).

Personification of the *Beauce* is characteristic of *La Terre.* Studying just a few examples, we can see how this procedure emanates from a very subjective perception of nature, similar to the nature sentiments found in Rousseau. The wheat fields of *La Beauce* stretch out endlessly in their immensity, and an emotion of sadness is associated with them:

> ... la Beauce, flagellée, s'étendait, d'une tristesse morne (395).

> Au fond de ce trou perdu, à la lisière de la triste
> Beauce... (403).
> ... cette plate Beauce, dont le déroulement à l'infini
> noyait son coeur de tristesse (757).
> ... le désir de revoir une fois encore se dérouler la
> plaine immense, la triste Beauce, qu'il avait fini
> par aimer... (797).

Complementing these subjective landscape are the consistent
personifications of the land as a bountiful mother in times of
good crops, and an indifferent mistress in times of drought.
All the peasants enter into an intimate and almost sexual
relationship with the earth. Less symbolic forms, however,
appear to be nothing more than personified intensifications of
the lyrical feeling just observed:

> ainsi, la Beauce, devant lui, déroula sa verdure, de
> novembre à juillet... (531).
> ... il entendait la Beauce boire, cette Beauce sans
> rivières et sans sources, si altérée (535).
> La Beauce, à l'infini, s'étendait, écrasée sous un
> sommeil de plomb (619).

This procedure is similar to the one employed for the various
moods of the sea in *La Joie de vivre.* Moreover, with a poetic
eye which exactly duplicates the imagery of the symbolist
poets, the land is frequently compared to the sea, and the sea
to wheat fields.

Paris, in its many moods, and in its attributes, remains one
of the main personifications of the *Rougon-Macquart.* In *La
Curée,* the Seine takes on the attributes of elegantly dressed
young girls. Under the impact of the commune (*Débâcle,*
857-912), the city, personified, pulsates with collective reactions. Likewise, intimate relationships are established between parts and the whole. The animated life on the interior
of the department store produces a reaction in the entire city:
«Au loin, Paris grondait» (*Bonheur,* 719), for the city will
always be able to supply a sufficient and ever-increasing number
of customers:

> ... il ne restait, au-delà du grand murmure de la
> vente, que le sentiment de Paris immense, d'une

immensité qui toujours fournirait des acheteuses (*Bonheur*, 492).

As in *Le Ventre de Paris* where direct relationship are establis-hed between the market and the city: «Paris mâchait les bouchées à ses deux millions d'habitants» (*Ventre*, 631), the monster store is a source of alimentation for the monster city. It is characteristic of Zola to start with a concrete detail, in this instances the sound of the *fiacres* and move on to the personified voice of the city:

> Du dehors, ne venaient plus que les roulements des derniers fiacres, au milieu de la voix empâtée de Paris, un ronflement d'ogre repu, digérant les toiles et les draps, les soies et les dentelles, dont on le gavait depuis le matin (*Bonheur*, 499).

Personification of nature is very characteristic of the art of Zola and all that could be basically said about this technique is to be found in the work of Joan Dangelzer, particularly on *La Faute de l'abbé Mouret*. The feminization of nature, viewing nature as an exotic and erotic woman, is an essential part of the late nineteenth century movement known as Natu-rism. Several aspects of this phenomenon in Zola perhaps need some clarification.

Personification of nature seems first of all to be a rather poetic fancy on the part of Zola, not unlike the exaggerated personifications of nature found in Chateaubriand. Thus the apricot trees of *La Faute* become:

> ... des *abricotiers patriarches,* qui portaient *gaillar-dement* leur grand âge, paralysés déjà d'un côté, avec une forêt de bois mort, pareil à un échafau--dage de cathédrale... (1361).

There is also the need for the hypersensitive descendants of Rousseau to be aware of the vitality of nature, and to enter into *correspondances* with it. Serge inquires of Albine how she found the tree:

> Je ne sais pas ... Les plantes ... avaient toutes l'air de me pousser de ce côté. Les branches longues me fouettaient par-derrière, les herbes ménageaient des

pentes, les sentiers s'offraient d'eux-mêmes. Et je crois que les bêtes s'en mêlaient aussi... (*Faute,* 1401-1402).

Thus a personification not just in the style of Zola, but in the words of Albine, quite sentimental in the manner of Walt Disney. Angélique of *Le Rêve* is a bit like Albine, the river speaks to her (*Rêve,* 861-862); she also hears the cathedral, and angels and saints (942).

Rousseau had established vague, floating and indefinite relationships between himself and nature. If there is sexuality therein, it is well camouflaged. Zola will start with the same vague *rapports* and build them into a metaphorical sexual structure. We read in *La Fortune:* «Il leur semblait que toute la langueur du ciel entrait en eux» (198-199). Similarly, the opening descriptions of the effect of the Bois de Boulogne on Renée at first seem innocent enough, but rapidly become explicit:

> Elle était mollement envahie par l'ombre du crépuscule; tout ce que cette ombre contenait d'*indécise tristesse,* de *discrète volupté,* d'*espoir inavoué,* la *pénétrait,* la *baignait* dans une sorte d'air alangui et morbide (*Curée,* 328).

That is, Rousseau corrupted, or Rousseau unveiled, as the language of Zola rapidly moves from the *imprécis* to the *précis,* for it is his intention in this novel to show the Bois de Boulogne as the over-refined and artificial paradise of the Second Empire. This perverting influence on an already perverted family will be further explored in the next chapter, with Renée in the sensually exploding *serre chaude.* From the first novels on, then, nature is seen as extraordinary, larger than life, unrestrained, and stylistically rendered as a mirror image of human biological acts. Zola has intensified Rousseau's bucolic scene; he speaks of «La vie ardente des herbes et des arbres...» (*Fortune,* 6); «Dans cette allée ... règnent encore la végétation puissante...» (*Fortune,* 8). The next step is the creation of figurative fields where nature takes on the attributes of a woman:

... des ténèbres grises flottaient, pareilles aux crêpes

musqués d'une toilette de femme ... ces crêpes, comme parfumés et tièdes encore des épaules voluptueuses de la nuit... (*Fortune,* 200).

Here Zola is working within a very old tradition, one which Hatzfeld has traced back to Buffon and Diderot and the spirit of the rococo (3), mainly bypassed by the romantics, and not gaining ascendancy until the second half of the nineteenth century, starting with Baudelaire, and then drawing in the Symbolists poets, the so-called *école naturiste* of poetry, and a whole line of female poets extending into the twentieth century, such as the Comtesse de Noailles. It is a literary pansexualism which extends well into the twentieth century in the prose writings of Colette, Gide, Giono and even Camus. It may be the ultimate meaning of Rousseauism. Zola is in this line. Renée's sexuality is best expressed across her hothouse of which she is one of the most artificial flowers. And Zola's thesis on the positive value of the natural life could not find better expression than in the intimate fusion of Albine with the great flowers and vegetation of *Le Paradou.* The field of woman-light-color-nature is very dense in *La Faute de l'abbé Mouret* and may truly be considered as a type of personification, much as the Seine river is personified in *La Curée* as a beautiful woman, who according to time of day and season, is displayed in different colored dresses of many textures on which the sunlight plays. In one way, Zola's approach looks a bit like that of Baudelaire who makes several poems fusing person and nature, particularly «La Géante» in which the poet deliberately confuses an amazon, a giantess about whom he can have sexual fantasies, with a mountain range, the hamlet of which is transformed into the poet. As in the poem, the majority of fusions of nature and woman in Zola are permeated by a rampant sexuality which becomes an integral part of the structure.

Epithet, including metaphor and comparison functioning as epithet, is an essential part of the figurational system of Zola. Clinging tenaciously, like a familiar piece of clothing, or physical or psychological trait, Zola's personages cross the pages of his novels accompanied by a consistent tag or meta-

---

(3) Hatzfeld, *Literature Through Art,* 107.

phor. Its purpose is to stabilize and freeze the characterization.

Sometimes Zola's epithets look strongly Balzacian, La Trouille, for example, with her «... museau effronté de chèvre...» (*Terre*, 400). They also recall Chateaubriand when old Fouan is named «... chef de la famille paysanne» (*Terre*, 389). Usually they are original and coincide with the theme of a particular novel, as when Sandoz refers to Claude Lantier as «... le soldat de l'incréé...» (*Oeuvre*, 243).

The language of the people, creative and inventive, nicknames others, sometimes positively, usually pejoratively. Denise is looked down upon by other employees in the store and is often referred to as «... la mal peignée...» (*Bonheur*, 505). In *L'Assommoir* Gervaise becomes «La Blonde» and Virginie «La Brune»; *Le Ventre de Paris* sustains the opposition of Lisa as «La belle charcutière» and Louise Méhudin the fishmonger as «La Normande,» «La belle Normande,» «la poissonnière.»

More interesting is the use of metaphorical variations to surround a character, with all of the images aimed at supporting a single moral or psychological aspect. Mlle Saget who is inordinately curious about the lives of others, and envious, is also forced to live from food rejected by others. In both the moral and physiological sense she becomes «... un fumier vivant, une bête immonde nourrie de pourritures...» (*Ventre*, 842). Mme Méchain of *L'Argent* profits from the suffering of others. Consequently she is consistenly tagged as a bird of prey:

> ... le corbeau qui suivait les armées en marche... (25).
> ... flairât l'air, attendant les cadavres... (*Ibid.*).
> ... avec son louche commerce d'oiseau de carnage...» (291).
> ... elle guettait les morts, telle que le corbeau vorace qui suit les armées, jusqu'au jour du massacre (332).

La Grande of *La Terre* has similar attached figures appropriate for a novel of the land: «... la tête décharnée d'un oiseau de proie...» (393); «... son air sauvage de vieux vautour déplumé» (394). Nana is accompanied by a series of related epithets, the most common of which is «... la mangeuse d'hommes...» (1393), with variations such as «... chatte de race...» (1346).

Clara of *Au Bonheur des dames* is hardly ever described without the horse head tag: «... cette grande rousse à tête de cheval...» (*Bonheur*, 679), and Irma Bécot of *L'Oeuvre* looks like a Titian painting:

> ... la tête faite avec un art de cabotine, le front diminué par la frisure des cheveux, la face tirée en longueur ... rousse ardente de blonde pâle qu'elle était, si bien qu'une courtisane du Titien semblait maintenant s'être levée du petit voyou de jadis (*Oeuvre*, 176).

Once established, the epithet sticks:

> Seulement, ma chère, tu fais craquer ton Titien (178).
> Regarde! le revoilà, mon Titien! (179).
> Tu sais, ma tête pour les jobards, mon Titien, comme ils disent... (251).

Sustained epithet accompanies two great characterizations, Eugène Rougon and his brother, Aristide Saccard. In a novel of sexual politics it is more than fitting that Eugène should be dubbed «taureau»:

> ... Rougon, qui gardait à son banc une attitude superbe de taureau assoupi (*Son Excellence*, 27).
> ... se ruait avec un souffle haletant de taureau échappé (*Son Excellence*, 118).
> ... son cou de taureau éclatait... (*Son Excellence*, 122).
> Ses muscles de taureau rendaient simplement sa chute plus retentissante... (*Son Excellence*, 344).

Saccard (*L'Argent*) is aptly depicted as a pirate: «... le terrible corsaire...» (130); «... en capitaine d'aventure...» (255); «... ce terrible aventurier...» (266); «... Saccard, ce corsaire au coeur tanné par vingt ans de brigandage...» (331); «... avec sa passion voleuse de corsaire sans scrupules» (336).

Moving directly into the field of metaphor it might be asked if there is a discernible metaphorical system across the *Rougon-Macquart*. A careful reading of the twenty volumes isolates the main figurative fields of Zola which attach themselves to his general philosophical beliefs as they are revealed in his aesthetic choices. Without attempting to be exhaustive or to make any total catalogue of the metaphorical fields, it is possible to isolate the dominant ones.

The basic metaphor, from the viewpoint of Zola's philosophy of seizing life, is that of the sun which is put into opposition with the shadow of those forces opposing life. Representative metaphors of this variety are found in the concluding paragraph of Chapter II of *La Faute de l'abbé Mouret* where the sun «L'astre triomphant...» (1226) dominates over the cross of Christ. The sun is the life giving force of the conclusion of Germinal where the April earth finds itself pregnant with the hope of the future under the «... rayons enflammés de l'astre...» (1591). The triumph of *plein air* painting over academic art is centralized in the sun: «... le coup de soleil avait passé là» (*Oeuvre*, 297). Destruction of the old order is also implied: «Bientôt, les murs tomberaient, la grande nature entrerait, car la brèche était large...» (*Ibid.*). The child of Clotilde and Dr. Pascal is the symbol of hope for the future of mankind in the concluding page of the last volume, and it opens its eyes «... désireux de la lumière» (*Pascal*, 1220).

It is under this sun that the human drama is enacted. The human condition is often ant-like, dehumanized, especially in a novel like *Germinal* in which Catherine, working alone in the mine, seems «... pareille à une maigre fourmi noire en lutte contre un fardeau trop lourd» (*Germinal*, 1179). But the image of working ants can indicate industry, such as the founding of a new civilization in the Middle East:

> ... les fourmis humaines s'étaient multipliées, changeaient la face de la terre (*Argent*, 59).

The ant image accurately betrays German efficiency during the battles of the Franco-Prussian war:

> ... de vraies fourmilières, des files de fourmis noires, si bien que, quand il n'y en avait plus, il y en avait encore (*Débâcle*, 450).

The ants of the *Rougon-Macquart* organize and form new nations, they become a *peuple*. It may be no more than the self-contained world of the department store: «... un coin perdu du vaste monde où s'agitait le peuple du *Bonheur des dames*» (*Bonheur,* 716); or the collective image of the miners: «... un peuple de mineurs...» (1199, 1379); «... tout un peuple le maudissait d'une voix peu à peu tonnante...» (*Germinal,* 1519); or the defeated French waiting for a new world to be born following *La Débâcle:* «... il y avait là tout un peuple dans l'attente...» (867). These few examples are typical of metaphorical fields scattered generously through the volumes.

Contrasted with the ants and the people are the artificial women of the Second Empire, the *poupées* (4), vain, self-centered dolls wearing Ionescan masks. To them, Zola contrasts the healthy image of maternity, the true mark of womanhood in his system. The *Rougon-Macquart* frequently evokes transvestism as a sign of the decadence of the times, such as Georges dressed in women's clothing in *Nana* (VI): «Elle le tournait comme une poupée» (1237). The doctor and priest of *Pot-Bouille* analyze the moral climate of the times: «... les unes qu'une éducation de poupée corrompait ou abêtissait...» (363). Rose Campardon of the same novel is a prototypical antiseptic doll woman.

There are other dominant metaphorical fields in the *Rougon-Macquart.* They are so pervasive and so multi-layered in meaning that they can be considered as leitmotives. These are the fields of military conquest; fissures, *fêlures* and *lézardes;* religious imagery; and the sea.

---

(4) A study of Zola's newspaper articles complements any study of the metaphorical procedures of the *Rougon-Macquart.* The articles prove that he thinks primarily by analogy and not analytically. An article entitled «Catherine» in *La Cloche* of 18 April, 1870 is appropriate to this discussion of the *poupée* analogy. «Catherine» is an allegorical article on the moral state of modern France, Catherine being a doll who at one and the same time anticipates Nana, contrasts the *honnête femme* with the courtesan, and the idea of vice with that of maternity. Zola states that he has a little friend named Rose who has received as a gift a doll named Catherine. According to Zola this doll is dangerous and symbolic of bourgeois corruption. The body of this doll moves in all ways: «Catherine a des formes souples et arrondies. Catherine est une femme faite, et bien faite.» (2). She has many dresses, jewerly, even a bedroom «... garnie de tous les engins que nécessite aujourd'hui la toilette d'une femme comme il faut.» (2) Rose, who is hardly much bigger than the doll, calls it her daughter, but Zola suspects that it is

For the first, terms associated with military operations seem more than appropriate for the agressive spirit of the series. The nineteenth century novel depicts the *arrivistes* engaging in the battle of Paris. Without making any analysis, the following list may be seen as representative of this metaphorical field:

> Il avait la vision très nette de la bataille qu'il venait livrer (*Curée*, 359).
> Il voulait rester jusqu'à la fin sur le champ de bataille... (*Curée*, 386).
> ... elle prit un air terrible d'homme de guerre qui conduisait ses filles au massacre... (*P. B.*, 81).
> ... il faut bien conquérir Paris (*P. B.*, 13).
> ... l'air d'un capitaine satisfait de ses troupes... (*Bonheur*, 426).
> ... tu n'as qu'à me suivre, si tu veux tout voir, car aujourd'hui je reste sur la brèche (*Bonheur*, 482).
> C'étaient comme les détonations d'une artillerie géante ... qui ressemblait à un craquement continu de fusillade (*Joie*, 828).

Fêlure and *lézarde* seem to be key metaphors in the Zola

---

the doll who is instructing Rose. Reacting against this artificial education of the child, Zola recalls *Mes fils* of Michelet wherein the basic educational principle is found in action: «Il faut que l'enfant agisse, crée. Instruire, c'est apprendre à agir et à créer.» He concludes by finding the Empire guilty of having corrupted even the dolls of the children. He recommends that Rose be given a good old-fashioned doll which will teach her motherhood. Another article, «Causerie —sur les dix-sept années d'Empire de la France. Zola souhaite à cette jeune fille de prendre pour mari le Peuple,» which appeared in *La Tribune*, 3 January, 1869, p. 7, also reveals the parabolic method of Zola. Speaking of earlier marriages of the Empire's older sisters, he recommends that the young France marry a good boy of the people: «A une bonne fille, il faut un bon garçon. J'ai voulu que ton fiancé eût ton courage, ta santé, ta gaîté large et heureuse. Il aime comme toi la liberté et la justice, il travaille du matin au soir en chantant tes chansons. A tous deux vous formerez un couple puissant, et de votre étreinte féconde naîtra une nation de géants ... Tu me demandes, n'est-ce pas? le nom du jeune homme. Il s'appelle Peuple. Tel est mon cadeau de nouvel an.»

system (5). They occur for the first time in *Nana* as the reporter Fauchery, a sort of moral commentator in spite of his own immorality, evaluates the moral facade of the Muffat salon, and intuitively guesses that the structure is collapsing:

> Et ces rires, dans la solennité de la vaste pièce, prenaient un son dont Fauchery resta frappé; ils sonnaient le cristal qui se brise. Certainement, il y avait là un commencement de fêlure (*Nana*, 1155).

This idea is picked up again (*Nana*, 1429) when the real crack has occurred, and Fauchery recalls his original evaluation. Thereafter it is a common enough figure in the novels. Lazare's inconsistencies are explained by Zola: «C'était en lui la lésion première, la fêlure de l'artiste, que l'on aurait retrouvée chez le savant et l'industriel avortés» (*Joie*, 886). Old friendships break up in *L'Oeuvre*:

> La fissure était là, la fente à peine visible, qui avait fêlé les vieilles amitiés jurées, et qui devaient les faire craquer, un jour, en mille pièces (198).

Jacques Lantier meditating his own poor mental health recalls his family: «La famille n'était guère d'aplomb, beaucoup avaient une fêlure» (*Bête*, 1043). This figurative language is picked up by Dr. Pascal as he defends his work to his mother:

> Mais vous ne m'entendez guère, si vous imaginez que je crois à l'effondrement final, parce que je montre les plaies et les lézardes (*Pascal*, 999).

This metaphorical field is employed constantly across *L'Argent*: Gundermann awaits the interior collapse of the rival bank:

> Cette Universelle bruyante ... qui se dressait comme une menace devant la haute banque juive, il atten-

_____

(5) The literary source of this metaphor may well be the concluding one of Chapter IV, Part II of *Madame Bovary* (94): «Elle ne savait pas que, sur la terrasse des maisons, la pluie fait des lacs quand les gouttières sont bouchées, et elle fût ainsi demeurée en sa sécurité, lorsqu'elle découvrit subitement une lézarde dans le mur.»

dait froidement qu'elle se lézardât d'elle-même...
(*Argent*, 202).
Que faisait-on, rue de Londres? n'était-ce point, à
cette seconde précise, que se produisait la lézarde
dont périrait l'édifice? (*Argent*, 230).
Déjà, des écroulements partiels s'étaient produits,
le marché exténué, trop chargé, se lézardait de toutes parts (*Argent*, 326).
Vingt-quatre heures suffirent, la maison s'était lé-
zardée... (*Argent*, 366).

Religious imagery presents one of the most interesting but
peculiar aspects of Zola's system. Tante Dide's forty years in
the asylum (*Pascal*, 974) or the servant Martine's life-long
service to Pascal: «Depuis qu'elle veillait ainsi sur eux, elle
avait retrouvé sa petite figure blanche de nonne vouée au
célibat...» (*Pascal*, 1115) are normal enough and apt similes
as is the calvary metaphor for the despairing French army:
«Elle allait monter son calvaire jusqu'au bout...» (*Débâcle*,
460; 507). Of course, *calvaire* has become a term for suffering,
as a lexical metaphor of the language. Furthermore, the
description of quiet and peaceful atmospheres in terms of
cloisters also seems appropriate. Plassans is described as a
city which avoids active life: «Il n'y a pas de cité, je crois,
qui se soit entêtée si tard à s'enfermer comme une nonne»
(*Fortune*, 38). Or the bourgeois apartment house: «L'escalier
retrouvait son recueillement de chapelle bourgeoise» (*P. B.*,
227; 292; 342). The department store in the summer months
has very few customers:

C'était une somnolence, une sieste d'été, au milieu
du vide élargi des comptoirs, pareils à des chapelles,
où l'ombre dort, après la dernière messe (*Bonheur*,
540).

Beyond this point, however, a unique and original religious
imagery issues forth from Zola. He senses that the materialism
of the period has been destroying family relationships and
creating new goddesses, some sexless, such as Rose Campardon,
who «... s'enfonçait dans son égoïsme d'idole sans sexe»
(*P. B.*, 213); or the newly enshrined Nana who «... prenait
le rayonnement mystérieux d'une idole chargée de pierreries»

— 289 —

19

(*Nana*, 1471-1472). The basis of this new liturgy is «L'argent, l'argent roi, l'argent Dieu...» (*Argent*, 220), the hidden «... dieu repu et accroupi...» (1141; 1193; 1324) of *Germinal*. Berthe Josserand has been raised in this new religion: «... toute cette religion de l'argent dont elle avait appris le culte dans sa famille...» (*P. B.*, 243). The department store of *Au Bonheur des dames* becomes the cathedral of the new religion, its new entryway on the rue Neuve-Saint-Augustin described as «Cette porte, haute et profonde, comme un porche d'église...» (*Bonheur*, 611). Its new galleries are «... pareilles aux bas-côtés d'une église» (767). Mouret even has the idea of having the store blessed by the curé from the Madeleine (765). Denise has fears of the hall of silks «... dont ... l'air d'église lui faisait peur» (434). Mouret is asked: «Où prendriez-vous la clientèle pour emplir pareille cathédrale?» (457). Zola's narrative voice makes it clear that these modern French women, their Christian faith lost, have replaced it with faith in the store. Where they used to spend their time in chapels, they are now attached to a new religion where the confessional and the altar have been suppressed (797-798). These images are too explicit and analytical to enjoy any symbolic thrust, but they are striking as consistent and sustained metaphorical constructions:

> Mouret laissait ainsi passer la brutalité d'un juif vendant de la femme à la livre: il lui élevait un temple, la faisait encenser par une légion de commis, créait le rite d'un culte nouveau (461).

Similar religious images surround the creation of Saccard's bank in *L'Argent* (139).

Zola's psyche makes even stronger and stranger uses of religious imagery. Beyond chapel, church, cathedral, there is a daring and neurotic use of more solemn terms, such as tabernacle, *chapelle ardente,* and monstrance. Florent arriving at Les Halles sees the market transformed:

> ... les culs de charrettes ouverts montraient des chapelles ardentes, des enfoncements de tabernacle, dans les lueurs flambantes de ces chairs réguliè-res... (*Ventre*, 632).

No one is allowed in Dr. Pascal's bedroom which «... restait close, ainsi qu'un tabernacle» (*Pascal,* 939).

Religious imagery becomes entangled with sexual imagery. Claude Lantier, now insane, is back at work on his great nude painting:

> ... il peignait le ventre et les cuisses en visionnaire affolé ... ces cuisses se doraient en colonnes de tabernacle ... Une si étrange nudité d'ostensoir... (*Oeuvre,* 343).

After hanging himself, Claude's face is «... tournée vers le tableau, tout près de la Femme au *sexe fleuri d'une rose mystique*» (352). His wife Christine feels the painting is a rival woman, a goddess «... au fond d'un tabernacle farouche...» (244).

La Terre contains the most bizarre religious metaphors of the entire work. Lise gives birth to her child, and Zola describes the vagina as «... une vraie cathédrale où le mari devait loger tout entier» (589). Religious tradition is inverted with the character of Jésus-Christ, described as having «... une face de Christ ravagé, un Christ soûlard, violeur de fille et détrousseur de grandes routes» (380). He has the «... bonhomie d'apôtre soûlard» (415). Arriving at a dance with stolen money he shows a coin about the room, «... qu'il promena ensuite comme un ostensoir» (560).

Finally Zola reserves religious imagery for descriptions of his secular city of the future, the brave new world from which the old religion will have been restricted. In *Germinal* he speaks of the «... immense cathédrale du monde futur» (1347). The love between Dr. Pascal and Clotilde will engender a new race, resuscitate a dying one with a new eighth sacrament:

> Elle, au retour, l'adorait ... comme si leur amour était le soulagement qu'ils portaient en viatique au pauvre monde (*Pascal,* 1107).

In a return to the pantheistic vocabulary of the eighteenth century, he announces in the last volume, the new or rather old epithet for God, *le grand moteur, il primo motore* (Dante) which is life itself: «La vie était l'unique manifestation divine.

La vie, c'était Dieu, le grand moteur, l'âme de l'univers»
(*Pascal,* 947).

It is with the metaphor of the sea that Zola most approaches the figurative procedures of the symbolist poets. He
may be attracted to the sea image because of the ever-changing
aspects of great bodies of water, fluidity and formlessness. As
a metaphorical device the sea metaphor makes of the verifiable
raw material, a higher, aesthetic reality.

Since *L'Oeuvre* is about *plein air* painting, the importance
of sun and light, Zola seeks to translate the idea of sun in as
many ways as possible. His procedure thus is to go from
tour de force light and color descriptions to ever denser literary
fields of simile and metaphor which are accomplishing the same
mission as the light descriptions. Most of these metaphors
are of seas and lakes because of the quality of fluid, of liquid,
to indicate movement and change.

But the sea metaphor can be quite frozen as in «Dans cette
mer de créanciers...» (*Argent,* 34) or «... la mer des dossiers»
(*Argent, 35*).

The sea is mainly utilized to describe mass and space, such
as the accumulation of merchandise: «C'était une mer montante
de teintes neutres, de tons sourds de laine...» (*Bonheur,* 485).

The sea metaphor enhances cityscapes and landscapes. In
La Curée there is «... cet océan de maisons aux toits bleuâtres...» (387) as in *Une Page d'amour* there is Paris which
«... déroulait devant elle la mer houleuse de ses toitures»
(822). Landscapes are habitually so described by Zola: «... des
mers grises d'oliviers...» (*Fortune,* 209); «Une mer de verdure,
en face, à droite, à gauche, partout» (*Faute,* 1327); «... la
vaste mer de betteraves et de blé...» (*Germinal,* 1247); «... les
vastes champs plats ... n'étaient plus qu'une mer blanche...»
(*Bête,* 1167); «Toute la vallée noire se creusa, roulant sa mer
de ténèbres» (*Débâcle,* 533); «... derrière la ligne d'horizon,
nette et ronde comme sur une mer» (*Terre,* 367).

The following examples from *La Terre* present the sea by
allusion: «Elle avait ce coup d'oeil de matelot, cette vue longue
des gens de plaine...» (372); «Ils avaient la face rêveuse et
figée, la songerie des matelots...» (396); «On aurait dit une
de ces masures de pêcheurs, au bord de l'océan, dont pas une
fente ne regarde le flot» (465).

As to Zola's imagery in general, comparison, of course,

dominates, and the two terms are kept apart as abstractions. As the metaphors invade more and more of the space of the novels, however, the procedure raises the potential for making the material truly symbolic.

In summary, single vocabulary items have been seen repeating across a single novel or group of novels. These repeating elements by their very nature are tinged with figurative concepts, giving a highly subjective substratum to the narration. We thus observe single elements turning into larger syntactical units of metaphor which must now be called sustained metaphorical structure.

This procedure is illustrated by *L'Argent*. The theme is conquest, Saccard's conquest of Paris with his fraudulent bank scheme. At the minimal level this idea is reinforced by repetitions and variations of the noun *conquête* and the verb *conquérir*. In the first pages, Saccard walks across Paris «... avec ses bottes éculées, son paletot graisseux, pour la conquérir!» (*Argent*, 16). The same page speaks of his fever to «reconquérir,» to put his foot on «... la cité conquise» Yet, Saccard's conquest is just the basic narrative level of this theme. The socialists dream of the just city of the future, while the gullible Catholics, investing in Saccard's bank, dream of the new Jerusalem, reconquered for the Church. Saccard, the anti-semite, fears «... la conquête finale de tous les peuples par les juifs...» (*Argent*, 92). Now the idea of conquest in the Middle East suggests another level of interpretation, and consequently the image of Napoleon is fused into the metaphorical structure. Likewise, since Saccard mixes banking and Catholicism and the Near East, another type of conquest, that of crusade, is introduced. The two ideas appear as couplets in several sections of the novel:

> ... un immense empire reconstruit, Napoléon couronné à Constantinople, empereur d'Orient et des Indes. ... Et ce que les Croisades avaient tenté, ce que Napoléon n'avait pu accomplir, c'était cette pensée gigantesque de la conquête de l'Orient qui enflammait Saccard... (*Argent*, 78).
> Ce que Napoléon n'avait pu faire avec son sabre, cette conquête de l'Orient, une Compagnie financière le réalisait.
> ... Et la croisade des femmes surtout triomphait,

aux petites réunions intimes de cinq heures... (*Argent*, 253).

As Saccard's financial empire collapses, the images of conquest must be reversed, and Zola will maintain the metaphorical unity and density of the novel by changing Saccard into a Napoleon, and the floor of the stock market into the battlefield of Waterloo. At this point the novel begins to look like Victor Hugo's «Expiation» poem:

> Au lieu des secours attendus, était-ce une nouvelle armée ennemie qui débouchait des bois voisins? Comme à Waterloo, Grouchy n'arrivait pas, et c'était la trahison qui achevait la déroute (328).
> Alors, pendant la dernière demi-heure, ce fut la débâcle, la déroute s'aggravant et emportant la foule en un galop désordonné (329).
> Il n'y avait plus d'acheteurs, la plaine restait rase, jonchée de cadavres (*Ibid.*).
> Mais, dans la salle, la panique venait surtout de souffler autour de Saccard, et c'était là que la guerre avait fait ses ravages. Sans comprendre au premier moment, il avait assisté à cette déroute, faisant face au danger. Pourquoi donc cette rumeur? n'étaient-ce pas les troupes de Daigremont qui arrivaient? (330).

A similar if less tightly constructed metaphorical field is found in the proliferated idea of royalty in *Le Docteur Pascal* (6).

Perhaps no metaphor is more central or sustained in the *Rougon-Macquart* than that of the sea of gold, the rain of gold, the dance of gold, movement metaphors which are found in many of the volumes beginning with *La Curée*. Saccard finds himself «... au beau milieu de la pluie chaude d'écus tombant dru sur les toits de la cité» (*Curée*, 368). He knows that «... la pluie d'or qui en battait les murs tomberait plus

---

(6) Although I am discussing sustained metaphorical fields, the whole concept of royalty in *Le Docteur Pascal* has been fully discussed by Michel Butor, «Zola's blue flame,» *Yale French Studies*, 42 (1969), 9-25. For those interested in checking out the royal references in the *Pascal*, see pages 925, 926, 965, 1009, 1094, 1097, 1104, 1105, 1206, 1213.

dru chaque jour» (*Curée,* 387). At the costume cotillion, two Lesbian ladies dressed as Gold and Silver dance together: «L'Or et l'Argent dansaient ensemble, amoureusement» (*Curée,* 579). Octave Mouret plans to associate himself with Mme Hédouin in order to «... commencer la danse des millions» (*P. B.,* 339). As children, Pauline and Lazare would swim at la baie du Trésor, so-called because of its «... flot solitaire qui semblait rouler des pièces de vingt francs» (*Joie,* 842). Later (865) Lazare decides to install his algae factory at that location, hoping to reap a profit. The generous and altruistic Angélique is generous to the poor. She dreams of marrying a rich prince which will enable her to be even more generous: «Ce beau soleil criblant les rues, c'était comme la pluie d'or, les aumônes des contes de fées...» (988). After a period of aridity it finally rains in La Beauce and Buteau says: «Allez, allez, donc! ... C'est des pièces de cent sous qui tombent!» (*Terre,* 536). Since Saccard again emerges as hero in *L'Argent,* this famous metaphor as expected makes multiple appearances: «... cette folle danse de millions...» (55); «... la grêle des pièces d'or, la danse des millions...» (116); «... la pluie d'or qui allait pleuvoir sur lui et autour de lui» (127). The image proliferates and frequently develops in a very complex manner. In *La Curée,* Saccard's vision of an expanding financial empire is described in terms of an ever-expanding body of water, a lake being transformed into ocean, and in the midst of this we see Saccard the hearty and agile *nageur.* We follow, amazed at his natatory skill:

> Il lui semblait qu'une mer de pièces de vingt francs s'élargissait autour de lui, de lac devenait océan, emplissait l'immense horizon avec un bruit de vagues étrange, une musique métallique qui lui chatouillait le coeur; et il s'aventurait, nageur plus hardi chaque jour, plongeant, reparaissant, tantôt sur le dos, tantôt sur le ventre, traversant cette immensité par les temps clairs et par les orages, comptant sur ses forces et son adresse pour ne jamais aller au fond (*Curée,* 416).

The most famous and developed of these images is of course the rain of gold scene as Saccard and his wife look down on Paris from a restaurant high on Montmartre. Here, another element must be added, that of impressionistic description as Zola transforms Paris into a city from a fairytale. It is another impressionistic sunset:

> ... le soleil se couchait dans un nuage rouge, et, tandis que les fonds s'emplissaient d'une brume légère, une poussière d'or, une rosée d'or tombait sur la rive droite. ... C'était comme le coin enchanté d'une cité des *Mille et Une Nuits,* aux arbres d'émeraude, aux toits de saphir, aux girouettes de rubis. Il vint un moment où le rayon qui glissait entre deux nuages, fut si resplendissant, que les maisons semblèrent flamber et se fondre comme un lingot d'or dans un creuset (*Curée,* 388).

It is with such descriptions that we arrive at a true juncture in the art of Emile Zola, for as shall be made clear in the concluding chapter, impressionism and symbolism will be furthering the narrative structure, acting as complementary layers. Zola as painter presents a Paris sunset transformed into something enchanting and rich out of a fairy tale. But the same sunset is also viewed by Saccard. Following the above cited description, Saccard exclaims: «Oh! vois, dit Saccard, avec un rire d'enfant, il pleut des pièces de vingt francs dans Paris!» (*Curée,* 388). The impressions of the sunset have one meaning for Saccard and another for Zola and the sensitive reader.

Lest we become too tempted, however, to view Zola as a real impressionist or a true symbolist, it should not be forgotten that always, across the *Rougon-Macquart,* there is the correcting factor of the exact simile, a type of *mot juste,* the simile out of everyday familiar speech, and of course the crude and rough naturalistic detail. These are just as essential to Zola's structure as the metaphorical fields. Nana at thirteen was «... grande déjà comme une asperge montée...» (*Assommoir,* 678); at fifteen she had grown «... comme un veau...» (*Assommoir,* 708). She takes to vice «... comme un poisson dans l'eau» (*Assommoir,* 720). Clotilde at her piano was «... comme une écuyère sur son cheval» (*P. B.,* 82). The weak supports in the mine are «... ainsi que des béquilles trop faibles» (*Germinal,* 1167). Lise's child is born: «... comme d'une femme canon, l'enfant sortit...» (*Terre,* 588).

When trying to estimate the true nature of Zola's symbolism, at all times the persistency of the naturalistic detail must be kept in mind: «... il n'y avait, sous le flamboiement du gaz, qu'un pot de chambre oublié...» (*Nana*, 1223); «... dans la crotte noire des rues...» (P. B., 22); «Son corps imbibé d'alcool se ratatinait comme les foetus qui sont dans des bocaux, chez les pharmaciens» (*Assommoir*, 745); «Dans l'obscurité, elle tira son pot, s'accroupit, s'épuisa en efforts inutiles» (*P. B.*, 368).

Erotic and scatological detail are on rampant display throughout the *Rougon-Macquart*, counterbalancing the impressionistic paintings and allegorical constructions in a tension which may ultimately be seen as the unifying aesthetic structure of Zola's novels. We do not raise the question whether or not the crude barnacles of life, taken over as such, unbalance the impressionistic-symbolic structure, which they certainly do for the moralist, but rather how all these elements work together in Zola's aesthetics.

CHAPTER VII

SYMBOLIST AND IMPRESSIONIST STRUCTURES
IN THE NOVEL

The novel, a bastard aesthetic form unless one is convinced of the contrary by the formularies of the *nouveaux romanciers,* traditionally has borrowed heavily from its ancestor, the medieval verse romance. Consequently, it is normal to find as constituents of its structure the very formal figures of poetry —simile and metaphor, and sometimes the very highest forms of figuration, which lead to symbolism.

If Balzac and Zola made the aesthetic mistake of confusing the ends of sociology and those of art, it was only in intention, for the structures themselves prove otherwise. Even those critics who would mainly read the *Rougon-Macquart* as history, sociology or politics (1) ultimately see the super structure of an attempted symbolism, and a major Zola scholar of our time, Guy Robert, speaking of *La Terre,* while affirming the «realistic» level of the novel, insists upon a higher level of reading which is the true source of the work's vitality (2).

While this study would hope to have analyzed the major aspects of symbolism and impressionism as they inter-relate with novelistic goal, it is not within its scope to make a total analysis of symbolic systems. A close reading of Zola, for example, makes the reader aware of the fact that there is a vast and complex (even contradictory) symbolic system at work therein. But, is such a system reducible to aesthetic goals?

---

(1) Pierre Abraham, «Lire Zola,» *Europe* (nov.-déc., 1952), 4-5.
(2) Guy Robert, *La Terre d'Emile Zola* (Paris, 1952), 169.

Inter-locking symbolic structures which lead somewhere are multiple in the twenty novels, among which can be cited the windows of envy, the question of open and locked doors, closed and open properties (3). This seems, in the long and open form of the novel, as opposed to the short and closed form of the hermetic poem, a system which may be open to aesthetic analysis, perhaps with the help of the new French criticism, but one which may also lead to complex psychological categories explaining more the man and less the work. Yet, such an approach, leaving aside traditional literary categories, rhetorical devices, and accepted mythic traditions, can provide, by the freshness of its approach, new perspectives on old ideas (4).

This concluding chapter, therefore, will follow the same methodology used in the preceding ones, starting with the most simple categories and then moving progressively into complex uses of symbol and impression as they act upon the basic structure of story telling.

To speak of symbolism is perhaps one of the most dangerous acts of literary criticism. Does this mean ideological or philosophical system, or is it more simply a matter of stylistic technique and structure? If the latter, are there not degrees or levels of complexity, of ambiguity which must be accounted for? The romantic poet, Alfred de Vigny, was long classified by literary history as the sympolist poet of romanticism. Yet his poems are clearly, in rhetorical terms, allegories, while his highly subjective landscapes seem symbolic.

The novels of Zola present even more difficult problems. The form of the novel itself and Zola's own theoretical statements could almost banish symbolism from his work. Moreover, analysis of the novels yields a harvest of good and bad fruit, for on a conscious level his symbolism is broad and melodramatic, a bad and cheap romantic sensationalism.

Blood spilling, from the death of Silvère on (*Fortune*), must be seen as part of a very transparent symbolic system. While ultimately the shedding of blood works into a complex if

---

(3) See Naomi Schor, «Zola: from window to window,» *Yale French Studies*, 42 (1969), 38-51, and Philip Walker, «The mirror, the window and the eye in Zola's fiction,» 52-67 of the same issue.

(4) See Jean Borie, *Zola et les mythes ou de la Nausée au salut* (Paris, 1971).

apparent web (joining with fires and sunsets) indicating appeasement, expiation, chastisement, and purification, on the lowest level it remains an obvious sign for guilt and bad conscience. In *Nana,* young Georges attempts suicide by plunging scissors into his chest, and for all their efforts, Nana's servants cannot get the stains of blood out of the carpet «C'était, au seuil même de la chambre, comme un trait de sang qui barrait la porte» (1447). Octave's wife, Mme Hédoin, visiting the construction site of the new department store, slips and falls into a hole, an accident from which she dies. Quite literally, «Il y a de son sang sous les pierres de la maison» (*Bonheur,* 408), meaning that the new enterprise has been established «... sur le sang de ses membres» (*Bonheur,* 503).

Likewise, a strong, if not totally convincing case can be made for a color symbolism in the *Rougon-Macquart.* Symbolic colors do work within particular narratives. Félicité assembles her allies in her *salon jaune* which seems representative of her envy and ambition, and in Volume 4, where we see her as a success, she has an elegant *salon vert* appropriate to an Empire *arriviste.* The *chambre rouge* at la Croix-de-Maufras has to be an obvious symbol of perversion and murder in *La Bête humaine.* Pink is the color of *La Curée;* it corresponds to Renée's inner feelings about herself. As the chosen color for her bedroom and bath it is an extension into space of the body of a naked woman. Higher and more idealistic types of love are accorded very refined colors. *Une Page d'amour* is done in pastels; gold and white dominate *Le Rêve* as symbols of purity and royalty; dawn color indicates a symbolic new day in *Le Docteur Pascal.* Blackness pervades *La Débâcle* and *Germinal,* the latter also utilizing the red of revolution (the blood of the wounded and murdered), and concluding with a very high type symbolic green of hope.

Zola's landscapes are often very subjective and seem to be lending themselves to psychological purpose in indirect and suggestive manners. Renée's ennui and lassitude, indicative of her latent sexuality, are felt in the opening pages of *La Curée* as she infects the landscapes of the Bois de Boulogne and the parc Monceau with her vague feelings. The same may be said of the atmospheres of Les Halles which are transformed into grotesque Brueghelian nightmares by the disturbed mind of Florent (Chapter III, the description of the fish market).

Sexually explicit materials create obvious allegorical landscapes which are restatements of the psychological character analysis. This is exactly the situation in the barn scene of *Son Excellence Eugène Rougon* (117), Désirée's barnyard, the *Paradou* of *La Faute de l'abbé Mouret,* and the hothouse scene of *La Curée.*

The best use of landscape is to be found in the use of pathetic fallacy, in a refreshing impressionistic manner, to express the sentiment of budding love as is found in the lyrical swing ride of Hélène in *Une Page d'amour.* Here the procedure is similar to that of Balzac describing Eugènie's new love for her cousin Charles in *Eugènie Grandet,* wherein the hope of love in the heart is transformed to a description of a morning garden over which the sun is casting its rays. Zola announces that Hélène is for the first time out from under her widow's sorrow. The passage increases in intensity as Hélène goes higher and higher in the air, putting into nature her new feelings of on-coming life (for spring is not too far away), which, at this moment in the narration, cannot be associated by her with her subconcious feelings for Dr. Deberle. What is new with Zola, continuing the tradition of using nature to explore psychology, is the dominance of impressionistic elements utilized to express a lyric intoxication with nature:

> ... elle entrait dans le soleil, dans ce blond soleil de février, pleuvant comme une poussière d'or. Ses cheveux châtains ... s'allumaient ... elle flambait tout entière ... ses noeuds de soie mauve, pareils à des fleurs de feu, luisaient sur sa robe blanchissantes ... le printemps naissait, les bourgeons violâtres mettaient leur ton fin de laque sur le bleu du ciel (*Page,* 843).

The extent to which Zola wanted to impose symbolism on narrational happening may be measured by isolating things or object as they are presented in the narration. Here again the symbolic intent is often very obvious and can be seen as a form of novelistic allegory. The ringing of the bell of alarm, the *tocsin,* is transparent in its meaning in *La Fortune des Rougon* where it signals the end of liberty with the coup d'état of Napoleon, and in *La Débâcle* where the end of the Empire is sounded. The uncontrolled train of *La Bête humaine* is explained to us by Zola as a train to the future (1053), a visionary new world exploited across a spatial perspective. Napoleon III, lost and wandering across a devastated France, finds himself sheltered in a small room decorated with two prints, Rouget de l'Isle singing the Marseillaise, and the last Judgment (*La Débâcle*, 727). The sexual symbolism of *La Faute de l'abbé Mouret* and of *La Curée* proves a conscious building-in of a reinforcing symbolic layer. The mountain ash tree is a phallic symbol, nature penetrating and destroying the church (*Faute*, 1418), as is the tree of knowledge under which Serge and Albine consummate their love. That Zola is consciously creating these symbols is demonstrated by *La Curée*. Renée's incestuous love for Maxime is first explained as she chews on the leaf of the *Tanghin* plant, «... une plante maudite...» (358) according to Zola. Is this plant the source of her perverted love? It would seem so:

> D'habitude, les amants se couchaient sous le Tanghin de Madagascar, sous cet arbuste empoisonné dont la jeune fille avait mordu une feuille (488).

Yet Zola is capable of a more nuanced thing symbolism, where the meaning is more covert. After four years in the country Claude and Christine return to Paris. A short visit back to the country is unsuccessful, they are unable to retrieve the magic of bygone days. With skill, Zola describes the decay of their old boat, but not dwelling on it, goes on to state that they no longer are interested in boating, that country life now bores them. Yet we see the boat as symbolic of a lost joy of life:

> Leur barque pourrie, défoncée, avait coulé au fond de la Seine. Du reste, ils n'avaient même plus l'idée de se servir du canot que les Faucheur mettaient à leur disposition. La rivière les ennuyait... (*Oeuvre*, 167).

They are tired of eternal nature. It is to be wondered if such would not have been the fate of Serge and Albine had their idyll not been interrupted.

Chapter IV of *Son Excellence Eugène Rougon* which describes the official ceremonies at Notre-Dame for the baptism of the imperial prince very successfully builds an ominous symbol into the descriptive materials. The chapter focuses on the assembly of a great crowd of Parisians outside the cathedral. The thematic thrust is the apotheosis of the Second Empire. Into this description, Zola inserts three constants which reappear as frames for the scene: (1) a rowing team in the Seine (87, 98); (2) a group of *laveuses* pounding their laundry (87, 98, 109); and (3) an enormous advertisement for men's clothing (86, 97, 109). At first glance these elements might be viewed as descriptive decorations in the tableau. Then they might also be considered as constants of on-going activity, lack of interest in the ceremony. The third element, the *réclame,* however, makes it clear that what appears on the surface to be objective reporting is truly a symbolic and ironic commentary on the events, for the advertisement figure looks much like Napoleon I. Thus Zola works into his novel an ironic symbol not unlike the procedure of Victor Hugo in *Les Châtiments*:

> ... on apercevait de toute part ... sur la muraille nue d'une maison à six étages, dans l'île Saint-Louis, une redingote grise géante, peinte à fresque, de profil, avec sa manche gauche pliée au coude, comme si le vêtement eût gardé l'attitude et le gonflement d'un corps. ... Cette réclame monumentale prenait, dans le soleil, au-dessus de la fourmilière des promeneurs, une extraordinaire importance (86).
> Au loin ... se dressait, comme fond à ce tableau, la réclame monumentale peinte sur le mur d'une maison à six étages de l'île Saint-Louis, la redingote grise géante, vide de corps, que le soleil battait d'un rayonnement d'apothéose (97).
> ... dans le léger brouillard qui montait de la Seine ... on ne distinguait plus ... que la redingote géante, la réclame monumentale, accrochant, à quelque clou de l'horizon, la défroque bourgeoise d'un titan, dont la foudre aurait mangé les membres (109).

This stable object has been subjected to atmospheric changes which finally make it the only perceptible element, symbol brought about by the *mise en relief* of the fog which ends the sun-filled description of the triumph of the Empire.

Dynamic expansion and growth are also means for creating

symbolic effect. Nana's throne-bed, or the bed of Renée are presented as dominating structures. It is symbolic of her sexuality: «Il semblait que le lit se continuât, que la pièce entière fût un lit immense...» (*Curée*, 478). The corruption of the Muffat household is symbolically focused in a red chaise longue, the only modern piece of furniture when the novel opens. It is seen as a disturbing piece with its *ton brutal*, its *fantaisie troublante*, its *voluptueuse paresse* (*Nana*, 1153). At the conclusion of the novel, the new furniture and the new morality dominate the *hôtel* Muffat:

> On eût dit que la chaise longue de Sabine, ce siège unique de soie rouge, dont la mollesse autrefois détonnait, s'était multipliée, élargie, jusqu'à emplir l'hôtel entier d'une voluptueuse paresse, d'une jouissance aiguë, qui brûlait avec la violence des feux tardifs (*Nana*, 1419-20).

Characters also seem to undergo symbolic growth. The doll-like Rose Campardon spends much time in bed, eating and reading novels. She becomes an inflated symbol of the egocentrics of the day:

> Dans la chambre, Rose s'élargissait encore, au milieu du grand lit. Elle y trônait, avec son luxe de reine, sa tranquille sérénité d'idole (*P. B.*, 289).

Symbolic growths reach Ionescan proportions in *Pot-Bouille* as we follow the pregnancy of the *piqueuse de bottines*. This pregnancy acts as an affront to the bourgeois morality of the apartment house, especially as the growing stomach is observed by the hypocritical concierge M. Gourd. To him the stomach is filling the house with indecency. The progress of this stomach is observed across some pages (254-265) of which the following citation is quite typical:

> Le ventre ... semblait jeter son ombre sur la propreté froide de la cour, et jusque sur les faux marbres et les zincs dorés du vestibule. C'était lui qui s'enflait, qui emplissait l'immeuble d'une chose déshonnête, dont les murs gardaient un malaise (*P. B.*, 254).

20

The use of symbolic object then can be seen moving into deeper novelistic complexities and even ambiguities. The *grenadier* plant and the finch bird of *Le Ventre de Paris* seem to be functioning as symbolic objects whose exact meaning cannot be seized with any allegorical precision. Florent takes good care of this plant across the novel, it seems his companion as he works on his book on Cayenne and the administrative reform of the market. On the very day he is taken prisoner «... le grenadier était tout fleuri...» (*Ventre*, 887), and Florent frees the bird (889). Given the constancy of the plant across the novel, it would seem that Zola intends it to represent some sort of hope for the future as much as the freeing of the bird symbolizes ultimate liberty.

Zola's animals have always been seen as half-sentimental, half-symbolic representations. The horses of *Germinal*, confined to the dark mines, romantically dream of sunlight and green pastures. Less anthropomorphic is the rabbit *Pologne* of the same novel who seems to represent man's cruelty in harsh circumstances. Zola seems to have a predilection for cats, who can melodramatically represent conscience as in *Thérèse Raquin*. The theatre cats of *Nana*, however, are more difficult to assess. The big red cat appears at intervals across the novel (1198, 1224, 1226, 1332) and may have a function similar to the statue of a draped woman in the ball scene of *Madame Bovary*. The cat is always watching. Is it representative of sexual life, or of forces superior to sex, knowing more, indifferent to this banal life about it?

> Les yeux à demi clos, ce chat gardait seul la maison, pris de somnolence dans les odeurs enfermées et refroidies que les femmes laissaient là chaque soir (*Nana*, 1332).

Symbolism and psychologically fixing on object can combine, and such is the case with the *coquetier* of *Nana*. Fauchery, the reporter, is the true evaluator of social decadence in this novel. It is he who first observed the physical resemblance between Nana and Sabine. He also makes the connection between the red chaise longue and its invasion of the entire salon. He too had been present at the theatre when Muffat decided to buy Nana, risking his entire wealth and reputation.

At that decisive moment, in the props room, Muffat was fondling an egg cup:

> Muffat paraissait examiner avec attention le coquetier, qu'il tournait toujours.
> —C'est un coquetier, vint dire Bordenave obligeamment.
> —Tiens! oui, c'est un coquetier, répéta le comte (*Nana*, 1342).

A rather innocent looking bit of dialogue which could be accepted as realistic reporting. Yet, toward the conclusion, during a reception to celebrate the forthcoming marriage of Muffat's daughter, Fauchery, seeing moral collapse about him, recalls the scene at the theatre:

> Il revoyait le magasin des accessoires ... et Muffat s'y trouvait, tenant le coquetier, abusant de ses doutes. A cette heure, Muffat ne doutait plus, c'était un dernier coin de dignité qui croulait (*Nana*, 1428).

It would be naive and simplistic to interpret this egg cup in terms of existing symbols (eggs, fertility, sexuality). It seems to me to have two purposes which finally symbolize in the object the idea of the moral decay of the Count. It is first a means of exteriorizing in an object the decisive interior decision made by Muffat to sacrifice all so that he may enjoy the pleasures of Nana. The egg-cup is a means of emphasizing that Muffat knows what he is doing. That is, the affirmation, «oui, c'est un coquetier» means «I am aware of what I am doing.» Secondly, as a method of psychological recall on the part of Fauchery, it means replacing logical analysis by object analogy, or symbol. Fauchery thinks concretely, through object, which he makes representative.

The highest form of free thing symbolism must be found in *L'Assommoir* where the hopes of Gervaise for a better life, hardly possible with Goujet, are focused on the image of a goat tied to a post in a desolate landscape. Only the slightest of hope (green) can be found in this *terrain vague*:

> C'était, entre une scierie mécanique et une manu-facture de boutons, une bande de prairie restée

verte, avec des plaques jaunes d'herbe grillée; une
chèvre, attachée à un piquet, tournait en bêlant; au
fond, un arbre mort s'émiettait au grand soleil.
—Vrai! murmura Gervaise, on se croirait à la campagne (*Assommoir*, 613-614).

This *chèvre* must somehow stand for hope in the heart of
Gervaise. As the passage continues, Gervaise and Goujet enter
into a true proletarian meeting of souls (honest and authentic
by comparison with the insipid exchanges of Emma and Léon
of *Madame Bovary*), and Zola's description of nature accords
with their feelings:

Tous deux restèrent muets. Au ciel, le vol de nuages
blancs nageait avec une lenteur de cygne. Dans le
coin du champ, la chèvre, tournée vers eux, les regardait en poussant à de longs intervalles réguliers
un bêlement très doux (*Assommoir*, 615-616).

Symbol for an impossible love? It must mean in some manner,
liberation, freedom from the city, the joys of country living.
It is thus that Nana expresses her desire to live in the country,
for as a child, she had seen the same goat:

Etant petite, longtemps elle avait souhaité vivre
dans un pré, avec une chèvre, parce qu'un jour, sur
le talus des fortifications, elle avait vu une chèvre
qui bêlait, attachée à un pieu (*Nana*, 1244).

In addition to object, personage can be interpreted as
symbolic. The child of Clotilde and Pascal has been born to
redeem a perverted world: «L'enfant était venu, le rédempteur
peut-être» (*Pascal*, 1218), «... du messie attendu; ... l'éternelle
espérance...» (*Ibid.*). This is Zola's own and explained
symbolism. There is also the symbolism felt by the reader,
but not perceived by other characters as such. The ill-treated
Mère Pérou of *Pot-Bouille* is a poignant incarnation of human
misery. La Mère Fétu appears as a constant figure across the
pages of *Une Page d'amour* as a link between Hélène and
Dr. Deberle. With her constant religious ejaculations and
blessings she seems like an escapee from a Spanish novel,
particularly of Galdós. Her particular function is to focus the
reader's attention on the relationship between the couple. As

Hélène and Dr. Deberle meet on their charity rounds we ponder the words of this old beggar-woman to them: «... on peut bien dire que vous faites la paire ... les braves gens se comprennent» (*Page*, 827). Practically each encounter with this woman can be read as an indirect statement on the potential relationship between Hélène and the doctor. Encountering Mère Fétu (with her ominous name hinting at baby killing) outside the church after May devotions, the old woman tells Hélène that Henri is waiting for her, and utters a prayer that all of Hélène's wishes may be fulfilled: «Que le ciel exauce vos désirs, que toutes ses bénédictions soient avec vous!» (*Page*, 920). But is la mère Fétu a force to bring them together, or a symbol of their impossible love? As Henri escorts Hélène home with little Jeanne, the old woman is heard behind them:

> ... derrière eux, le pas de la mère Fétu semblait être l'écho des leurs. Elle se rapprochait; on entendait ce bout de phrase latine: «Ave Maria, gratia plena», sans cesse recommencé sur le même bredouillement. La mère Fétu disait son chapelet en rentrant chez elle (*Page*, 924).

There are several more appearances of the old woman built centrally into the intrigue (989, 998), culminating in the cemetery encounter in the closing pages of the novel. The old woman speaks of the new child in the Deberle family and of the tragic loss of Jeanne. Thus she summarizes the meaning of the novel: the death of Jeanne signals the end of the love of Hélène and Dr. Deberle; the birth of the new baby signals the continuity of the Deberle *foyer*.

Characters may also perform the function of moral evaluators. The valet Baptiste of *La Curée* certainly must be seen as conscience judging the immoral behaviour of Renée. Faucherey of *Nana* is not just a reporter, but a moral one, seeing the true meaning of the relationships in the novel. Although such personages are the vehicle by which we arrive at a moral conclusion, at the same time they actively participate in the narrative tale, and while the source of our conclusions, they themselves are not pure agents. Baptiste is an active homosexual, and Fauchery has an affair with Countess Muffat.

The most effective use of characters as symbol is when the protagonists themselves invest them with symbolic intent. This process relates to Emma Bovary's use of the beggar. A chilling example of this is found in *Nana* when Satin recounts to Nana the story of la reine Pomaré, a famous courtesan of bygone days who has been reduced by alcohol to ragpicking. She is spotted by Nana from her window, and Nana is forced to ponder her own final days —will they be similar, or can she hope for an aristocratic retreat like Irma d'Anglars:

> La chiffonnière, qui se trouvait sous sa fenêtre, leva la tête et se montra, à la lueur jaune de sa lanterne. C'était, dans ce paquet de haillons, sous un foulard en loques, une face bleuie, couturée, avec le trou édenté de la bouche et les meurtrissures enflammées des yeux (*Nana*, 1374).

The highest symbolism of this sort, of the leitmotive kind, is the reappearance across *L'Assommoir* of Le père Bazouge, the drunken undertaker. Zola has very astutely integrated this personage into the narrative. His first major encounter with Gervaise comes at the conclustion of the wedding chapter (III, 462-463) where he stumbles into Gervaise. The wedding has ended in such chaos, because of the conduct of the Lorilleux, that this encounter only increases Gervaise's anxieties and fears, and the chapter concludes with the *mot-clé* perhaps of the novel, the old man uttering: «Quand on est mort ... écoutez ça ... quand on est mort, c'est pour longtemps» (*Assommoir*, 463). His reappearances only confirm the idea that the novel, turning about the idea of the *déchéance* of Gervaise, means that on this level the work is announcing, from the moment of supposed happiness (the wedding), that death will be the only answer for Gervaise. Thus Zola builds into the structure the idea that père Bazouge, when sent for at the moment of the death of maman Coupeau (664), thought he had been called for Gervaise. Gervaise's desire for death, calling across the walls to père Bazouge to take her, may seem somewhat melodramatic (688); but we are convinced and can see Bazouge as a type of proletarian consoling angel when he speaks to the dead Gervaise:

> Tu sais ... écoute bien ... c'est moi, Bibi-la-Gaieté, dit le consolateur des dames ... Va, t'es heureuse. Fais dodo, ma belle! (*Assommoir*, 796).

Gervaise is perhaps more sensitive to Bazouge's symbolic role than Emma is to the beggar, but then Gervaise had always seen the ambiance about her in terms of threat and menace.

Sustained metaphorical transformations can so invade the descriptive process that true, objective, «realistic» novelistic description is obliterated. The novelist is using the procedure of the poet. The descriptions of the funerals of Geneviève and of Mme Baudu in *Au Bonheur des dames* illustrate how a novelist can abandon temporarily, for symbolic intent, the normal narrative procedure, transforming the raw material into a highly subjective and metaphorical description. Taking the body of Geneviève from Saint-Roch, the procession is obliged to pass a second time in front of the huge department store, the indirect cause of her demise. The real funeral thus becomes a symbolic movement around the enemy:

> C'était une obsession, ce pauvre corps de jeune fille était promené autour du grand magasin, comme la première victime tombée sous les balles en temps de révolution (742).

Bourras rides along with Denise, and as he speaks of the ruin of all the small merchants by the great store, his figurative speech presents a unified pattern of defeat as illness, with intensification, each suceeding term being more drastic. This is not unlike the process in high symbolist poetry, wherein an original analogy engenders even more drastic ones, as in Baudelaire's «Cloche fêlée» poem where the analogy of poet and cracked bell finally leads to the image of a soldier dead next to a lake of blood. These are Bourras' words to Denise about the other merchants:

> —Ce pauvre Robineau est *fichu,* il a une figure d'homme qui *se noie* ... les Vanpouille, ça *ne tient plus debout,* c'est comme moi, les *jambes cassées.* Deslignières *crèvera* d'un *coup de sang,* Piot et Rivoire ont eu la jaunisse. Ah! nous sommes tous jolis, un beau *cortège de carcasses* ... Ça doit être drôle, pour les gens qui regardent défiler cette *queue de faillites.* ... D'ailleurs, il paraît que *le nettoyage* va continuer. ... Le *choléra* souffle jusqu'à la rue Sainte-Anne... (743).

Zola's imagery joins that of Bourras. He sees Uncle Baudu marching behind with «... la marche aveugle et muette de boeuf assommé...» (*Ibid.*), and the uncle himself seems to hear «... le piétinement d'un troupeau conduit à l'abattoir...» (*Ibid.*). Now, some months later, Mme Baudu has died, another funeral procession has formed. What was seen above metaphorically now seems to be the reality:

> On y vit les frères Vanpouille, blêmes de leurs échéances de décembre. ... Bédoré et soeur s'appuyait sur une canne, travaillé de tels soucis, que sa maladie d'estomac s'aggravait. Deslignières avait eu une attaque... (755).

Reliance upon existing myths is another avenue to symbolism for Zola. In greater and lesser degrees the twenty volumes either resuscitate existing legends, or proceed to create new ones. It may be simply in the form of a comparison: Madame Josserand «... rentra dans sa chambre, avec une dignité de Cérès colossale, aux triples mamelles...» (*P. B.*, 232). It is interesting that her retarded son, reversing the myth, is named Saturnin. In *L'Oeuvre,* Claude Lantier tries to make a living woman out of his painting, giving a hint at least to the Pygmalion story. Clorinde Balbi, depending on her mood, is either a dominating huntress, Diana, or a passive Venus: «Et, brusquement, elle ne fut plus Diane. Elle laissa tomber son arc, elle fut Vénus» (*Son Excellence,* 65). Her Diana pose is ridiculous enough for Zola, however: «C'était une Diane à mettre sur une boîte de pastilles» (*Son Excellence,* 80).

Biblical allusion is equally employed, the most complicated being the Adam and Eve replay in *La Faute de l'abbé Mouret,* which interplays with other structures. Lazarus of *La Joie de vivre* is certainly intended to recall the New Testament account of the friend of Jesus since the novel's thrust is to affirm life over death. In *La Conquête de Plassans,* Marthe, as she comes more under the influence of the abbé Faujas, abandons her household duties to become a fake mystical Mary (989), recalling Martha and Mary, the friends of Jesus. Claude Lantier, who had invented the parable of the fat and the thin, easily transforms it: «Caïn était un gras et Abel un Maigre» (*Ventre,* 805).

The single most sustained mythic structure in the *Rougon-Macquart* is the Phaedra legend of *La Curée* in which Renée becomes Phaedra, Maxime, Hippolytus, and Saccard, Theseus. Zola knew what he was about: «Décidément, c'est une nouvelle Phèdre que je vais faire.» (5) While indeed the Phaedra motif will be accompanied by related mythic fields (6), it is the Phaedra story which Zola builds into his novel, hitting the main points of the legend. Renée's fateful passion is underlined by the eating of the leaf of the Tanghin plant. Two sentences recapitulate the end of the legend:

> ... elle lui (Saccard) raconta que, le jour où il l'avait surprise avec Maxime, c'était celui-ci qui la poursuivait depuis longtemps, qui cherchait à la violenter. ... Il dut se fâcher avec son fils, cesser de le voir (*Curée*, 589).

Other single details of the legend are evoked. On an excursion to a seaside resort, Maxime refuses to go swimming: «Jamais Renée ne put décider Maxime à se baigner. Il avait une peur abominable de l'eau...» (*Curée*, 497). After seeing a performance of *Phèdre*, Zola brings the legend down to realistic interpretation, for Maxime cannot help but make a funny remark: «C'est moi ... qui avais raison de ne pas m'approcher de la mer, à Trouville» (*Curée*, 509). Renée, however, has more serous reactions to the performance than her lover. Like Emma Bovary seeing *Lucia di Lammermor*, or Hélène reading Scott's *Ivanhoe*, she identifies with the play, and seeks psychological explanation of herself through it:

> Phèdre était du sang de Pasiphaé, et elle se demandait de quel sang elle pouvait être, elle, l'incestueuse des temps nouveaux (*Curée*, 508).

Symbolism best serves the novel when it forms part of a

---

(5) *Fr. Nouv. Acq.* 10282, *feuillet* 298.
(6) Renée is a «... Messaline géante...» (489), «... un sphinx...» (358), «... une grande chatte accroupie...» (488). In the sub-structure of the *tableau vivant*, Maxime plays Narcissus and Renée the nymph Echo (537-548). At the end, so aware of her nakedness, Renée is like Eve, about to be expelled from the garden (573-580).

multilayered construction, meaning that the novel cannot be read or interpreted simply on the basis of its raw narration, or within the limits of a single myth. Six of the novels present diverse aspects of this kind of creation: the theme of the rival woman in the painting of *L'Oeuvre,* the doll episodes of *Une Page d'amour,* the failure to create a new myth out of Genesis in *La Faute de l'abbé Mouret,* the multiple readings of the Silvère-Miette idyll in *La Fortune des Rougon,* the successful replay of an Old Testament story in *Le Docteur Pascal,* and the creation of a complex and modern novelistic myth in *Nana.*

L'Oeuvre is constructed almost as a symbolist novel in the rivalry established between the real woman and the painted one, the conflict between aesthetic and conjugal love (7). The hostility between human love and art is felt from the beginning of the work, Christine resentful of Claude's painting in general, and then more specifically, of the colossal nude he is always trying to paint. The painting has created a terrible *ménage à trois,* the rival being represented as «... cette concubine, si envahissante et si terrible...» (*Oeuvre,* 244). Claude, himself, unable to complete the painting takes a knife to the painting killing the painted woman (246), but repairs it, and continues with his work. The painting has become an obsession. The idea of the rival woman is so intertwined with the narration that it becomes difficult to separate the parts. Christine, for example, has been posing for Claude, but he complains that her skin absorbs the light. Then, one day, he finds the first big nude painting he had done, and rediscovers his wife at the age of eighteen. The real Christine has aged. Claude's mind sees something permanent about art which can be contemplated eternally as opposed to fragile human beauty which decays. These ideas work well with the psychological narration and Christine sees even a reason for her feelings of inferiority

---

(7) Structurally it resembles the novel of the symbolist poet, Georges Rodenbach, *Bruges-la-Morte,* wherein the protagonist, Hugues Viane, comes out of mourning for his beloved wife when he meets an actress who bears a striking resemblance to her. The pull of death is stronger than that of life, however, especially when the erotic actress, putting on his wife's clothing, becomes a parody of the original ideal. The equivalent to dead wife in *L'Oeuvre* is, of course, the woman in the painting who, paradoxically, is Christine at an earlier age.

by comparison with the painting: she should not have had their child, as maternity deforms the female shape (253-255). The novel concludes with Claude's total alienation and his desire to sleep with the ideal woman in the painting. His wife makes a final effort to regain him to life, but it is too late. He rejects life and his wife, and hangs himself. Joined to the motif of artistic *impuissance,* Zola's novel exploits in a high manner the central problem of life and aesthetics as it is mainly explored by poets since the time of romanticism: Musset, *Les Nuits*; Gautier, «Symphonie en blanc majeur;» Mallarmé, *Hérodiade*; Valéry, *La Jeune Parque.*

Une Page d'amour is one of Zola's most complex structures with both symbolism and impressionistic tableaux as component parts. For many reasons the love between Hélène and Dr. Deberle has to be an impossible love, the foremost reason being the unconscious rejection of this relationship by Jeanne who will die rather than accept it. On two occasions, Jeanne's dolls are used to symbolize the situation. M. Rambaud, Hélène's suitor, is repairing Jeanne's doll while Hélène speaks with her spiritual advisor. The priest presses to know the name of the man she loves. As she is about to reveal the name of Deberle, Rambaud sets the doll walking. It seems to represent Jeanne (who is asleep), who would want to know if her mother loved someone else:

> Elle hésistait (to tell the name), lorsqu'un bruit particulier lui fit tourner la tête. C'était la poupée qui, entre les doigts de M. Rambaud, reprenait peu à peu sa vie mécanique; elle venait de faire trois pas sur le guéridon, avec le grincement des rouages fonctionnant mal encore; puis, elle avait culbuté à la renverse, et, sans le digne homme, elle rebondissait par terre (*Page,* 970).

Almost as if the doll were dropping dead from the news, as Jeanne will. In addition, there is the big doll which truly represents Jeanne, and which Jeanne exposes to the rainstorm in Chapter V of Part IV, as she does herself. Now, as Jeanne, confined to bed, begins her death agony, she detaches herself from everyone, especially her mother, but she clings to the doll. Again the doll represents the girl: «La poupée ... était allongée comme une personne malade...» (*Page,* 1069), and when Jeanne does die: «La poupée, la tête renversée, les cheveux pendants, semblait morte comme elle» (*Page*, 1071).

Flaubert, realizing that there was no way to penetrate psychology as the ancients might have understood it, and yet wanting to write a historical novel without imposing on it modern psychology as the romantics had done, decided to explain the psychological love forces of *Salammbô* in terms of religious anthropology. Zola must have had a similar intent in the writing of *La Faute de l'abbé Mouret*, symbolic psychology through a rewriting of the story of Genesis. There is little authentic symbolism in this novel, however, for the multiple «symbolic» levels just hammer away at a Zola thesis, the goodness of the natural life, the perversion of Christianity. As we noted the single details of the *Phaedra* in *La Curée*, the same external parallels with the story of Adam and Eve are noticed: the tree of forbidden knowledge; Frère Archangias standing as an archangel guard at the entrance to the garden. *La Faute de l'abbé Mouret* has a dense formal structure which is too artificial. A whole series of problematic contrasts and oppositions pour forth from the novel. They do not fuse, however, as they would in an authentic symbolist structure, but appear as a series of analogous arguments in a pro-or anti-Christian argument. Serge himself moves from feminine religion (Mary) in Part I to masculine religion (Jesus) in Part III. Mary is contrasted with Eve; Mary, star of the sea, is opposed to the Venus star; mariology to sexology. The purity of the Virgin is paralleled with that of Albine. There are life forces (nature) and death forces (the Church), multiplying and decaying ones, active and passive ones. The opposition Christian-Pagan is established with the farmers, especially the young girls seen as «païennes,» thus fusing the actual root of the word «pagan» with its rustic etymology (païen < paganus, paysan). The redemptive act, conquering death with rebirth in Christ, is opposed to a pantheistic rebirth in nature. Nature is fertile, the Church sterile. Sexual fulfillment is opposed to chastity. The Church is related to the cemetery, the peasants to the soil. Nature is conscious, the Church is out of contact with the spirit of the planet. Nature is a woman, the Church is a eunuch, and Serge actually desires castration. In nature man feels comfortable with himself; the Church produces guilt feelings. May is the month of Mary, but it is also the time for May Pole rites. Jeanbernat is the natural man, Frère Archangias, the unnatural one. This listing could be extended, but the point is clear. All of these oppositions reduce themselves to a single argument (*pensée*) which makes them illustrative, and not symbolic.

La Faute de l'abbé Mouret illustrates the disadvantages of a formal and dense symbolic structure where none is called for. A novel should not be made of thesis. This novel could have been a psychological study of the emotional conflict of a celibate tempted by the flesh. That such a theme can be the source of great novels can be seen by the evidence of Bernanos' *Journal d'un curé de campagne* or by Graham Greene's *The Power and the Glory*. One hundred years later, the French playwright, Jean Genet, makes the same mistake as Zola, by endowing a fundamentally problematic theatre (*Le Balcon, Les Nègres*) with ritualistic ceremony, with an unnecessary symbolism.

The fusion of multi-layered structures is the basis for the success of the Silvère-Miette idyll which is certainly the aesthetically adhesive element of the first novel, *La Fortune des Rougon*. It is the means by which the other elements, the rising Rougon and the falling Macquart, can be put into some sort of moral perspective. And no thesis is involved. If a moral message issues forth, it is provoked by a fusion of lyricism and symbolism. This early novel is in the best tradition of symbolism in the novel, surpassing *Bruges-la-morte* of Rodenbach or Gide's *Voyage d'Urien*. In some ways, given the limitations and the exigencies of the novel, it looks like a Mallarmé poem. Such a daring statement, which should only lead to speculations and not to conclusions, cannot be made without distinguishing carefully what can be done by the poem and by the novel.

Unlike the symbolist poem, or at least the highly condensed Mallarmean form of symbolism, where the various shades and levels of meaning are extracted from single, brief, and unified lexicological fields and syntactical constructs, ambiguous and multi-layered structure in the novel with symbolist tendencies is dependent upon sustained development in the narration, author commentary, and the imagery of single but separate ideas which fuse in the reader's mind only as the totality of the work is absorbed (as page after page is read). The unity is not limited to the linguistic structure; the synthesis usually must be viewed as constructed and not inherent to the linguistic combination. That is, it is less dependent upon syntactical choice, arrangement, grouping, and more composed of interlocking themes imposed upon a single narration through sustained images, mythical and historical echo and allusion. Proof of this is found in the fact that, unlike the symbolist poem, the single layers of meaning can be separated from each other. The presence of such a structure in Zola does indicate, however, some parallels and parenty with symbolism. The novel must, however, by genre definition, support a discursive, analytical structure, which is never the goal of the high symbolist poem. The Silvère-Miette idyll demonstrates that Zola has superimposed on analysis, if not an intuitive inquiry, then at least a poetic evaluation of the events depicted. This procedure permits us to discuss the episode in terms of layers of meaning, using an exegetical procedure ordinarily reserved to the deep symbolist poem. That is, as long as we keep in mind the essential differences between a novel and a poem.

Silvère and Miette are certainly symbolic creations, their relationship to the events of the coup d'état providing, because of their innocent and pure love, the moral perspective in which Zola would have us view the happenings of the novel. Their goodness, and subsequent murder are to be contrasted with the evil ascendancy of the Rougons. Then, through symbolic construct, Zola will relate the innocence of the couple to the cause of republicanism and liberty. Like the young lovers, liberty dies. It is at this point that the material is given a mythical twist, partly derived from existing legend, partly attributable to Zola's naive concept of eschatology.

Depiction of young love in Zola has frequently been criticized as a romantic regression on his part, and indeed he may have so thought himself (8). The cold December rendez-vous of Silvère and Miette opens the work with descriptions

_____

(8) At least the notes for the *Fortune* indicate that his original intent with the episode did not have the proportions we are here suggesting. Zola writes of Chapter I: «Ce chapitre est un pur tableau pittoresque qui ouvre l'oeuvre.», *Fr. Nouv. Acq.* 10303, *feuillet* 39. For a very complete analysis of this episode see Olivier

of Miette in her cape, walking alongside Silvère, covering him with her cloak, an amorous Provençal promenade in the moonlight.

But this amorous couple makes echoes to other couples, for the episode can be seen as a modern replay of the legend of Pyramus and Thisbe. The lyrical aspects of Zola's tale are embellished by paralleling the lyrical highlights of the classical legend: the lovers occupy adjoining houses, the love frowned upon by the parents or guardians. Whereas in Pyramus and Thisbe, the lovers are separated by a wall, through a crack of which they speak, Zola gives a charming and unique rendering of the same ideas through the device of the *puits mitoyen,* the shared-well, divided at the top by a wall, but in which the lovers find each other reflected (*Fortune,* 179-180). As Pyramus and Thisbe go beyond the city to meet at the Tomb of Ninus, so also Silvère and Miette meet in an abandoned cemetery where they often sit together on an old tombstone.

By these allusions to the classical legend, Zola suggests that all human experience is replay, that there is nothing new, and by extension, no past or future, just an eternal present unfolding of the same human experience. Another layer appears to corroborate this interpretation, for Silvère seems to be re-experiencing, especially for grandmother Dide, the experience of her old lover, the smuggler Macquart. Melodramatically perhaps, an extraordinary number of identical situations are developed: Silvère's grandfather Macquart had been killed by a gendarme, and with his grandfather's gun, he puts out the eye of a gendarme, and finally is killed by one. Silvère's love for Miette is attached to the love of his grandmother for Macquart, through the episode of the secret door. Adélaïde and her lover had built a door in the wall between the two properties in the early days of their affair. After his death she had sealed the door. Silvère hopes to open the wall between the two properties, and succeeds in finding the key. The grandmother, discovering what has taken place, scolds Silvère, relocks the door and throws the key into the well. Zola's commentary leaves no question as to what this means:

Got, «L'Idylle de Miette et de Silvère dans *La Fortune des Rougon,»* *Les Cahiers naturalistes,* 46 (1973), 146-164.

> Une seconde fois, la porte était complice. Par où l'amour avait passé, l'amour passait de nouveau. C'était l'éternel recommencement, avec ses joies présentes et ses larmes futures (*Fortune*, 189).

Silvère's replaying of the life of Macquart is psychologically justified since it is mainly presented through the disturbed mind of the grandmother who frequently confuses the grandson with the lover.

The cemetery segment of the episode is given a curious anthropomorphic twist, as the dead, who only appear to be sleeping (9), intrude upon the present. The lovers meet at a tombstone simply marked *Ci-gist Marie*. We learn that Miette is a diminutive of Marie, and when Miette is killed, the grave marker becomes a sign of her death. Silvère is murdered at this very tombstone, and Zola concludes, with the dead and the cemetery welcoming Silvère to their midst (*Fortune*, 311-12). Needless to say, this is the least convincing layer of the idyll.

More convincing both psychologically and symbolically, is the fusion of the love element with republican ideas. The evidence for this is clearly established in the opening chapter when Silvère speaks of their life together, once political liberty is assured. In two instances the stress is on happiness associated with liberty (*Fortune*, 20; 21-22). Furthermore, Silvère mingles his love for the country and for the girl: «J'aime la République, vois-tu, parce que je t'aime» (*Fortune*, 22). Engaged in the reading of humanitarian and utopian social literature, Silvère muses on the creation of a social religion in which Miette figures prominently, not at all unlike the role of Clotilde de Vaux in the Positivist religion of Auguste Comte (*Fortune*, 185).

That Miette will become the symbol of the Republic is dramatically clear at the close of Chapter I. Intoxicated at the sight of the insurgents singing the Marseillaise, Miette, in a sweep of enthusiasm, picks up the flag and leads them into Plassans. At that moment she is liberty leading the people, the reincarnation of Marianne: «... elle fut la vierge Liberté»

---

(9) See the explanation by Professor Mitterand plus his duplication of an article by Zola recounting his visit to the tomb of Alfred de Musset in Père-la-chaise, I, Pléiade, 1545.

(*Fortune, 35*). While Zola is anxious for us to interpret Miette symbolically, he is careful to put realistic controls on the characterization. While to the insurgents she is the Republic, Miette confesses to Silvère her own interpretation: «il me semble que je suis à la procession de la Fête-Dieu, et que je porte la bannière de la Vierge» (*Fortune, 36*). Symbolic function is not allowed to interfere with psychological probing of character. The same is the case in the famous Liberty painting of Delacroix, evidently known to Zola. This is an instance of symbolism and realism fusing.

Le Docteur Pascal, the last novel, is proof that Zola never abandons the procedure just described for *La Fortune des Rougon.* In this instance, however, we are able to follow sequentially the unique elaboration of the myth of the old king comforted by a loving young girl. Dr. Pascal had raised and educated his niece, Clotilde ,and as the years passed, she became his assistant in his research. That Clotilde has the proper disciple respect for him is seen in her use of the term *maître,* with which she usually addresses the scholar-doctor. From this simple and ordinary locution, however, will develop a whole myth, which first will be exploited metaphorically, and in grammatical variations, before fully blooming into a mythic analogy in the structure.

Clotilde frequently would accompany Pascal on his house visits, and the people of Plassans find it charming to see the old man supported by such a sweet young girl:

> Et, à les revoir passer tous deux, l'ancien roi puissant et doux, appuyé à l'épaule d'une enfant charmante et soumise [recall the use of *maître* above], dont la jeunesse le soutenait... (*Pascal, 962*).

Their relationship changes, however, from that of master and disciple, or father and daughter, to that of lovers, with Zola stressing that Clotilde is giving the «royal» gift of her youth to her aged lover. Thus a series of motif-variations on «royalty» begins:

> ... le royal été qui dressait sa tente bleue... (1117).
> ... elle lui fit le royal cadeau de son corps (1128).
> ... dans sa nudité souveraine (1129).

... dans ce royal festin de jeunesse qu'elle lui servait et que des rois auraient envie (1130).
... en sujette qui s'était donnée à son vieux roi... (1138).
... la jeunesse, qui s'était royalement donné... (1150).

With such a preparation, the myth then begins to elaborate itself within the narrative structure. Pascal dreams of the arrival of a young girl who comes to him as a pilgrim of love to marry him: «Lui était le vieux roi et elle l'adorait...» (1048). Pascal also owns a fifteenth century Bible with engravings showing old king David going to his room with his hand posed on the nude shoulder of Abishag (Kings 1: 1-4):

«Nous chercherons une jeune fille vierge pour le roi notre seigneur, afin qu'elle se tienne en présence du roi, qu'elle puisse l'amuser, et que, dormant près de lui, elle réchauffe le roi notre seigneur» (*Ibid.*).

Consciously worked out by Zola, with the characters themselves aware of the fact that they seem like the biblical couple, the biblical echoes inundate the remaining structure of the work. Clotilde does a pastel drawing of King David and Abishag and Zola explains: «... le vieux roi David, c'était lui, et c'était elle, Abisaïg la Sunamite» (1078). The biblical reference engenders others as Clotilde has the desire to make pastels of Ruth and Boaz, of Abraham and Hagar, the latter especially relevant, since Clotilde will bear Pascal's child (Genesis, 16: 11, 12). The biblical allusions continue to manifest themselves (1087, 1122, 1124, 1125), and Clotilde even thinks of herself in terms of Albine of *La Faute de l'abbé Mouret,* in her mission of making green again the life of Pascal. Each personage thus replays a former one.

Nana is the novel in which Zola best utilizes symbolic procedures. Out of a sordid erotic story (which never contains the explicit sexual detail of novels like *La Terre* or *Pot-Bouille*), which at first glance might deserve the label of naturalism, Zola has been able to arrive at a universal significance —the corruption of France symbolized in Nana. For once Zola has understood that individual corruption does spread to destroy the body politic. The spirit of Nana leaves its imprint on the entire country. Nana is the unifying metaphor of perhaps the most tightly constructed novel of Emile Zola. Logical analysis and arrangement are difficult because of the complex symbolic weave.

The Nana myth as a sexual one is built formally in three parts: her representation in *La Blonde Vénus* (Chapter I) by which she captures Paris; Fauchery's newspaper article on *La Mouche d'Or* which gives her a reputation as the fly born on a dung heap which comes to destroy the aristocracy; her final theatrical appearance in *Mélusine* (legendary protectress of the house of Lusignan) at which point she is so legendary that, like a goddess, she does not even speak, but is admired all the same. From her first appearance in the play, her mythical status has been established:

> Quand elle passait en voiture sur les boulevards, la foule se retournait et la nommait, avec l'émotion d'un peuple saluant sa souveraine... (1346).

As Miette replays Marie (*Fortune*) and Clotilde replays Albine and the Old Testament young ladies (*Pascal*), so Nana seems to transmit her essence across her society. Fauchery notes (1163) that the Comtesse Muffat resembles Nana. Can this virtuous woman, who apparently has no lovers, be basically the same as Nana? By the end of the novel she is just a cheap imitation of her. Nana has corrupted not just the men but also the women.

At the racetrack we have the apotheosis of the new goddess. The cry for Nana first heard at the Théâtre des Variétés is heard again in the cry of the crowd for Nana. The appetite of the individual males for Nana has been transformed into the national spirit, the whole nation desiring Nana (a horse with the same color of hair as Nana (1400)) to win the race for France against the English horse: «Vive Nana! vive la France! à bas l'Angleterre!» (1404). In their enthusiasm for the French horse, the crowd does not yet realize that the real foreign enemy is Prussia.

The sub-theme of approaching war with Prussia, which runs throughout the novel, fuses with the Nana motif at the racetrack, with Nana being identified with the national spirit. Nana and Prussia, however, only cross in a tight manner, structurally, in the concluding chapter. The vigil over the dead

Nana is maintained as Paris prepares for war, and Zola contrasts this vigil with the repeated cry of the patriotic Frenchmen to march on Berlin. If at the racetrack, we are led to believe that a victory of the horse Nana is a victory for France, in the concluding chapter we must believe that the death of Nana means the death of a certain idea of France which will be destroyed by the victory of the Prussians. Has Nana something to do with the collapse of France? Like Carthage without the veil of its goddess, Tanit (*Salammbô*), corrupt France cannot survive without its goddess: «Vénus se décomposait» (1485).

On the level of character development it is interesting to note that Nana believes in her own myth. In cheering on the horse, she moves her own body in imitation of the animal's movements, without being aware of it (1403), and acclaims herself (1406). The crowd equally believes in her, confusing her with the horse: «... on ne savait plus si c'était la bête ou la femme qui emplissait les coeurs» (1405).

Her disappearance in the final chapter truly makes of her a subject for mythic gossip. It is rumored that she has gone to Cairo (1471), fabulous stories are told of her adventures, that she lives with a viceroy in a palace with two hundred slaves, whom she has decapitated at her whim (1471); someone claims to have seen her in Russia where she is the mistress of a prince (1471).

Zola does not believe in the myth, but he knows that it is effective. If Nana ever existed, she has become a myth in spite of herself:

> Et tandis que, dans une gloire, son sexe montait et rayonnait sur ses victimes étendues, pareil à un soleil levant qui éclaire un champ de carnage, elle gardait son inconscience de bête superbe, ignorante de sa besogne, bonne fille toujours (1470).

While the Nana myth may be related to existing ones within the western tradition, it can be analyzed without it. The materials are rich, complex, and original, which is why *Nana* is Zola's most successful use of symbol.

Nevertheless, we remain uneasy with Zola's symbolic system. While pointing out that they are obviously constructed, even the complex *Nana* —for the novel is not poem— the question remains as to why the same symbolic system is applied so indiscriminately across the series. *Le Rêve* sins as seriously in this regard as does *La Faute de l'abbé Mouret.* By what accident does the consistent Zola, technically, create a major novel such as *Nana,* and yet fall into either dogmatism or maudlin sentimentality? (10)

If, somehow, we could extract a naturalistic novel from *Le Rêve,* it would be that of a disturbed puberty. But this is almost impossible to find under the crush of a thick and contradictory symbolic system which, at best, approaches the oneiric fantasies of a Maeterlinck. Zola becomes lost in a symbolic system which crosses his traditional images of royalty with legends of the saints and the symbolism associated with their particular iconography (St. George, St. Agnes), obsessive legends, such as that of «la légende dorée» (549), and the addition of related materials, such as the Romeo and Juliette myth (910). The novel is truly disturbing to the system, which may explain why doctrinaire «naturalistic» critics have so little to say about it. It is the one novel in which one would have wished for more «naturalistic» detail, for, after all, Angélique is Saccard's niece.

Le Rêve is such an inferior novel that, in a way, it is proof that Zola felt that metaphorical and symbolic methods were true components of the novel, for it overdoes and contradicts what *Nana* states with such pure aesthetic integrity. Zola, as a novelist, would have benefited had he followed the path of Flaubert, had he not tried so hard to be of his time in all ways, trying to satisfy both the new craze for a naive science, and the wave of a contradictory symbolism (Maeterlinck, Villiers de l'Isle Adam, the young Claudel). Yet, as construct, *Le Rêve,* though more obvious, is built along the symbolic lines of the novels discussed so far. It remains the proof of the inauthenticity of *La Faute de l'abbé Mouret.*

Symbolism remained a major component of the novel as

---

(10) Mitterand cites a very revealing article of Jules Lemaître in *La Revue bleue* of 1888 in which this critic rightfully points out that there is no difference in the style of *Le Rêve, La Terre* or *L'Assommoir,* IV, Pléiade, 1654-55.

long as the novel remained a poem, although the symbolism in the romances remains a moot question. After the development of the prose romances, the novel is on its own, a bastard form to Boileau, but yet, a genre which gains ascendancy with the triumph of the bourgeoisie in 1789. Except for Flaubert, who truly tried to define it as a genre, its nineteenth century history is always one of borrowing from poetry, and, to a lesser degree, from theatre. The symbolist novel seems almost impossible. A brief consideration of Chapter IV of *L'Oeuvre* makes this point clear. Christine consents to pose, without clothing, for Claude's painting. At this point in the novel, she is not his mistress. She can handle the posing session, but at its conclusion, she feels ashamed, and Claude, likewise, averts his eyes so that she may dress. The artist has again become a man, and Christine is no longer nude, but naked. The point is: the novel cannot avoid moral questions, but the poem can. Mallarmé's «Une Dentelle s'abolit» or «Surgi de la croupe et du bond» both contain delicate questions of aesthetics, yet the inhabitants of the hermetically sealed poem have no history, no time, and consequently, there are no moral consequences. In the Mallarmé poems, the bed could have contained lovers, who could have had intercourse, and a child, perhaps, would have been born; or the poor sylph of the ceiling, had her mother and her lover drunk from the same *breuvage,* would have been born, and a flower would have issued forth from the vase. Zola's symbolism has to be limited by the very problematic nature of the novel in which people considered as real (hence the problem of «realism») live out moral and psychological stances in time and space.

Yet, if not as a perfect system, at least partially, across these long prose narratives is felt the true force of poetic motif. *L'Oeuvre* could be considered as a prose version of Mallarmé's obsession with his inability to write, for Claude Lantier remains fixed on the form which remains «informe,» the work which seeks to be born (249). Claude's pursuit of idealized womanhood in his painting recalls the satyr's chase after the elusive nymphs of *L'Après-midi d'un Faune*:

> Ah! les vouloir toutes, les créer selon son rêve, des
> gorges de satin, des hanches couleur d'ambre, des
> ventres douillets de vierges, et ne les aimer que

> pour les beaux tons, et les sentir qui fuyaient, sans
> pouvoir les étreindre! (*Oeuvre*, 243).

Claude, like the faun, must wonder if he has not just been dreaming. In the novel, dreaming is called insanity, and leads to suicide.

Similarly, *La Joie de vivre* recalls the early Mallarmé, the poet of «L'Azur» and of «Brise Marine,» the lyric cry of life and death while contemplating the sky and the sea —a tradition which stretches from Hugo to Valéry. Monsieur Chanteau, with terminal gout, looks out at the sea, and resembles the watcher of «L'Azur»:

> Et la mer l'intéressait, cet infini bleu où passaient
> des voiles blanches, cette route sans bornes, ouverte
> devant lui qui n'était plus capable de mettre un pied
> devant l'autre (1108).

Pauline Quenu's fascination with the sea must go back to the days when, in the *charcuterie,* she heard her Uncle Florent tell his stories. The sea of *La Joie de vivre* remains symbolic, for its meaning is never defined —it hovers between being a life force and a death force. It is certainly more attached to Hugo's «Oceano Nox» than to Mallarmé's «A la nue accablante tu...» in the sense that an exact novelistic (rational) meaning can ultimately be extracted from it.

La Terre has often been called the poem of the land. The motif of fecundity and renewal, by the density of its occurrence (a check would indicate 367, 368, 369, 372, 375, 377, 383, 388, 451, 452, 530, 531, 572, 575, 710, 720, 768), would certainly act as a salutary balm for the rough naturalistic detail.

The majority of the novels of the series seems to rely heavily on poetic synthesis (symbolism) to make the final point. Perhaps only *L'Assommoir* is the exception, making it, perhaps, Zola's unique contribution to the pure *genre romanesque.* Without the metaphorical and mythical structures which we have been discussing, Zola might have deserved the negative criticism he received from official criticism in his day.

Germinal would be a sad and sordid story of man's defeat without the almost Mallarmean poem which concludes it. The last paragraph, while constructed, summarizes the human condition in the form of a motif of hope, which transcends the implied socialist message of revolution. As the earth of *Germinal* turns green, so man will always have hope in his heart. Zola cannot be faulted for his optimistic belief in the dignity of the human race. Technically speaking, it is almost impossible to distinguish, grammatically, the spring growth from the eruption through the earth of the miners:

> ... le soleil d'avril rayonnait ... échauffant la terre qui enfantait. ... par cette matinée de jeunesse, c'était de cette rumeur que la campagne était grosse. Des hommes poussaient, une armée noire, vengeresse, qui germait lentement dans les sillons, grandissant pour les récoltes du siècle futur... (*Germinal*, 1591).

Allegory, but allegory reaching toward symbol, in a form not yet capable of symbolism, or in a form which should not use it. Yet, it is effective. In any case, *Germinal* expresses best Zola's idea of «... l'éternelle jeunesse de la terre» (*Faute*, 1226), meaning the eternal hope of man. This was the transcendency he aimed at in the *Rougon-Macquart*, and which he only achieved from time to time.

If this study began with an analysis of impressionistic technique in the *Rougon-Macquart*, and has been concluding with mainly a study of symbolic modes, it is because the heart of Zola's aesthetic system is found in the fusion of almost innate impressionistic linguistic tendencies which combine with proclivities towards the symbolic poem. While Zola's art is irregular and uneven, it is consistent in this regard. Late nineteenth century French literature has three movements contemporaneous to each other —naturalism, symbolism and impressionism. They are all mixed and uneven systems, technically and ideologically. Zola, of all the artists, seems the only one who combines these three tendencies. In the final analysis, would not his eclecticism help us to solve the riddle of categorization. Why not abandon the term naturalism, and speak of the entire nineteenth century in terms of a tendency towards realism, a term which easily can absorb impressionism and symbolism as mere techniques?

Three novels are exemplary for showing symbolism and impressionism in the service of the novel: *La Curée, Au Bonheur des dames,* and *Une Page d'amour.* Earlier, an analysis in terms of impressionistic technique was made of Renée's three sightings of the Boulevard des Italiens from the café Riche. Yet, over the entire light, color and shadow description, was felt the presence of the strolling prostitute. The seated whore, the whore waiting at the corner, and the whore still walking late at night are symbolic equivalents of the three impressionistic tableaux. They, perhaps, give meaning to the nuances of light seen by Renée, impart to the impressionism a novelistic meaning.

Similarly, an impressionistic analysis was made of the white sale in *Au Bonheur des dames.* Yet, this impressionism would be totally gratuitous were Zola not able to work it into the central intrigue. As lowly as the subject may seem, the lyrical rendering of the sale of towels, sheets and pillow slips has been prepared by Zola as an impressionistic background to the «royalty» of Denise, who will be the virgin bride of Octave Mouret. The department store becomes an entire kingdom of which Denise will be queen: «... le luxe de sa royale chevelure blonde» (645); «... la bonne reine de la maison» (783). The white sale dominates the final chapter so that Octave's proposal of marriage, coming only on the last page, makes valid the impressionistic description. The new queen, the good woman Denise, will purify Octave and his new style of capitalism, or at least, mitigate it. This work, like so many of the novels, shows how Zola will reiterate lexicological and metaphorical fields, manipulating them to a crescendo, often of hope and renewal, in the last pages of the work.

Une Page d'amour, by its very formal structure of five parts, each concluding with an impressionistic tableau of Paris, must be considered the highest formal fusing of impressionism and symbolism in the work of Zola. Here he has succeeded in combining what a whole line of prose writers since Rousseau had been trying to do: to exteriorize psychology into a landscape and to impose an already known superstratum upon the narration. Impressionism in the novel, since it is almost exclusively rendered in nature descriptions, can be seen as the ultimate precision of the pathetic fallacy introduced by Rousseau. Unlike the pastoral or *précieux* novels, Rousseau introduces a real landscape into literature. These landscapes will be used successively, and with greater nuance and precision, by Chateaubriand, Georges Sand, Balzac, Flaubert and, finally, Zola, who, following the lead of the painters, will render their subjectivity with great scientific accuracy. Hélène will use the cityscapes of Paris to try and figure out her sentiments. Zola's descriptive art, through its powerful color lyricism, will make the landscape indicative of Hélène's inner feelings.

Furthermore, following Flaubert, he will utilize high metaphorical analogy to complement the landscape. As Emma Bovary identifies with *Lucia di Lammermor,* so Hélène, looking out over Paris while reading *Ivanhoe,* will blend her personal life, the fiction of Scott, and the Paris horizon. Looking out over Paris at ten in the morning, the sky is described in terms meant to convey peace and harmony, emotions similar to her nascent but yet not precise feelings of love for the doctor:

> ... une paix souveraine et une gaieté tendre de l'infini, pendant que la ville ... paresseuse et som-nolente, ne se décidait point à se montrer sous ses dentelles (846).

There is a correspondance between the landscape and Hélène's feelings, positive atmosphere, pastel colors, possible happiness for her. Her thoughts are not yet precise, but she imparts on the landscape a certain melancholy and hope: «Hélène goûtait là toutes les mélancolies et tous les espoirs du large» (846-47). The narration then relates her feelings about the lies of fictions (*Ivanhoe*), but yet her mind returns to the story of Ivanhoe, loved by Rebecca and Lady Rowena, with whom she starts to identify. Now the idea of love, derived from the novel, crosses with the landscape, the sky becoming a sea on which her dream of love floats:

> Lentement, sur ces eaux blanches, si calmes, des ombres semblaient faire voyager des vaisseaux aux voiles roses que la jeune femme suivait d'un regard songeur. Aimer, aimer! et elle souriait à son rêve qui flottait (847).

Again, the book seems to her like *un beau mensonge,* a *jardin idéal,* and she puts down the book, recalls her marriage, and how little life she has had compared to the fictions (848).

The landscape is again filled with movement, color nuance and change. This pattern of vacillation continues, between the temptation of life found in the novel and in the sky, and the duties of a regulated life (memories of her dead father, found hung, duties to her child). Yet, the Paris landscape seems to be beckoning Hélène to participate in life, Paris itself seems to incarnate life:

> Sous cette radieuse matinée, la ville, jaune de soleil, semblait un champ d'épis mûrs, et l'immense tableau avait une simplicité, deux tons seulement, le bleu pâle de l'air et le reflet doré des toits (850).

The entrance of Jeanne interrupts this meditation of love, with Hélène concluding that she should be happy in her simple life with the love of her daughter. The child asks Hélène to identify various buildings of Paris, which she is unable to do: «Alors, elles continuèrent à regarder Paris, sans chercher davantage à le connaître» (854). At this point, Hélène is not going to explore any more deeply the city or her feelings for the doctor. As Zola writes, she is on the threshold of a world which she can always see, but which she will ultimately refuse to enter (854). The tableau concludes with a total fusion of Hélène's sentiment for the doctor with Lady Rowena of the Scott novel, and the Paris landscape.

The imprecision of Hélène's thought has been effected through the novelistic use of the Scott novel and the Paris scene. The idea of Paris (freedom and life) surging forth from the impressionistic colorations (abstract pastel dreams in the blue and pinks of the first part of the description) parallels her musings on the Ivanhoe story. As Paris becomes more dominant as the morning advances, she makes a total identification with Lady Rowena. The final correspondance in this pastel dream of possible future happiness is made possible through the odiferous flowers brought in by her daughter. Nevertheless, the whole chapter summarizes the problem of the entire novel, to choose life or to retire from life, and we know that Hélène will choose the minor joy. The whole thrust of the novel can be found in this impressionistically rendered landscape conjoined to a symbolism emanating from the Scott novel. All of the elements have been intertwined, but with great psychology and impressionism, the like of which cannot be found in the Silvère-Miette idyll of *La Fortune des Rougon*.

All of the tableaux of *Une Page d'amour* show intimate union between psychology and landscape to a degree not seen in the novel before Zola. An impressionistic sunset conveys the deep passion of Hélène. Ultimately, her maternal and bourgeois character will win out. After the death of her daughter, Hélène returns to Paris on a snowy day to visit Jeanne's tomb. The final scene has her again looking out over Paris. The city, metaphorically and impressionistically, is transformed by the snowstorm; its true form is beyond recognition. But has it not always been so for Hélène:

> Alors, Hélène, une dernière fois, embrassa d'un regard la ville impassible, qui, elle aussi, lui restait inconnue (1091-92).

Musing on Henri a page earlier, we find that he also is a stranger to her:

> Et Hélène se disait qu'elle ne connaissait pas Henri ... Elle ne le connaissait pas, elle faisait un immense effort sans pouvoir comprendre. D'où venait-il? comment se trouvait-il près d'elle? quel homme était-ce, pour qu'elle lui eût cédé, elle qui serait plutôt morte que de céder à un autre? ... Au dernier comme au premier jour, il lui restait étranger (1090).

Impressionism, then, can be more than a picturesque tableau. The dense impressionistic descriptions with which this study began perhaps are only thinner distillations of the highly subjective landscapes used in the structure of *Une Page d'amour*.

Naturalism seemed the best term for Zola to describe his art, and most of us have so believed for almost one hundred years. It may be time for a change in literary terminology. The substitute term cannot be impressionism, nor may it be symbolism, as this and other parts of this work have tried to demonstrate.

If the term naturalism is to be retained, however, its traditional definition must be modified. Impressionistic technique, stylistically and novelistically, must be included. Serious attention must also be given to the role of metaphor and symbol, which seems to be derived from a very subjective general semantic field in the *Rougon-Macquart*. In any case, impressionism and symbolism have a larger and more systematic role in the *Rougon-Macquart* than may have been expected. Both may be at the heart of its aesthetic effects. There are, naturally, implications here for the relationship between literature and art, but in literature alone, the technical relationships between poetry and prose in the late nineteenth century still deserve our serious attention. Thus our study, seeing Zola in a new key, may open also a new view on the literary scene of the late nineteenth century.

SELECTED BIBLIOGRAPHY

It would be redundant, given the interest today in the work of Zola, to reproduce here the Zola bibliography. This bibliography, therefore, will only list those items which are considered primary for the discussion in this work. For the reader who seeks as much source information as possible, we point out the recent work of Professor David Baguley, *Bibliographie de la critique sur Emile Zola, 1864-1970,* (University of Toronto Press, 1976) and his bibliographical articles since 1970 in *Les Cahiers naturalistes;* the bibliographical essay of Professor Philip D. Walker in his *Emile Zola* (New York, 1968), and the chronological and rather complete bibliography of Professor Patrick Brady, at the conclusion of his *'L'Oeuvre' de Emile Zola* (Geneva, 1968).

Beuchat, Charles. *Histoire du naturalisme français.* Paris, 1949.

Bruneau, Alfred. *A l'Ombre d'un grand coeur.* Paris, 1931.

Brunetière, Ferdinand. *Le Roman naturaliste.* Paris, 1892.

Dangelser, Joan-Yvonne. *La Description du milieu dans le roman français de Balzac à Zola.* Paris, 1938.

Desprez, Louis. *L'Evolution naturaliste.* Paris, 1884.

Frey, John A. «A Nineteenth-Century Stylistician, Louis Desprez and his *Evolution naturaliste*,» *Romance Notes,* XII, no. 2, 1971, 1-5.

Gaufinez, Eugène. *Etudes syntaxiques sur la langue de Zola dans 'Le Docteur Pascal'.* Bonn, 1894.

Grant, Elliot M. *Emile Zola.* New York, 1966.

Hamon, Philippe. «A propos de l'impressionnisme de Zola,» *Les Cahiers naturalistes,* 34 (1967), 139-147.

Hatzfeld, Helmut A. *Initiation à l'explication de textes français.* Munich, 1975.

— *Literature Through Art.* Chapel Hill, 1969.

Hauser, Arnold. *The Social History of Art.* New York, 1952.

Hemmings, F. W. J. «Zola, Manet and the Impressionists, 1875-80,» *PMLA,* 73 (1958), 407-417.

Johnson, J. Theodore, Jr. «Literary Impressionism in France: A Survey of Criticism,» *Esprit créateur,* 13 (1973), 271-297.

Le Blond, Maurice. *Emile Zola, son évolution, son influence.* Paris, 1903.

Mallarmé, Stéphane. *Dix-neuf lettres de Stéphane Mallarmé à Emile Zola.* Paris, 1929.

Moser, Ruth. *L'Impressionnisme français.* Geneve, 1952.

Newton, Joy. «Emile Zola impressionniste,» *Les Cahiers naturalistes,* 33 (1967), 39-52; 34 (1967), 124-138.

— «Zola et l'expressionnisme: le point de vue hallucinatoire,» *Les Cahiers naturalistes,* 41 (1971), 1-14.

— «Emile Zola and the French Impressionist Novel,» *Esprit créateur,* 13 (1973), 320-328.

Nochlin, Linda. *Realism.* Baltimore, 1970.

Nordau, Max. *Degeneration.* New York, 1895.

Powell, Silas Robert. «Impressionistic Art in *Le Ventre de Paris* of Emile Zola,» (The George Washington University), Washington, 1967.

Robert, Guy, editor. *Lettres inédites de Louis Desprez à Emile Zola.* Paris, 1952.

Rosenblum, Robert. *Modern Painting and the Northern Romantic Tradition, Friedrich to Rothko.* New York, 1975.

Sherard, Robert. *Emile Zola; a Biographical and Critical Study.* London, 1893.

Sypher, Wylie. *Rococo to Cubism in Art and Literature.* New York, 1960.

Wilson, Angus. *Emile Zola, an Introductory Study of his Novels.* London, 1952.

INDEX

A

Bourgeoisie, 5, 29, 39, 45, 55, 103, 109, 110, 111, 134, 136, 137, 138, 139, 145, 151, 172, 173, 213, 217, 220, 230, 237, 238, 241, 245n, 246, 262, 264, 267, 286n, 289, 326, 332; speech, 221-29, 249, 250.
Bourras, 311-12.
Bovary, Emma, 5, 59, 60, 69, 86, 103, 108, 114, 123, 151, 173, 174, 223, 238, 255, 307, 310, 311, 313, 330.
Brady, Patrick, 164-165n, 335.
Brown, Calvin S., 38n.
Brueghel, Pieter, 301.
Bru-Laloire, Louis, 176.
Bruneau, Alfred, 10n, 335.
Brunetière, Ferdinand, 3n, 8n, 335.
Buffon, Georges de, 282.
Busch (Sigismond), 122, 271.
Buteau (Fouan, Jules), 41, 106, 112, 136, 162, 229, 242-43, 295.
Butor, Michel, 294n.

C

Cadine, 193, 195.
Campardon (Rose), 227, 267, 286, 289, 305.
Camus, Albert, 133, 282.
Capitalism, 110, 257, 258-59.
Catholicism, 78, 93, 106, 248, 262, 263, 293, 316.
Cézanne, Paul, 3n, 6, 90, 164n, 216.
Change (Impressionistic), 13, 52, 55-68, 96, 117.
Chanteau (Lazare), see Lazare.
Chanteau (mme), 74, 75, 106, 125, 140, 148, 159, 235, 242; (monsieur), 101, 327.
Chateaubriand, François-René, 17, 18, 34, 86, 89, 102, 118, 180, 180n, 181, 198, 209, 242, 280, 283, 330.
Chaval, 202, 250, 256.
Christine (Hallegrain), 16, 18, 46, 66, 67, 103, 111, 149, 157, 158, 162, 171, 178, 275, 291, 303, 314-315, 326.
Citron, Pierre, 53n.

Clarisse (Bocquet), 103, 138, 139, 222, 228.
Classicism, 20, 134, 180.
Claude (Lantier), 16, 18, 27, 31, 44, 46, 60, 62, 64, 66, 67, 88, 103, 104, 106, 111, 112, 119, 121, 134, 135, 143, 145, 149, 157, 158, 162, 165-66, 171, 178, 201, 202, 216, 222, 263, 283, 291, 303, 312, 314, 315, 326-27.
Claudel, Paul, 325.
Clause, 43, 189-90, 197, 198, 199, 200, 208.
Clorinde (Balbi), 77, 139, 140, 188, 242, 264, 312.
Clotilde (Rougon), 101, 107, 117, 118, 141, 211, 217, 285, 291, 308, 321-22, 323.
Cohen, Marcel, 247n.
Collapse, 47, 64, 110-23, 134-41, 150, 158, 266, 270, 274, 275, 294.
Color, 13, 15, 19-41, 44, 46, 49, 52, 53, 55, 57-64, 71, 74, 75, 90, 91, 127, 141, 143-45, 162, 178, 198, 282, 292, 329-31.
Commune, 44, 271.
Comte, Auguste, 99, 320.
Conjunction, 148, 178, 187, 190, 195, 197, 198, 199, 200, 201, 202-03, 204, 205, 208.
Connectives, 205, 206, 208.
Conquest, 171, 203, 204, 266, 293-94.
Corot, Camille, 90.
Couleur de, 24.
Coupeau, 106, 118, 119, 126, 135, 214, 240, 241, 242, 248, 250, 255, 256.
Coupeau (Nana), see Nana.
Courteline, Georges, 103.
Creativity, 13, 143-45, 272.
Cubism, 13.
Cursus, 180-81.

D

Dangelser, Joan-Yvonne, 9n, 92, 105, 106, 278, 280, 335.
Dante, 291.
Daudet, Alphonse, 8, 12, 183n.
Deberle (Henri), 5, 15, 18, 45, 46, 85, 104, 302, 308-09, 315, 332.

L

Language, 143-260.
Lantier (Auguste), 125, 196, 199-200, 240, 256.
Lantier (Claude), see Claude.
Lantier (Etienne), see Etienne.
Lantier (Jacques), 122, 136, 150, 216, 218, 288.
Lamartine, Alphonse de, 34, 102, 131, 147.
Larbaud, Valery, 169.
Lattre, Alain de, 13n.
Lazare (Chanteau), 75, 89, 101, 106, 111, 121, 129, 130, 135, 141, 151, 159, 171, 177, 235, 242, 251-52, 261, 288, 295, 312.
LeBlond, Maurice, 3n, 8n, 106n, 335.
Lecoeur (mme), 80, 82, 83.
Léger, Fernand, 62, 94.
LeHavre, 16, 123, 278.
LeHir, Yves, 163n.
Lemaitre, Jules, 325n.
Lerch, Eugen, 176, 179, 183.
Levasseur (Maurice), see Maurice.
Lézarde, 275, 286-88.
Liaisons dangereuses, Les, 130.
Light, 13, 15, 16, 19, 20, 21, 22, 24, 25, 26, 28, 29, 30, 31, 32, 33, 34, 35, 36, 37, 38, 39, 40, 42, 44, 45, 46, 49, 52, 53, 54, 55, 56, 57, 58, 59, 60, 61, 62, 63, 64, 65, 67, 74, 76, 77, 80, 90, 91, 93, 130, 141, 143, 144, 145, 165, 169, 185, 192, 273, 274, 282, 292, 329.
Lipps, Marguerite, 247n.
Lombroso, Cesare, 214-15.
Lösch, Georg, 163n.
Loti, Pierre, 21, 134, 164, 165.
Lourdes, 217.
Love (and speech), 239-42.
Lubbock, Percy, 181n, 209.
Lugné-Poe, Aurélien-Marie, 12.
Lukács, Georg, 212n.
Lyricism, 3, 16, 18, 19, 31, 32, 33, 39, 40, 45, 46, 49, 52, 54, 55, 64, 66, 67, 90, 91, 100, 106, 178, 179, 242, 279, 302, 319, 327, 330.

M

Macquart (Antoine), 170, 216, 240, 243-44.
Macquart (Gervaise), see Gervaise.
Macquart (Jean), 100, 112, 135, 136, 171, 246.
Macquart (Lisa), 61, 62, 122, 201, 283.
Maeterlinck, Maurice, 325.
Maheu (Catherine), 202, 250, 256, 285.
Maheude (la), 110, 226, 233, 240, 249.
Maigrat, 148, 154, 243.
Mallarmé, Stéphane, 10, 11, 12, 29, 43, 48, 49, 90, 134, 164, 315, 317, 326, 327, 336.
Manet, Edouard, 6, 12.
Marjolin, 193, 195.
Marxism, 212n, 234, 265.
Materialism, 12, 77, 151, 211, 268, 289.
Maupassant, Guy de, 3n, 12, 252.
Mauriac, François, 252.
Maurice (Levasseur), 122, 171, 218, 259.
Max, Stefan, 51n.
Maxime (Rougon), 56, 84, 117, 140, 244, 303, 313.
Maynial, Edouard, 206.
Metamorphosis, 29, 32, 36, 40, 43, 46, 47, 48, 49, 53, 85, 126, 192, 208, 275, 277.
Metaphor, 12, 29, 30, 36, 43, 44, 45, 47, 48, 49, 53, 58, 62, 63, 64, 65, 66, 67, 68, 74, 79, 81, 88, 127, 149, 150, 158, 159, 160, 161, 162, 191, 209, 211, 234, 239, 257, 258, 263, 264, 265, 266-67, 268, 269, 270, 271, 274, 275, 280, 281, 282, 283, 284, 285, 286, 287, 288, 293, 294, 296, 299, 311, 321, 322, 325, 330, 333.
Michelet, Jules, 183n, 287n.
Miette, 31, 84, 100, 101, 314, 317-21, 323, 332.
Milieu, 123-33.
Military (metaphor), 286-87.
Misard (Flore), see Flore.

10, 11, 12, 13, 14, 44, 164n, 296; lyricism, 3, 16, 18, 19, 40, 52, 178, 209; morality, 209, 213, 214, 215, 239; Naturalism, 1-14; nature, 15, 16, 18, 19, 40, 49, 210; painting, 7, 15, 29, 34, 48, 52, 164, 190, 296; poetry, 3, 11, 32, 190, 330; Provençal origins, 16; Romanticism, 3, 16, 18, 99, 131; science, 3, 12, 19, 30, 205, 209, 214, 215, 216, 254, 265; subjectivity, 10, 10n, 12, 15, 33, 208-19, 263; symbolism, 1, 10, 11, 12, 13, 14, 296, 297; theatre, 7, 10, 52.

stuðia humanitatis

FORTHCOMING PUBLICATIONS

El cancionero del Bachiller Jhoan Lopez, edición crítica de Rosalind Gabin.

Studies in Honor of Gerald E. Wade, edited by Sylvia Bowman, Bruno M. Damiani, Janet W. Díaz, E. Michael Gerli, Everett Hesse, John E. Keller, Luis Leal and Russell Sebold.

HELMUT HATZFELD, *Essais sur la littérature flamboyante.*

MARIO ASTE, *La narrativa di Luigi Pirandello: Dalle novelle al romanzo «Uno, Nessuno, e Centomila».*

JOSEPH BARBARINO, *The Latin Intervocalic Stops: A Quantitative and Comparative Study.*

NANCY D'ANTUONO, *Boccaccio's novelle in Lope's theatre.*

ANTONIO PLANELLS, *Cortázar: Metafísica y erotismo.*

Novelistas femeninas de la postguerra española, ed. Janet W. Díaz.

MECHTHILD CRANSTON, *Orion Resurgent: René Char, Poet of Presence.*

La Discontenta and La Pythia, edition with introduction and notes by Nicholas A. De Mara.

PERO LÓPEZ DE AYALA, *Crónica del Rey Don Pedro I,* edición crítica de Heanon and Constance Wilkins.

ALBERT H. LE MAY, *The Experimental Verse Theater of Valle-Inclán.*

CHESTER W. OBUCHOWSKY, *Mars on Trial: War as Seen by French Writers of the Twentieth Century.*

JEREMY T. MEDINA, *Spanish Realism: Theory and Practice of a Concept in the Nineteenth Century.*

ROBERT H. MILLER, ed. *Sir John Harington: A Supplie or Addicion to the «Catalogue of Bishops» to the Yeare 1608.*

María Elisa Ciavarelli, *La fuerza de la sangre en la literatura del Siglo de Oro.*

Mary Lee Bretz, *La evolución novelística de Pío Baroja.*

Dennis M. Kratz, *Mocking Epic.*